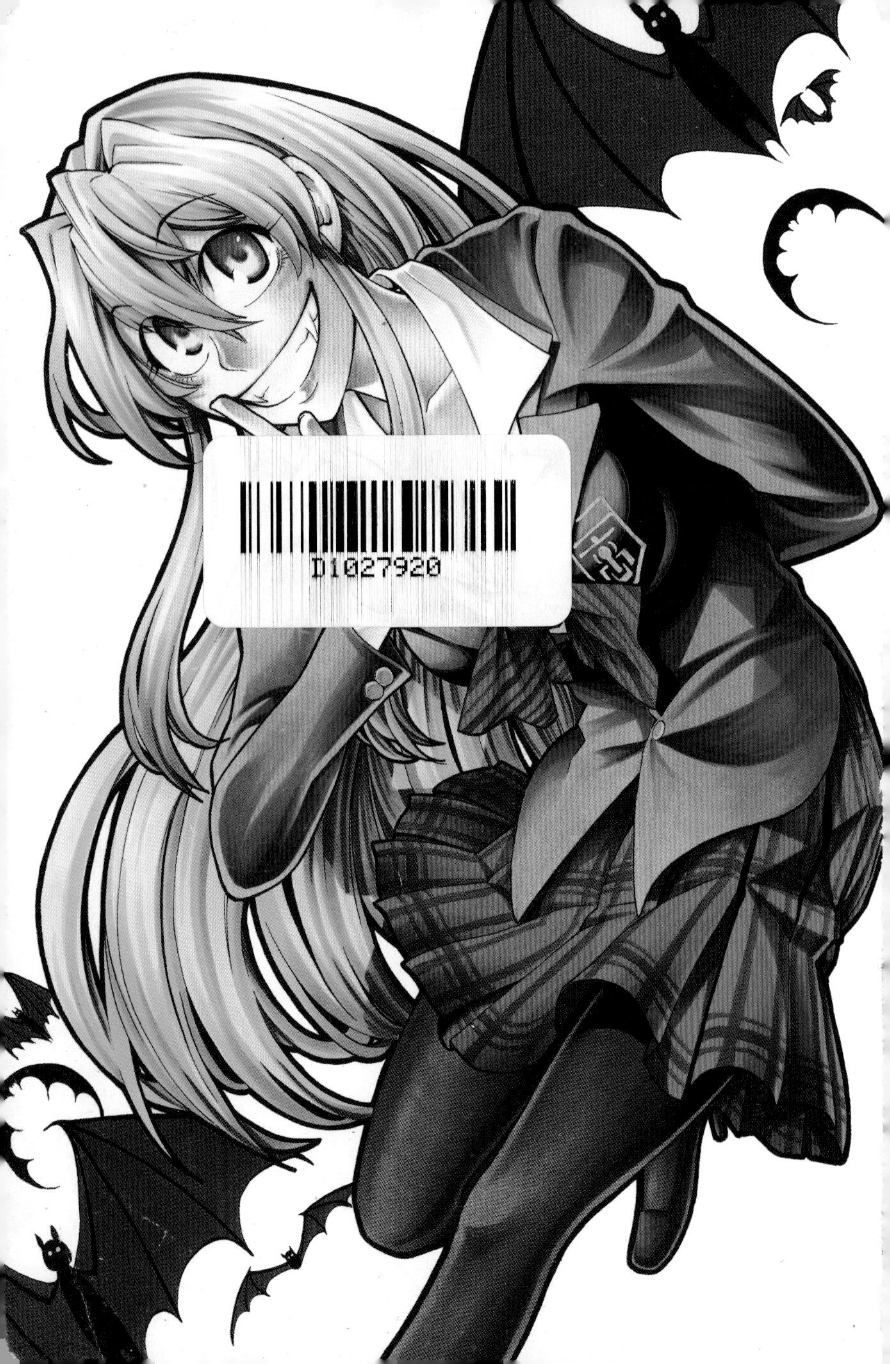

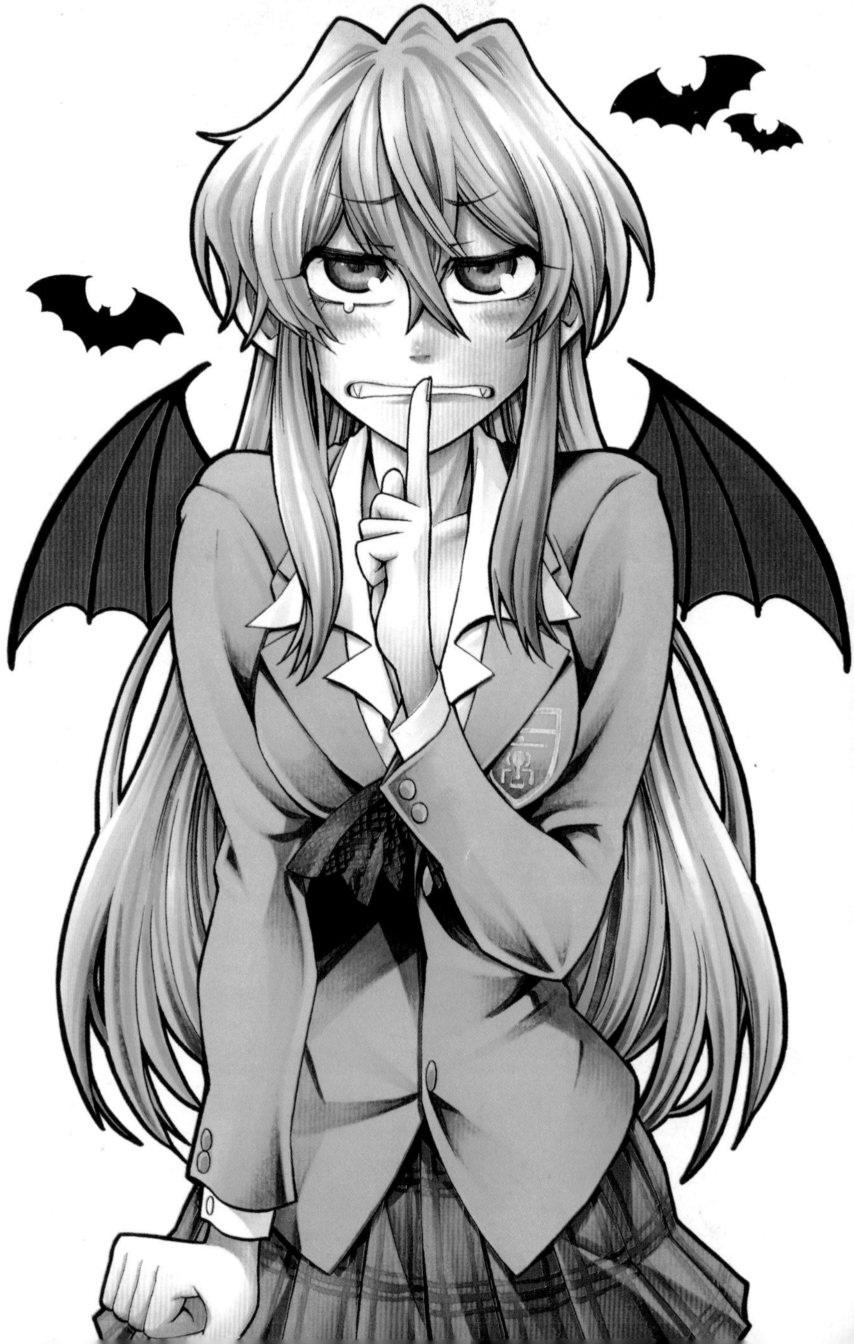

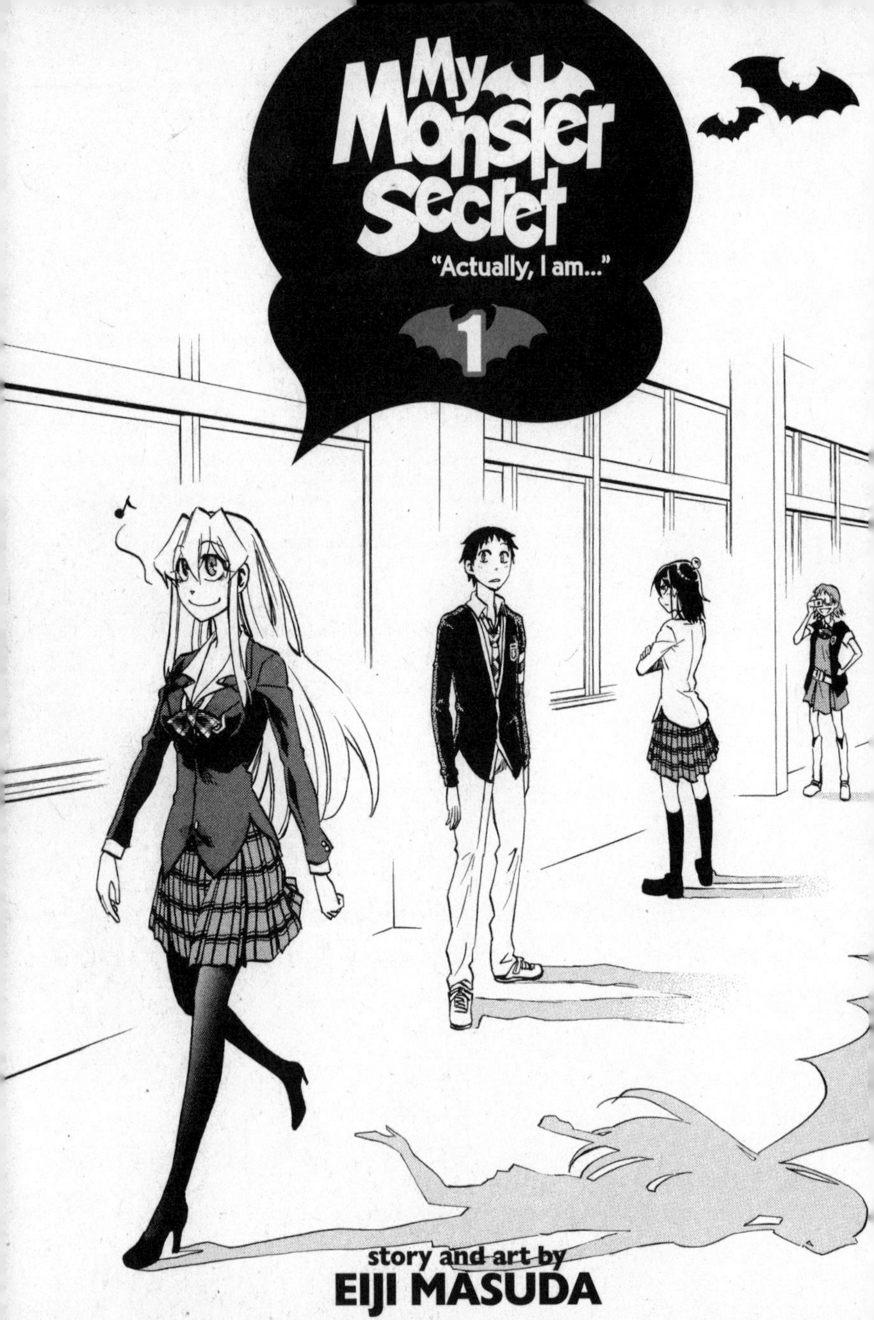
My Monster Secret
"Actually, I am..."
1

story and art by
EIJI MASUDA

SEVEN SEAS ENTERTAINMENT PRESENTS

My Monster Secret
"Actually, I am..."

story and art by Eiji Masuda

VOLUME 1

TRANSLATION
Alethea and Athena Nibley

ADAPTATION
Lianne Sentar

LETTERING AND LAYOUT
Annaliese Christman

LOGO DESIGN
Karis Page

COVER DESIGN
Nicky Lim

PROOFREADER
Shanti Whitesides

PRODUCTION MANAGER
Lissa Pattillo

EDITOR IN CHIEF
Adam Arnold

PUBLISHER
Jason DeAngelis

JITSUHA WATASHIHA Volume 1
© EIJI MASUDA 2013
Originally published in Japan in 2013 by Akita Publishing Co., Ltd.
English translation rights arranged with Akita Publishing Co., Ltd.
through TOHAN CORPORATION, Tokyo.

Seven Seas books may be purchased in bulk for educational, business, or
promotional use. For information on bulk purchases, please contact Macmillan
Corporate & Premium Sales Department at 1-800-221-7945 (ext 5442)
or write specialmarkets@macmillan.com.

Seven Seas and the Seven Seas logo are trademarks of
Seven Seas Entertainment, LLC. All rights reserved.

ISBN: 978-1-626922-38-9

Printed in Canada

First Printing: January 2016

10 9 8 7 6 5 4 3 2 1

FOLLOW US ONLINE: *www.gomanga.com*

READING DIRECTIONS

This book reads from *right to left*, Japanese style. If
this is your first time reading manga, you start
reading from the top right panel on each page and
take it from there. If you get lost, just follow the
numbered diagram here. It may seem backwards at
first, but you'll get the hang of it! Have fun!!

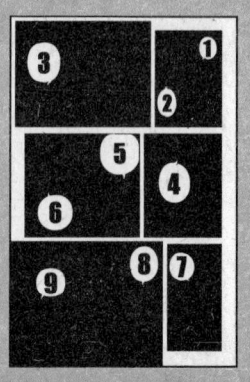

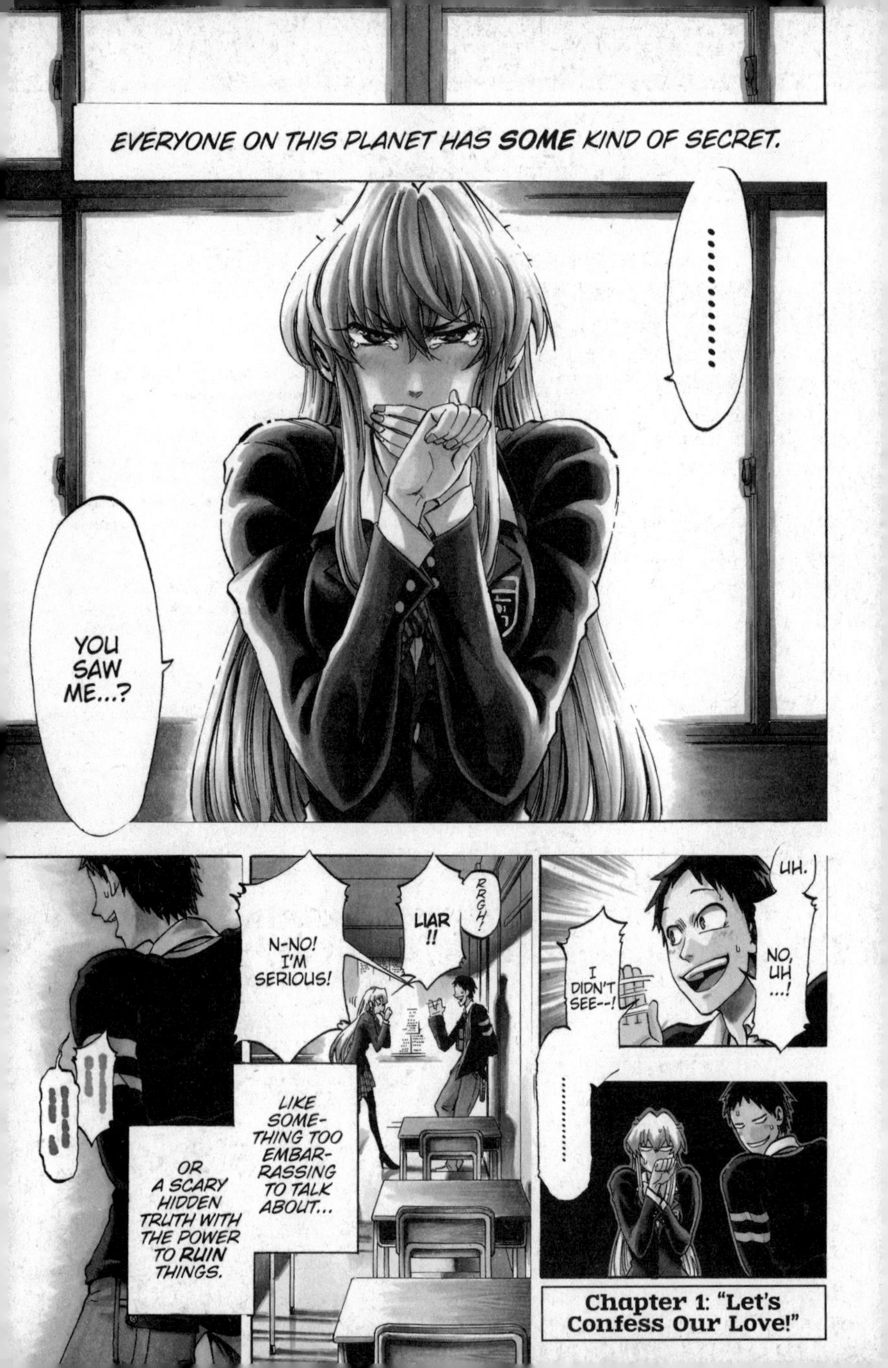
EVERYONE ON THIS PLANET HAS SOME KIND OF SECRET.
....
YOU SAW ME...?
UH.
NO, UH ...!
I DIDN'T SEE--!
......
Chapter 1: "Let's Confess Our Love!"
LIAR !!
RRGH!
N-NO! I'M SERIOUS!
LIKE SOMETHING TOO EMBARRASSING TO TALK ABOUT...
OR A SCARY HIDDEN TRUTH WITH THE POWER TO RUIN THINGS.

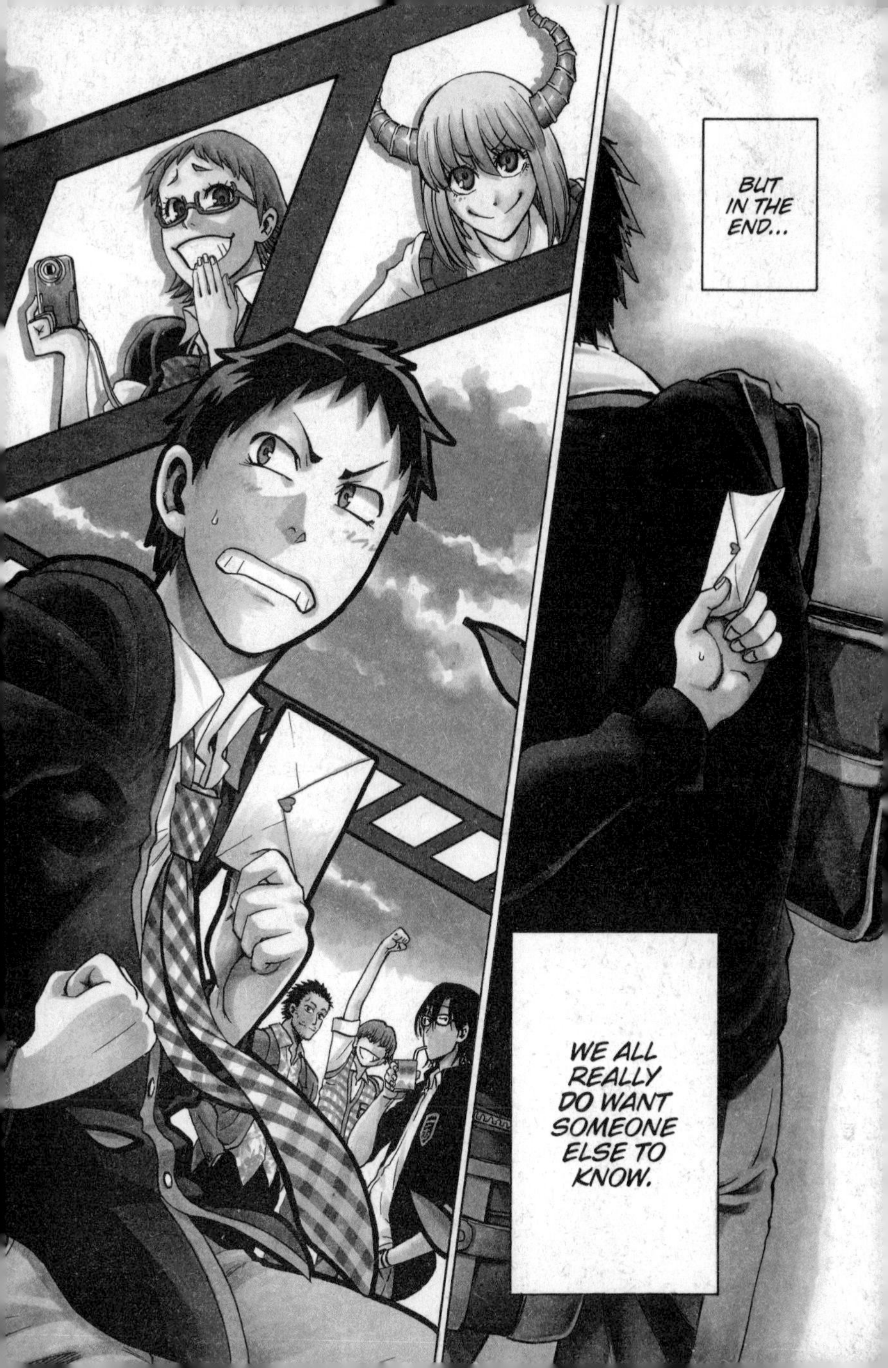
BUT IN THE END...
WE ALL REALLY DO WANT SOMEONE ELSE TO KNOW.

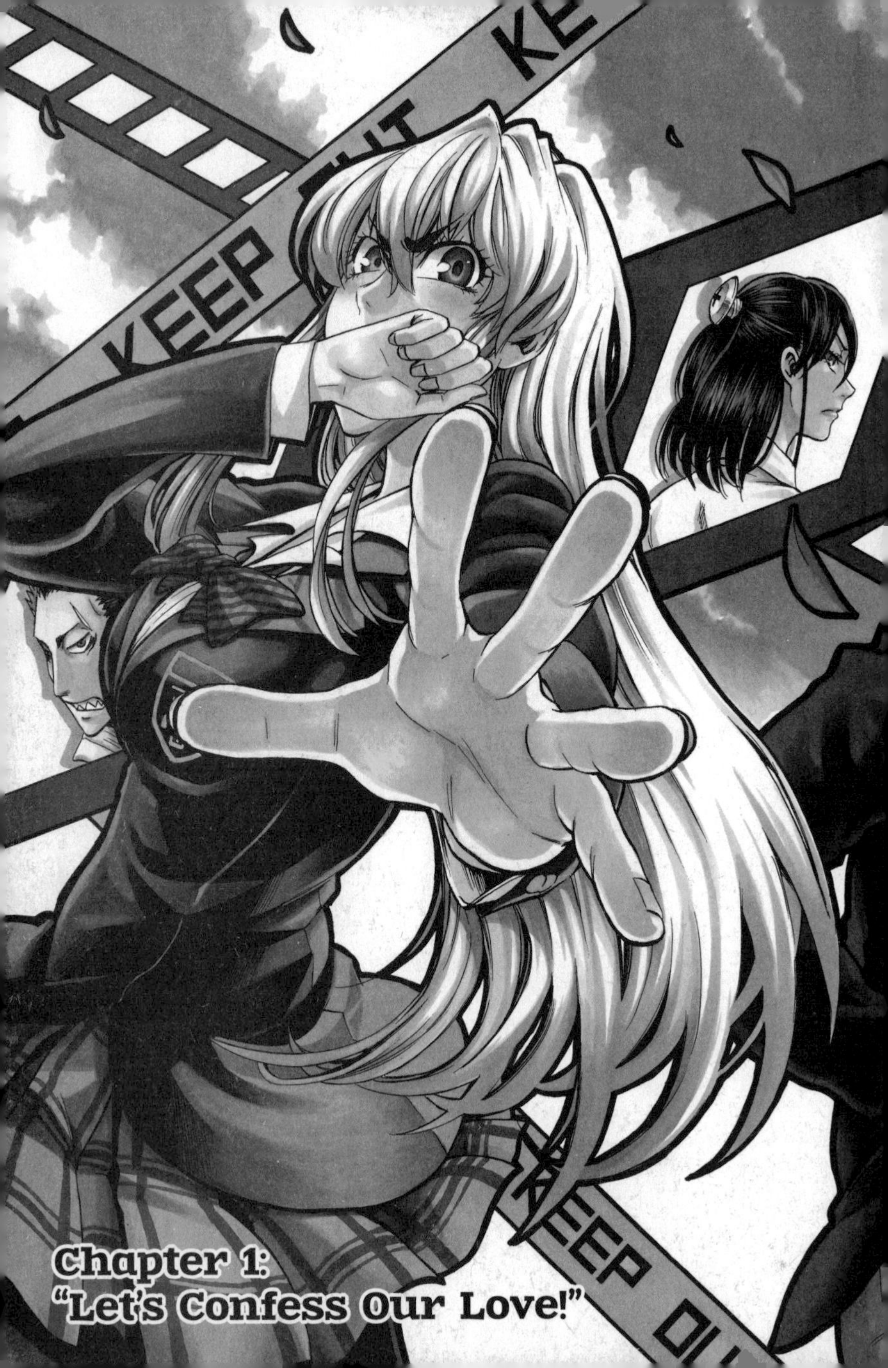
KE
KEEP
KEEP
Chapter 1:
"Let's Confess Our Love!"

TOP SECRET

My Monster Secret 1

?

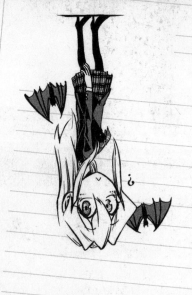

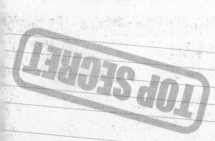

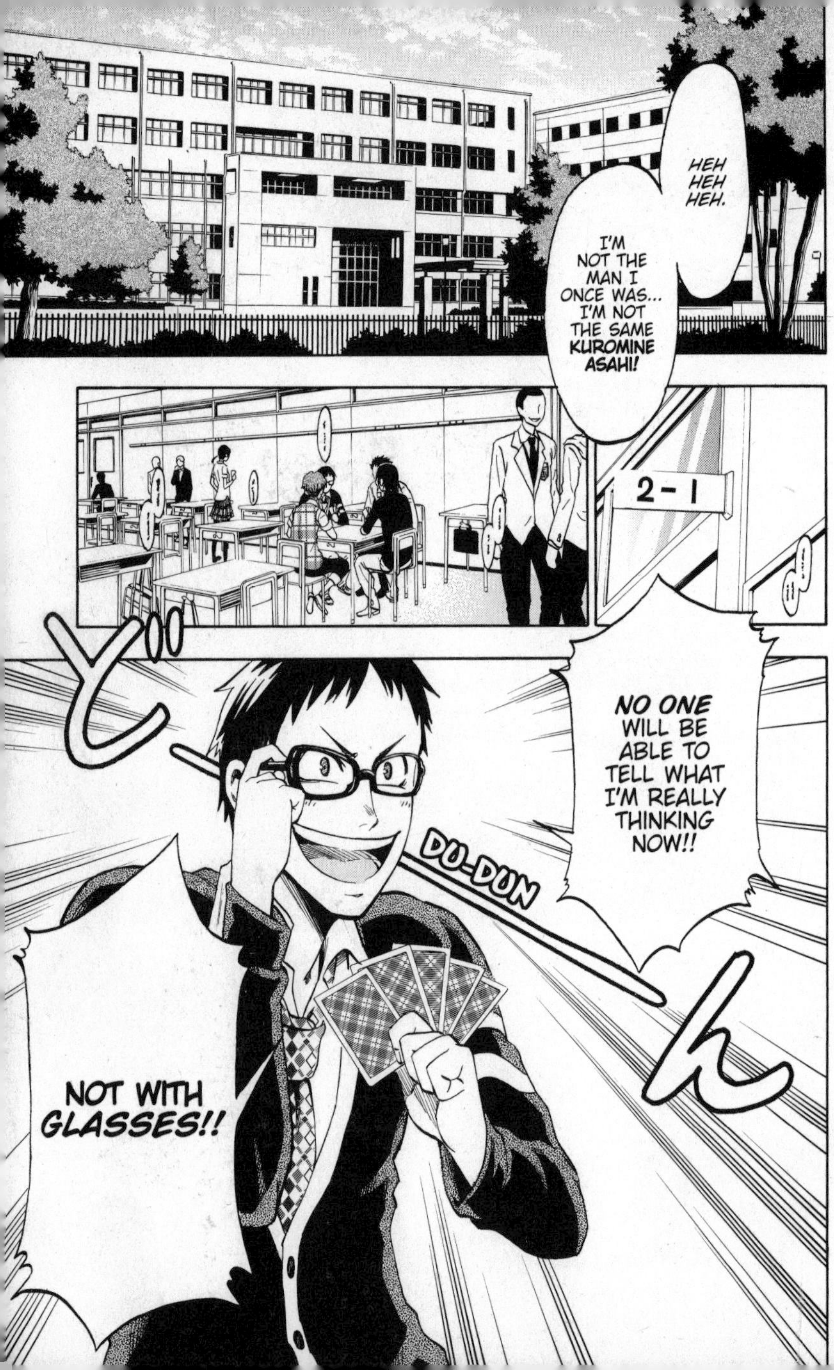
HEH HEH HEH.
I'M NOT THE MAN I ONCE WAS... I'M NOT THE SAME KUROMINE ASAHI!
2-1
NO ONE WILL BE ABLE TO TELL WHAT I'M REALLY THINKING NOW!!
DU-DUN
NOT WITH GLASSES!!

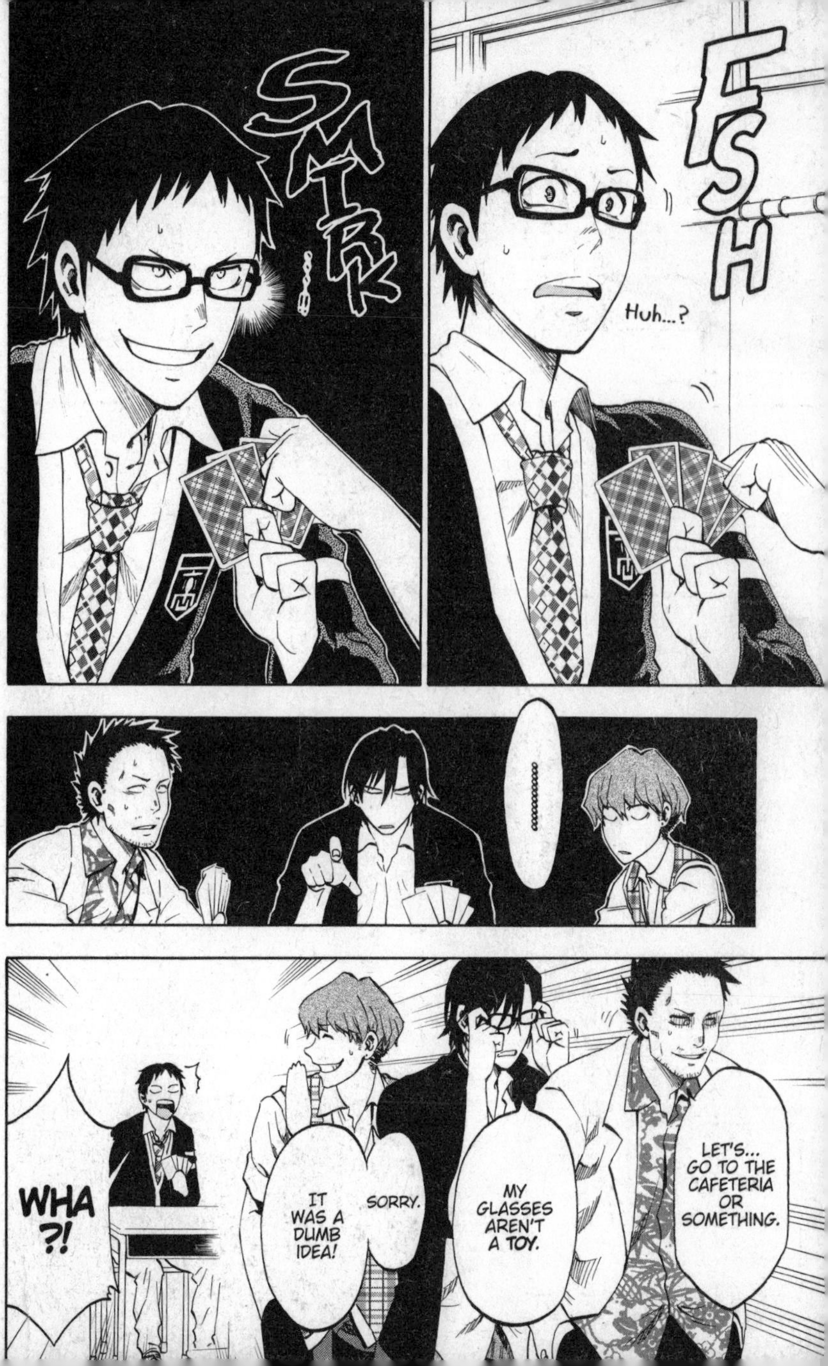
FSH
Huh...?
SMIRK
...!!
....
LET'S... GO TO THE CAFETERIA OR SOMETHING.
MY GLASSES AREN'T A TOY.
SORRY.
IT WAS A DUMB IDEA!
WHA ?!

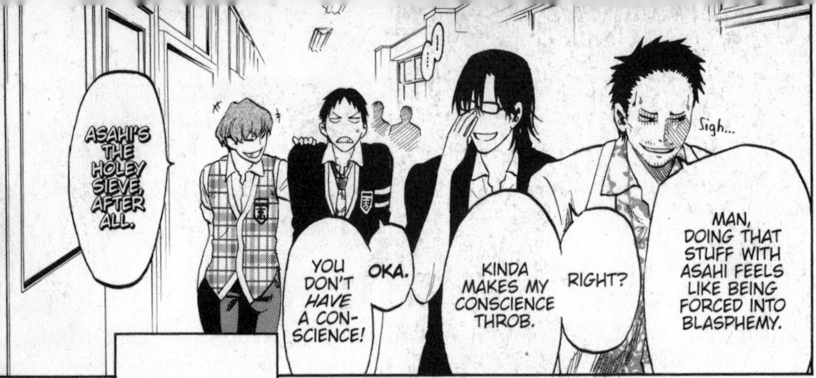
Sigh...
MAN, DOING THAT STUFF WITH ASAHI FEELS LIKE BEING FORCED INTO BLASPHEMY.
RIGHT?
KINDA MAKES MY CONSCIENCE THROB.
OKA.
YOU DON'T HAVE A CON-SCIENCE!
ASAHI'S THE HOLEY SIEVE, AFTER ALL.

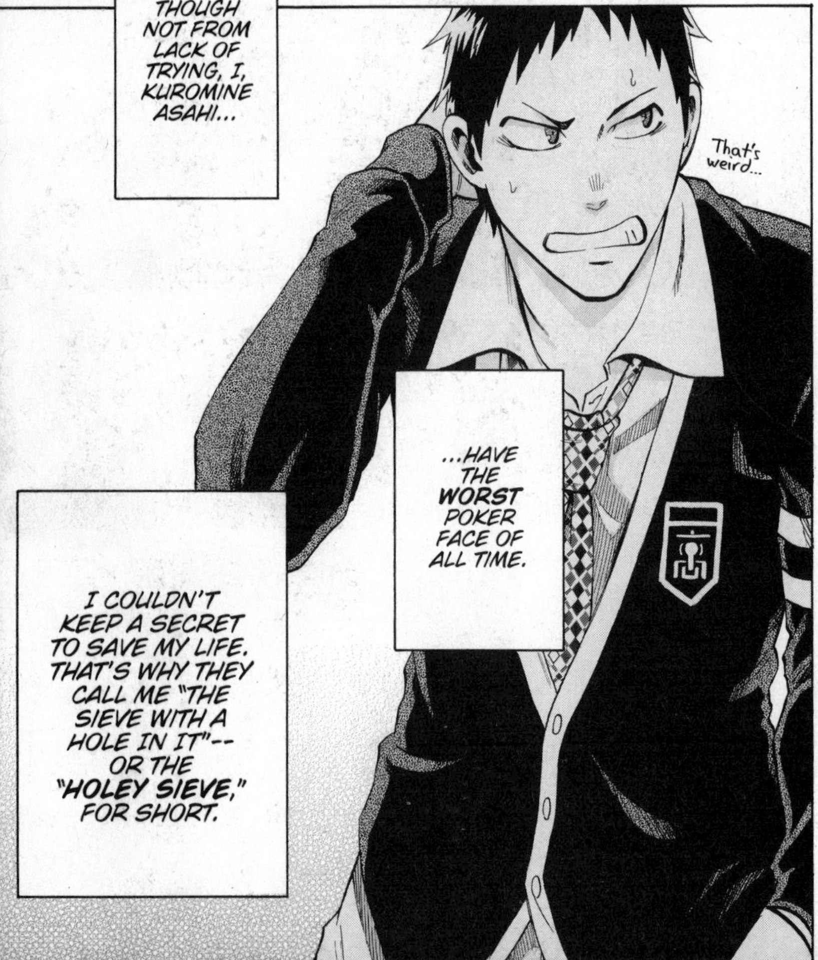
That's weird...
THOUGH NOT FROM LACK OF TRYING, I, KUROMINE ASAHI...
...HAVE THE WORST POKER FACE OF ALL TIME.
I COULDN'T KEEP A SECRET TO SAVE MY LIFE. THAT'S WHY THEY CALL ME "THE SIEVE WITH A HOLE IN IT"-- OR THE "HOLEY SIEVE," FOR SHORT.

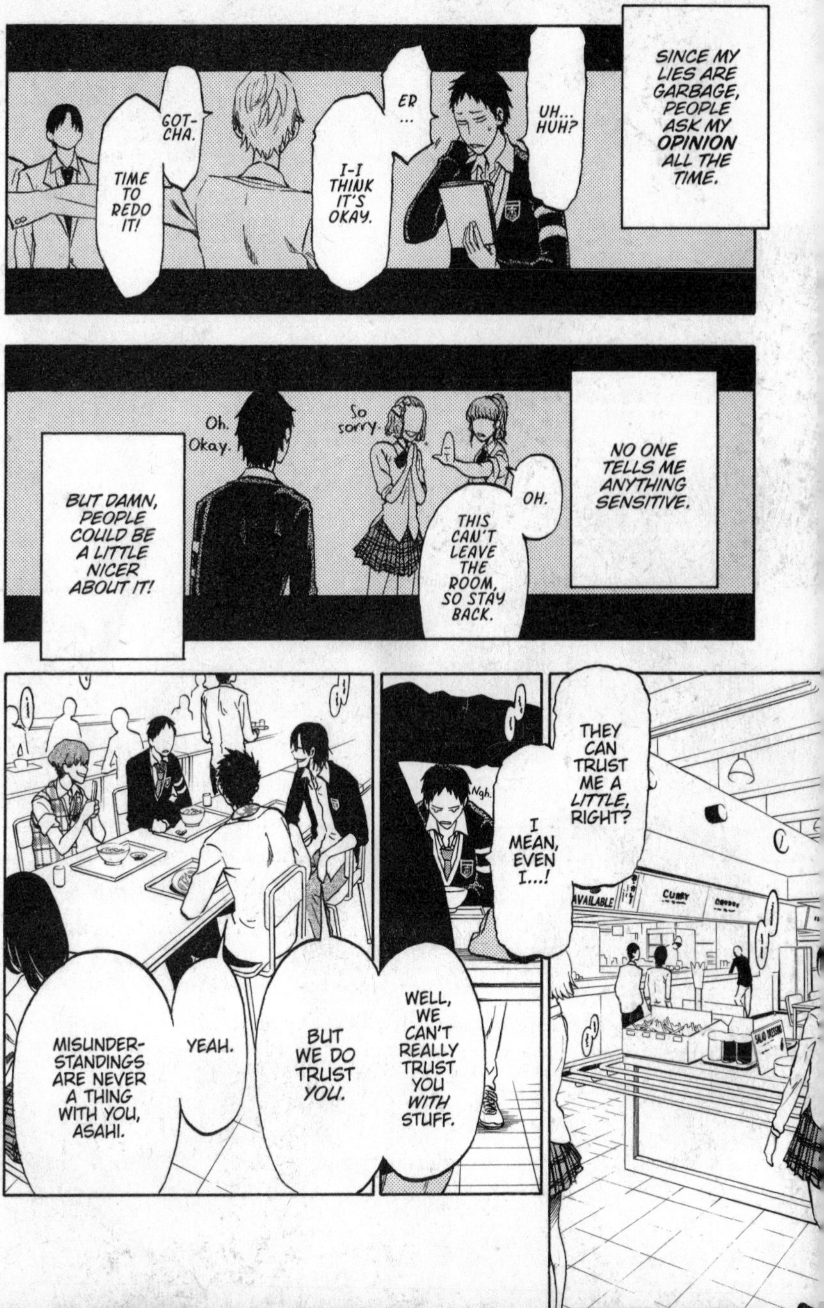
SINCE MY LIES ARE GARBAGE, PEOPLE ASK MY OPINION ALL THE TIME.
UH... HUH?
ER ...
I-I THINK IT'S OKAY.
GOT-CHA.
TIME TO REDO IT!
NO ONE TELLS ME ANYTHING SENSITIVE.
OH.
THIS CAN'T LEAVE THE ROOM, SO STAY BACK.
So sorry.
Oh. Okay.
BUT DAMN, PEOPLE COULD BE A LITTLE NICER ABOUT IT!
THEY CAN TRUST ME A LITTLE, RIGHT?
I MEAN, EVEN I...!
Ngh.
WELL, WE CAN'T REALLY TRUST YOU WITH STUFF.
BUT WE DO TRUST YOU.
YEAH.
MISUNDER-STANDINGS ARE NEVER A THING WITH YOU, ASAHI.

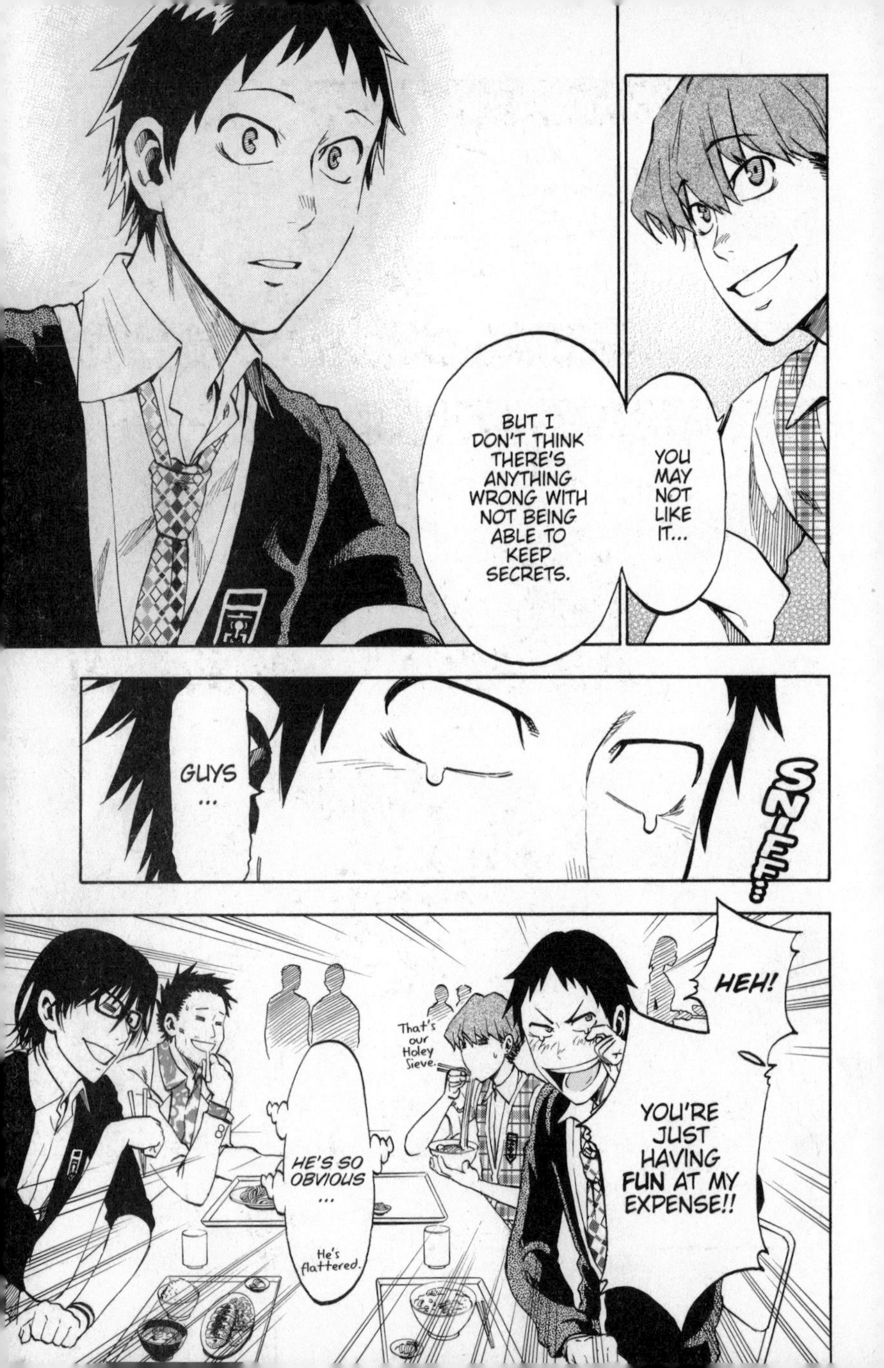
YOU MAY NOT LIKE IT...
BUT I DON'T THINK THERE'S ANYTHING WRONG WITH NOT BEING ABLE TO KEEP SECRETS.
SNIFF...
GUYS ...
HEH!
YOU'RE JUST HAVING FUN AT MY EXPENSE!!
That's our Holey Sieve.
HE'S SO OBVIOUS ...
He's flattered.

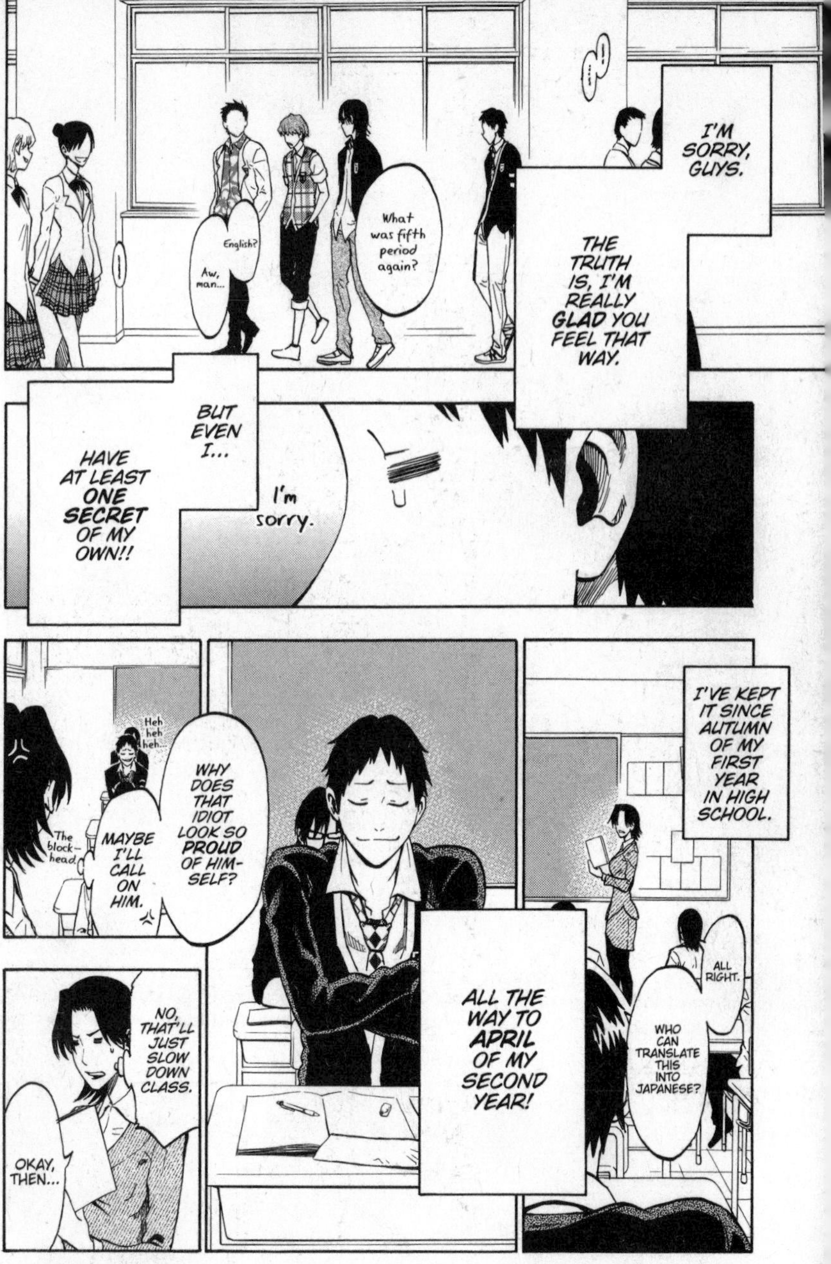
I'M SORRY, GUYS.
...!
THE TRUTH IS, I'M REALLY GLAD YOU FEEL THAT WAY.
What was fifth period again?
English?
Aw, man...
!
I'm sorry.
BUT EVEN I...
HAVE AT LEAST ONE SECRET OF MY OWN!!
I'VE KEPT IT SINCE AUTUMN OF MY FIRST YEAR IN HIGH SCHOOL.
ALL RIGHT.
WHO CAN TRANSLATE THIS INTO JAPANESE?
ALL THE WAY TO APRIL OF MY SECOND YEAR!
Heh heh heh...
WHY DOES THAT IDIOT LOOK SO PROUD OF HIMSELF?
MAYBE I'LL CALL ON HIM.
The blockhead.
NO, THAT'LL JUST SLOW DOWN CLASS.
OKAY, THEN...

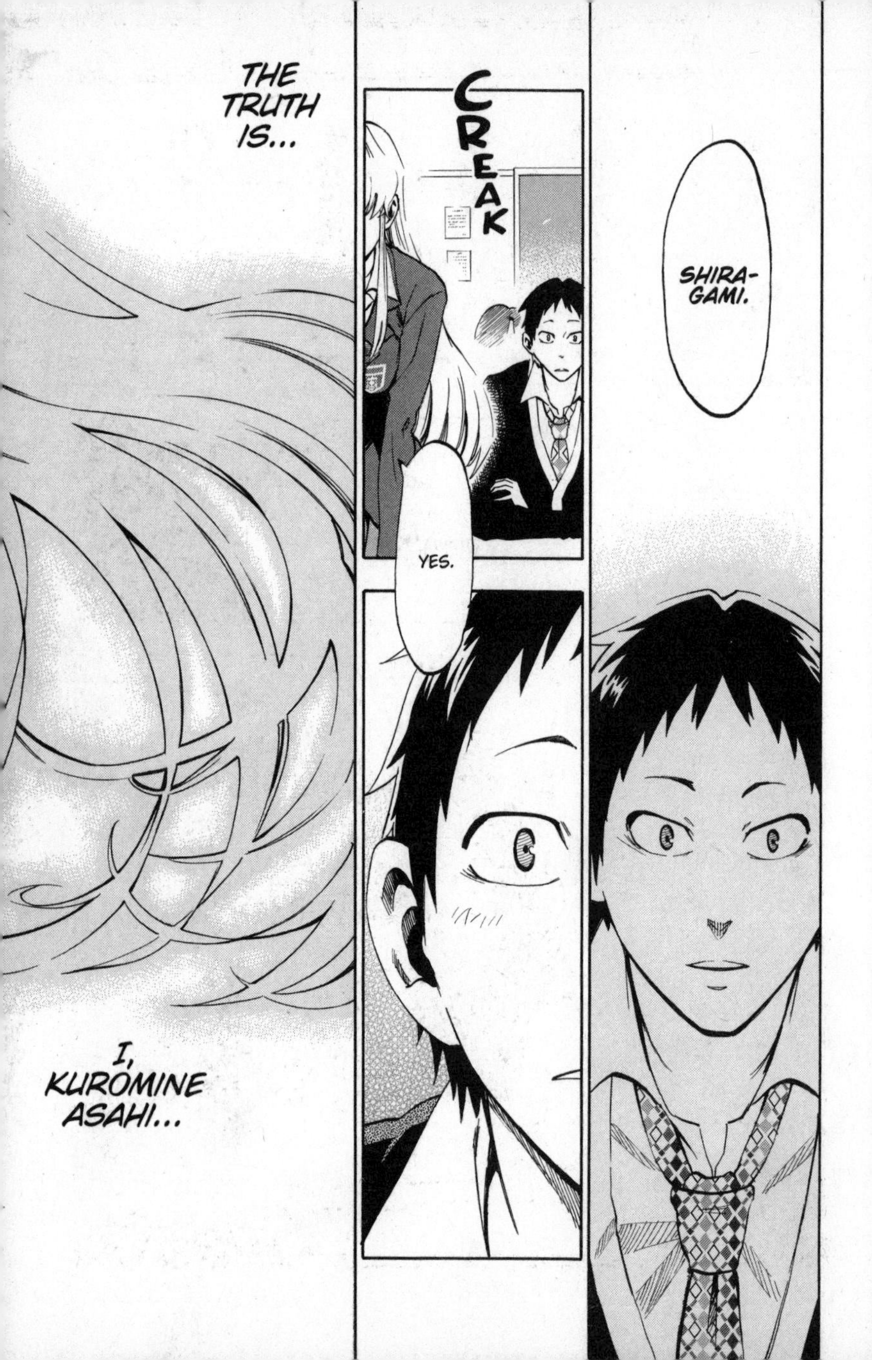
SHIRA-GAMI.
CREAK
YES.
THE TRUTH IS...
I, KUROMINE ASAHI...

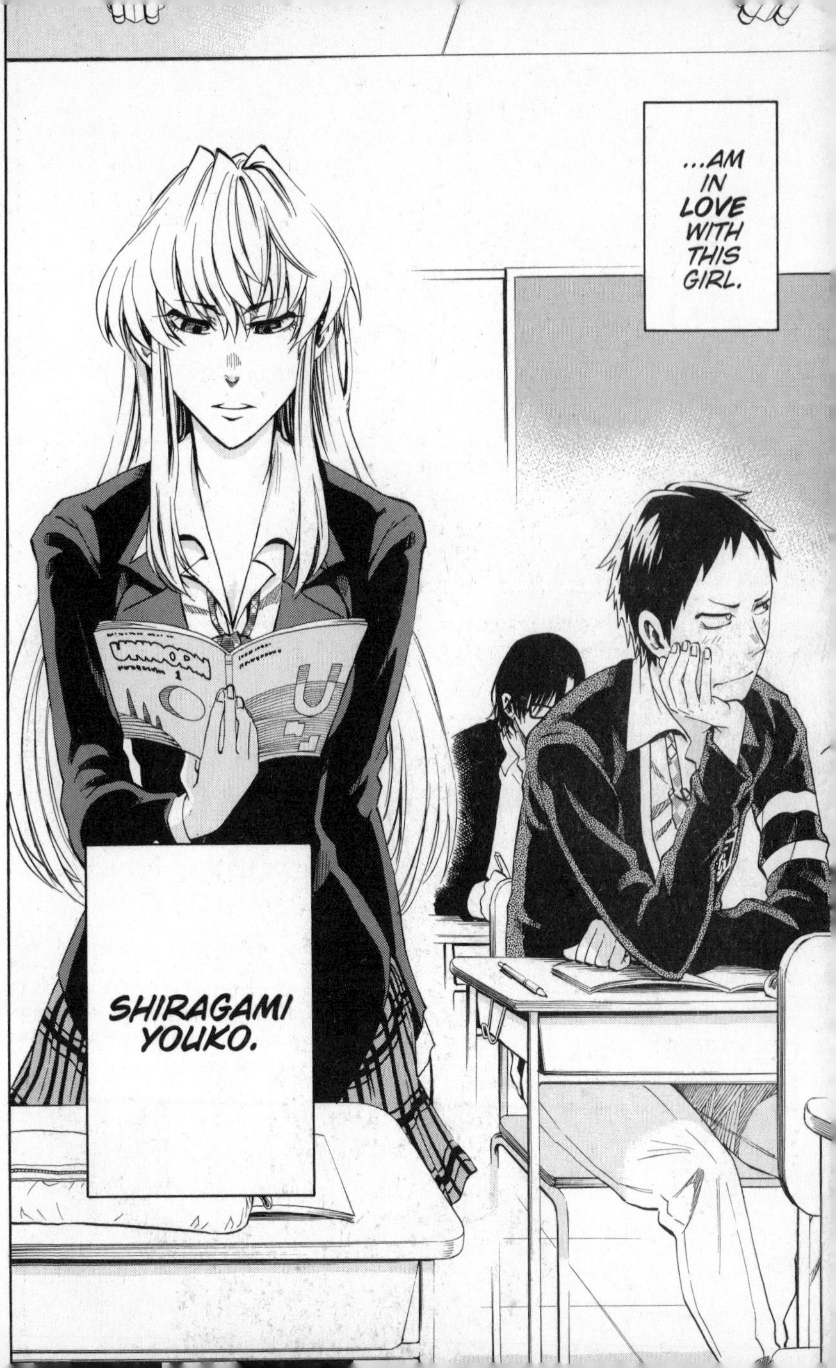
...AM IN LOVE WITH THIS GIRL.
SHIRAGAMI YOUKO.

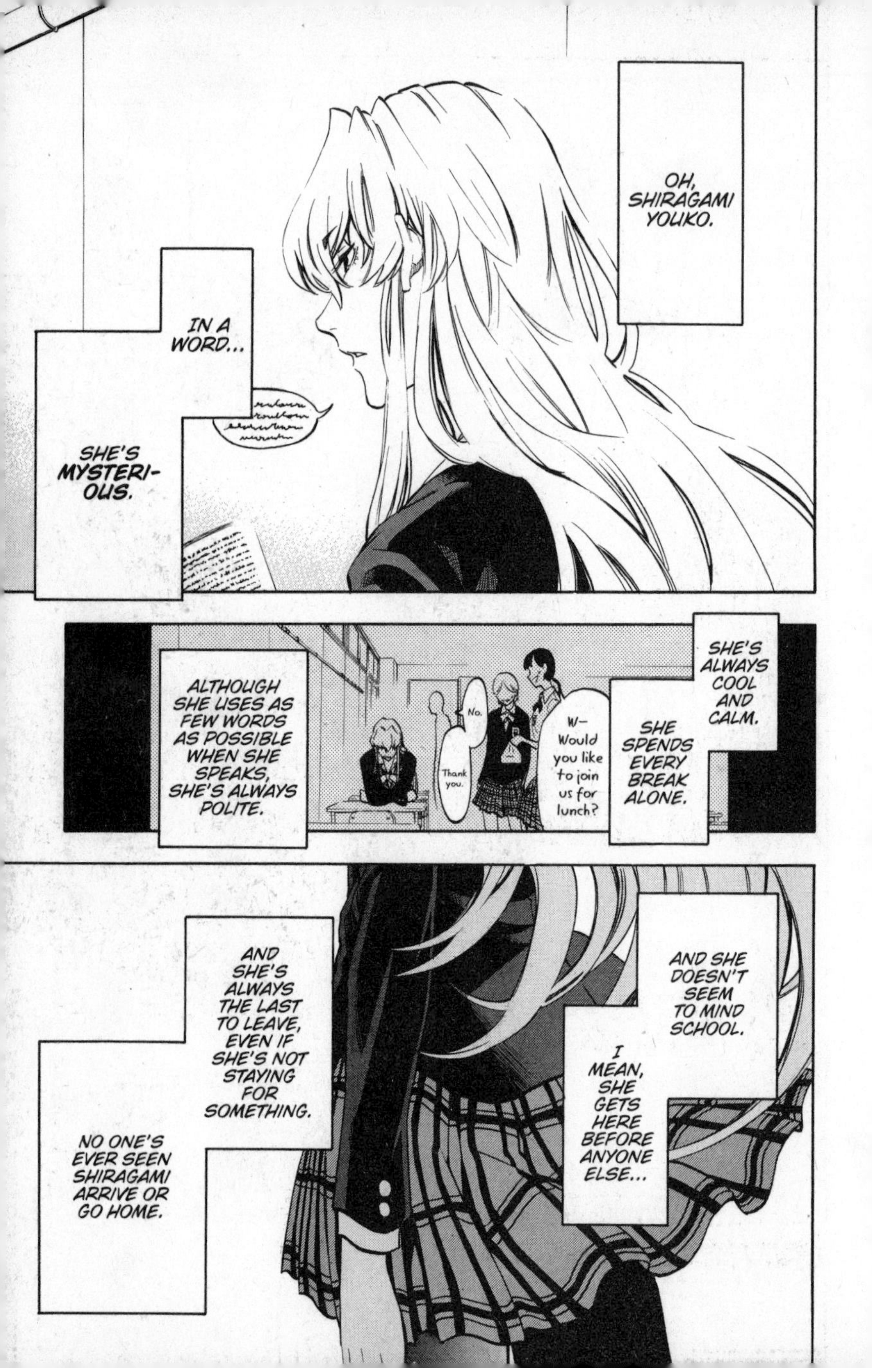
OH, SHIRAGAMI YOUKO.
IN A WORD...
SHE'S MYSTERI-OUS.
SHE'S ALWAYS COOL AND CALM.
SHE SPENDS EVERY BREAK ALONE.
W— Would you like to join us for lunch?
No.
Thank you.
ALTHOUGH SHE USES AS FEW WORDS AS POSSIBLE WHEN SHE SPEAKS, SHE'S ALWAYS POLITE.
AND SHE DOESN'T SEEM TO MIND SCHOOL.
I MEAN, SHE GETS HERE BEFORE ANYONE ELSE...
AND SHE'S ALWAYS THE LAST TO LEAVE, EVEN IF SHE'S NOT STAYING FOR SOMETHING.
NO ONE'S EVER SEEN SHIRAGAMI ARRIVE OR GO HOME.

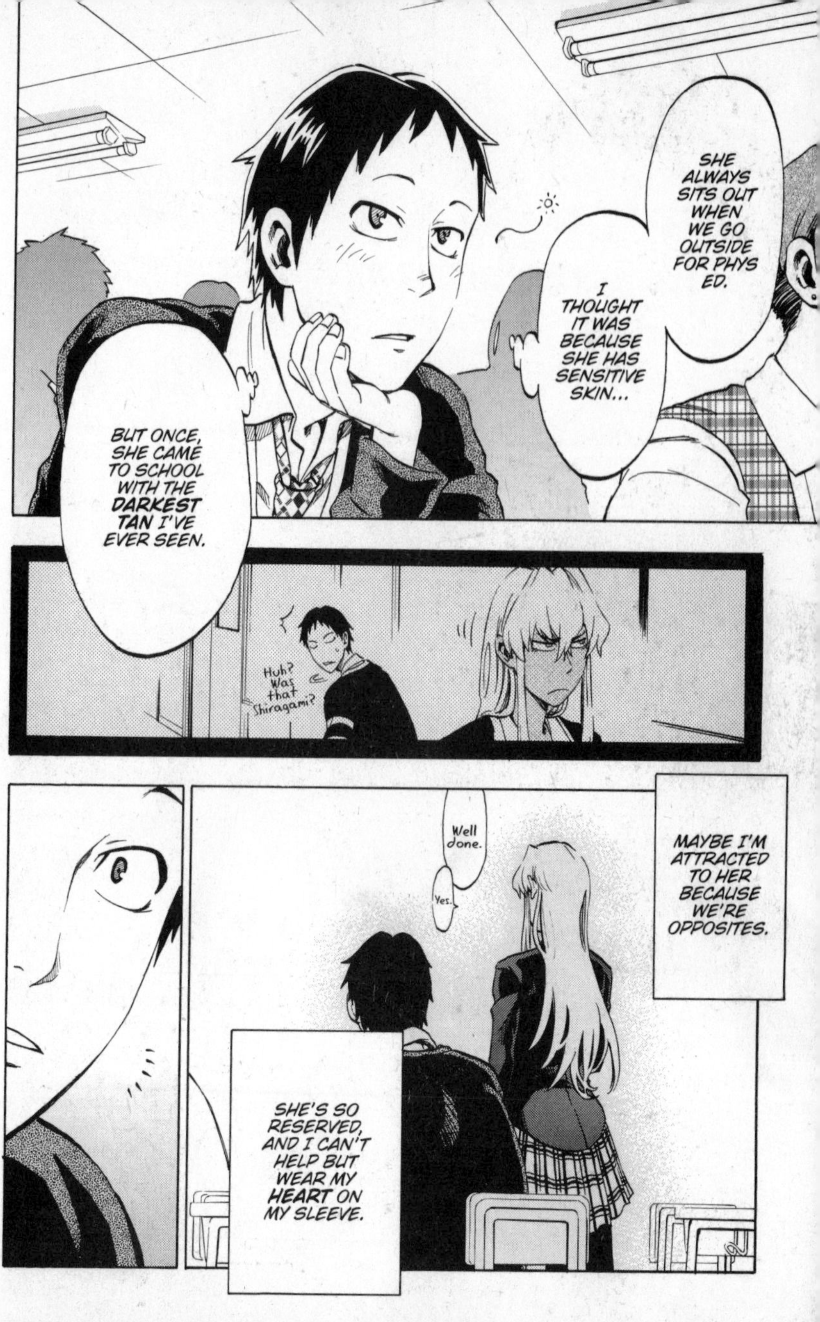
SHE ALWAYS SITS OUT WHEN WE GO OUTSIDE FOR PHYS ED.
I THOUGHT IT WAS BECAUSE SHE HAS SENSITIVE SKIN...
BUT ONCE, SHE CAME TO SCHOOL WITH THE **DARKEST TAN** I'VE EVER SEEN.
Huh? Was that Shiragami?
MAYBE I'M ATTRACTED TO HER BECAUSE WE'RE OPPOSITES.
Well done.
Yes.
SHE'S SO RESERVED, AND I CAN'T HELP BUT WEAR MY **HEART** ON MY SLEEVE.

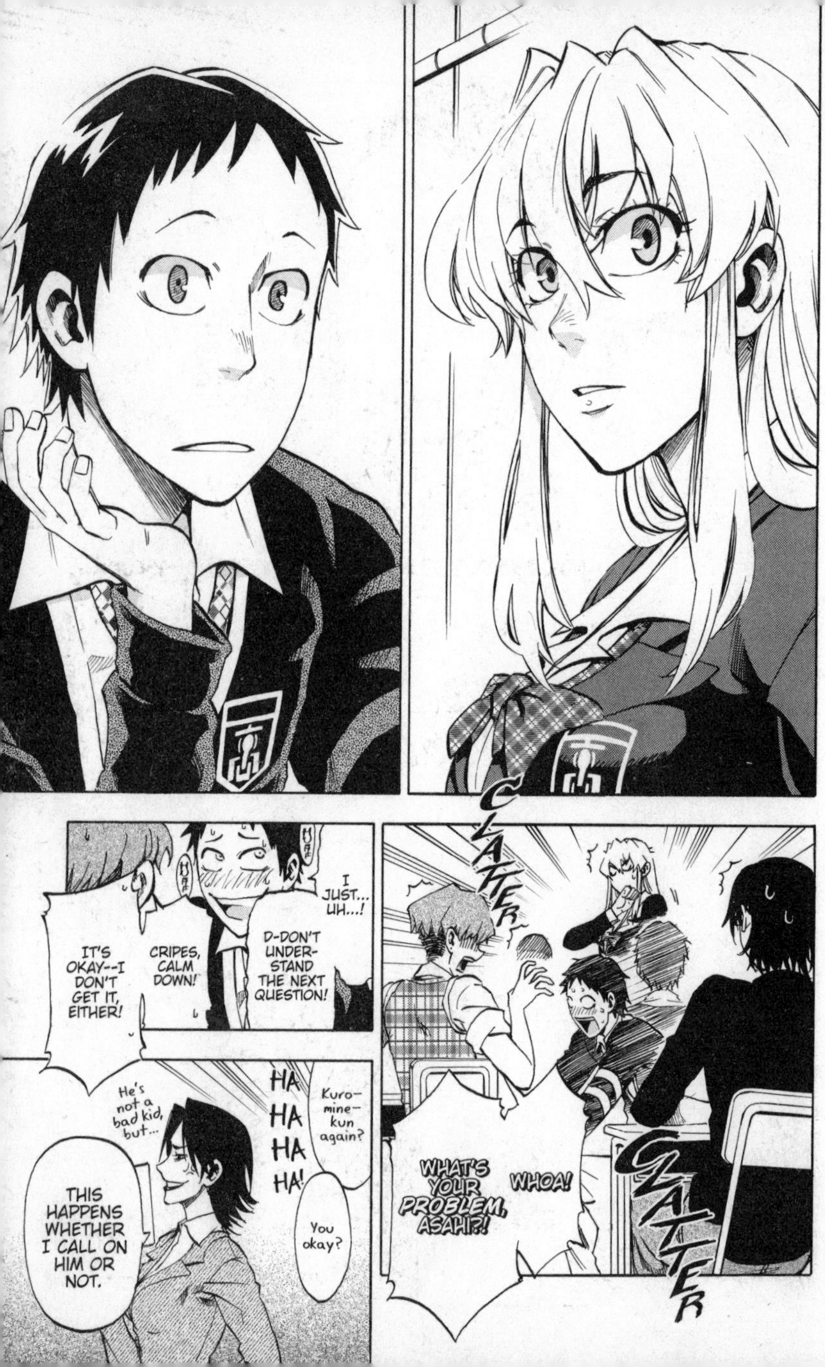
CLATTER
CLATTER
WHOA!
WHAT'S YOUR PROBLEM, ASAHI?!
I JUST... UH...!
D-DON'T UNDERSTAND THE NEXT QUESTION!
CRIPES, CALM DOWN!
IT'S OKAY--I DON'T GET IT, EITHER!
Kuromine-kun again?
HA HA HA HA!
He's not a bad kid, but...
You okay?
THIS HAPPENS WHETHER I CALL ON HIM OR NOT.

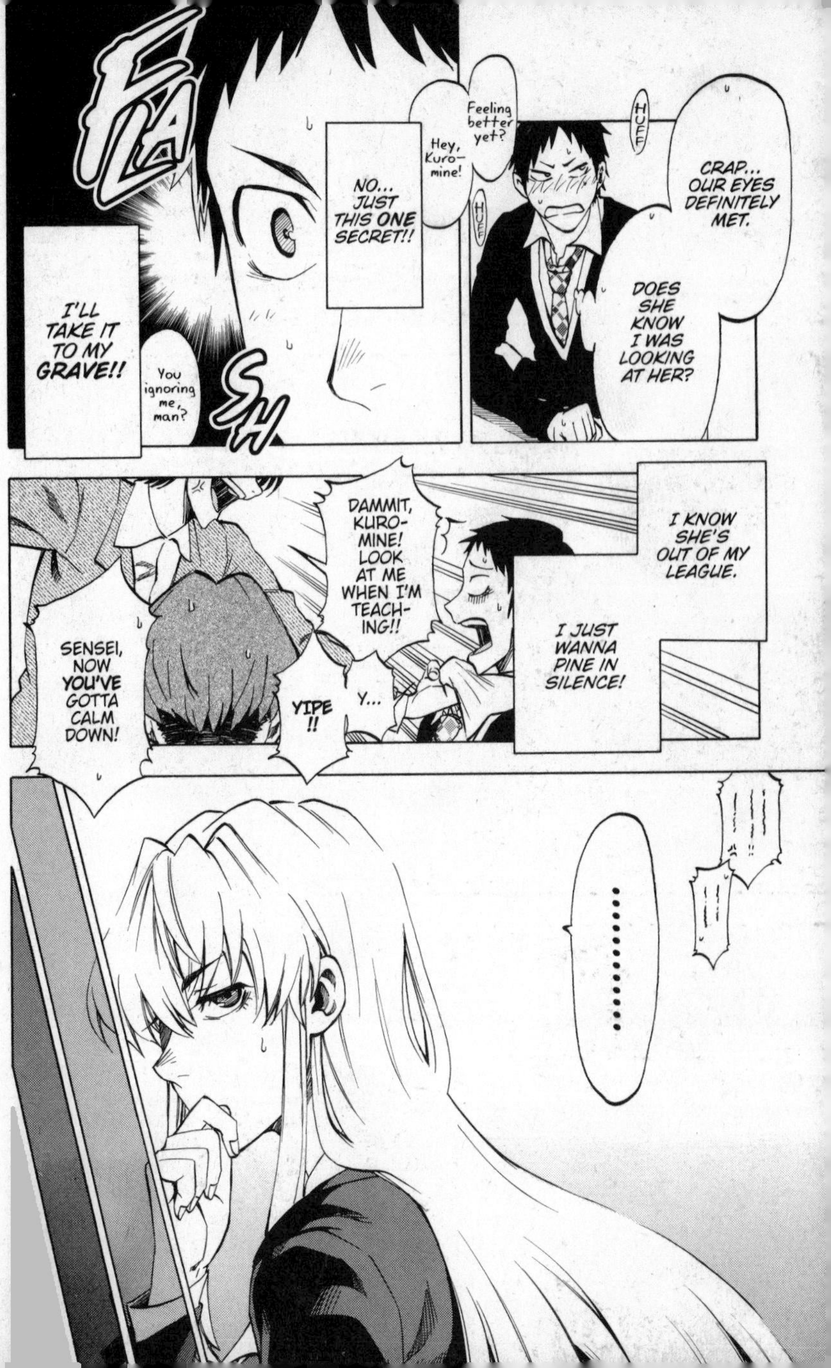
CRAP... OUR EYES DEFINITELY MET.
DOES SHE KNOW I WAS LOOKING AT HER?
HUFF
HUFF
Feeling better yet?
Hey, Kuro-mine!
NO... JUST THIS ONE SECRET!!
FLA
SH
You ignoring me, man?
I'LL TAKE IT TO MY GRAVE!!
I KNOW SHE'S OUT OF MY LEAGUE.
I JUST WANNA PINE IN SILENCE!
DAMMIT, KURO-MINE! LOOK AT ME WHEN I'M TEACHING!!
Y...
YIPE!!
SENSEI, NOW YOU'VE GOTTA CALM DOWN!
....

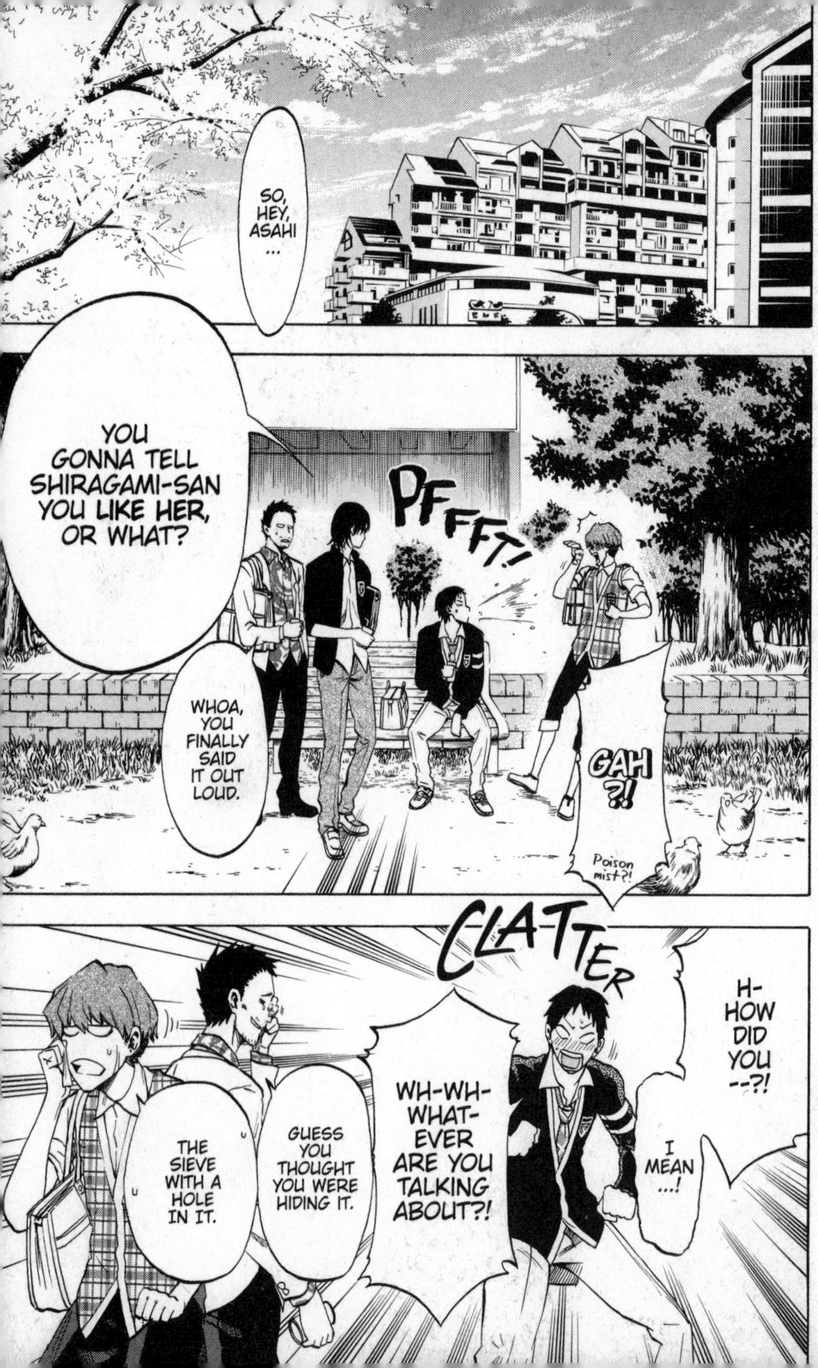
SO, HEY, ASAHI...
YOU GONNA TELL SHIRAGAMI-SAN YOU LIKE HER, OR WHAT?
PFFFT!
GAH?!
Poison mist?!
WHOA, YOU FINALLY SAID IT OUT LOUD.
CLATTER
H-HOW DID YOU--?!
I MEAN...!
WH-WH-WHATEVER ARE YOU TALKING ABOUT?!
GUESS YOU THOUGHT YOU WERE HIDING IT.
THE SIEVE WITH A HOLE IN IT.

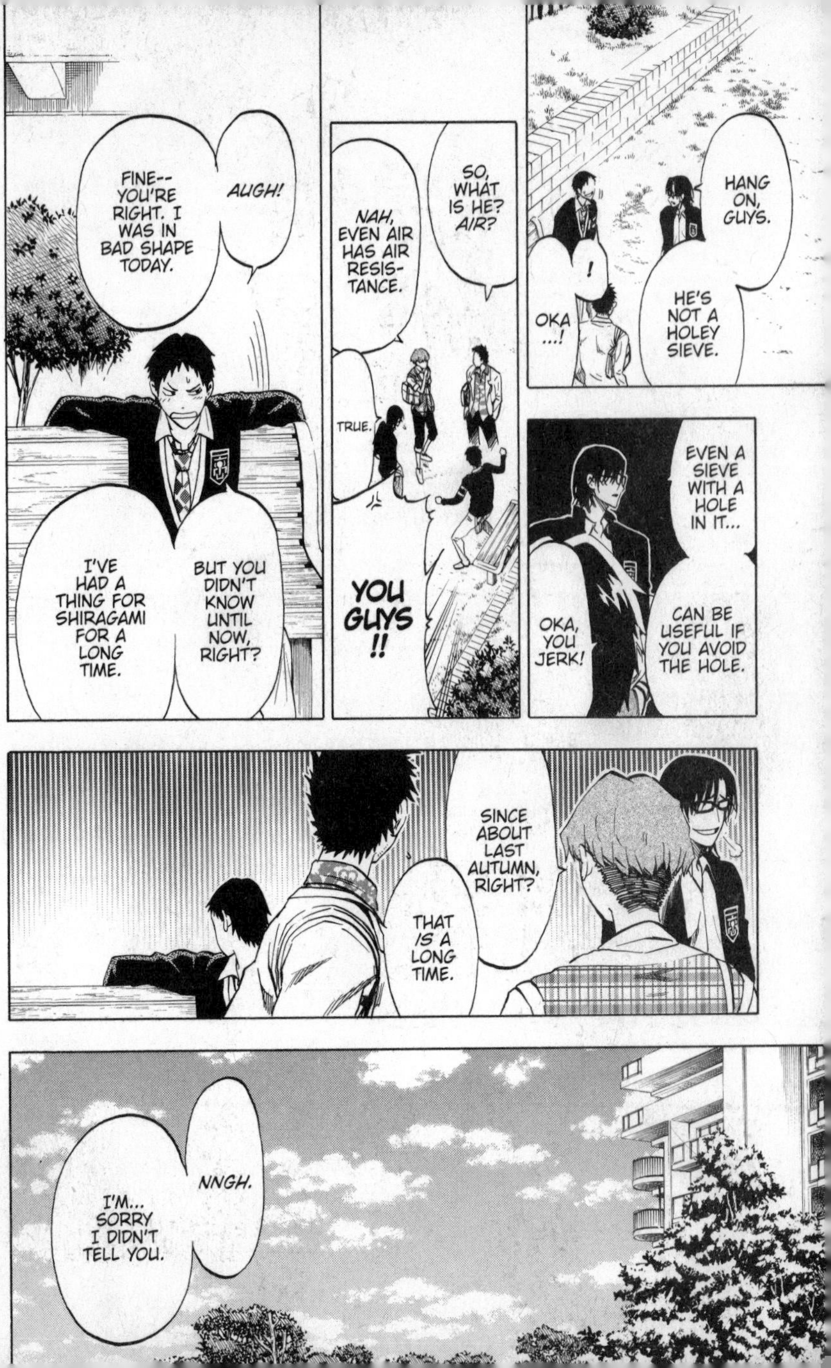
HANG ON, GUYS.
HE'S NOT A HOLEY SIEVE.
!
OKA ...!
EVEN A SIEVE WITH A HOLE IN IT...
CAN BE USEFUL IF YOU AVOID THE HOLE.
OKA, YOU JERK!
SO, WHAT IS HE? AIR?
NAH, EVEN AIR HAS AIR RESIS-TANCE.
TRUE.
YOU GUYS !!
AUGH!
FINE-- YOU'RE RIGHT. I WAS IN BAD SHAPE TODAY.
BUT YOU DIDN'T KNOW UNTIL NOW, RIGHT?
I'VE HAD A THING FOR SHIRAGAMI FOR A LONG TIME.
SINCE ABOUT LAST AUTUMN, RIGHT?
THAT IS A LONG TIME.
NNGH.
I'M... SORRY I DIDN'T TELL YOU.

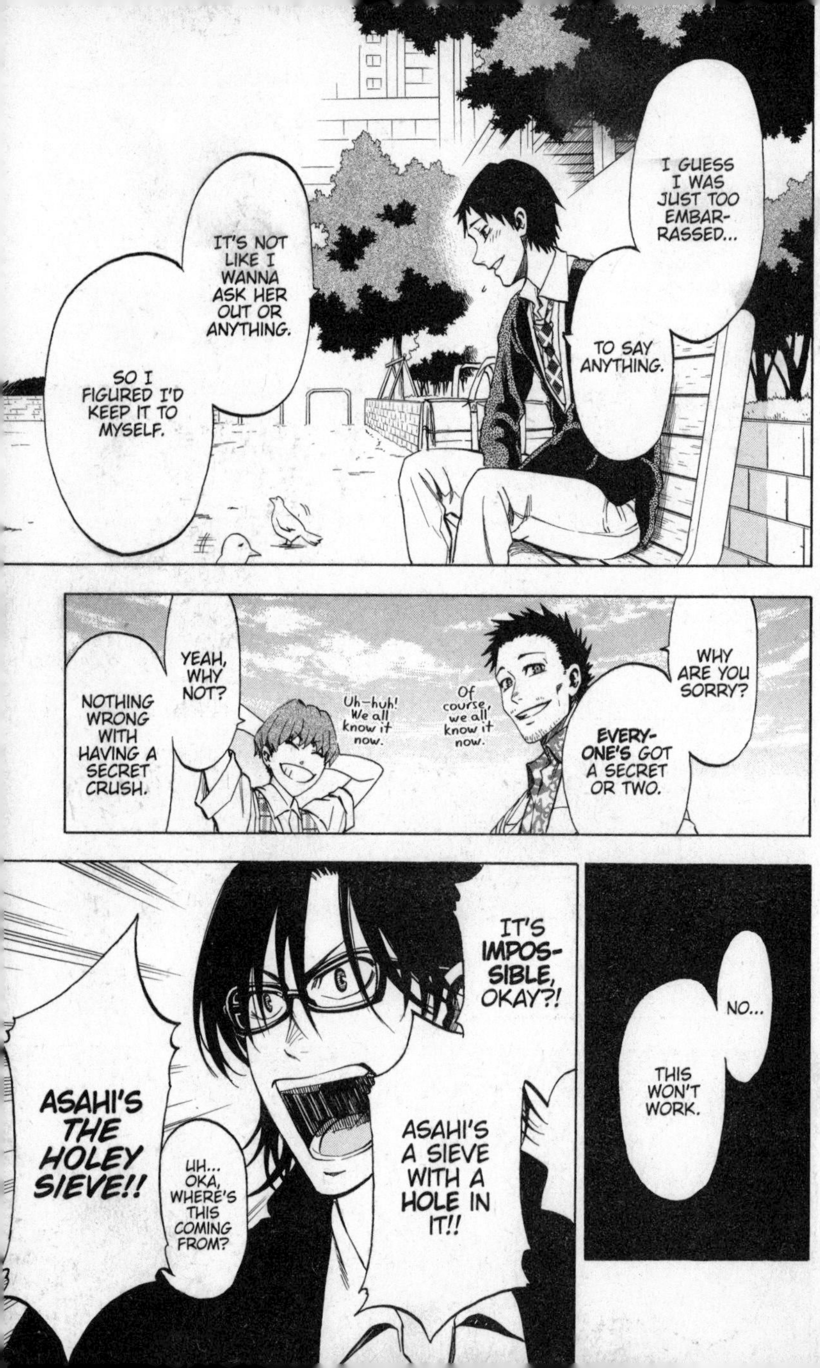
I GUESS I WAS JUST TOO EMBAR-RASSED...
TO SAY ANYTHING.
IT'S NOT LIKE I WANNA ASK HER OUT OR ANYTHING.
SO I FIGURED I'D KEEP IT TO MYSELF.
WHY ARE YOU SORRY?
EVERY-ONE'S GOT A SECRET OR TWO.
Of course, we all know it now.
Uh-huh! We all know it now.
YEAH, WHY NOT?
NOTHING WRONG WITH HAVING A SECRET CRUSH.
NO...
THIS WON'T WORK.
IT'S IMPOS-SIBLE, OKAY?!
ASAHI'S A SIEVE WITH A HOLE IN IT!!
UH... OKA, WHERE'S THIS COMING FROM?
ASAHI'S THE HOLEY SIEVE!!

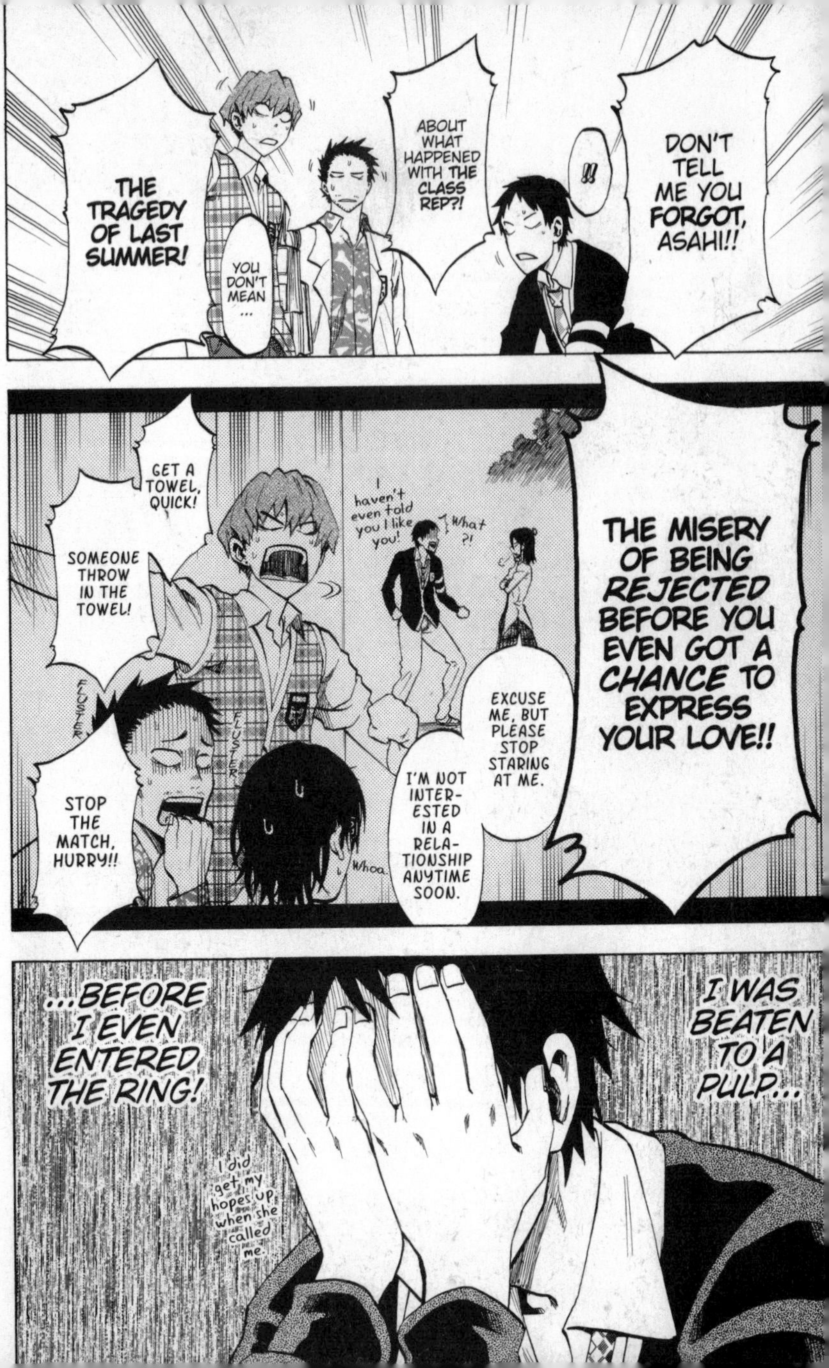
DON'T TELL ME YOU FORGOT, ASAHI!!
!!
ABOUT WHAT HAPPENED WITH THE CLASS REP?!
THE TRAGEDY OF LAST SUMMER!
YOU DON'T MEAN ...
THE MISERY OF BEING REJECTED BEFORE YOU EVEN GOT A CHANCE TO EXPRESS YOUR LOVE!!
I haven't even told you I like you!
What ?!
EXCUSE ME, BUT PLEASE STOP STARING AT ME.
I'M NOT INTERESTED IN A RELATIONSHIP ANYTIME SOON.
Whoa.
GET A TOWEL, QUICK!
SOMEONE THROW IN THE TOWEL!
FLUSTER FLUSTER
STOP THE MATCH, HURRY!!
I WAS BEATEN TO A PULP...
...BEFORE I EVEN ENTERED THE RING!
I did get my hopes up when she called me.

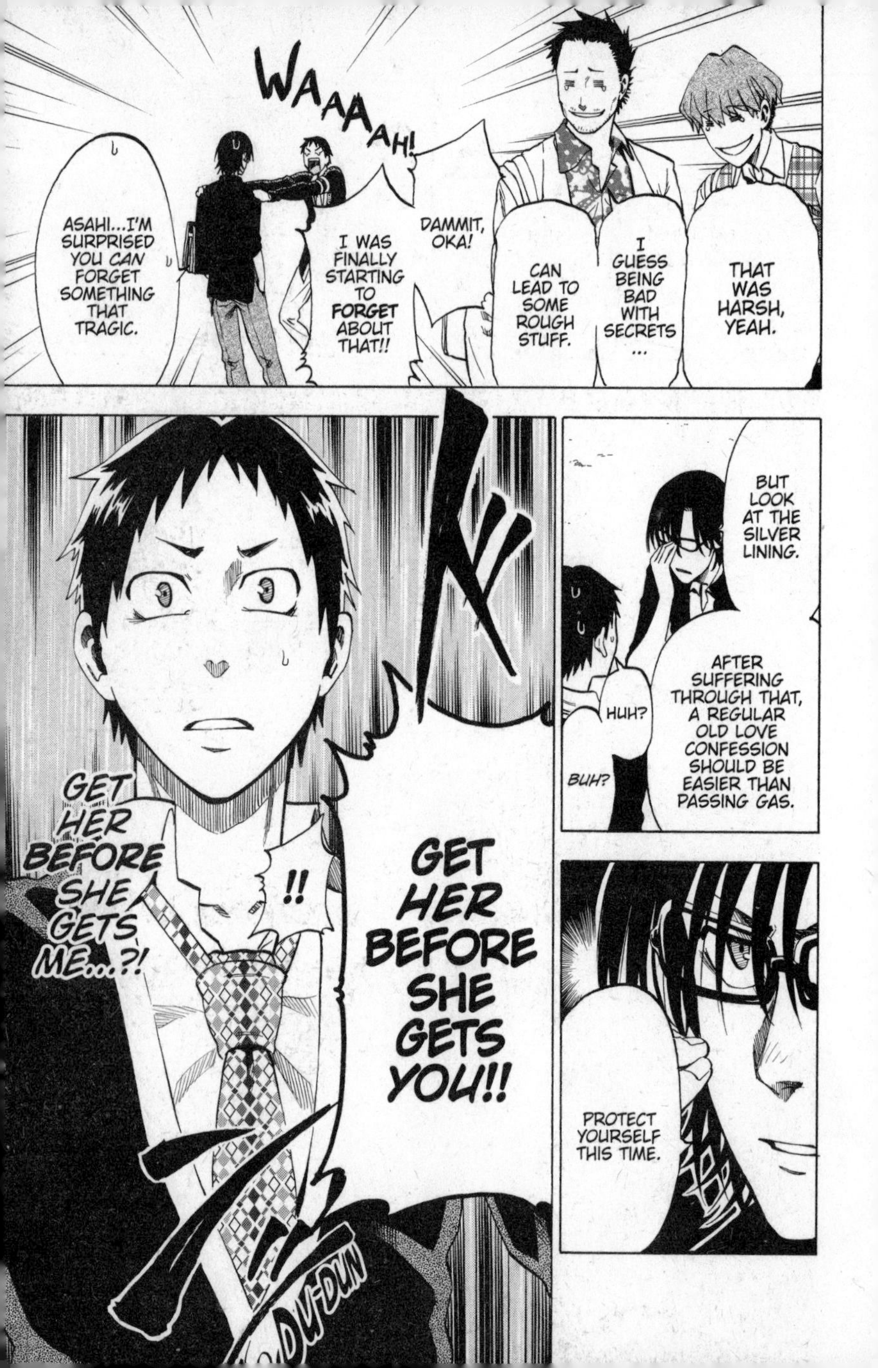
THAT WAS HARSH, YEAH.
I GUESS BEING BAD WITH SECRETS...
CAN LEAD TO SOME ROUGH STUFF.
DAMMIT, OKA!
WAAAAAH!
I WAS FINALLY STARTING TO **FORGET** ABOUT THAT!!
ASAHI...I'M SURPRISED YOU CAN FORGET SOMETHING THAT TRAGIC.
BUT LOOK AT THE SILVER LINING.
AFTER SUFFERING THROUGH THAT, A REGULAR OLD LOVE CONFESSION SHOULD BE EASIER THAN PASSING GAS.
HUH?
BUH?
PROTECT YOURSELF THIS TIME.
GET HER BEFORE SHE GETS YOU!!
!!
GET HER BEFORE SHE GETS ME...?!
DU-DUN

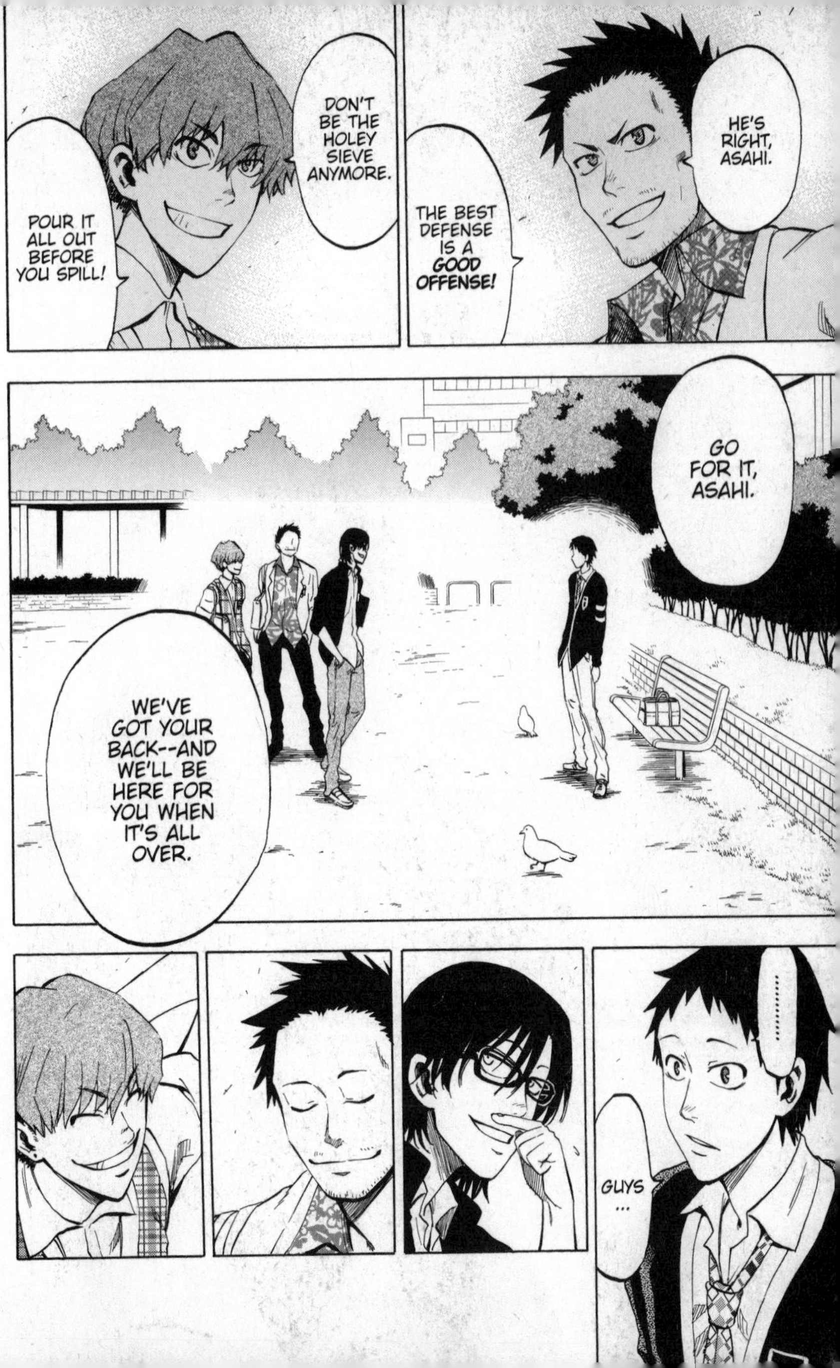
HE'S RIGHT, ASAHI.
THE BEST DEFENSE IS A GOOD OFFENSE!
DON'T BE THE HOLEY SIEVE ANYMORE.
POUR IT ALL OUT BEFORE YOU SPILL!
GO FOR IT, ASAHI.
WE'VE GOT YOUR BACK--AND WE'LL BE HERE FOR YOU WHEN IT'S ALL OVER.
......
GUYS ...

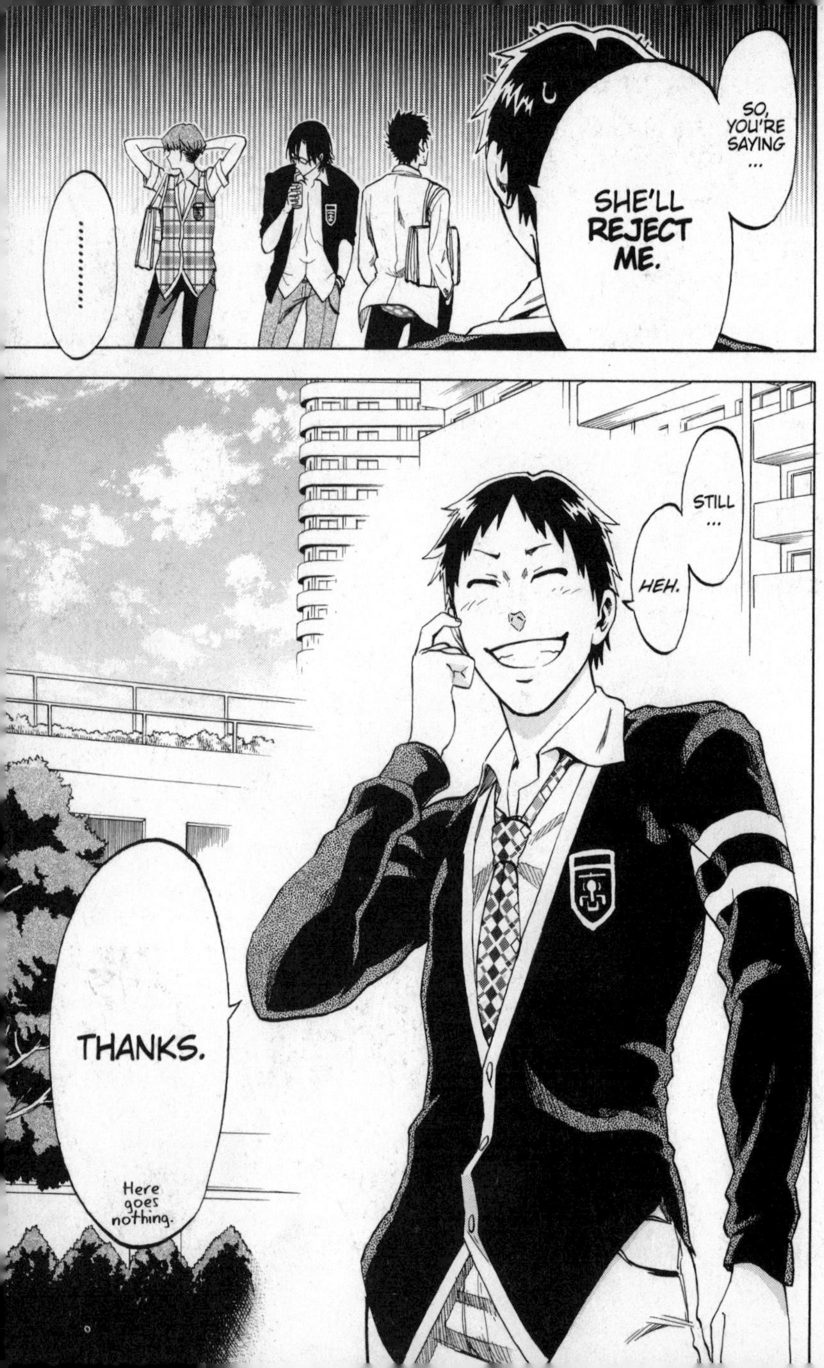
SO, YOU'RE SAYING ...
SHE'LL REJECT ME.
....
STILL ...
HEH.
THANKS.
Here goes nothing.

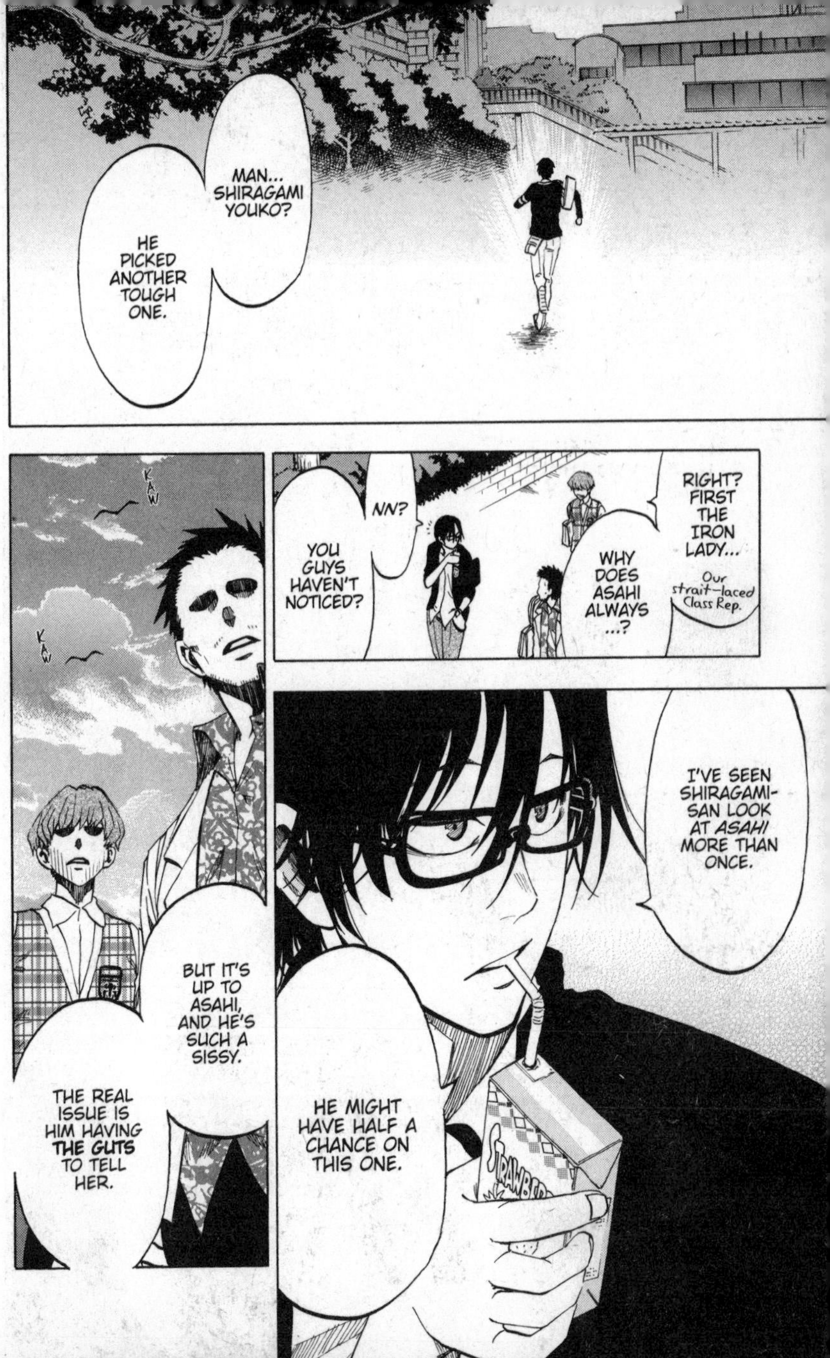
MAN... SHIRAGAMI YOUKO?
HE PICKED ANOTHER TOUGH ONE.
RIGHT? FIRST THE IRON LADY...
Our strait-laced Class Rep.
WHY DOES ASAHI ALWAYS ...?
NN?
YOU GUYS HAVEN'T NOTICED?
I'VE SEEN SHIRAGAMI-SAN LOOK AT ASAHI MORE THAN ONCE.
HE MIGHT HAVE HALF A CHANCE ON THIS ONE.
KAW
KAW
BUT IT'S UP TO ASAHI, AND HE'S SUCH A SISSY.
THE REAL ISSUE IS HIM HAVING **THE GUTS** TO TELL HER.

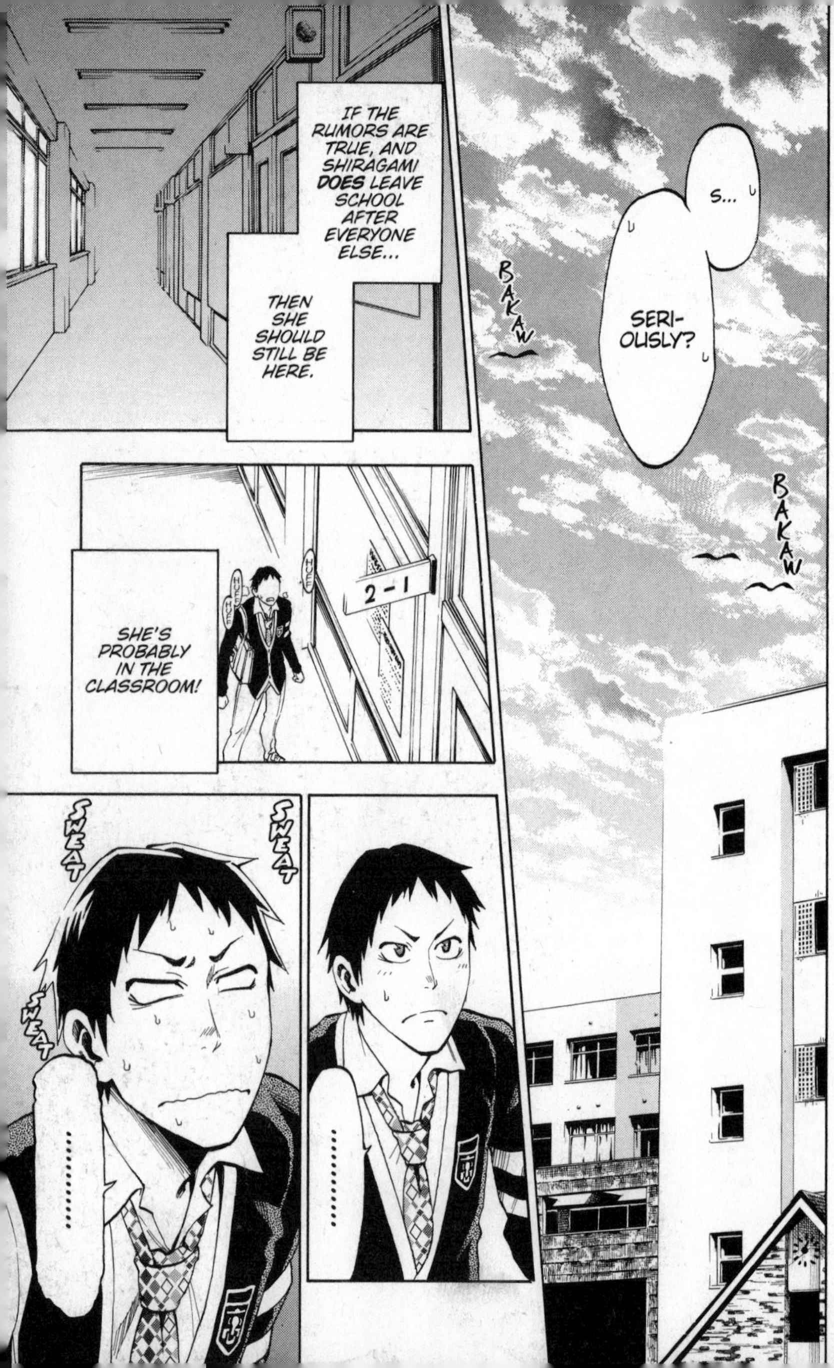
S...
SERI-OUSLY?
BAKAW
BAKAW
IF THE RUMORS ARE TRUE, AND SHIRAGAMI DOES LEAVE SCHOOL AFTER EVERYONE ELSE...
THEN SHE SHOULD STILL BE HERE.
SHE'S PROBABLY IN THE CLASSROOM!
HUFF
HUFF
HUFF
2-1
SWEAT
......
SWEAT
SWEAT
......

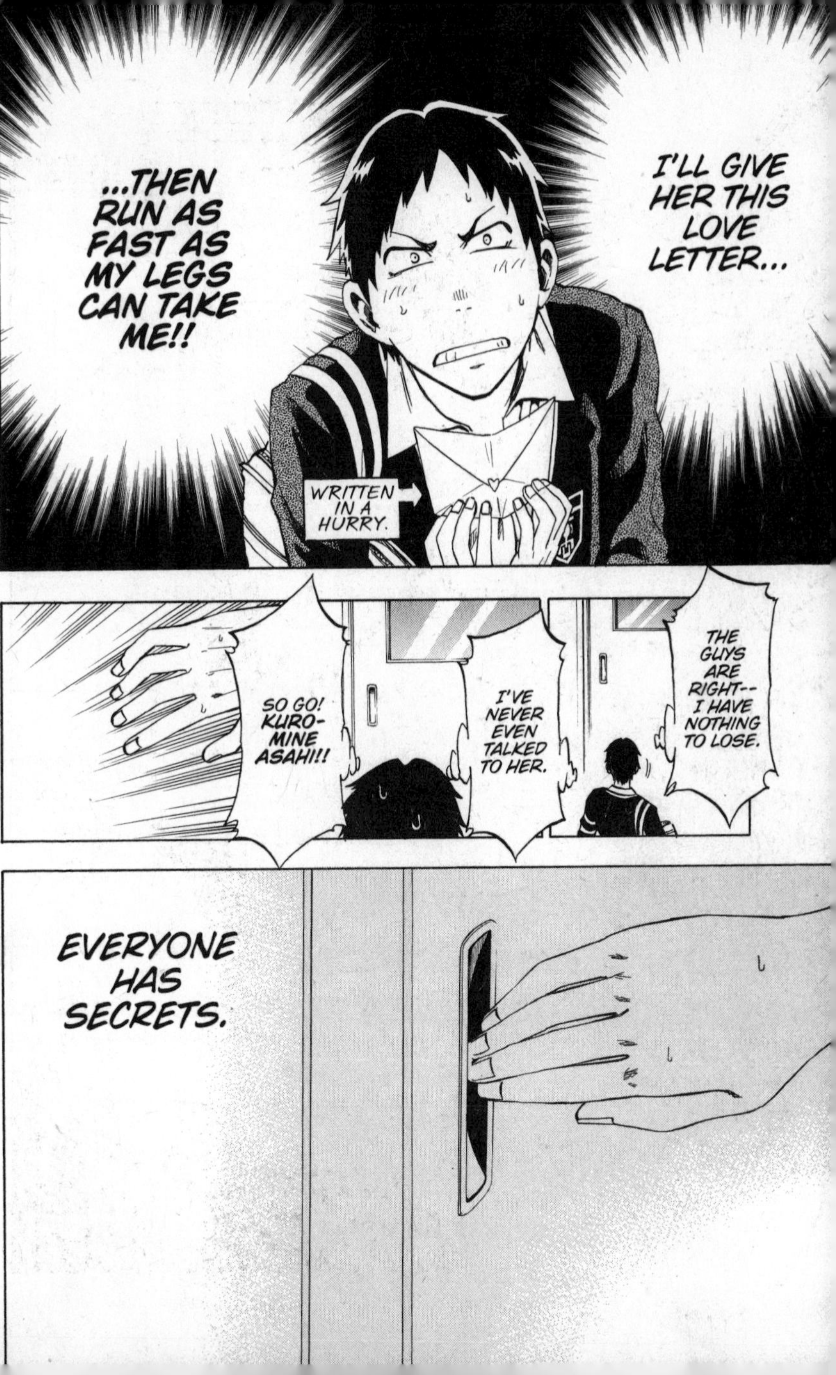
I'LL GIVE HER THIS LOVE LETTER...
...THEN RUN AS FAST AS MY LEGS CAN TAKE ME!!
WRITTEN IN A HURRY.
THE GUYS ARE RIGHT-- I HAVE NOTHING TO LOSE.
I'VE NEVER EVEN TALKED TO HER.
SO GO! KURO-MINE ASAHI!!
EVERYONE HAS SECRETS.

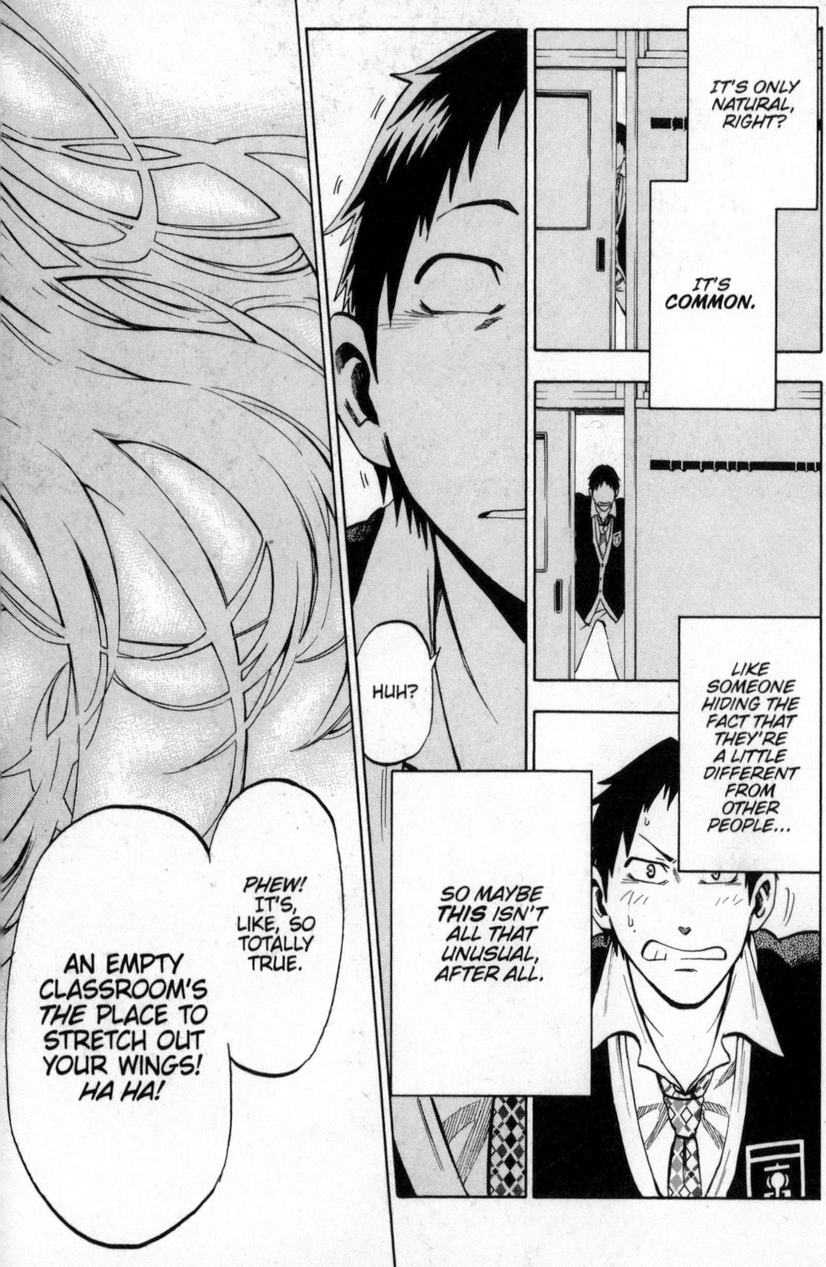
IT'S ONLY NATURAL, RIGHT?
IT'S COMMON.
LIKE SOMEONE HIDING THE FACT THAT THEY'RE A LITTLE DIFFERENT FROM OTHER PEOPLE...
SO MAYBE THIS ISN'T ALL THAT UNUSUAL, AFTER ALL.
HUH?
PHEW! IT'S, LIKE, SO TOTALLY TRUE.
AN EMPTY CLASSROOM'S THE PLACE TO STRETCH OUT YOUR WINGS! HA HA!

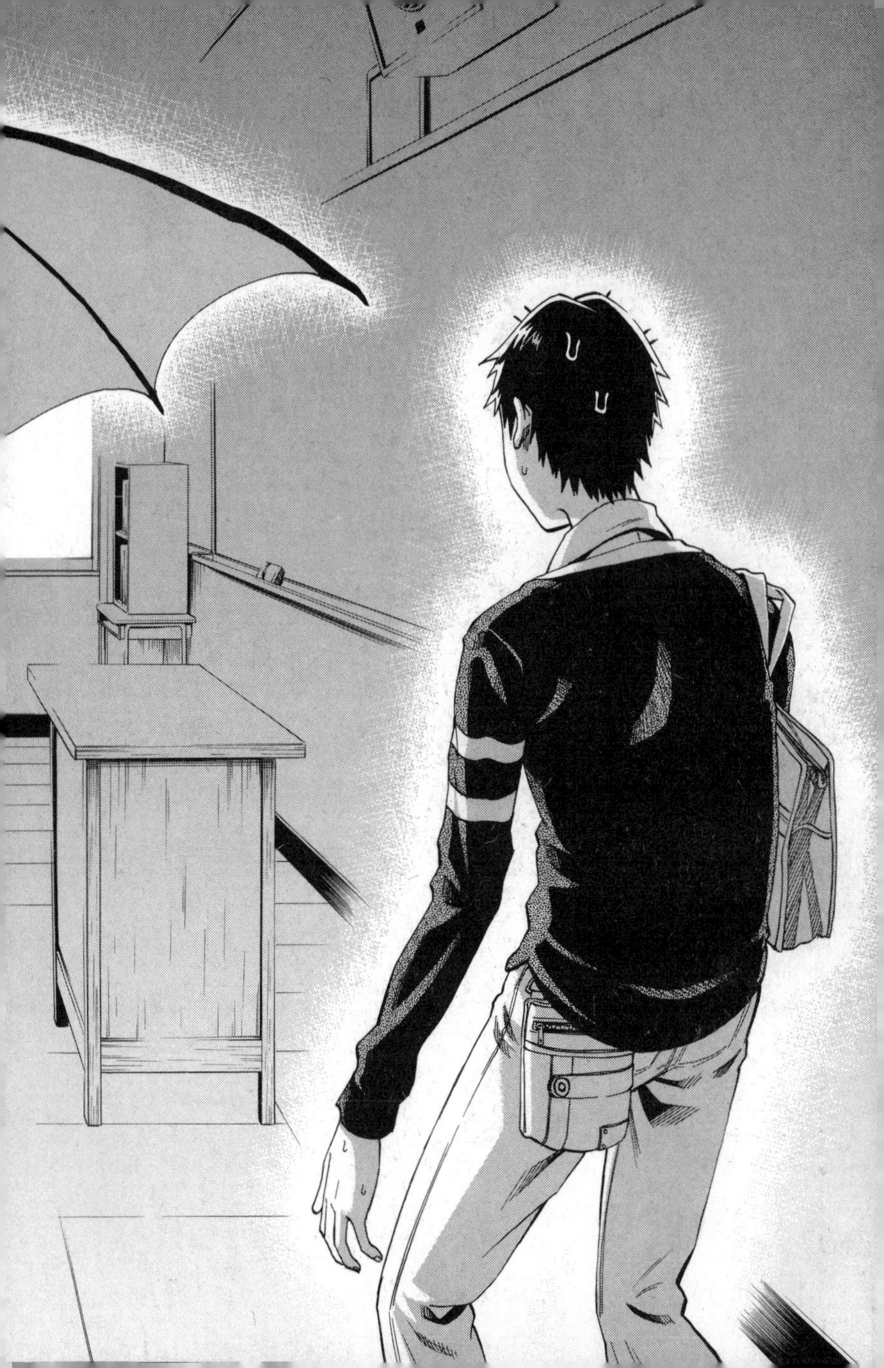

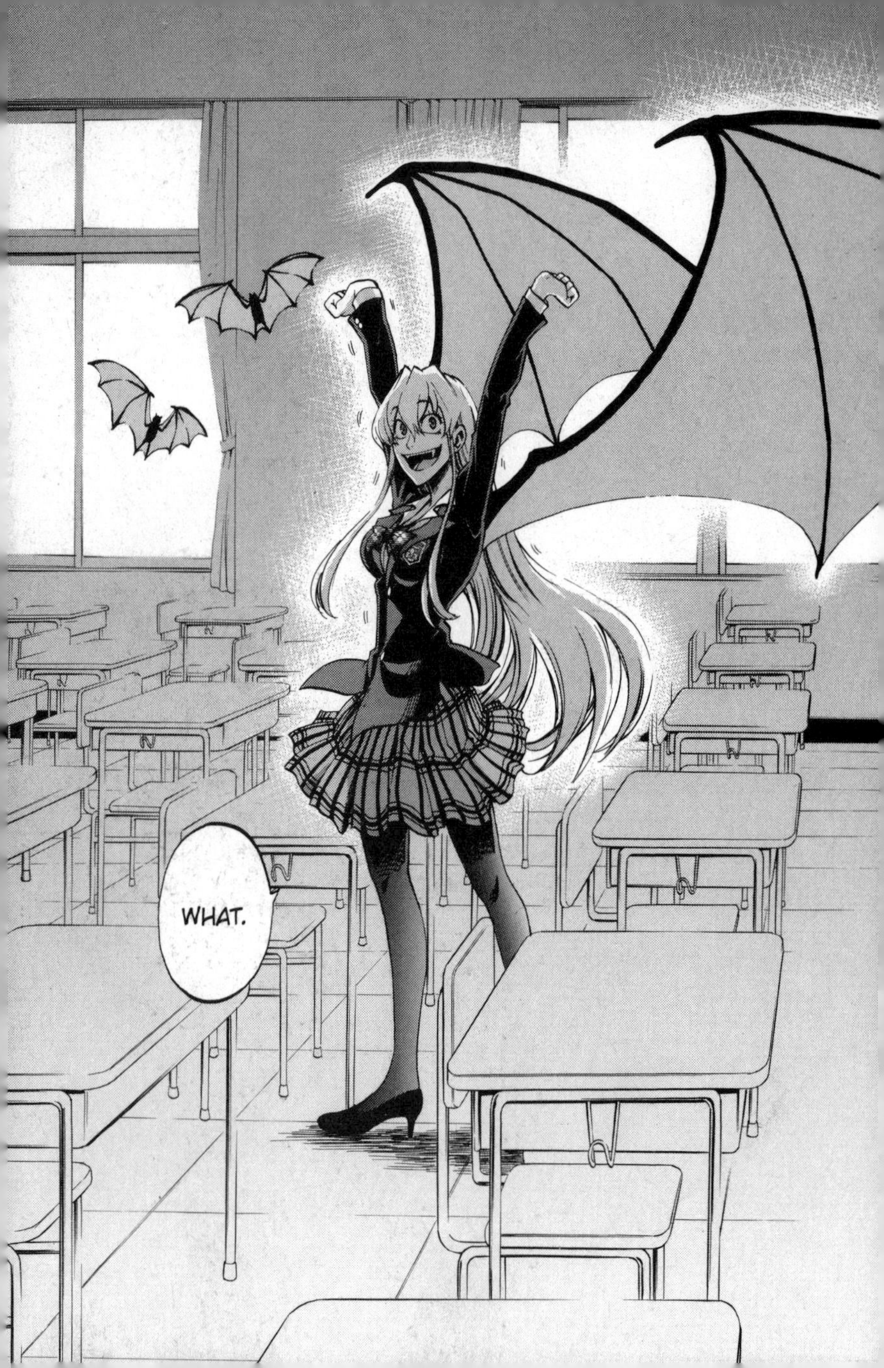
WHAT.

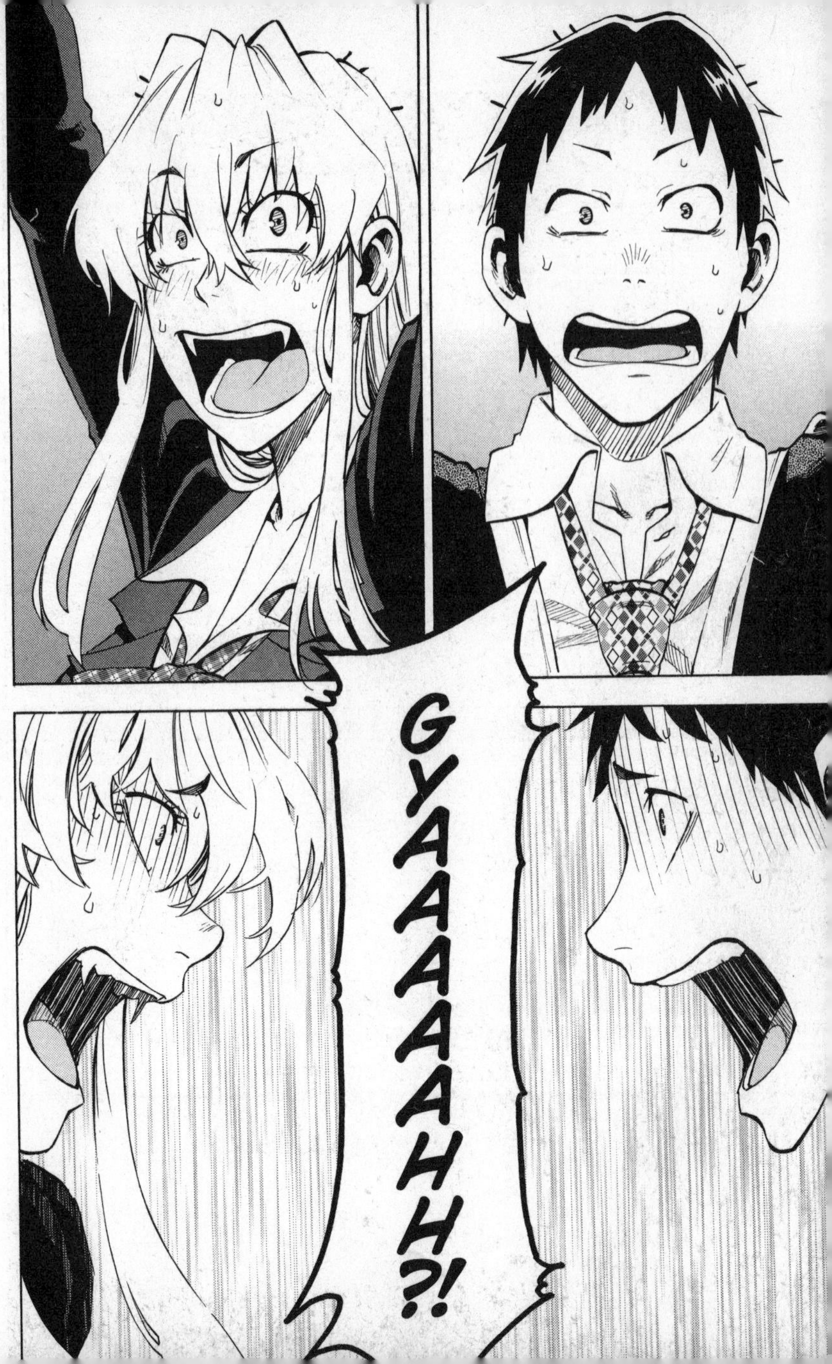
GYAAAAAHH?!

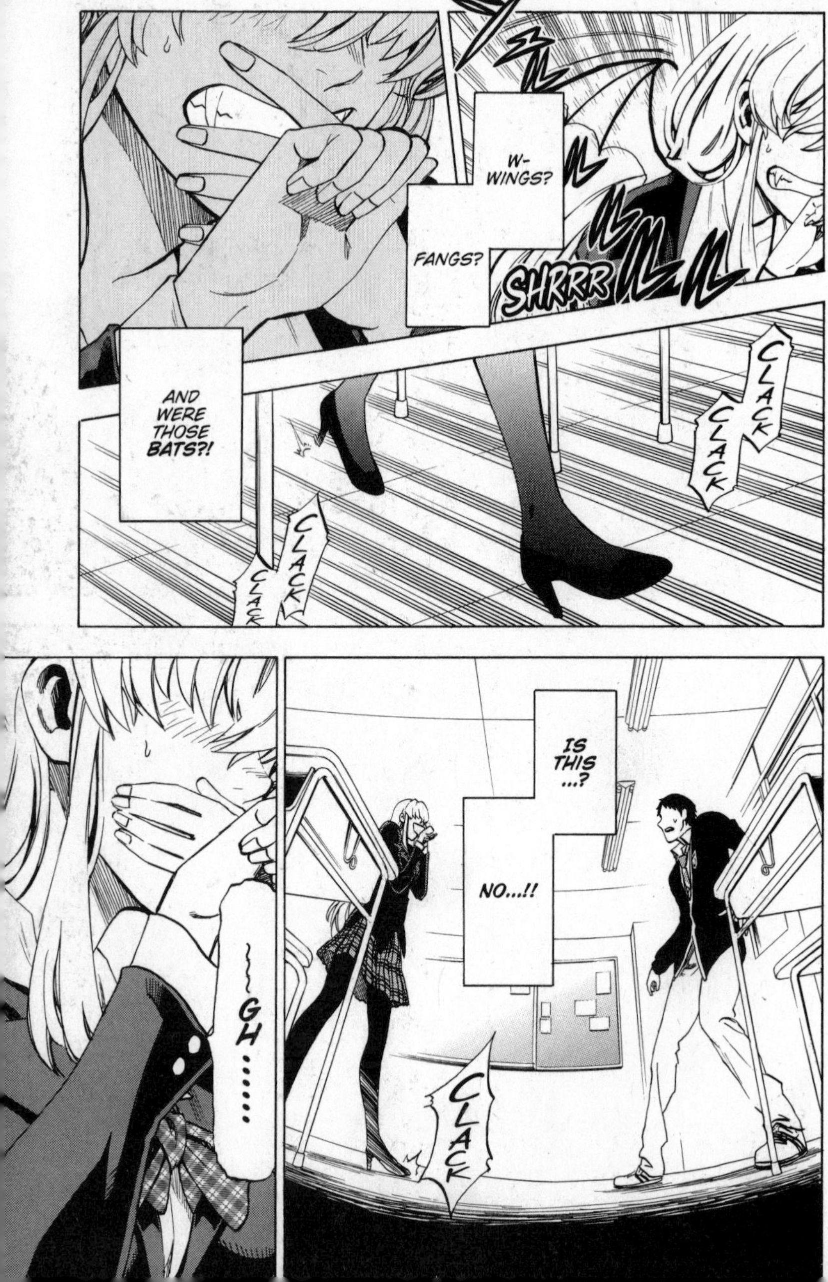
W-
WINGS?
FANGS?
SHRRR
AND WERE THOSE BATS?!
CLACK CLACK
CLACK CLACK
IS THIS ...?
NO...!!
CLACK
GH......

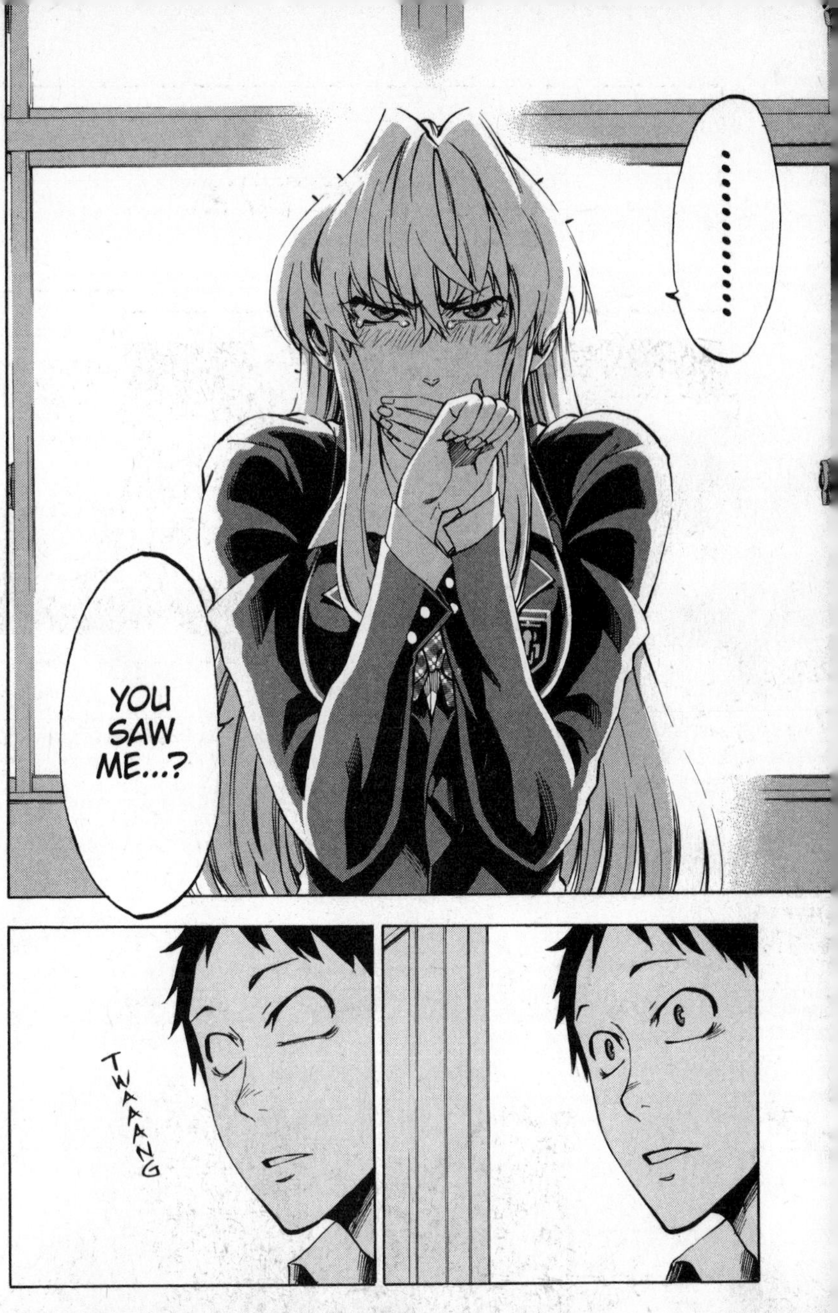
……
YOU SAW ME…?
TWAAANG

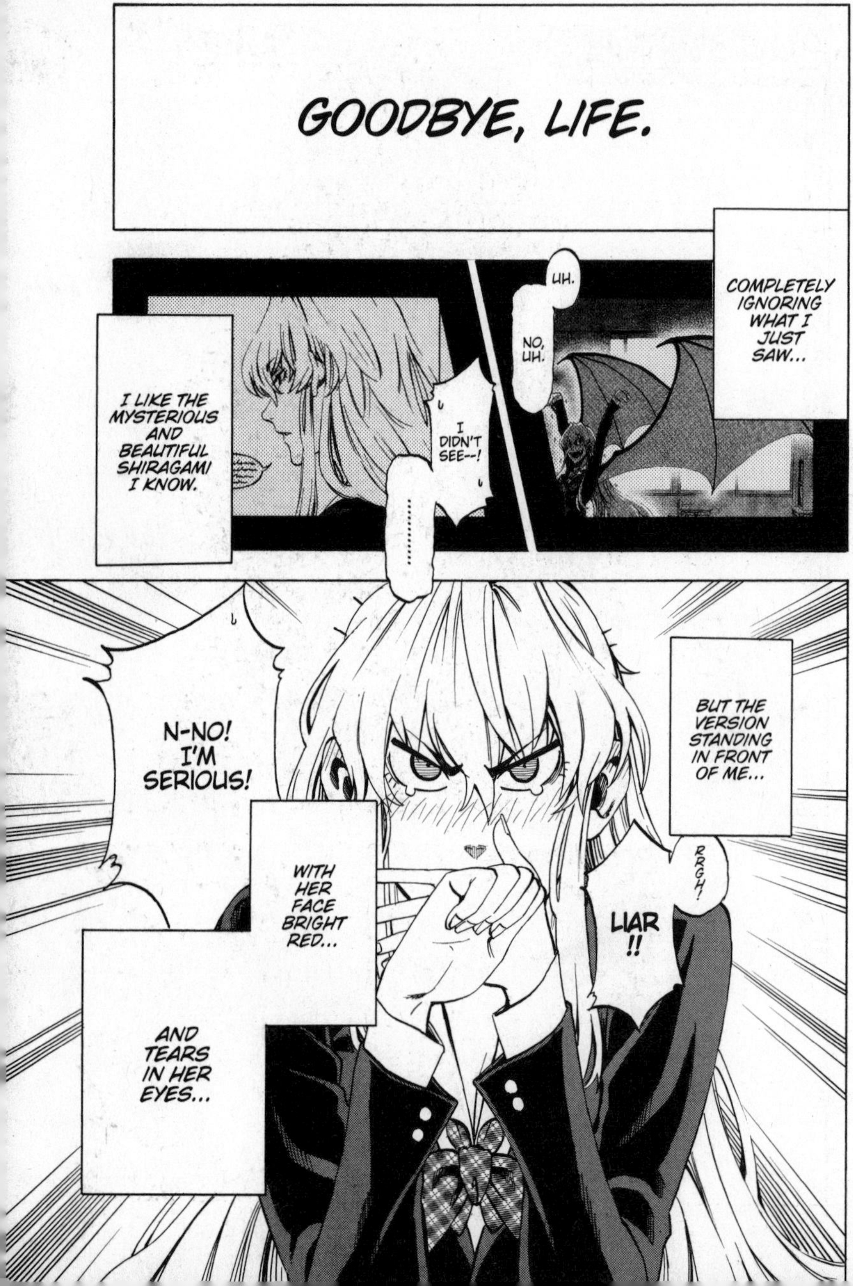
GOODBYE, LIFE.
COMPLETELY IGNORING WHAT I JUST SAW...
UH.
NO, UH.
I DIDN'T SEE--!
......
I LIKE THE MYSTERIOUS AND BEAUTIFUL SHIRAGAMI I KNOW.
BUT THE VERSION STANDING IN FRONT OF ME...
RRGH!
LIAR!!
N-NO! I'M SERIOUS!
WITH HER FACE BRIGHT RED...
AND TEARS IN HER EYES...

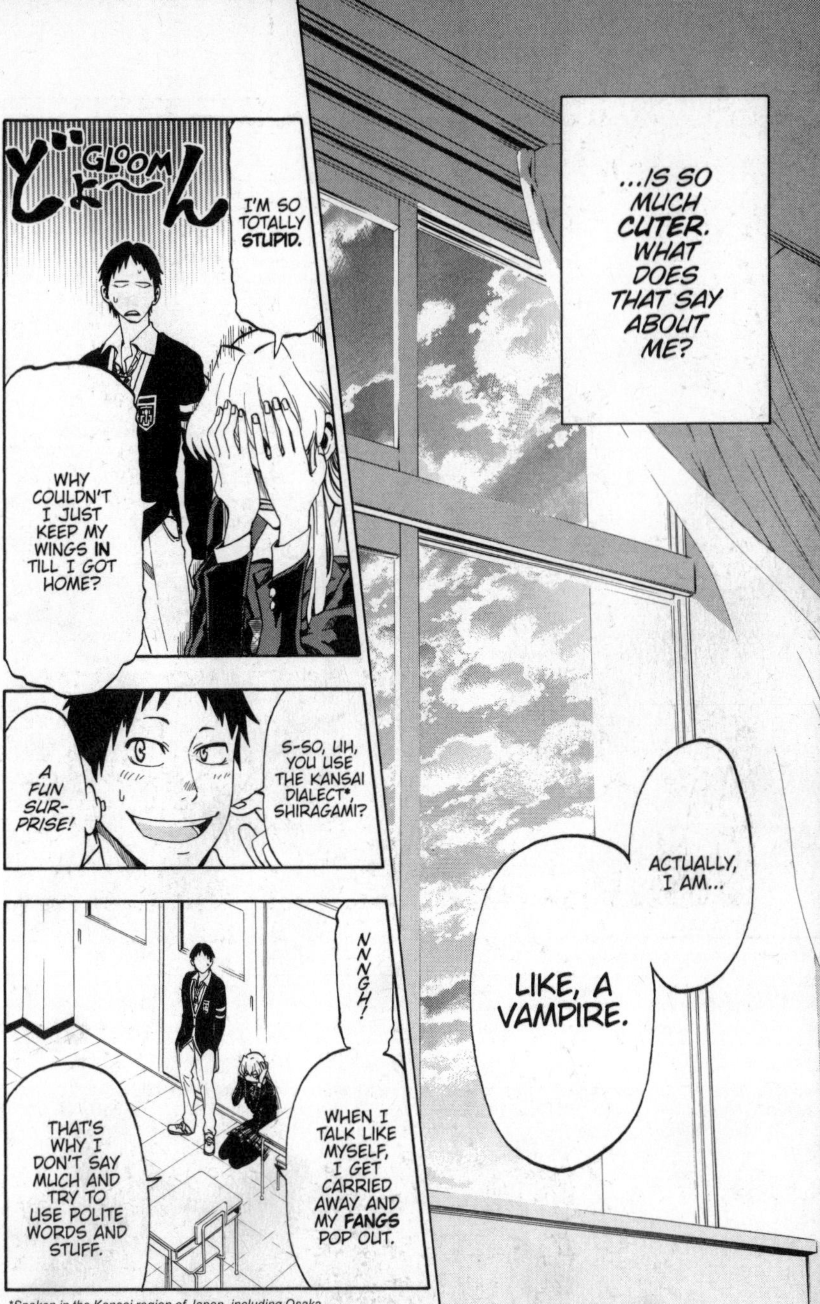
...IS SO MUCH CUTER. WHAT DOES THAT SAY ABOUT ME?
ACTUALLY, I AM...
LIKE, A VAMPIRE.
I'M SO TOTALLY STUPID.
どよ〜ん GLOOM
WHY COULDN'T I JUST KEEP MY WINGS IN TILL I GOT HOME?
S-SO, UH, YOU USE THE KANSAI DIALECT*, SHIRAGAMI?
A FUN SUR-PRISE!
NNNGH!
WHEN I TALK LIKE MYSELF, I GET CARRIED AWAY AND MY FANGS POP OUT.
THAT'S WHY I DON'T SAY MUCH AND TRY TO USE POLITE WORDS AND STUFF.

*Spoken in the Kansai region of Japan, including Osaka. Stereotyped as passionate...and honest.

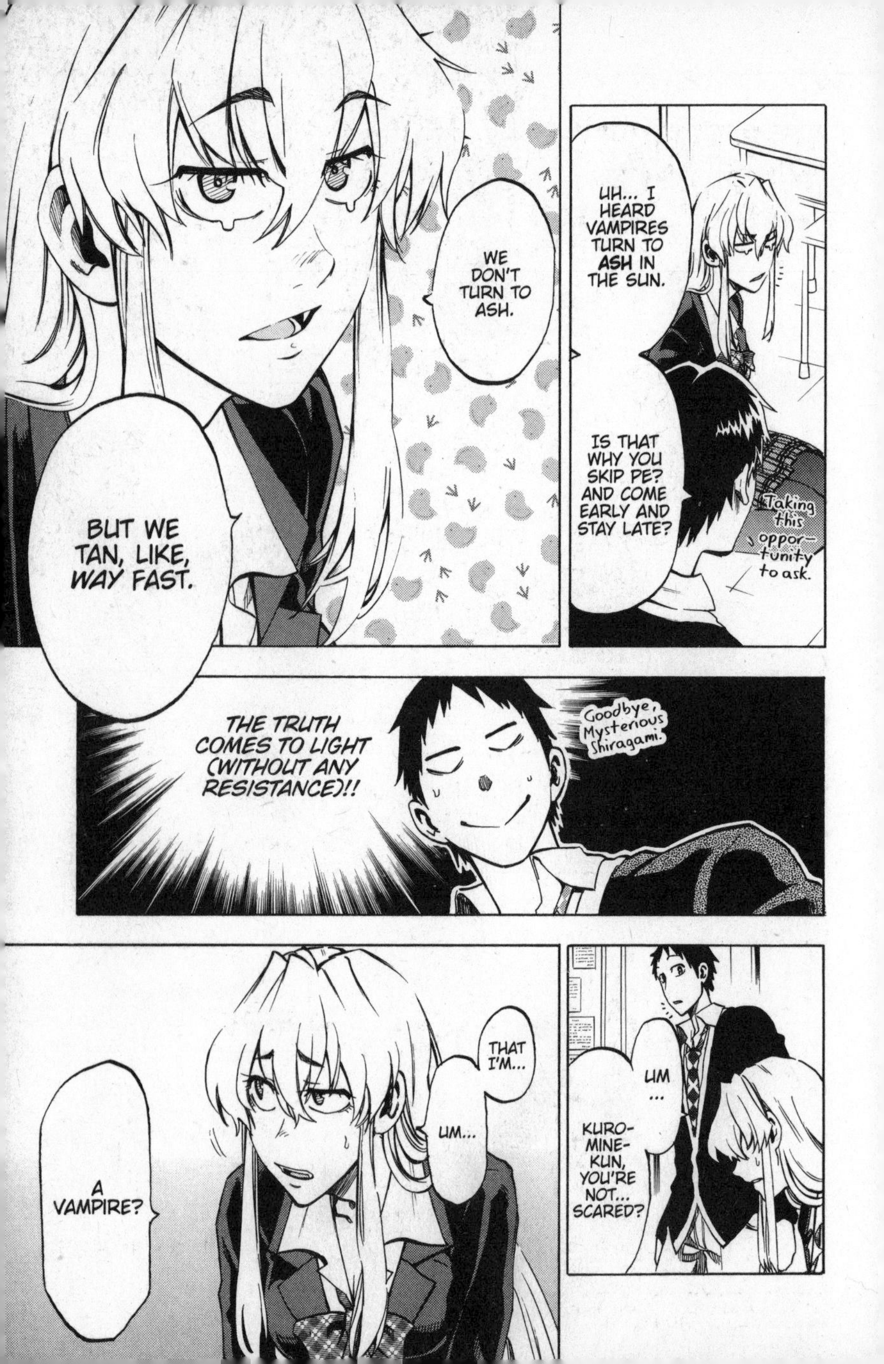
UH... I HEARD VAMPIRES TURN TO ASH IN THE SUN.
IS THAT WHY YOU SKIP PE? AND COME EARLY AND STAY LATE?
Taking this oppor-tunity to ask.
WE DON'T TURN TO ASH.
BUT WE TAN, LIKE, WAY FAST.
Goodbye, Mysterious Shiragami.
THE TRUTH COMES TO LIGHT (WITHOUT ANY RESISTANCE)!!
UM ...
KURO-MINE-KUN, YOU'RE NOT... SCARED?
THAT I'M...
UM...
A VAMPIRE?

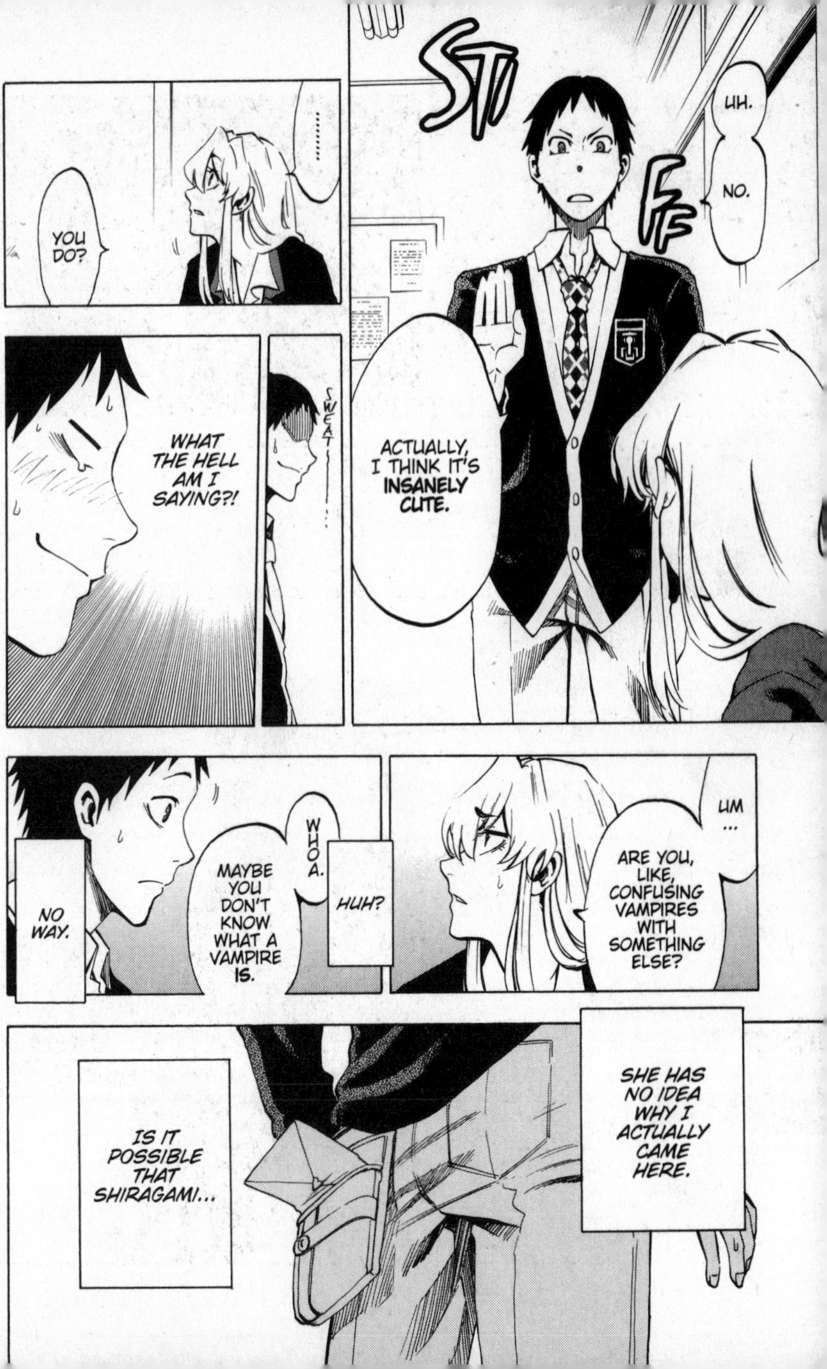
UH.
NO.
STIFF
ACTUALLY, I THINK IT'S INSANELY CUTE.
YOU DO?
....
SWEAT ....
WHAT THE HELL AM I SAYING?!
UM ...
ARE YOU, LIKE, CONFUSING VAMPIRES WITH SOMETHING ELSE?
HUH?
WHOA.
MAYBE YOU DON'T KNOW WHAT A VAMPIRE IS.
NO WAY.
SHE HAS NO IDEA WHY I ACTUALLY CAME HERE.
IS IT POSSIBLE THAT SHIRAGAMI...

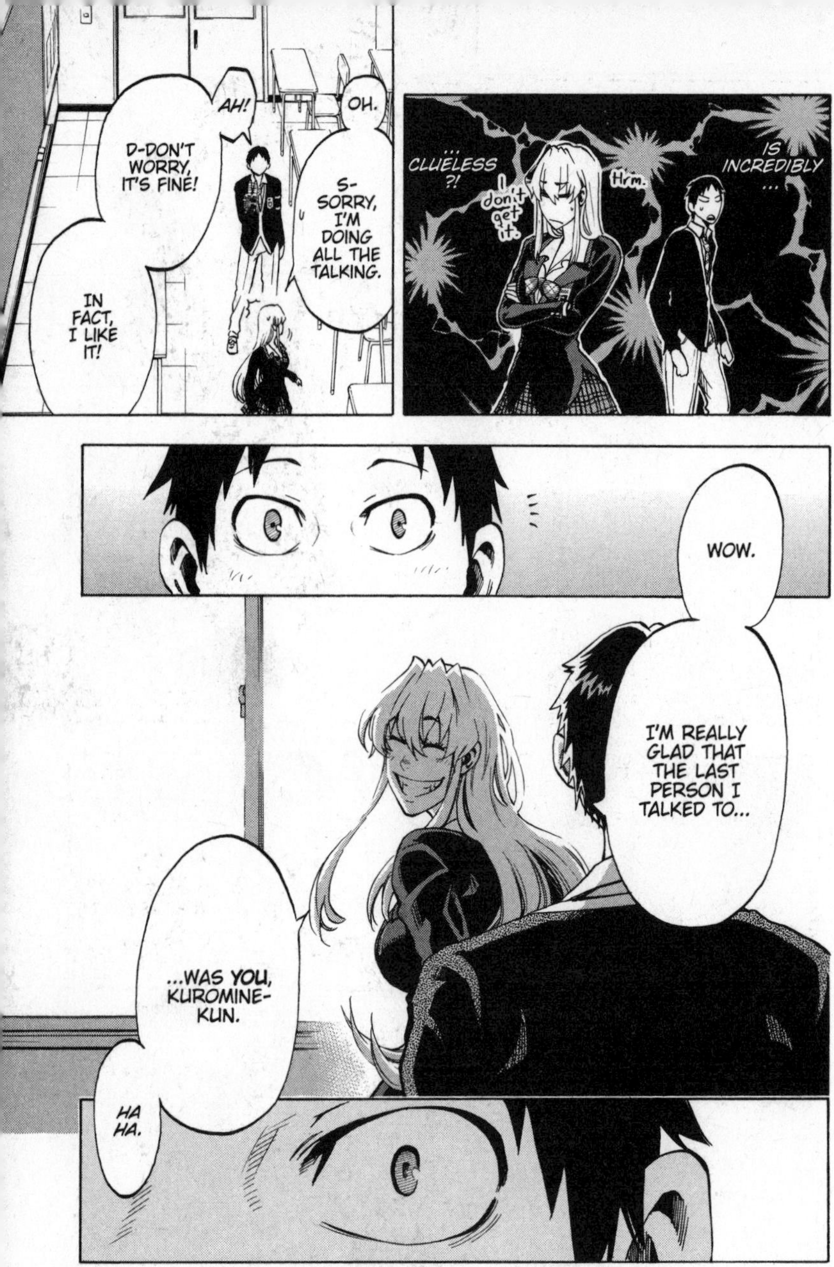
IS INCREDIBLY ...
... CLUELESS ?!
Hrm.
I don't get it.
OH.
S-SORRY, I'M DOING ALL THE TALKING.
AH!
D-DON'T WORRY, IT'S FINE!
IN FACT, I LIKE IT!
WOW.
I'M REALLY GLAD THAT THE LAST PERSON I TALKED TO...
...WAS YOU, KUROMINE-KUN.
HA HA.

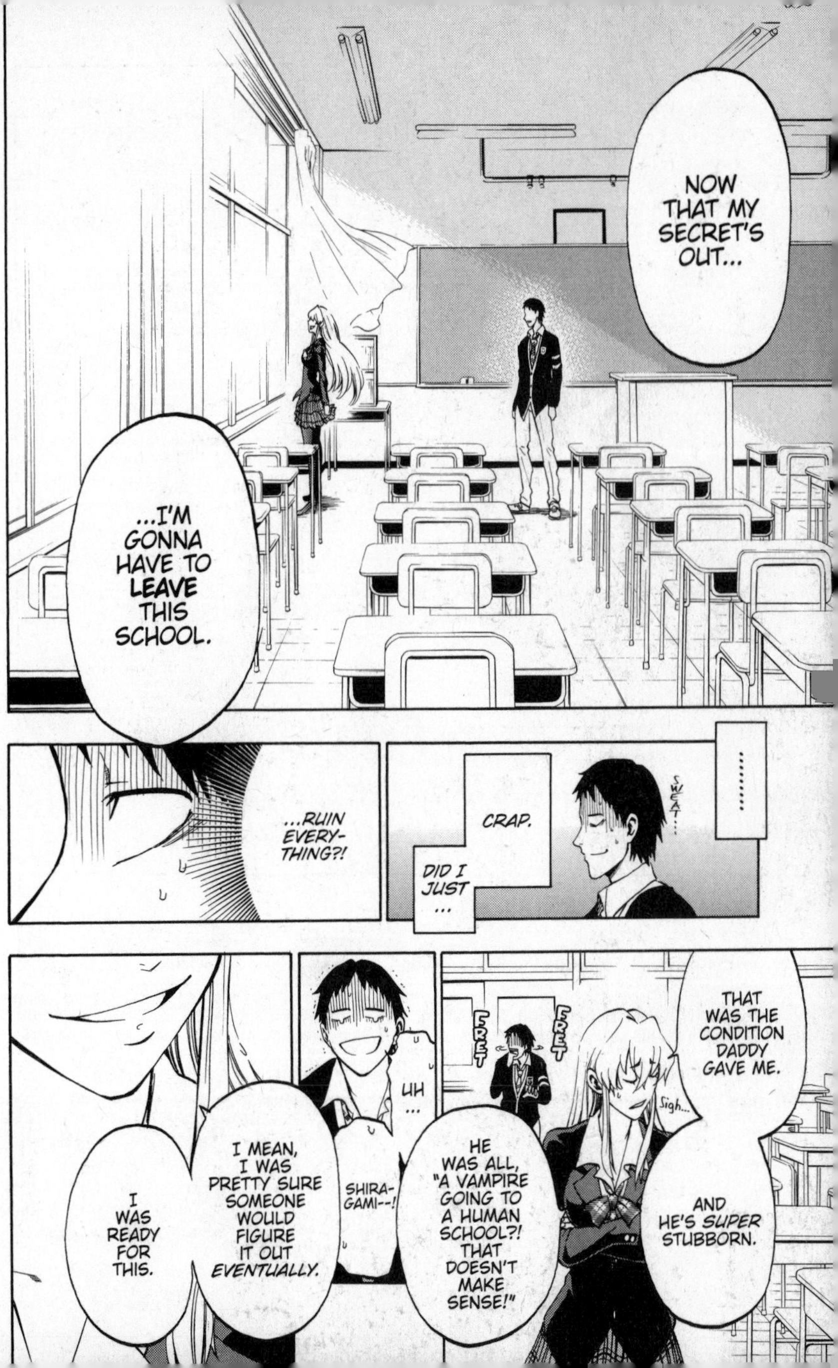
NOW THAT MY SECRET'S OUT...
...I'M GONNA HAVE TO LEAVE THIS SCHOOL.
......
SWEAT...
CRAP.
DID I JUST ...
...RUIN EVERY-THING?!
THAT WAS THE CONDITION DADDY GAVE ME.
Sigh...
AND HE'S SUPER STUBBORN.
FRET
FRET
HE WAS ALL, "A VAMPIRE GOING TO A HUMAN SCHOOL?! THAT DOESN'T MAKE SENSE!"
UH ...
SHIRA-GAMI--!
I MEAN, I WAS PRETTY SURE SOMEONE WOULD FIGURE IT OUT EVENTUALLY.
I WAS READY FOR THIS.

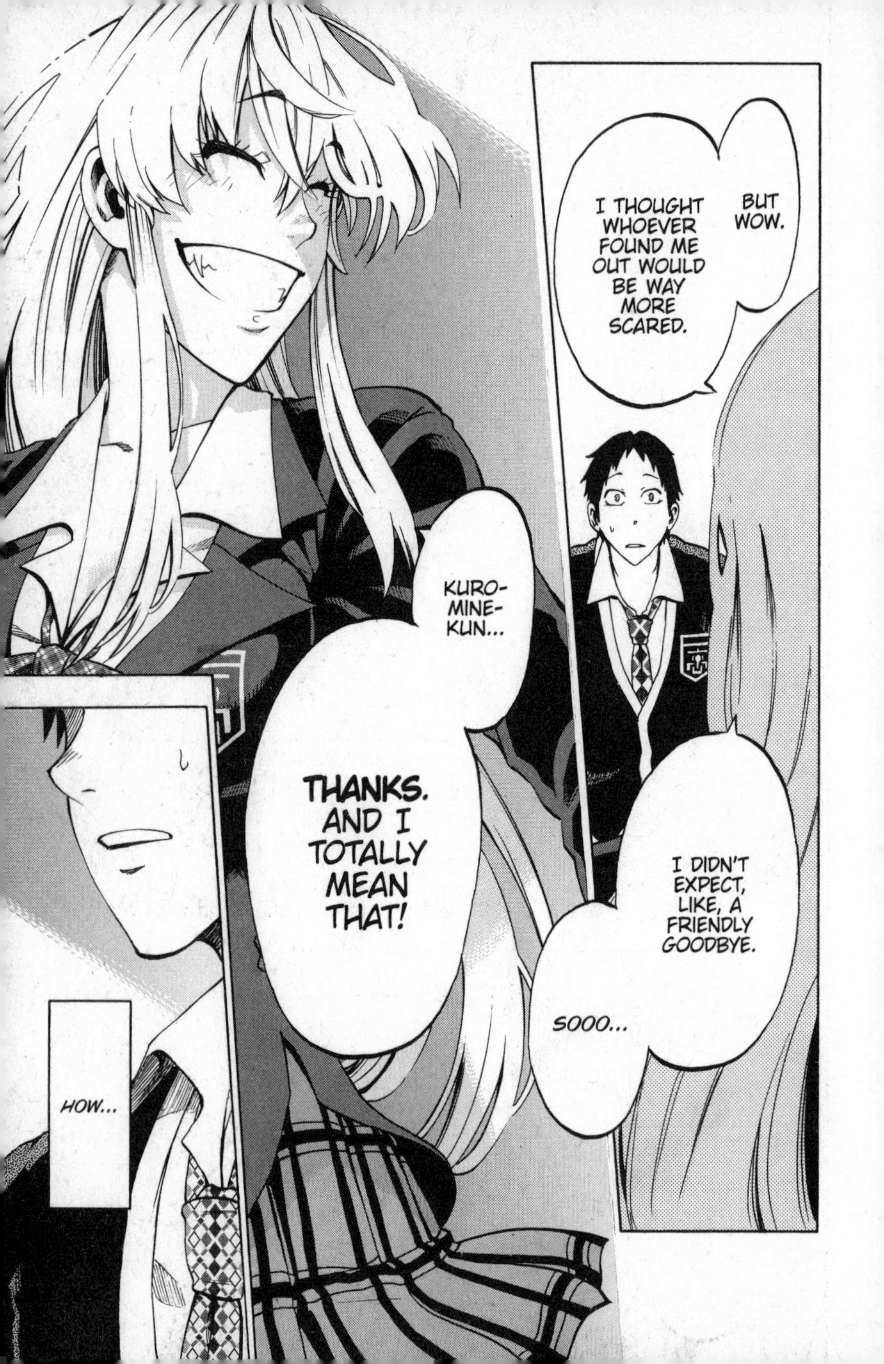
BUT WOW.
I THOUGHT WHOEVER FOUND ME OUT WOULD BE WAY MORE SCARED.
I DIDN'T EXPECT, LIKE, A FRIENDLY GOODBYE.
SOOO...
KURO-MINE-KUN...
THANKS. AND I TOTALLY MEAN THAT!
HOW...

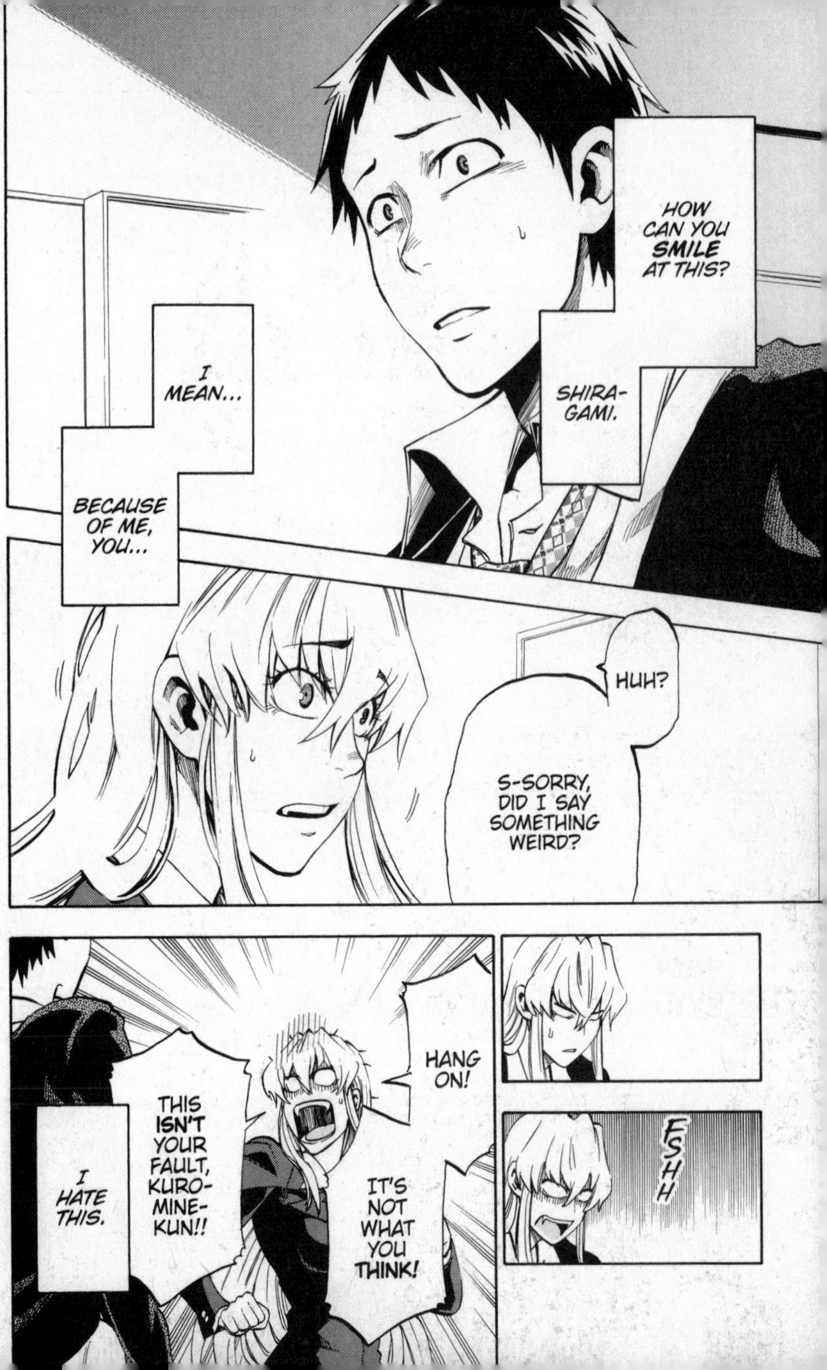
HOW CAN YOU SMILE AT THIS?
SHIRA-GAMI.
I MEAN...
BECAUSE OF ME, YOU...
HUH?
S-SORRY, DID I SAY SOMETHING WEIRD?
FSHH
HANG ON!
IT'S NOT WHAT YOU THINK!
THIS ISN'T YOUR FAULT, KURO-MINE-KUN!!
I HATE THIS.

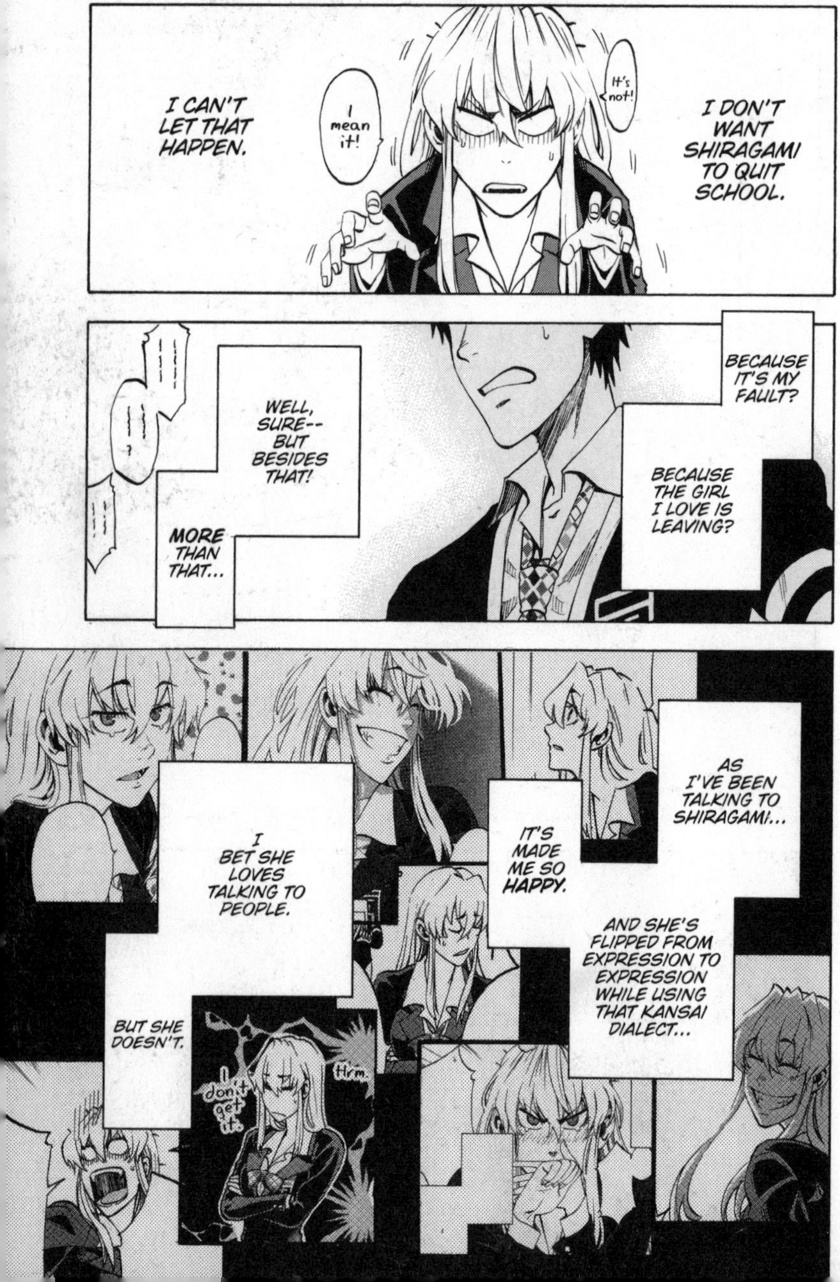
I DON'T WANT SHIRAGAMI TO QUIT SCHOOL.
It's not!
I mean it!
I CAN'T LET THAT HAPPEN.
BECAUSE IT'S MY FAULT?
BECAUSE THE GIRL I LOVE IS LEAVING?
WELL, SURE-- BUT BESIDES THAT!
MORE THAN THAT...
AS I'VE BEEN TALKING TO SHIRAGAMI...
IT'S MADE ME SO HAPPY.
AND SHE'S FLIPPED FROM EXPRESSION TO EXPRESSION WHILE USING THAT KANSAI DIALECT...
I BET SHE LOVES TALKING TO PEOPLE.
BUT SHE DOESN'T.
Hrm.
I don't get it.

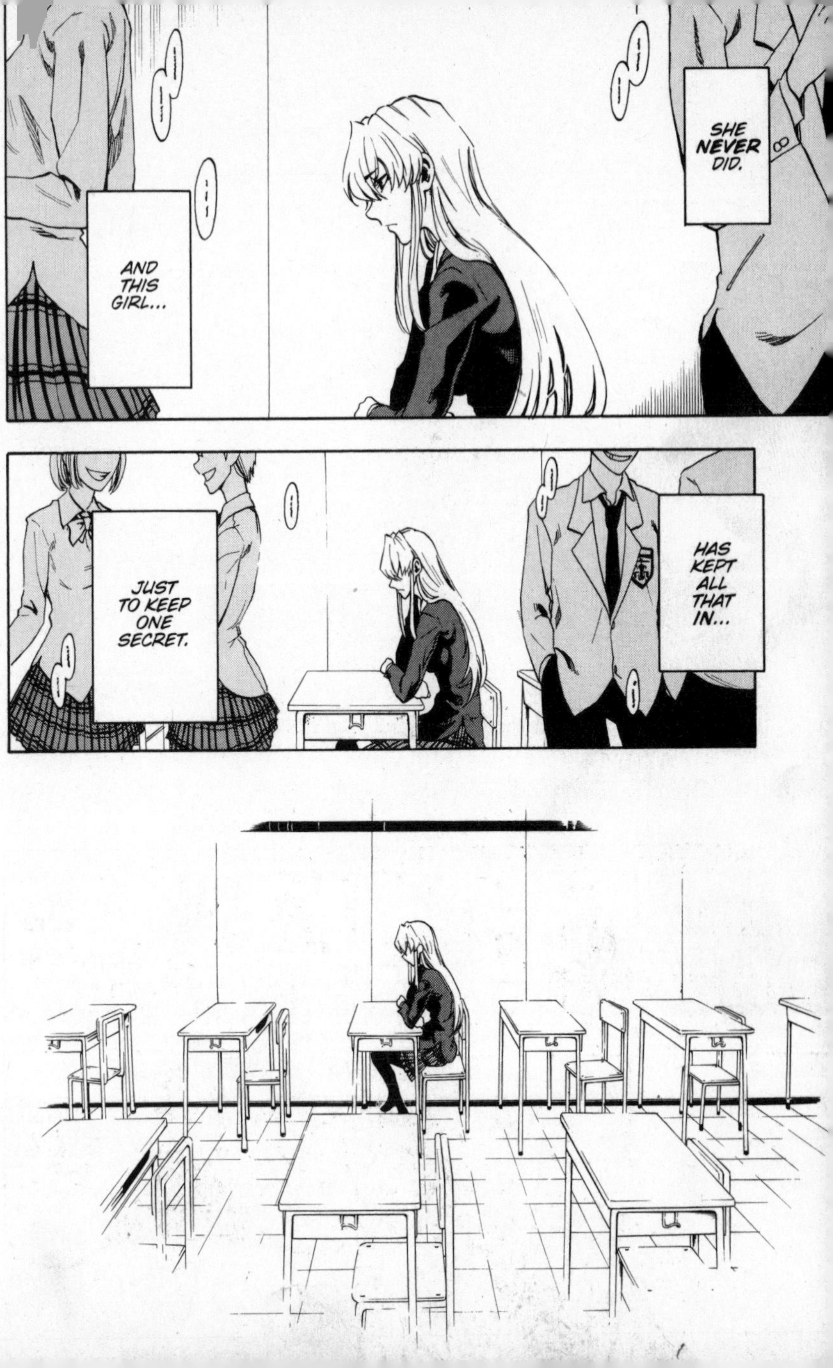
SHE NEVER DID.
AND THIS GIRL...
HAS KEPT ALL THAT IN...
JUST TO KEEP ONE SECRET.

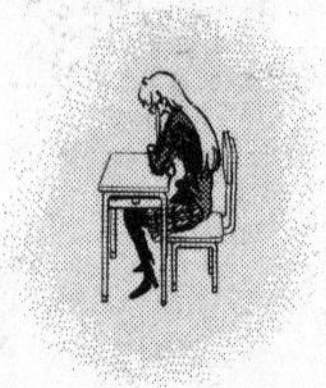

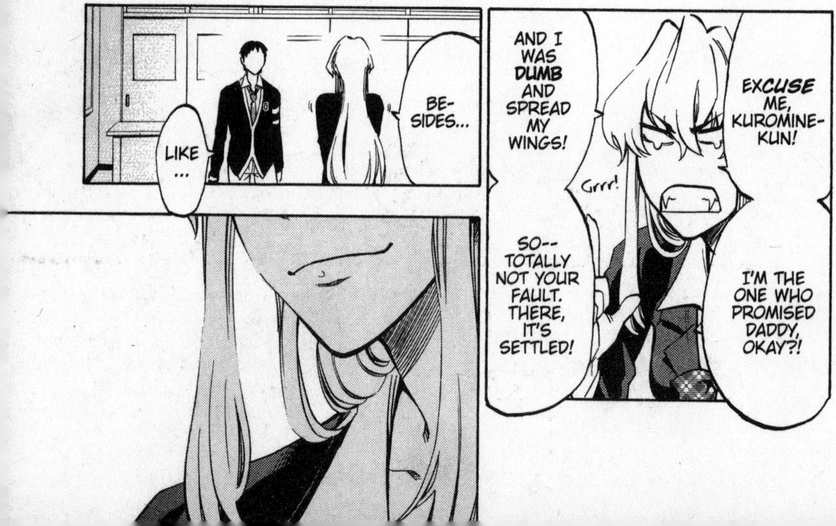
EXCUSE ME, KUROMINE-KUN!
I'M THE ONE WHO PROMISED DADDY, OKAY?!
AND I WAS DUMB AND SPREAD MY WINGS!
Grrr!
SO-- TOTALLY NOT YOUR FAULT. THERE, IT'S SETTLED!
BE-SIDES...
LIKE ...

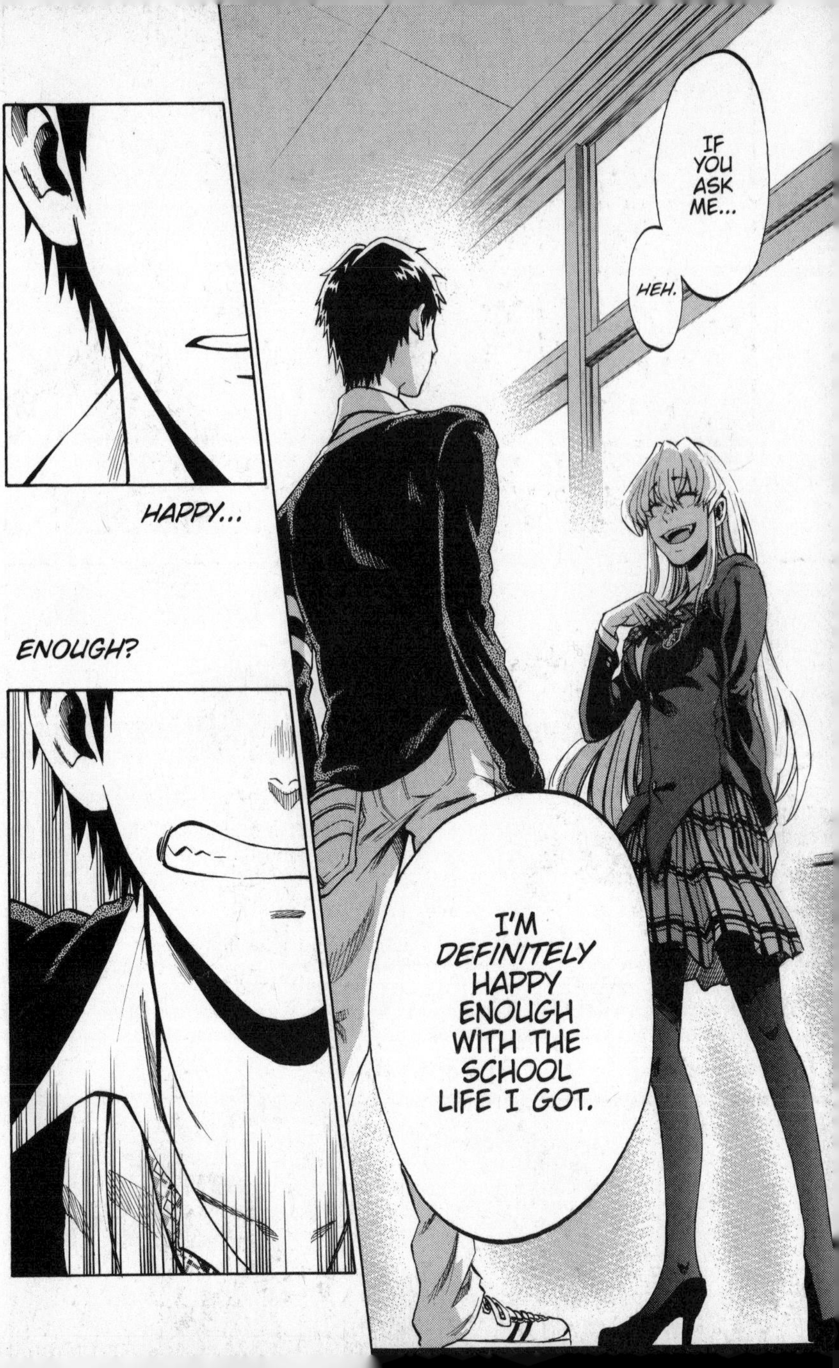
IF YOU ASK ME...
HEH.
I'M DEFINITELY HAPPY ENOUGH WITH THE SCHOOL LIFE I GOT.
HAPPY...
ENOUGH?

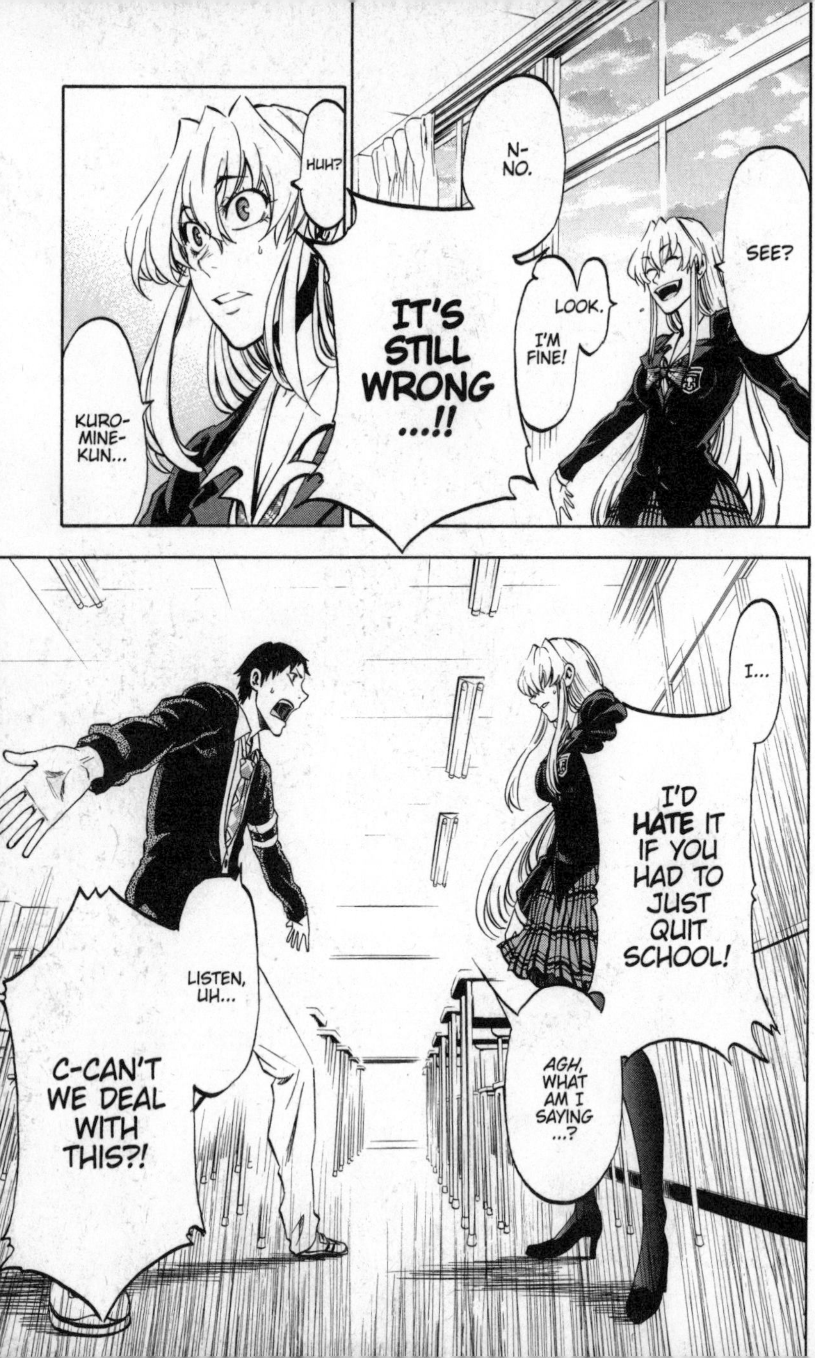
SEE?
LOOK.
I'M FINE!
N-NO.
HUH?
KURO-MINE-KUN...
IT'S STILL WRONG ...!!
I...
I'D HATE IT IF YOU HAD TO JUST QUIT SCHOOL!
AGH, WHAT AM I SAYING ...?
LISTEN, UH...
C-CAN'T WE DEAL WITH THIS?!

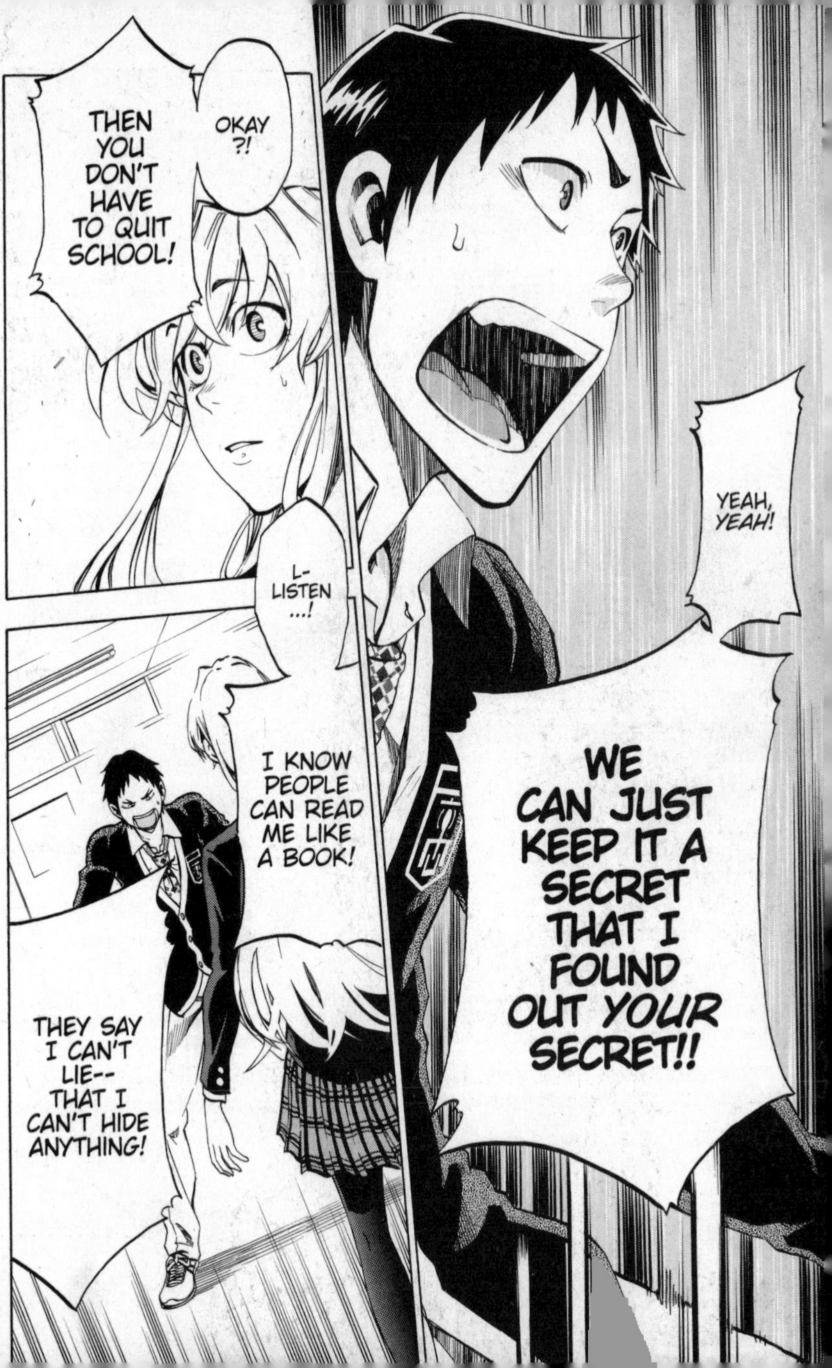
YEAH, YEAH!
WE CAN JUST KEEP IT A SECRET THAT I FOUND OUT YOUR SECRET!!
OKAY ?!
THEN YOU DON'T HAVE TO QUIT SCHOOL!
L- LISTEN ...!
I KNOW PEOPLE CAN READ ME LIKE A BOOK!
THEY SAY I CAN'T LIE-- THAT I CAN'T HIDE ANYTHING!

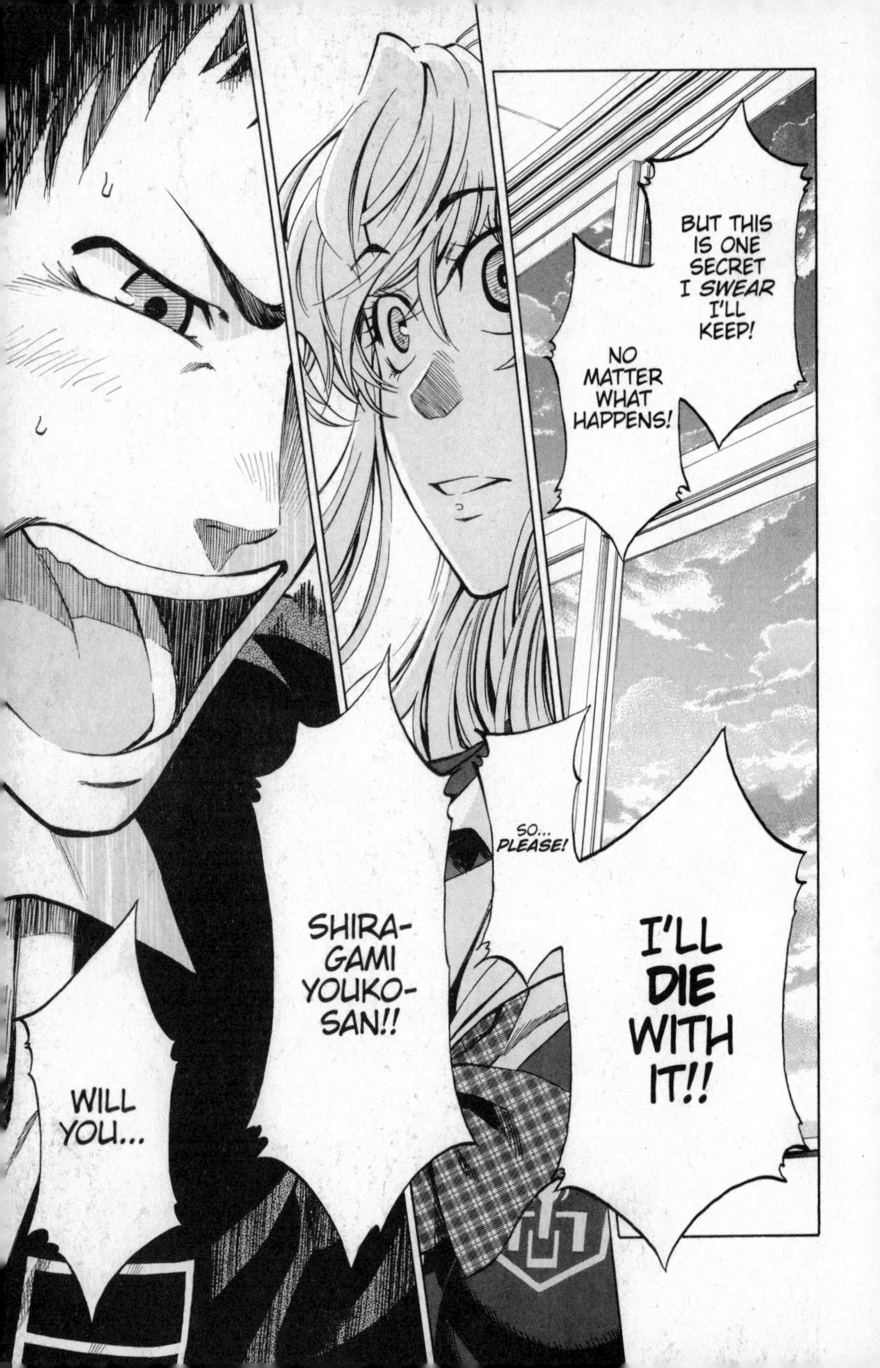
BUT THIS IS ONE SECRET I *SWEAR* I'LL KEEP!
NO MATTER WHAT HAPPENS!
SO... PLEASE!
I'LL DIE WITH IT!!
SHIRA-GAMI YOUKO-SAN!!
WILL YOU...

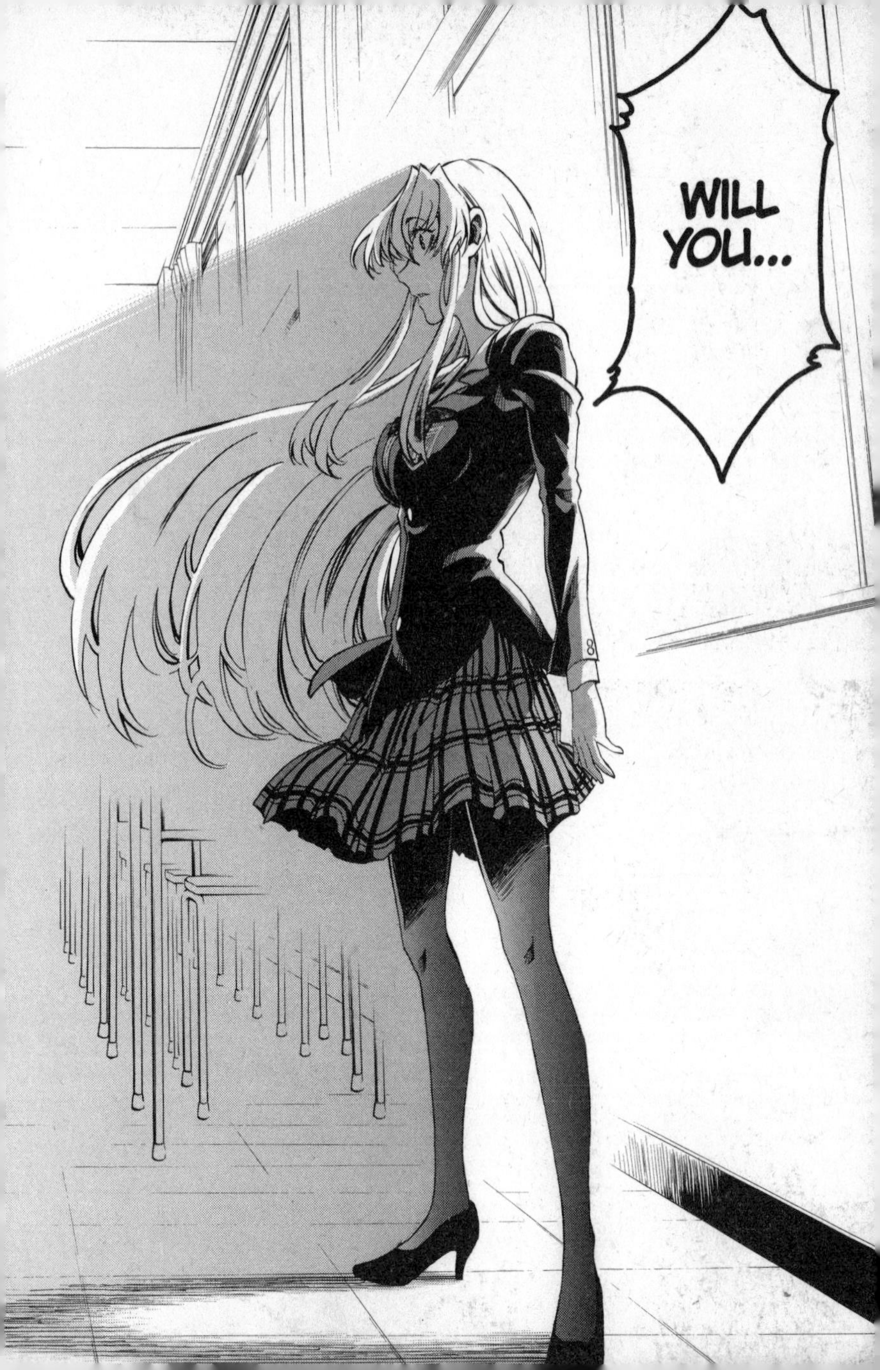
WILL YOU...

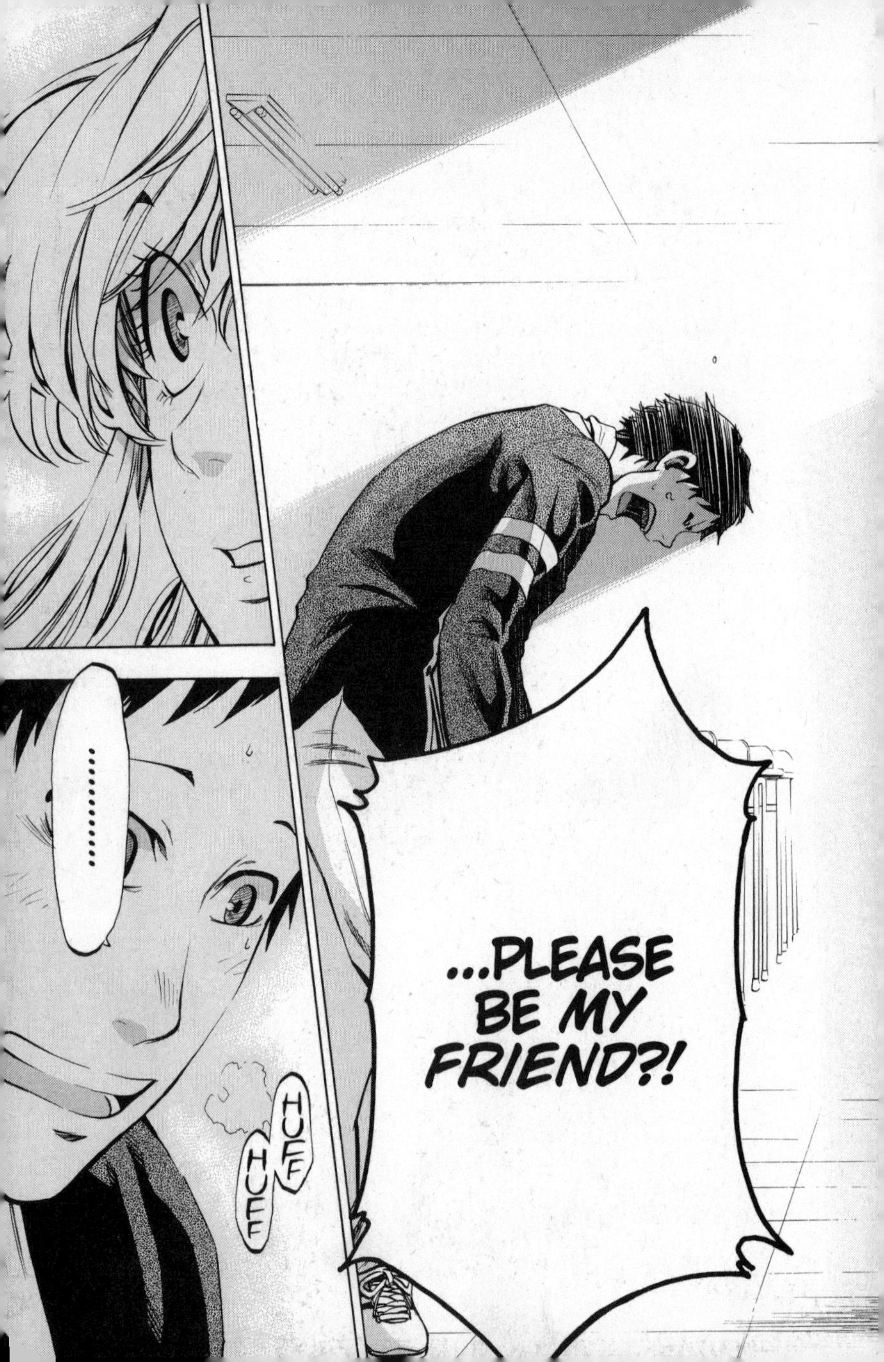
...PLEASE BE MY FRIEND?!
HUFF
HUFF
....

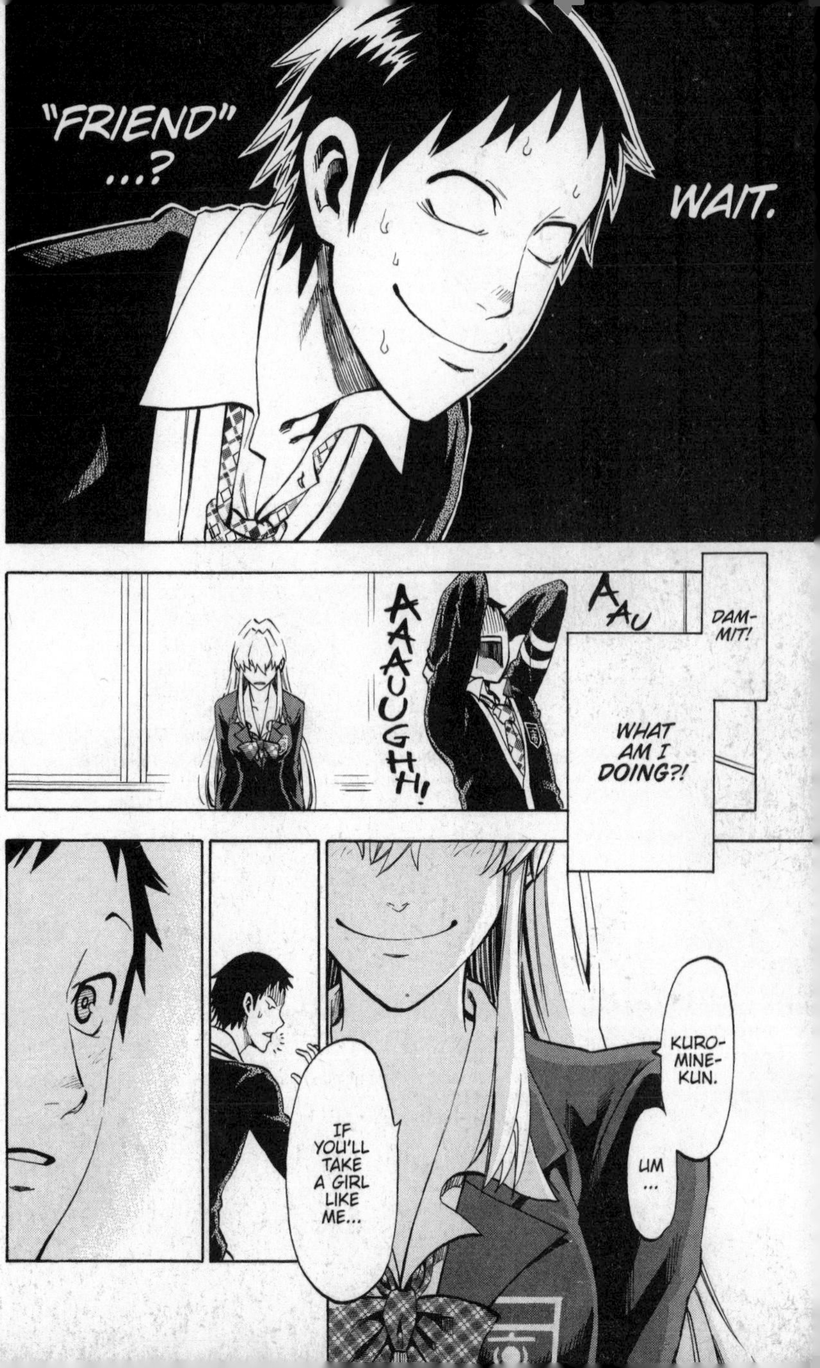
WAIT.
"FRIEND" ...?
DAM-MIT!
WHAT AM I DOING?!
AAU
AAAAUGHH!
KURO-MINE-KUN.
UM ...
IF YOU'LL TAKE A GIRL LIKE ME...

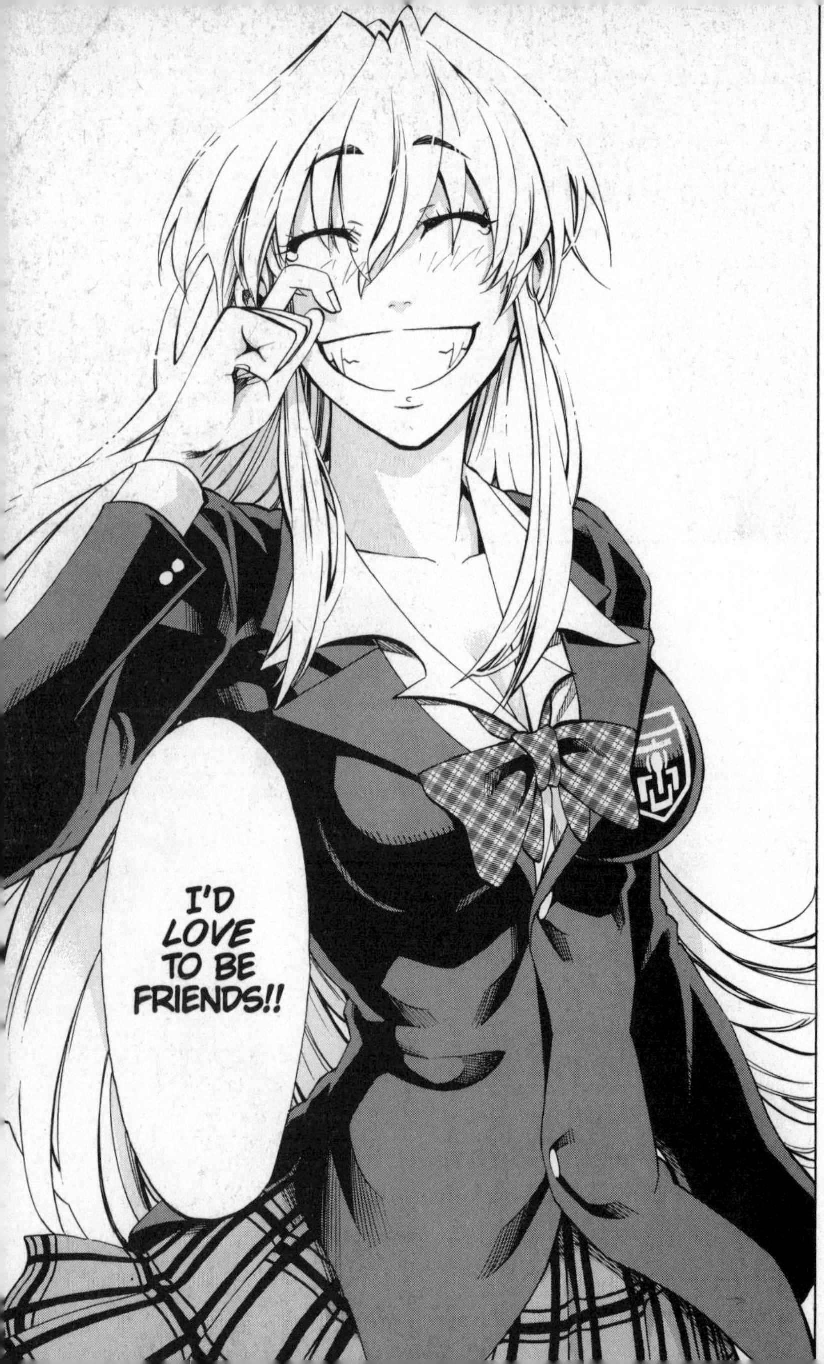
I'D LOVE TO BE FRIENDS!!

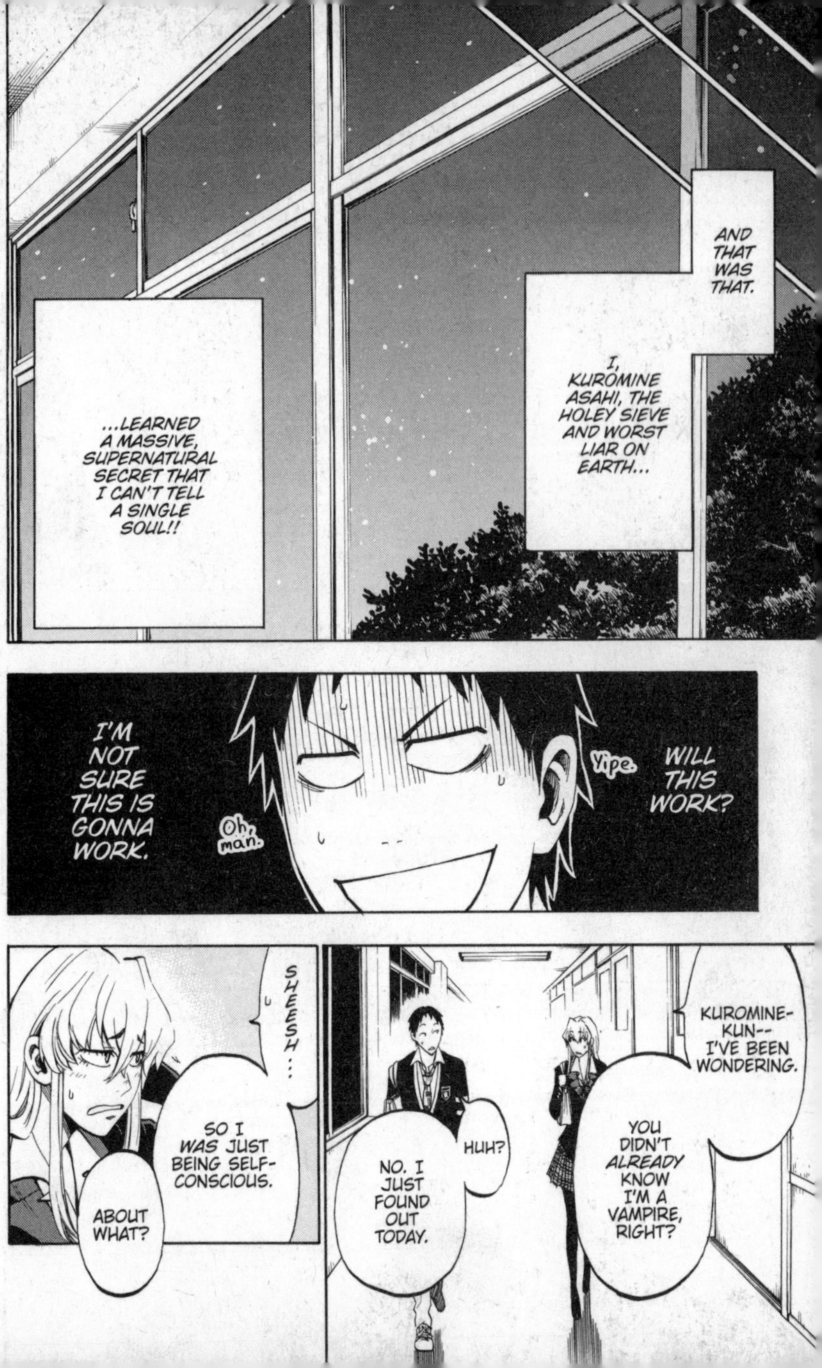
AND THAT WAS THAT.
I, KUROMINE ASAHI, THE HOLEY SIEVE AND WORST LIAR ON EARTH...
...LEARNED A MASSIVE, SUPERNATURAL SECRET THAT I CAN'T TELL A SINGLE SOUL!!
WILL THIS WORK?
Yipe.
Oh, man.
I'M NOT SURE THIS IS GONNA WORK.
KUROMINE-KUN-- I'VE BEEN WONDERING.
YOU DIDN'T ALREADY KNOW I'M A VAMPIRE, RIGHT?
HUH?
NO. I JUST FOUND OUT TODAY.
SHEESH...
SO I WAS JUST BEING SELF-CONSCIOUS.
ABOUT WHAT?

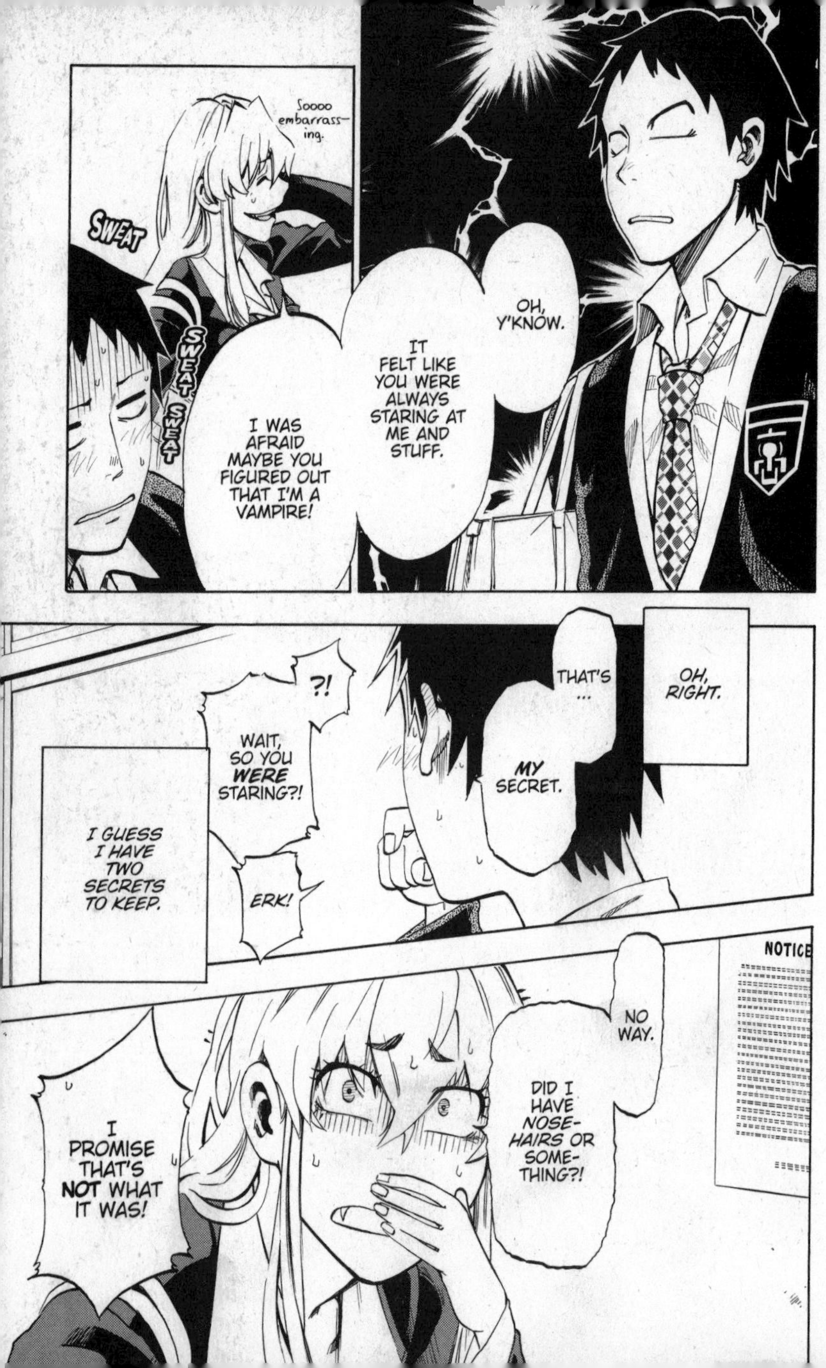
OH, Y'KNOW.
IT FELT LIKE YOU WERE ALWAYS STARING AT ME AND STUFF.
I WAS AFRAID MAYBE YOU FIGURED OUT THAT I'M A VAMPIRE!
Soooo embarrass-ing.
SWEAT
SWEAT SWEAT
OH, RIGHT.
THAT'S ...
MY SECRET.
?!
WAIT, SO YOU WERE STARING?!
ERK!
I GUESS I HAVE TWO SECRETS TO KEEP.
NOTICE
NO WAY.
DID I HAVE NOSE-HAIRS OR SOME-THING?!
I PROMISE THAT'S NOT WHAT IT WAS!

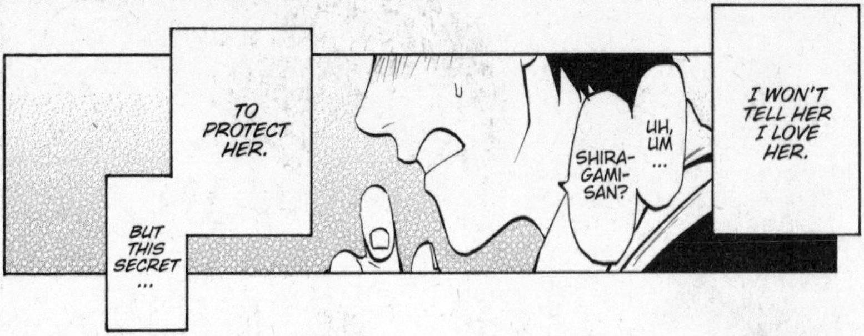
I WON'T TELL HER I LOVE HER.
UH, UM ...
SHIRA-GAMI-SAN?
TO PROTECT HER.
BUT THIS SECRET ...

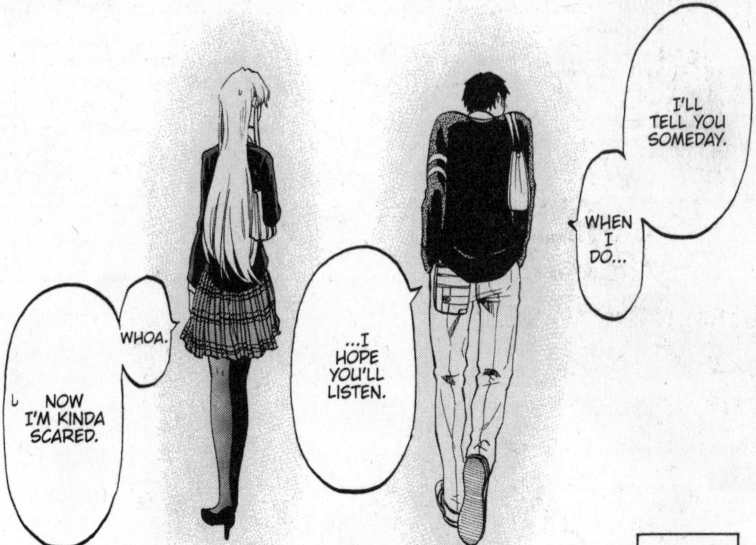
I'LL TELL YOU SOMEDAY.
WHEN I DO...
...I HOPE YOU'LL LISTEN.
WHOA.
NOW I'M KINDA SCARED.

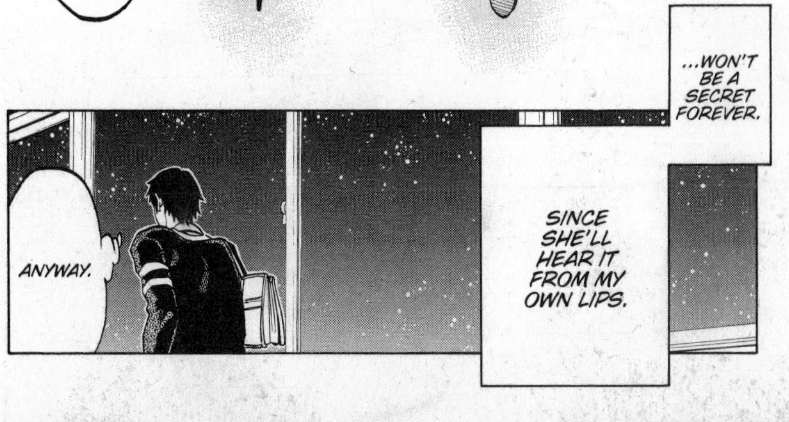
...WON'T BE A SECRET FOREVER.
SINCE SHE'LL HEAR IT FROM MY OWN LIPS.
ANYWAY.

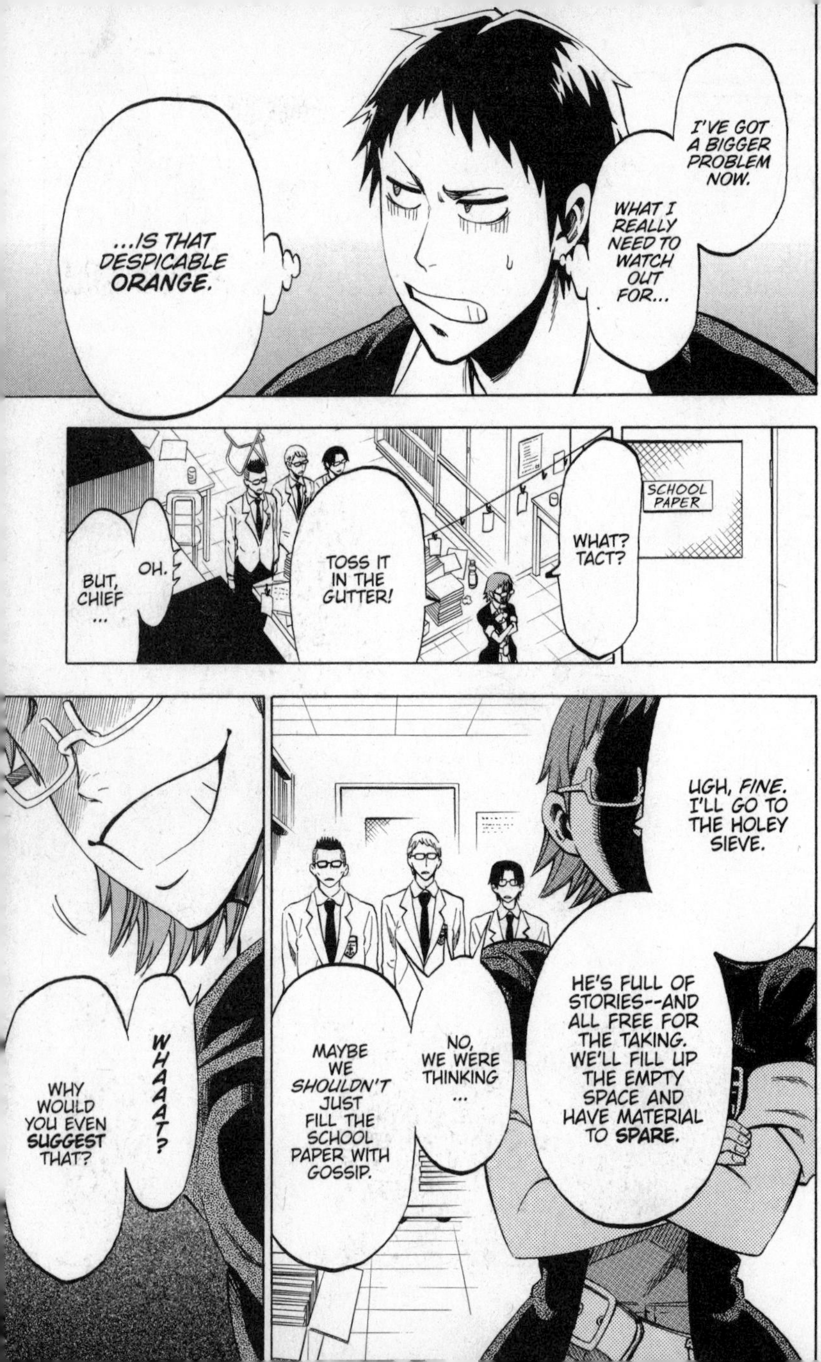
I'VE GOT A BIGGER PROBLEM NOW.
WHAT I REALLY NEED TO WATCH OUT FOR...
...IS THAT DESPICABLE **ORANGE**.
SCHOOL PAPER
WHAT? TACT?
TOSS IT IN THE GUTTER!
OH.
BUT, CHIEF ...
UGH, *FINE*. I'LL GO TO THE HOLEY SIEVE.
HE'S FULL OF STORIES--AND ALL FREE FOR THE TAKING. WE'LL FILL UP THE EMPTY SPACE AND HAVE MATERIAL TO **SPARE**.
NO, WE WERE THINKING ...
MAYBE WE *SHOULDN'T* JUST FILL THE SCHOOL PAPER WITH GOSSIP.
WHAAAT?
WHY WOULD YOU EVEN **SUGGEST** THAT?

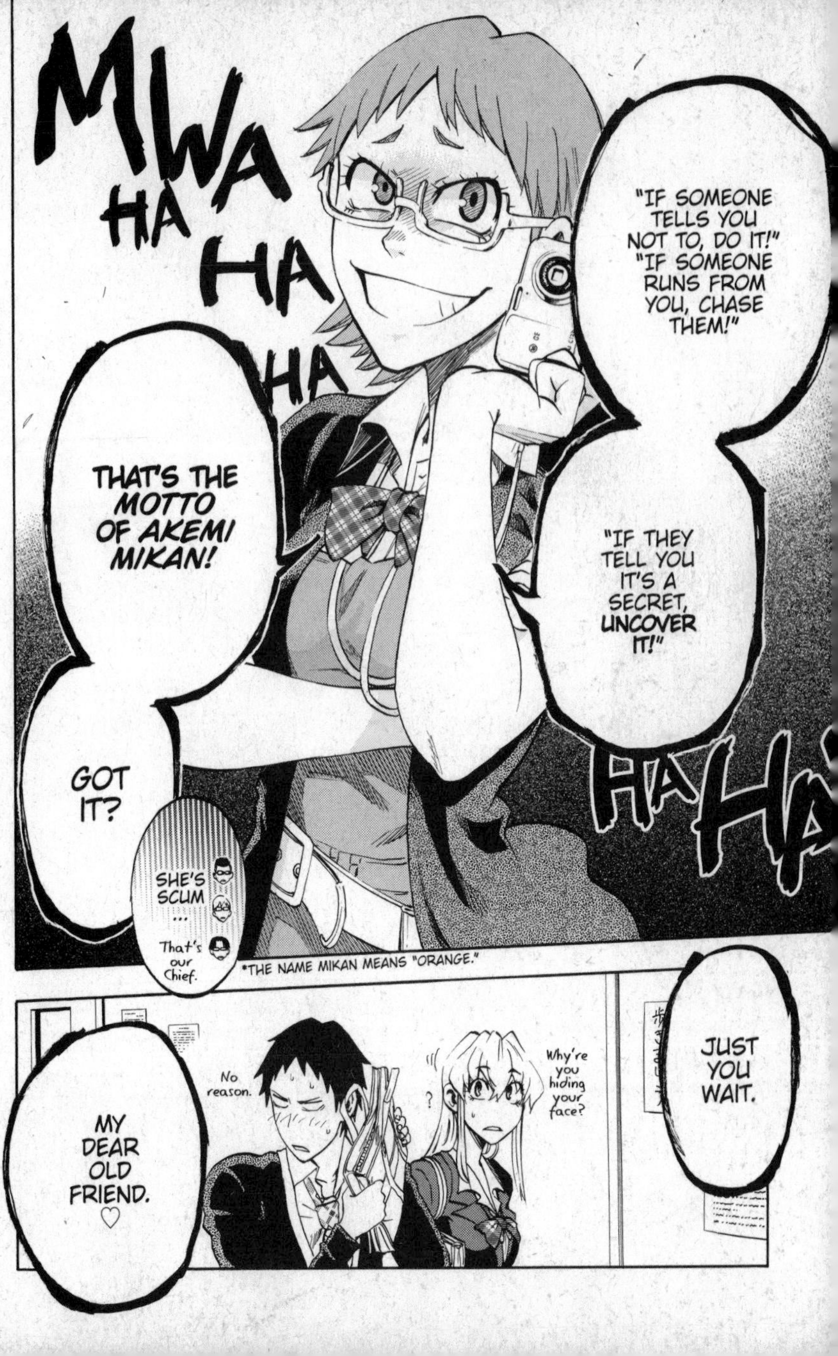
"IF SOMEONE TELLS YOU NOT TO, DO IT!" "IF SOMEONE RUNS FROM YOU, CHASE THEM!"
"IF THEY TELL YOU IT'S A SECRET, UNCOVER IT!"
MWA HA HA HA
THAT'S THE MOTTO OF AKEMI MIKAN!
GOT IT?
HA HA
SHE'S SCUM ...
That's our Chief.
*THE NAME MIKAN MEANS "ORANGE."
JUST YOU WAIT.
Why're you hiding your face?
?
No reason.
MY DEAR OLD FRIEND. ♡

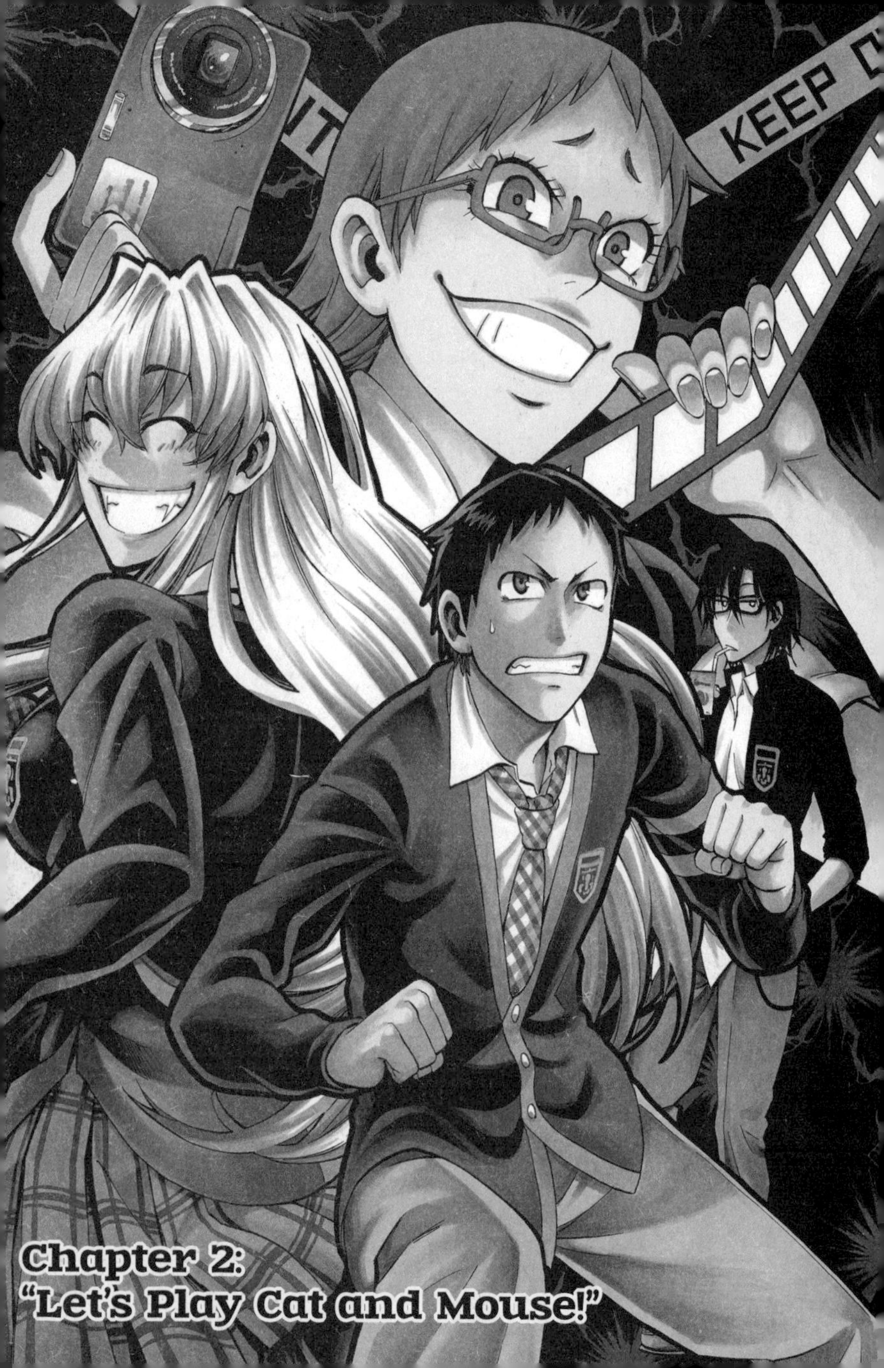
KEEP
Chapter 2:
"Let's Play Cat and Mouse!"

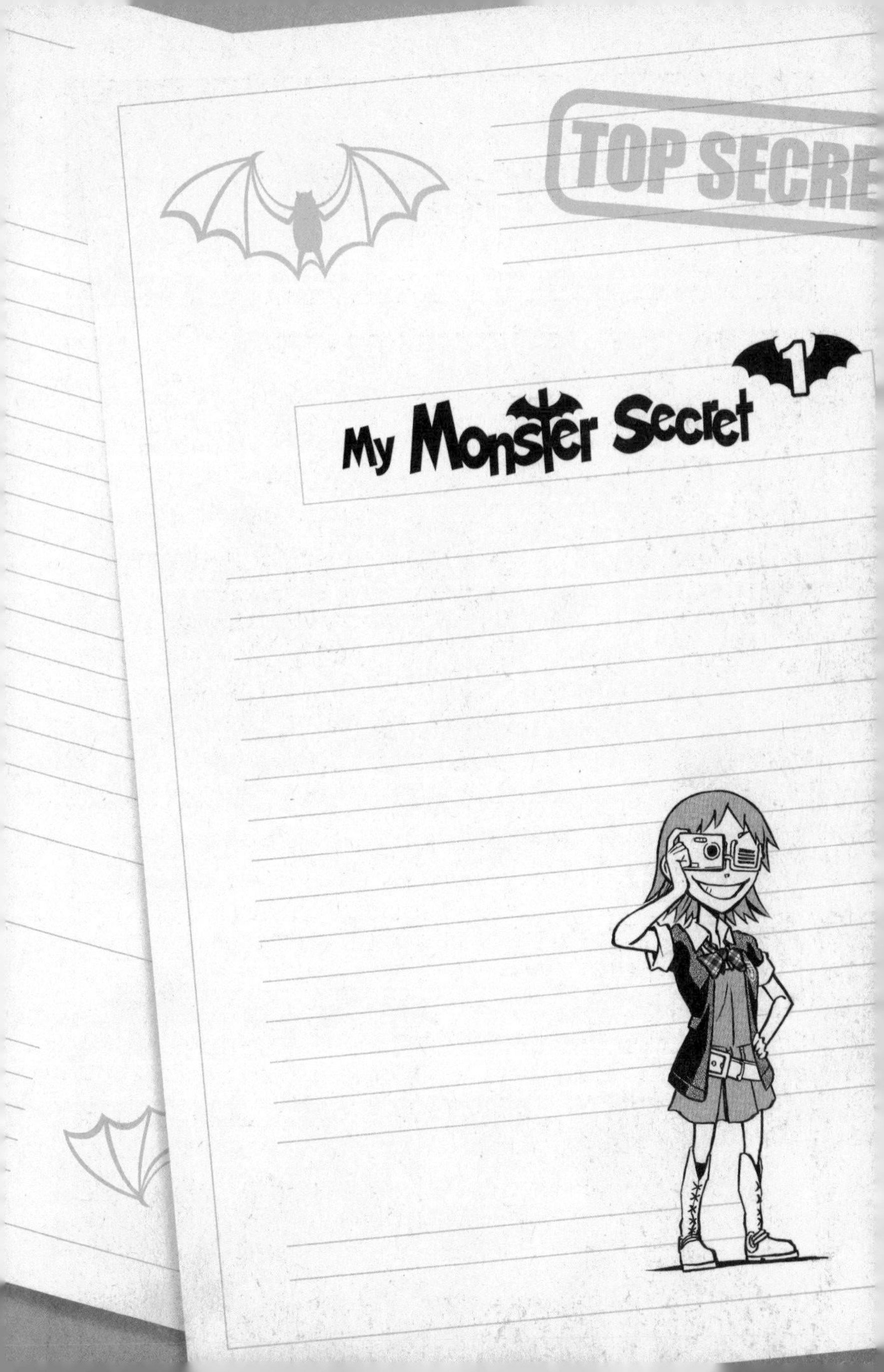
TOP SECRE
My Monster Secret
1

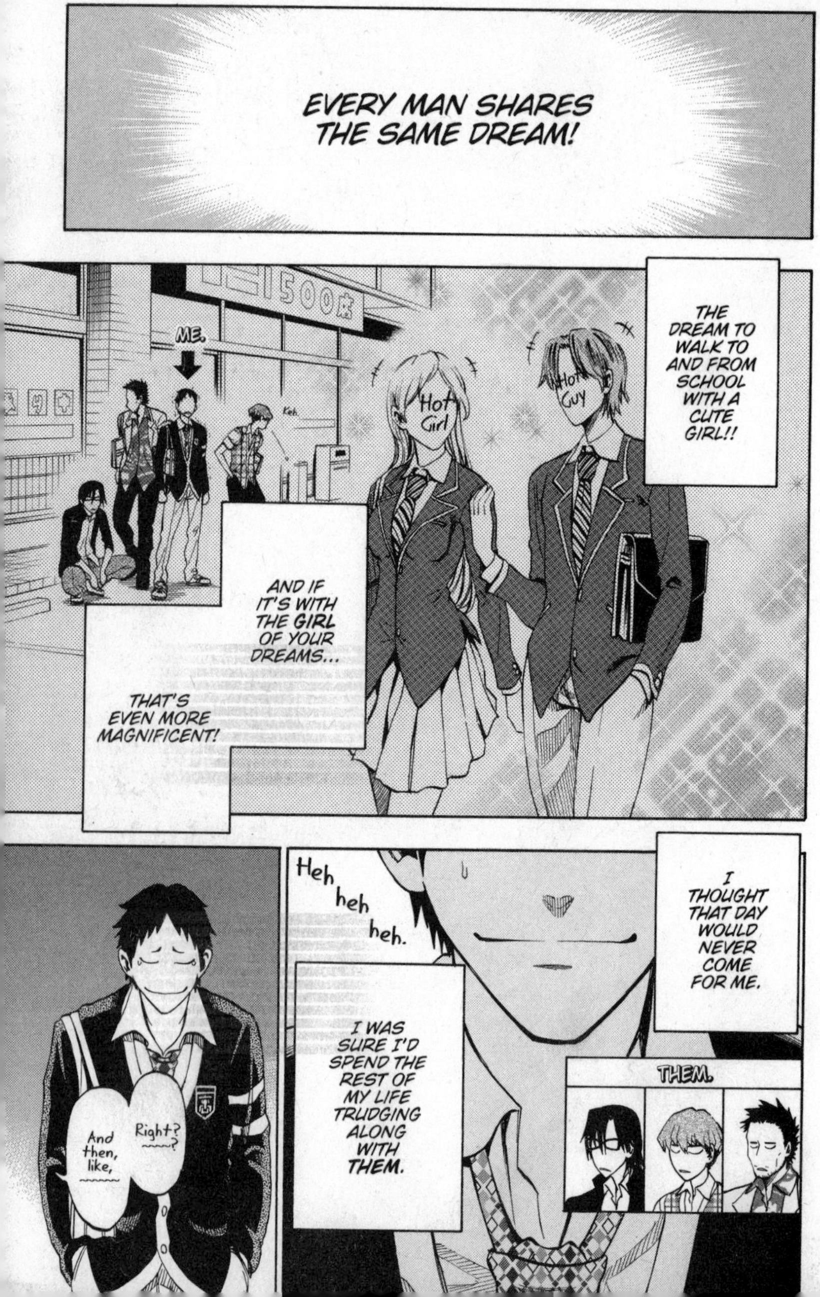
EVERY MAN SHARES THE SAME DREAM!
THE DREAM TO WALK TO AND FROM SCHOOL WITH A CUTE GIRL!!
Hot Guy
Hot Girl
Keh.
ME.
AND IF IT'S WITH THE GIRL OF YOUR DREAMS...
THAT'S EVEN MORE MAGNIFICENT!
I THOUGHT THAT DAY WOULD NEVER COME FOR ME.
THEM.
I WAS SURE I'D SPEND THE REST OF MY LIFE TRUDGING ALONG WITH THEM.
Heh heh heh.
Right? ~~~?
And then, like, ~~~~

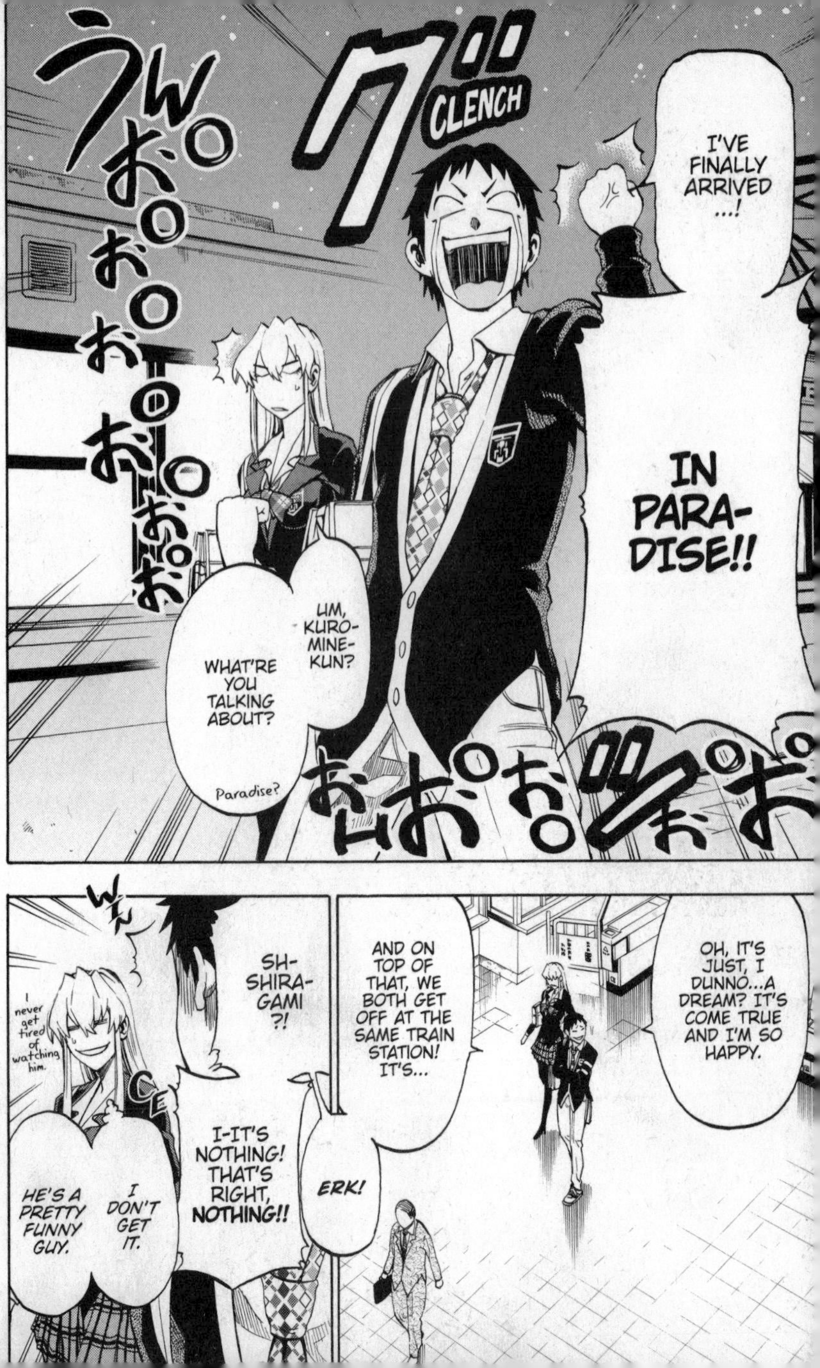
I'VE FINALLY ARRIVED ...!
クッ CLENCH
IN PARA-DISE!!
うwおおおおおおおおおおおおおおお
UM, KURO-MINE-KUN?
WHAT'RE YOU TALKING ABOUT?
Paradise?
OH, IT'S JUST, I DUNNO...A DREAM? IT'S COME TRUE AND I'M SO HAPPY.
AND ON TOP OF THAT, WE BOTH GET OFF AT THE SAME TRAIN STATION! IT'S...
ERK!
SH-SHIRA-GAMI?!
I-IT'S NOTHING! THAT'S RIGHT, NOTHING!!
I DON'T GET IT.
HE'S A PRETTY FUNNY GUY.
I never get tired of watching him.

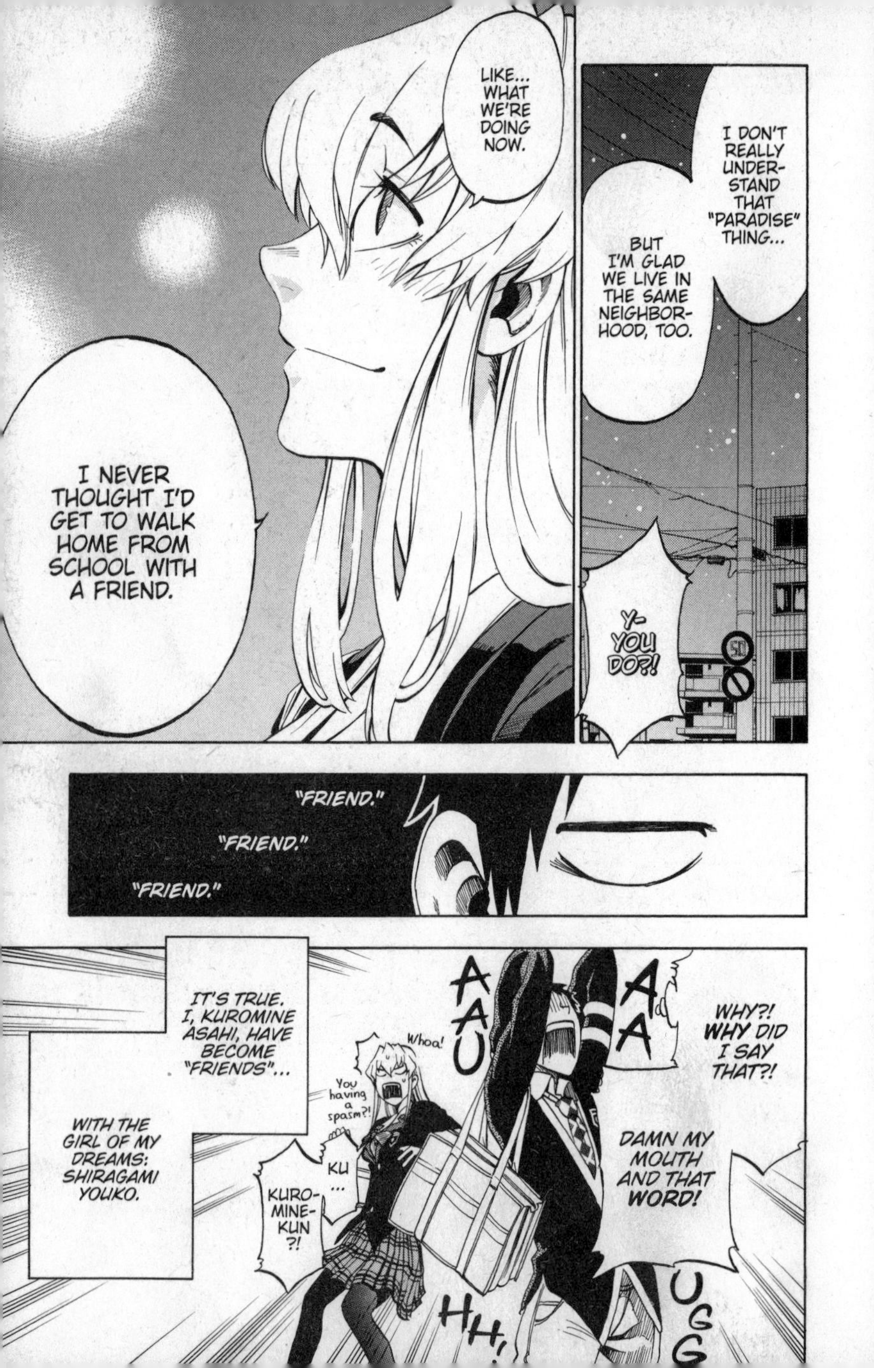
I DON'T REALLY UNDER-STAND THAT "PARADISE" THING...
BUT I'M GLAD WE LIVE IN THE SAME NEIGHBOR-HOOD, TOO.
Y-YOU DO?!
I NEVER THOUGHT I'D GET TO WALK HOME FROM SCHOOL WITH A FRIEND.
LIKE... WHAT WE'RE DOING NOW.
"FRIEND."
"FRIEND."
"FRIEND."
AAAAAU
WHY?! WHY DID I SAY THAT?!
DAMN MY MOUTH AND THAT WORD!
UGGHH!
Whoa!
You having a spasm?!
KU...
KURO-MINE-KUN?!
IT'S TRUE. I, KUROMINE ASAHI, HAVE BECOME "FRIENDS"...
WITH THE GIRL OF MY DREAMS: SHIRAGAMI YOUKO.

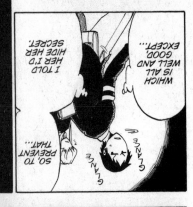

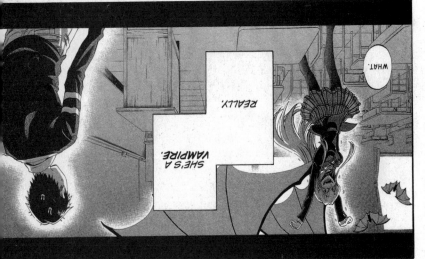

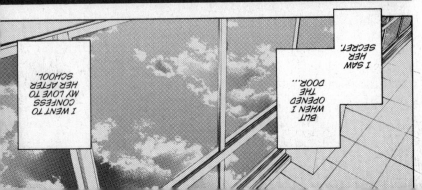

I WENT TO CONFESS MY LOVE TO HER AFTER SCHOOL.
BUT WHEN I OPENED THE DOOR...
I SAW HER SECRET.
SHE'S A VAMPIRE.
REALLY.
WHAT.
SHIRAGAMI MADE A PROMISE TO HER FATHER.
IF ANYONE FINDS OUT SHE'S A VAMPIRE, SHE HAS TO LEAVE SCHOOL.
SO, TO PREVENT THAT...
I TOLD HER I'D HIDE HER SECRET.
GLANCE
GLANCE
WHICH IS ALL WELL AND GOOD, EXCEPT...

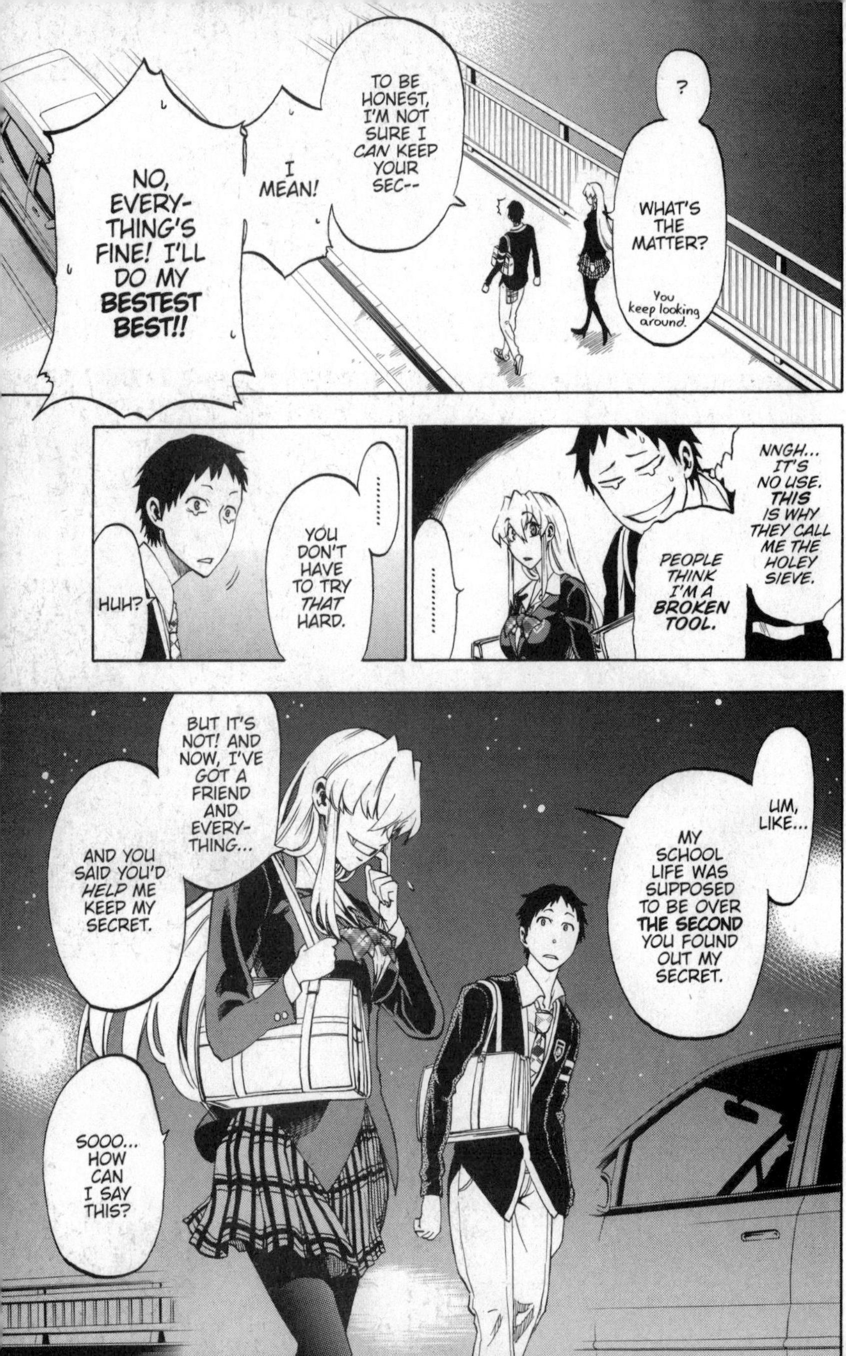
?
WHAT'S THE MATTER?
You keep looking around.
TO BE HONEST, I'M NOT SURE I CAN KEEP YOUR SEC--
I MEAN!
NO, EVERY-THING'S FINE! I'LL DO MY BESTEST BEST!!
NNGH... IT'S NO USE. THIS IS WHY THEY CALL ME THE HOLEY SIEVE.
PEOPLE THINK I'M A BROKEN TOOL.
......
......
YOU DON'T HAVE TO TRY THAT HARD.
HUH?
UM, LIKE...
MY SCHOOL LIFE WAS SUPPOSED TO BE OVER THE SECOND YOU FOUND OUT MY SECRET.
BUT IT'S NOT! AND NOW, I'VE GOT A FRIEND AND EVERY-THING...
AND YOU SAID YOU'D HELP ME KEEP MY SECRET.
SOOO... HOW CAN I SAY THIS?

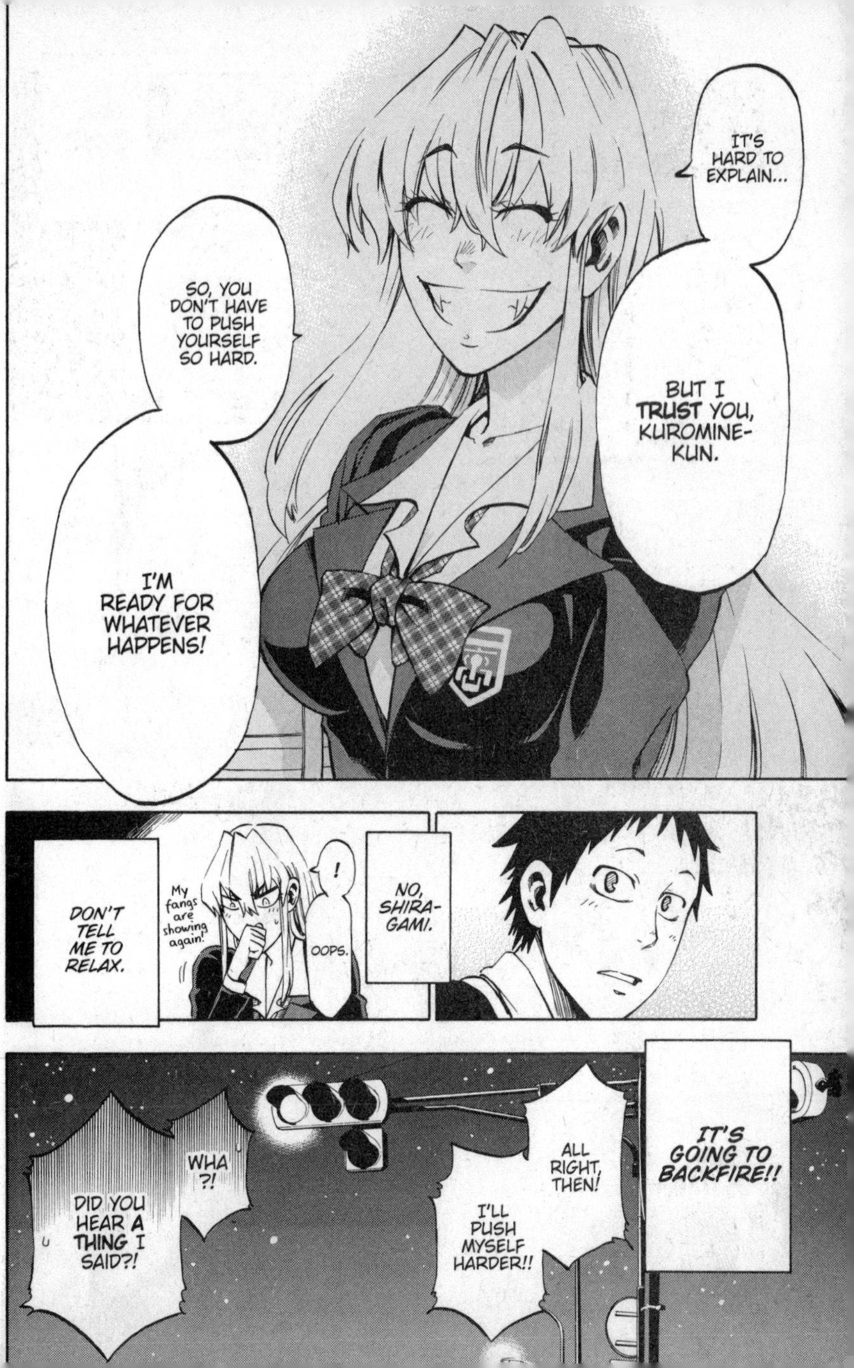
IT'S HARD TO EXPLAIN...
BUT I TRUST YOU, KUROMINE-KUN.
SO, YOU DON'T HAVE TO PUSH YOURSELF SO HARD.
I'M READY FOR WHATEVER HAPPENS!
NO, SHIRA-GAMI.
!
OOPS.
My fangs are showing again!
DON'T TELL ME TO RELAX.
IT'S GOING TO BACKFIRE!!
ALL RIGHT, THEN!
I'LL PUSH MYSELF HARDER!!
WHA ?!
DID YOU HEAR A THING I SAID?!

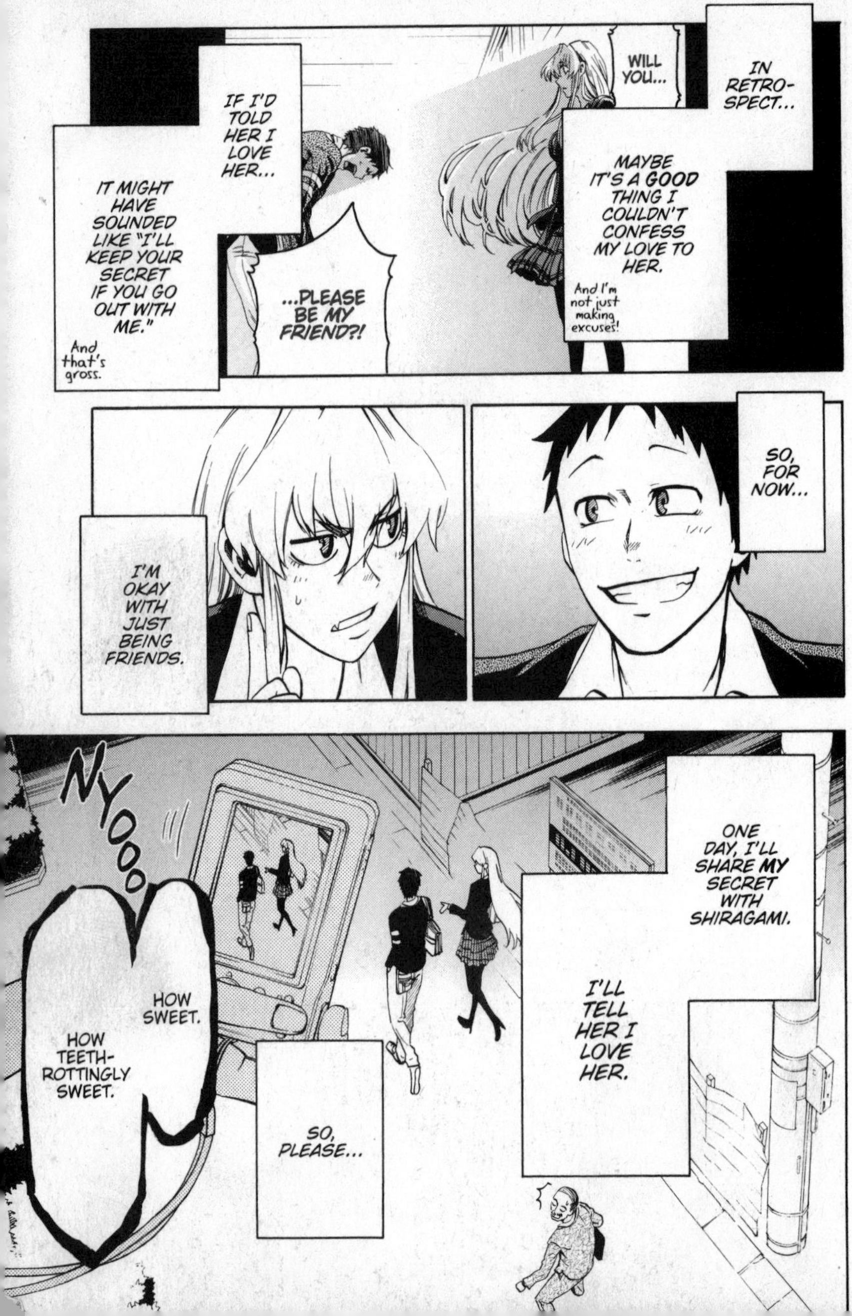
IN RETRO-SPECT...
WILL YOU...
MAYBE IT'S A GOOD THING I COULDN'T CONFESS MY LOVE TO HER.
And I'm not just making excuses!
IF I'D TOLD HER I LOVE HER...
IT MIGHT HAVE SOUNDED LIKE "I'LL KEEP YOUR SECRET IF YOU GO OUT WITH ME."
And that's gross.
...PLEASE BE MY FRIEND?!
SO, FOR NOW...
I'M OKAY WITH JUST BEING FRIENDS.
ONE DAY, I'LL SHARE MY SECRET WITH SHIRAGAMI.
I'LL TELL HER I LOVE HER.
SO, PLEASE...
NYOOO
HOW SWEET.
HOW TEETH-ROTTINGLY SWEET.

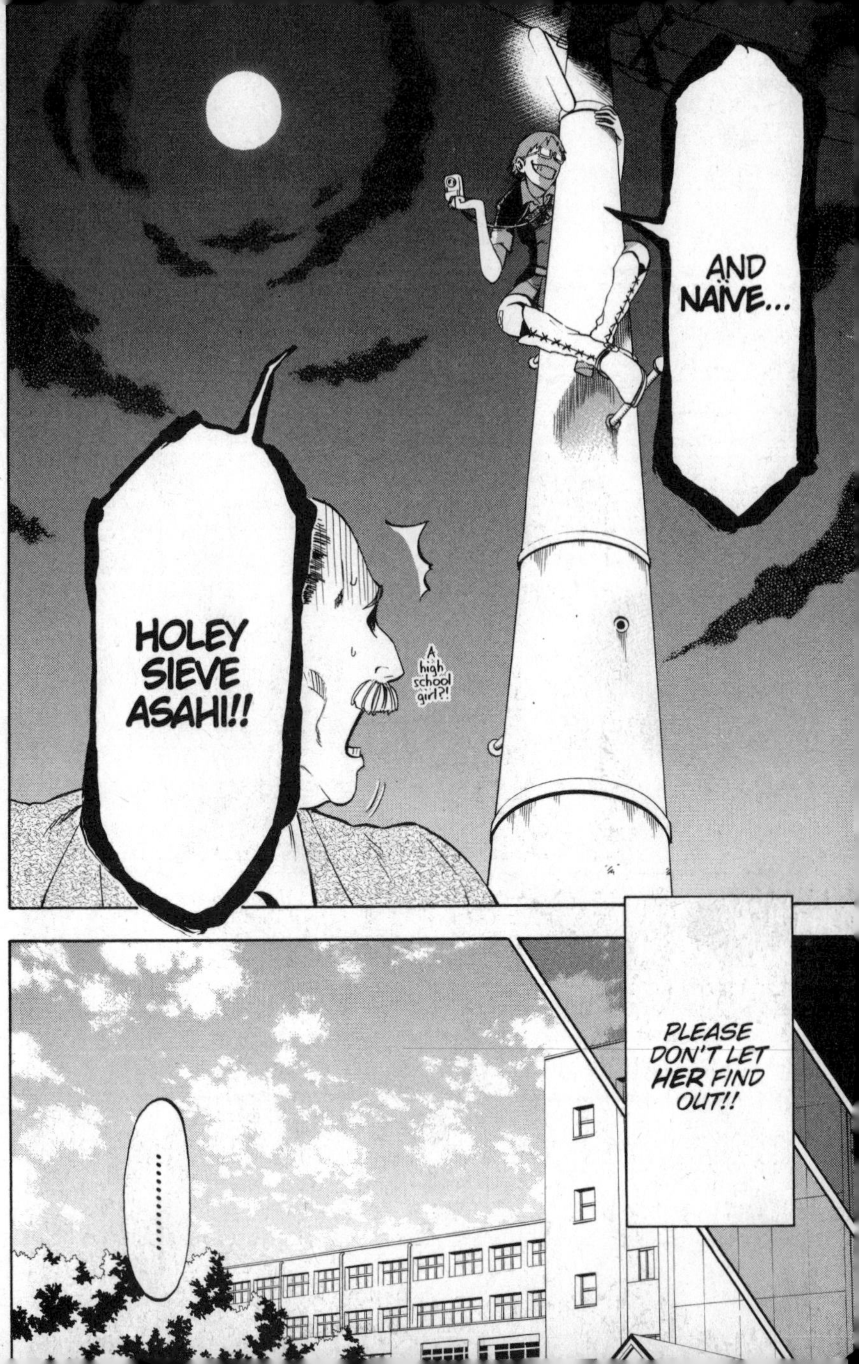
AND NAÏVE...
HOLEY SIEVE ASAHI!!
A high school girl?!
PLEASE DON'T LET HER FIND OUT!!
....

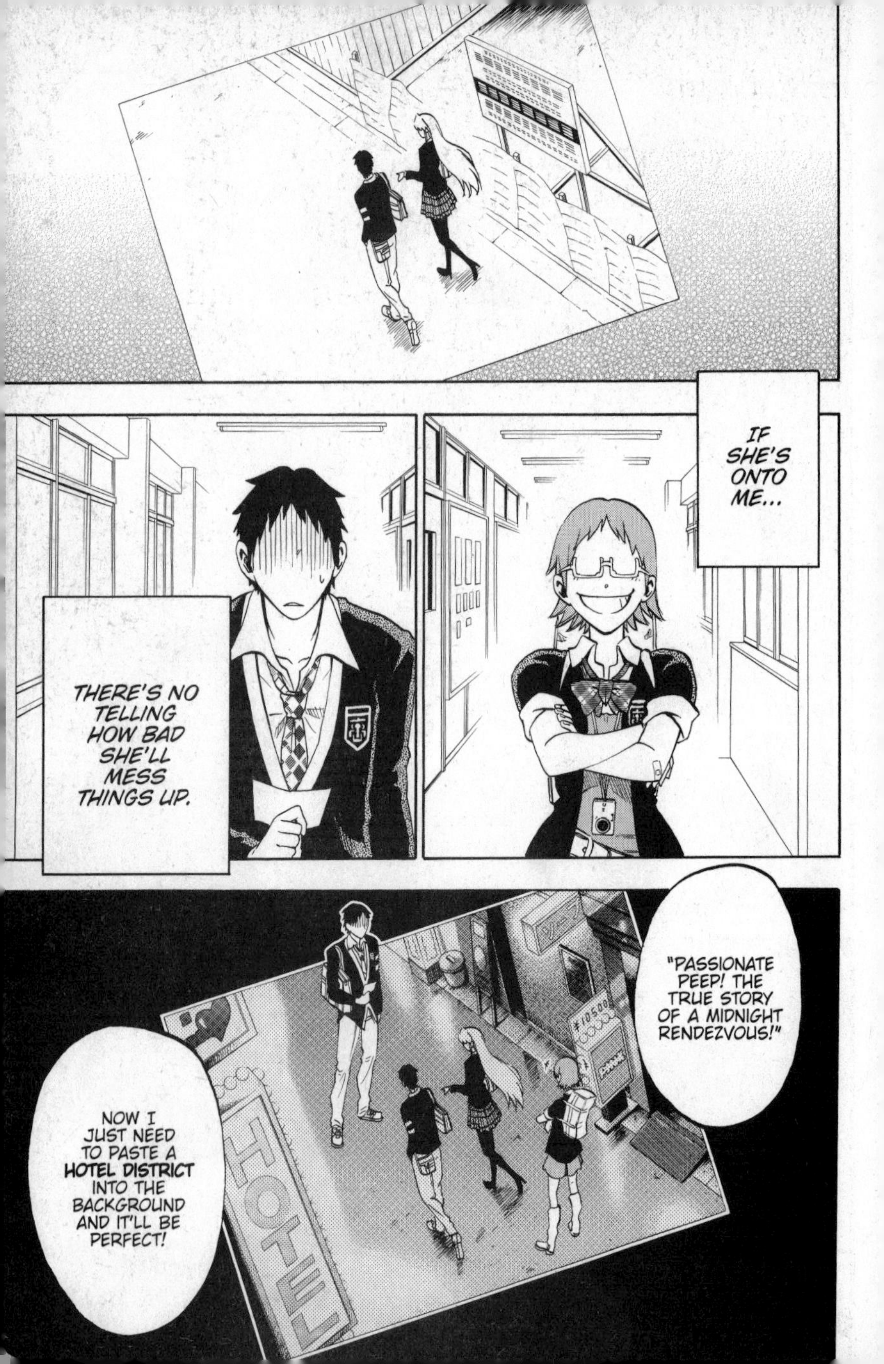
IF SHE'S ONTO ME...
THERE'S NO TELLING HOW BAD SHE'LL MESS THINGS UP.
"PASSIONATE PEEP! THE TRUE STORY OF A MIDNIGHT RENDEZVOUS!"
NOW I JUST NEED TO PASTE A **HOTEL DISTRICT** INTO THE BACKGROUND AND IT'LL BE PERFECT!
HOTEL

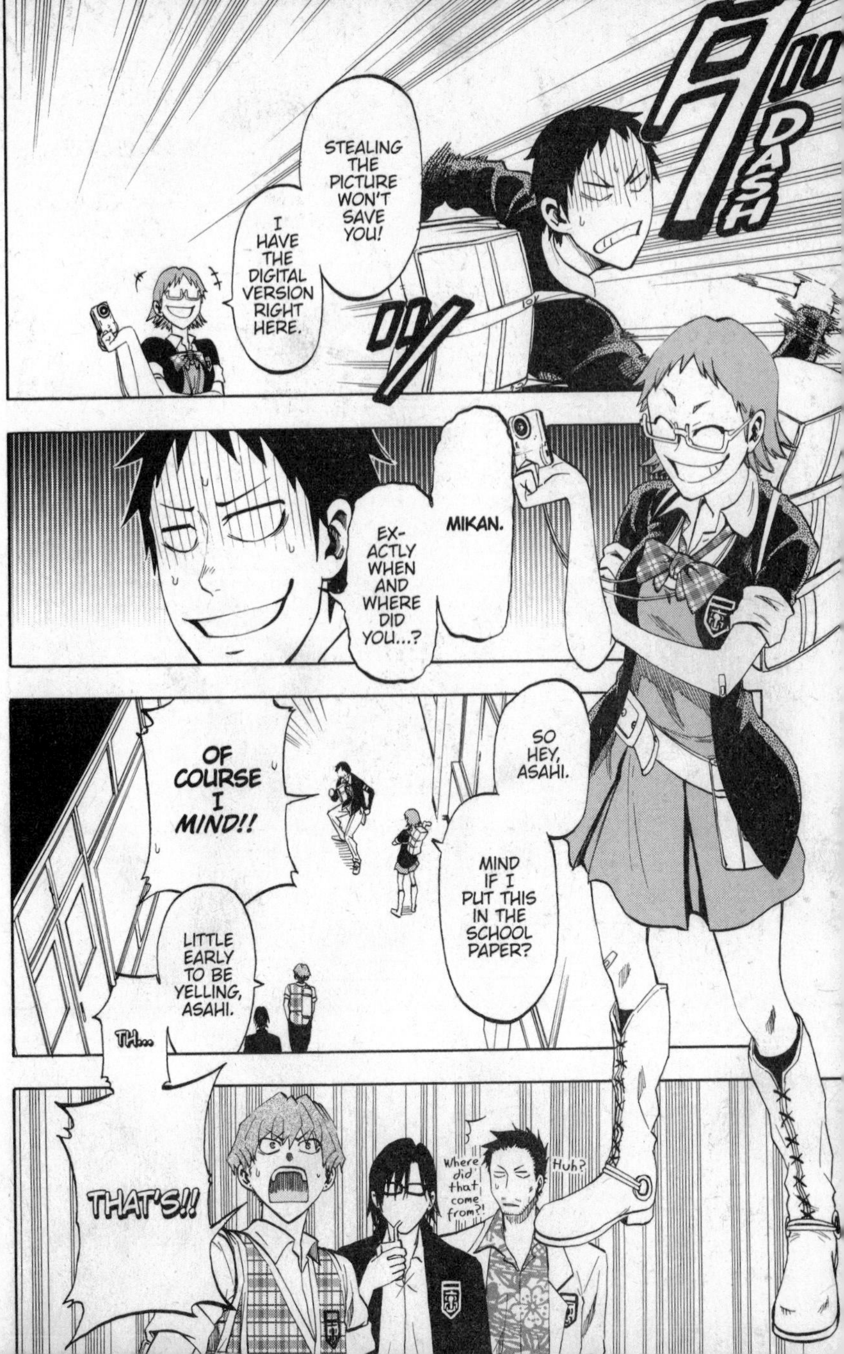
DASH
STEALING THE PICTURE WON'T SAVE YOU!
I HAVE THE DIGITAL VERSION RIGHT HERE.
MIKAN.
EX-ACTLY WHEN AND WHERE DID YOU...?
SO HEY, ASAHI.
MIND IF I PUT THIS IN THE SCHOOL PAPER?
OF COURSE I MIND!!
LITTLE EARLY TO BE YELLING, ASAHI.
TH...
THAT'S!!
Huh?
Where did that come from?!

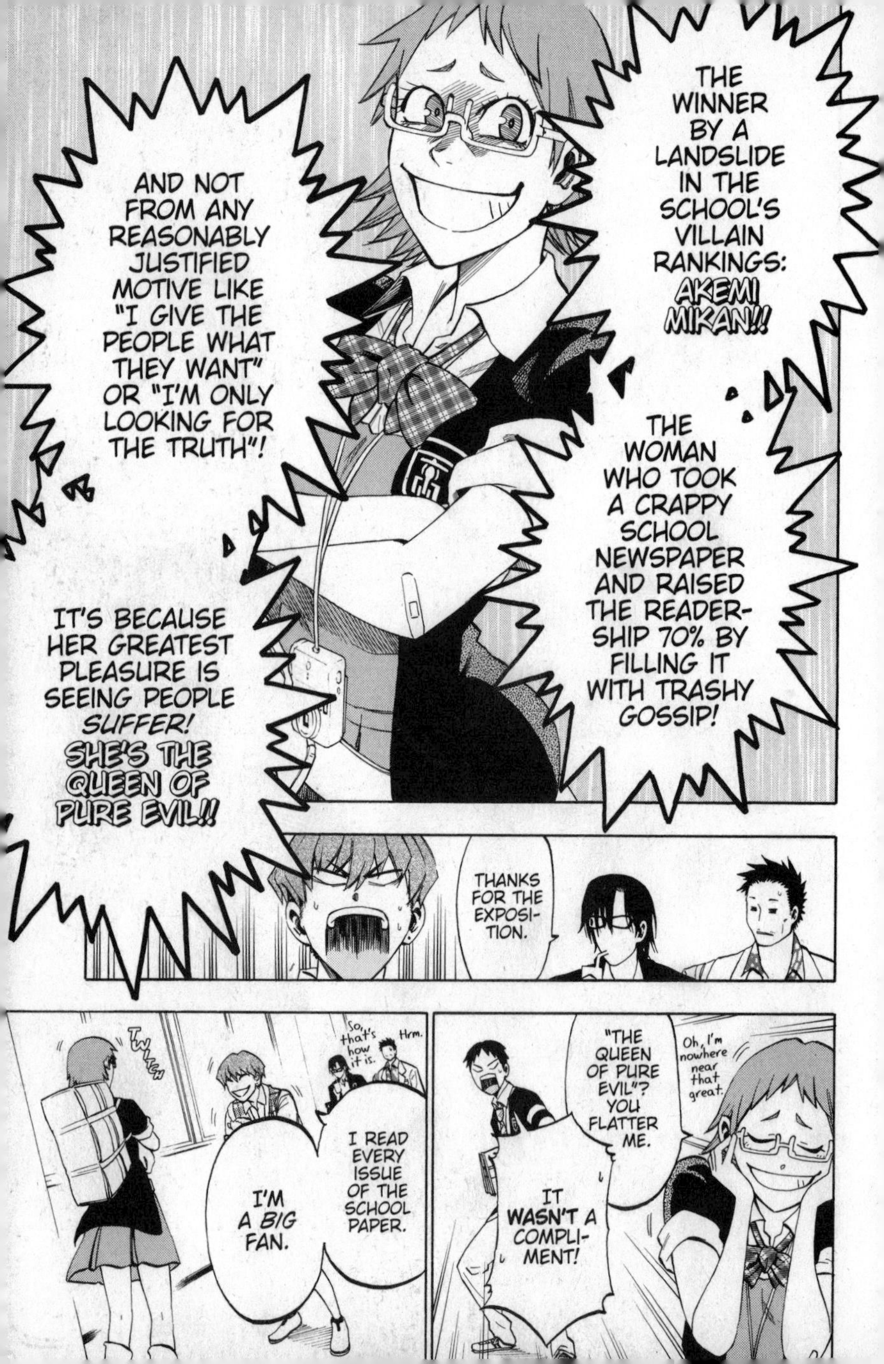
THE WINNER BY A LANDSLIDE IN THE SCHOOL'S VILLAIN RANKINGS: AKEMI MIKAN!!
THE WOMAN WHO TOOK A CRAPPY SCHOOL NEWSPAPER AND RAISED THE READER-SHIP 70% BY FILLING IT WITH TRASHY GOSSIP!
AND NOT FROM ANY REASONABLY JUSTIFIED MOTIVE LIKE "I GIVE THE PEOPLE WHAT THEY WANT" OR "I'M ONLY LOOKING FOR THE TRUTH"!
IT'S BECAUSE HER GREATEST PLEASURE IS SEEING PEOPLE SUFFER! SHE'S THE QUEEN OF PURE EVIL!!
THANKS FOR THE EXPOSI-TION.
Oh, I'm nowhere near that great.
"THE QUEEN OF PURE EVIL"? YOU FLATTER ME.
IT WASN'T A COMPLI-MENT!
Hrm.
So, that's how it is.
I READ EVERY ISSUE OF THE SCHOOL PAPER.
I'M A BIG FAN.
TWITCH

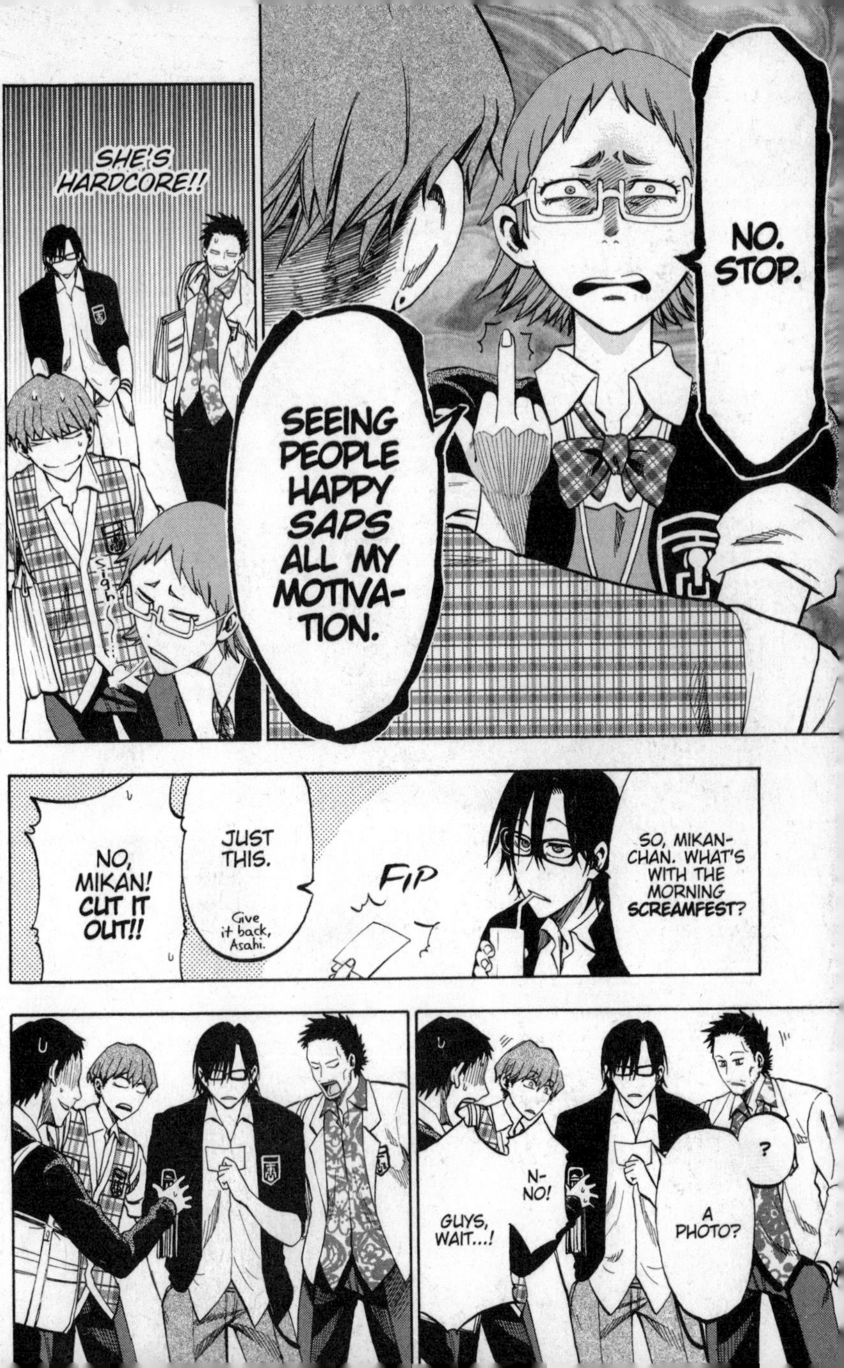
NO. STOP.
SEEING PEOPLE HAPPY SAPS ALL MY MOTIVA-TION.
SHE'S HARDCORE!!
Sigh...
SO, MIKAN-CHAN. WHAT'S WITH THE MORNING SCREAMFEST?
FIP
JUST THIS.
Give it back, Asahi.
NO, MIKAN! CUT IT OUT!!
?
A PHOTO?
N-NO!
GUYS, WAIT...!

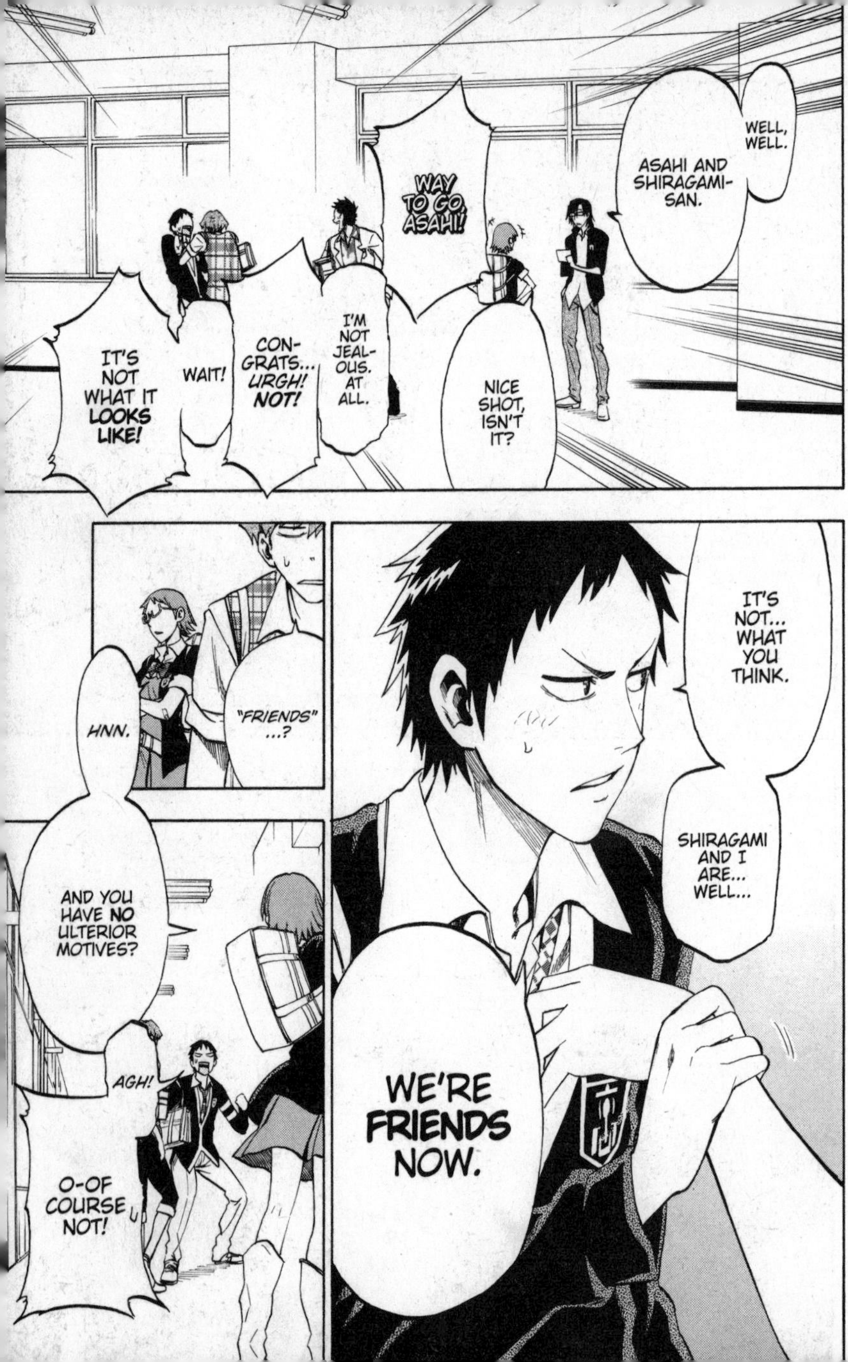
WELL, WELL.
ASAHI AND SHIRAGAMI-SAN.
WAY TO GO, ASAHI!
NICE SHOT, ISN'T IT?
I'M NOT JEALOUS. AT ALL.
CONGRATS... URGH! NOT!
WAIT!
IT'S NOT WHAT IT LOOKS LIKE!
IT'S NOT... WHAT YOU THINK.
SHIRAGAMI AND I ARE... WELL...
WE'RE FRIENDS NOW.
"FRIENDS"...?
HNN.
AND YOU HAVE NO ULTERIOR MOTIVES?
AGH!
O-OF COURSE NOT!

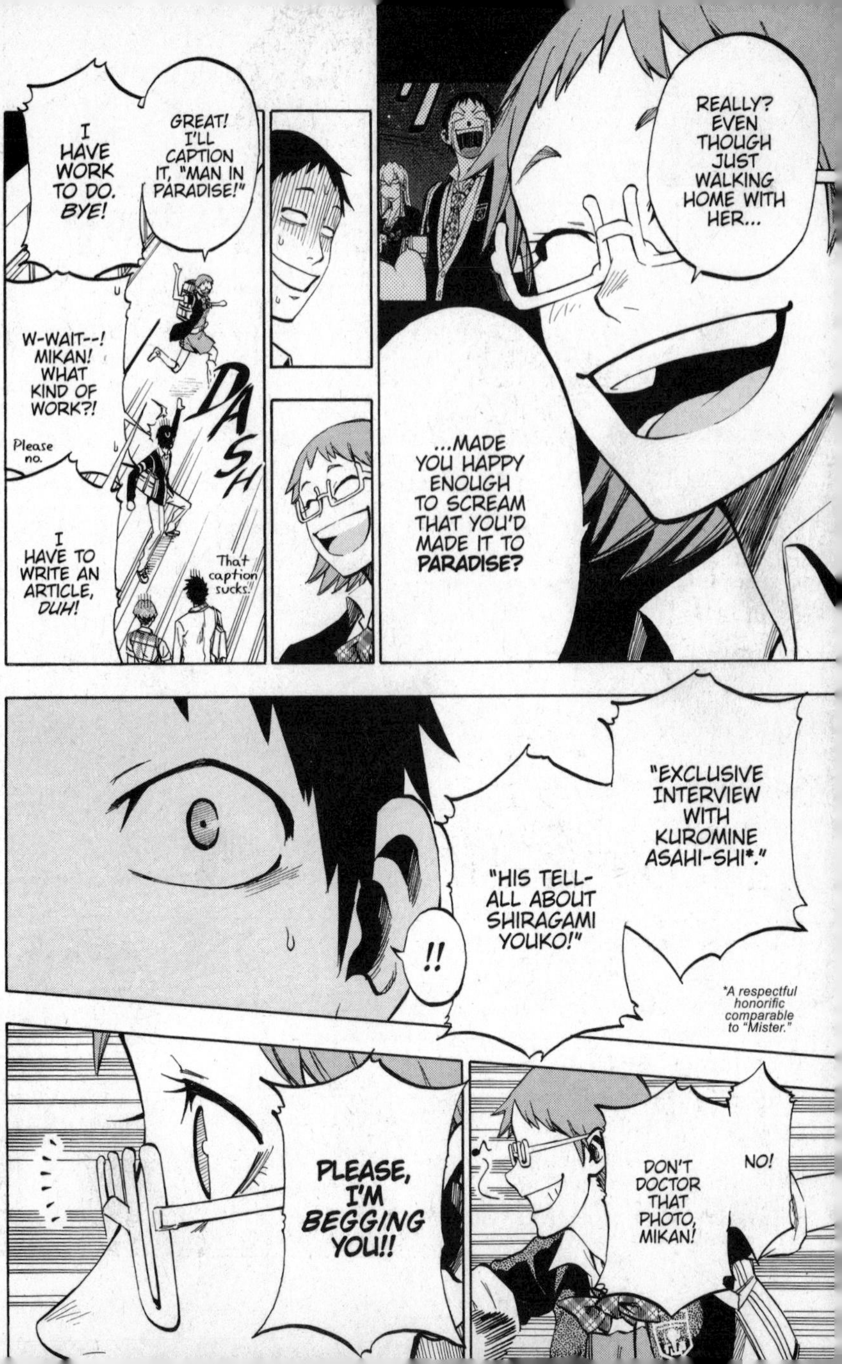
REALLY? EVEN THOUGH JUST WALKING HOME WITH HER...
...MADE YOU HAPPY ENOUGH TO SCREAM THAT YOU'D MADE IT TO PARADISE?
GREAT! I'LL CAPTION IT, "MAN IN PARADISE!"
I HAVE WORK TO DO. BYE!
W-WAIT--! MIKAN! WHAT KIND OF WORK?!
Please no.
DASH
I HAVE TO WRITE AN ARTICLE, DUH!
That caption sucks.
"EXCLUSIVE INTERVIEW WITH KUROMINE ASAHI-SHI*."
"HIS TELL-ALL ABOUT SHIRAGAMI YOUKO!"
!!
NO!
DON'T DOCTOR THAT PHOTO, MIKAN!
PLEASE, I'M BEGGING YOU!!
......
*A respectful honorific comparable to "Mister."

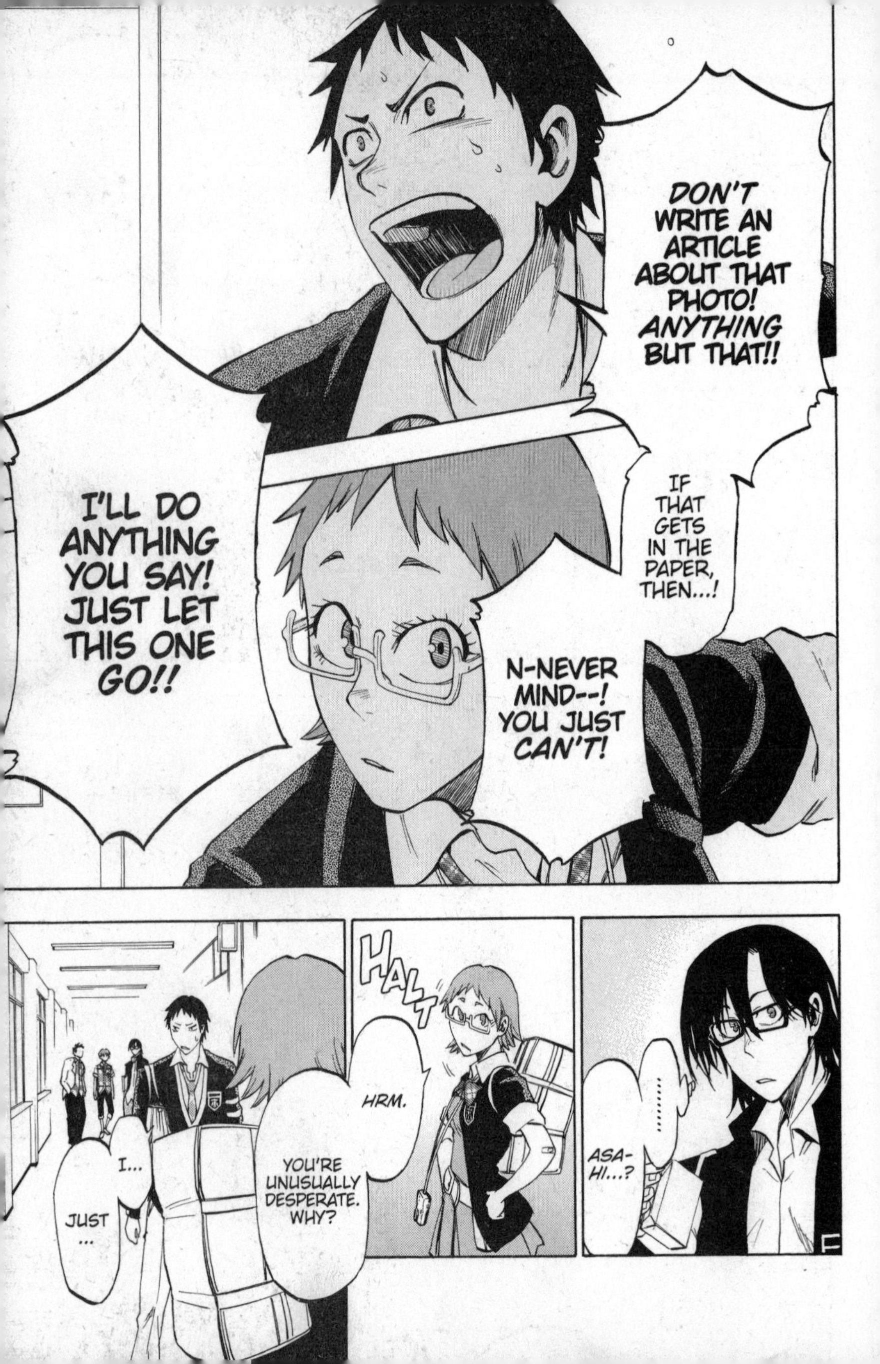
DON'T WRITE AN ARTICLE ABOUT THAT PHOTO! ANYTHING BUT THAT!!
IF THAT GETS IN THE PAPER, THEN...!
I'LL DO ANYTHING YOU SAY! JUST LET THIS ONE GO!!
N-NEVER MIND--! YOU JUST CAN'T!
......
ASA-HI...?
HALT
HRM.
YOU'RE UNUSUALLY DESPERATE. WHY?
I...
JUST ...

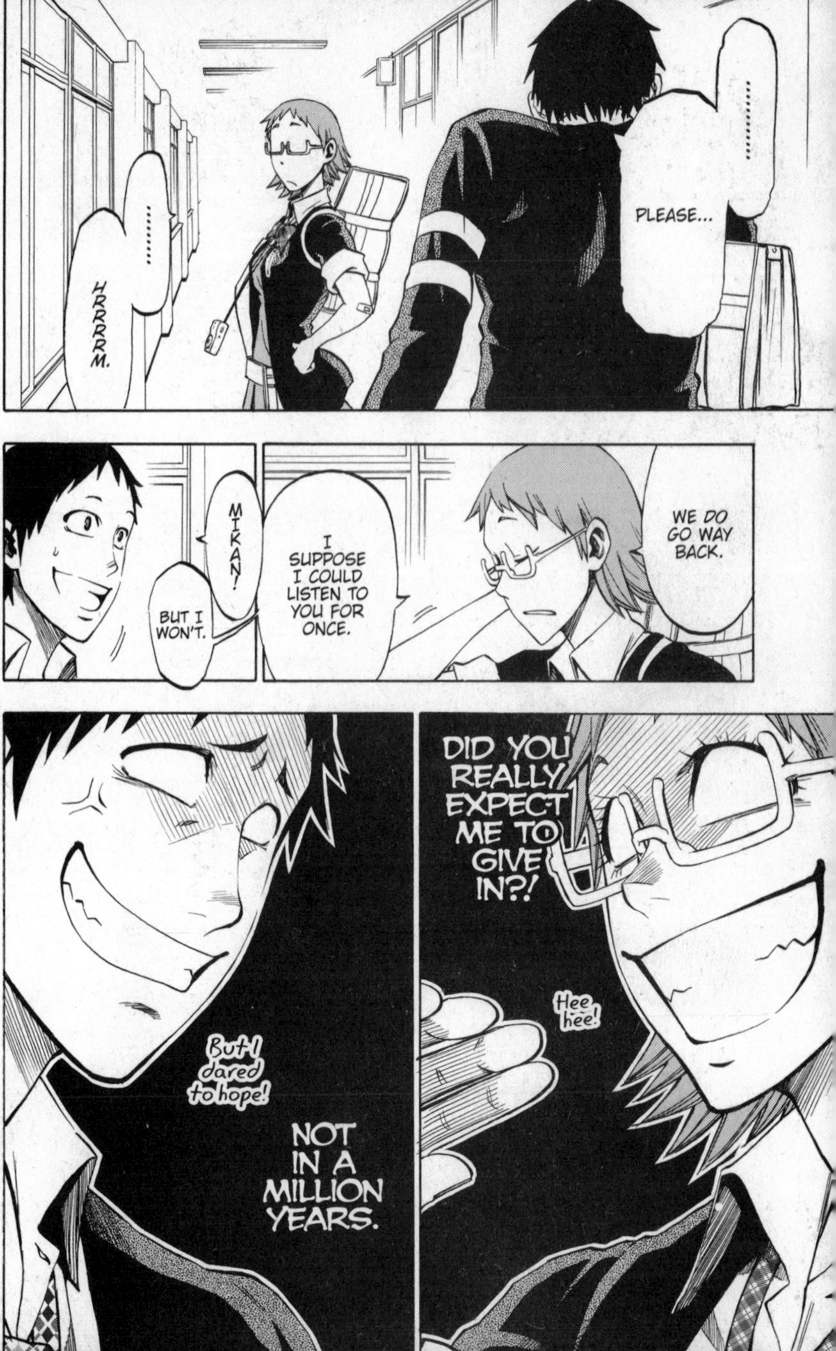
......
PLEASE...
......
HRRRRM.
WE DO GO WAY BACK.
I SUPPOSE I COULD LISTEN TO YOU FOR ONCE.
BUT I WON'T.
MIKAN!
DID YOU REALLY EXPECT ME TO GIVE IN?!
Hee hee!
NOT IN A MILLION YEARS.
But I dared to hope!

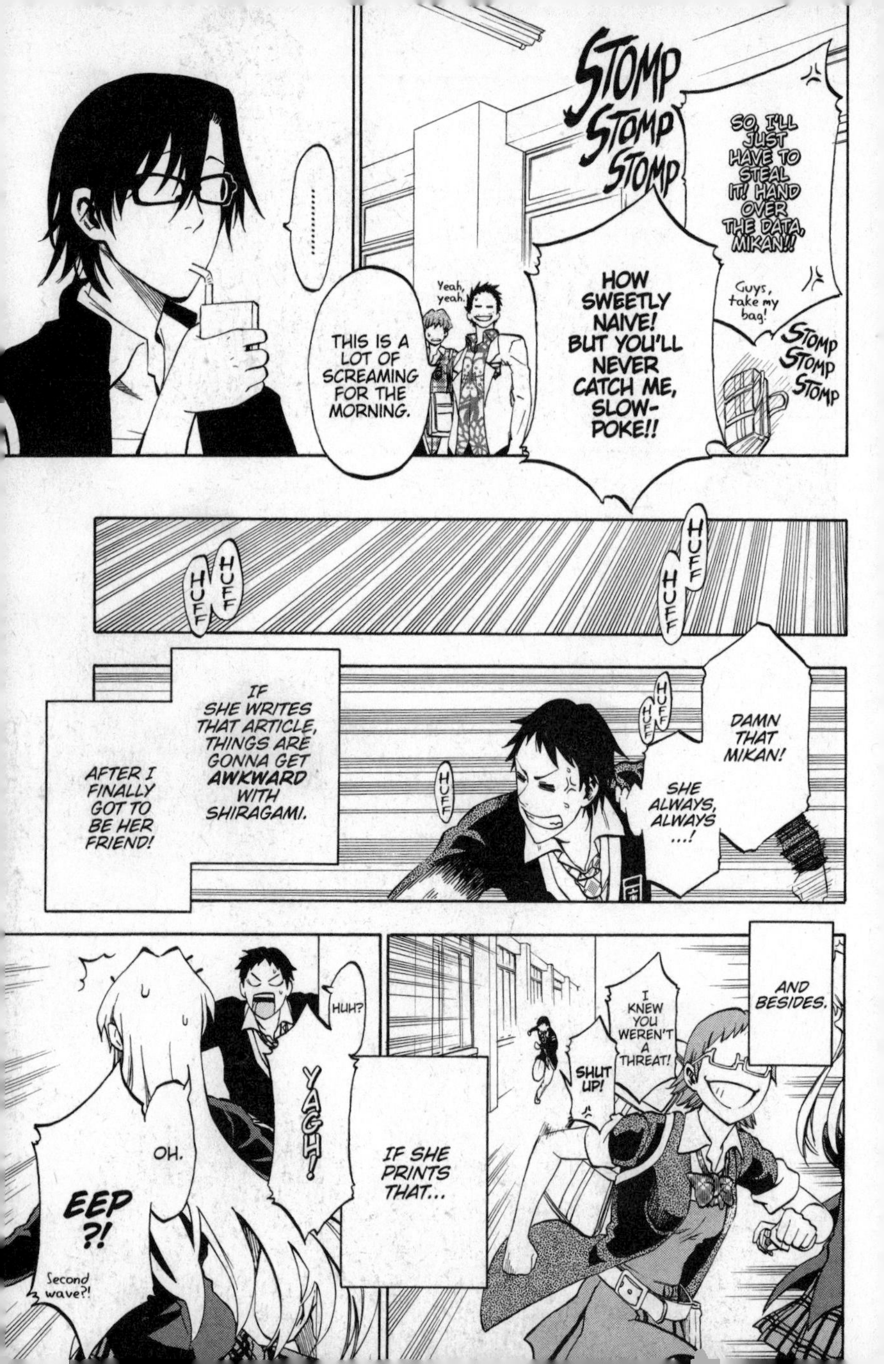
SO, I'LL JUST HAVE TO STEAL IT! HAND OVER THE DATA, MIKAN!!
Guys, take my bag!
STOMP STOMP STOMP
STOMP STOMP STOMP
HOW SWEETLY NAIVE! BUT YOU'LL NEVER CATCH ME, SLOW-POKE!!
Yeah, yeah.
THIS IS A LOT OF SCREAMING FOR THE MORNING.
......
HUFF HUFF
HUFF HUFF
DAMN THAT MIKAN!
SHE ALWAYS, ALWAYS ...!
HUFF HUFF
HUFF
IF SHE WRITES THAT ARTICLE, THINGS ARE GONNA GET AWKWARD WITH SHIRAGAMI.
AFTER I FINALLY GOT TO BE HER FRIEND!
AND BESIDES.
I KNEW YOU WEREN'T A THREAT!
SHUT UP!
IF SHE PRINTS THAT...
HUH?
YAGH!
OH.
EEP?!
Second wave?!

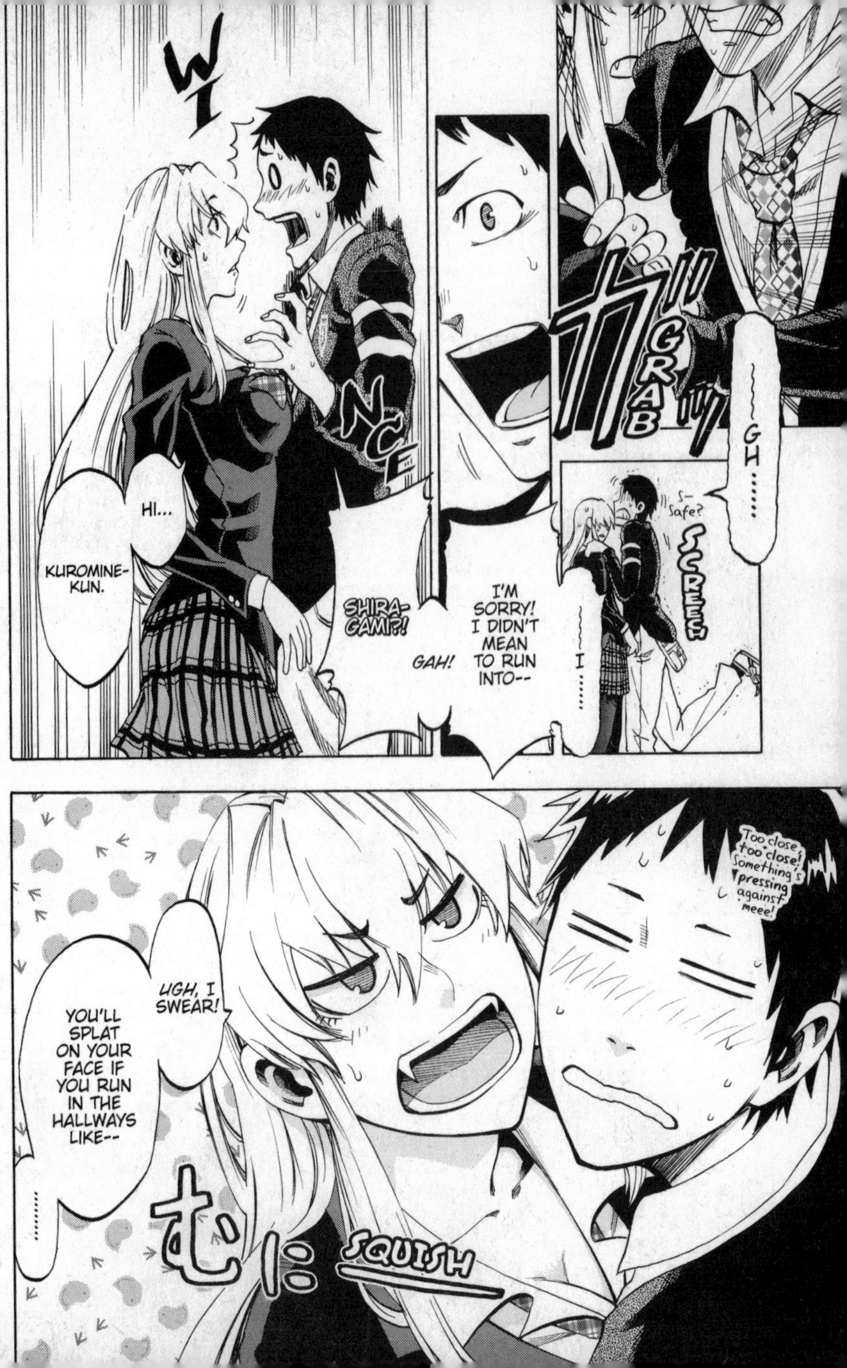

GRAB
GH......
S-Safe?
SCREECH
I......
I'M SORRY! I DIDN'T MEAN TO RUN INTO--
GAH!
SHIRA-GAMI?!
WINCE
HI...
KUROMINE-KUN.
Too close, too close! Something's pressing against meee!
UGH, I SWEAR!
YOU'LL SPLAT ON YOUR FACE IF YOU RUN IN THE HALLWAYS LIKE--
......
SQUISH

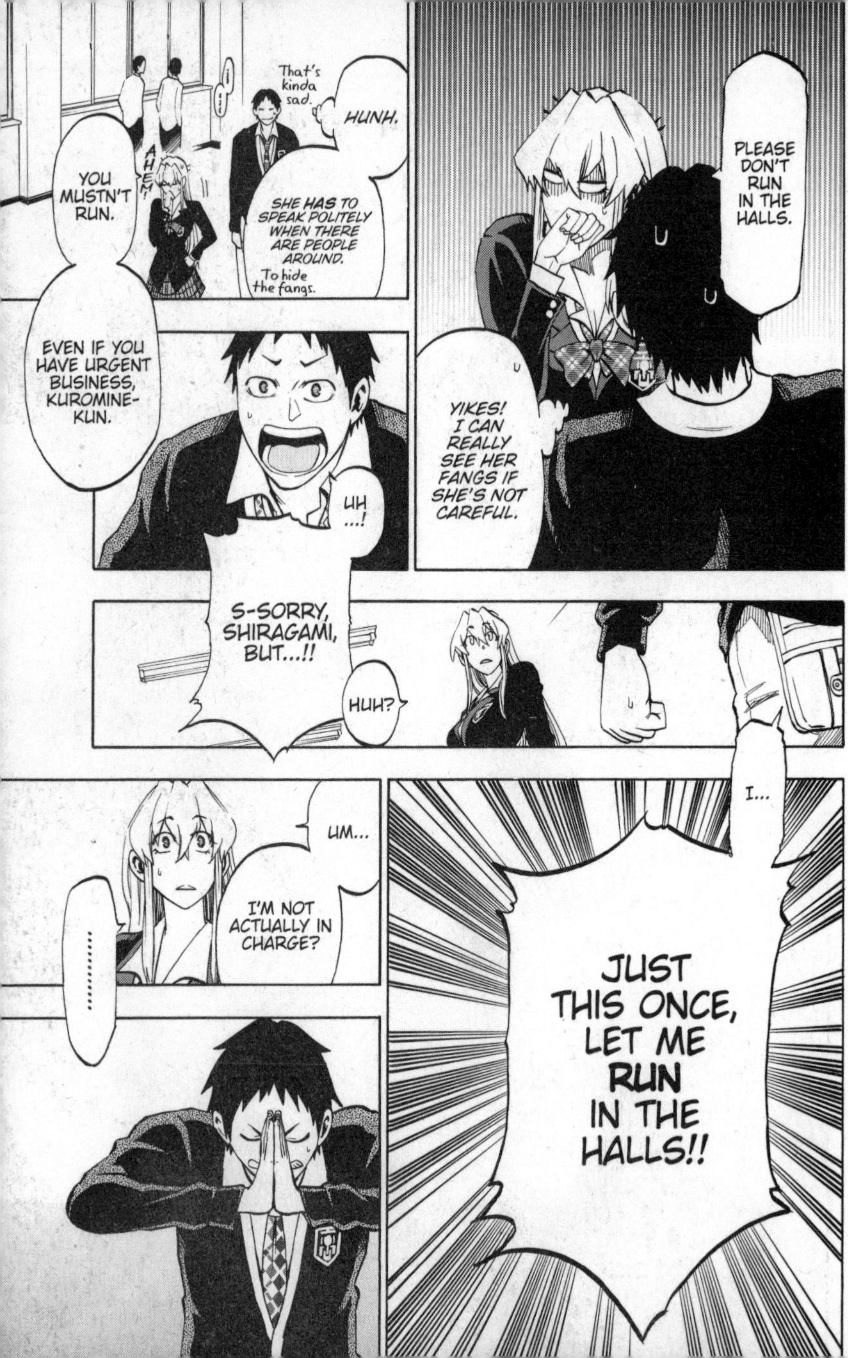
PLEASE DON'T RUN IN THE HALLS.
YIKES! I CAN REALLY SEE HER FANGS IF SHE'S NOT CAREFUL.
HUNH.
That's kinda sad.
...!
YOU MUSTN'T RUN.
AHEM!
SHE HAS TO SPEAK POLITELY WHEN THERE ARE PEOPLE AROUND.
To hide the fangs.
EVEN IF YOU HAVE URGENT BUSINESS, KUROMINE-KUN.
UH ...!
S-SORRY, SHIRAGAMI, BUT...!!
HUH?
I...
JUST THIS ONCE, LET ME RUN IN THE HALLS!!
UM...
I'M NOT ACTUALLY IN CHARGE?
....

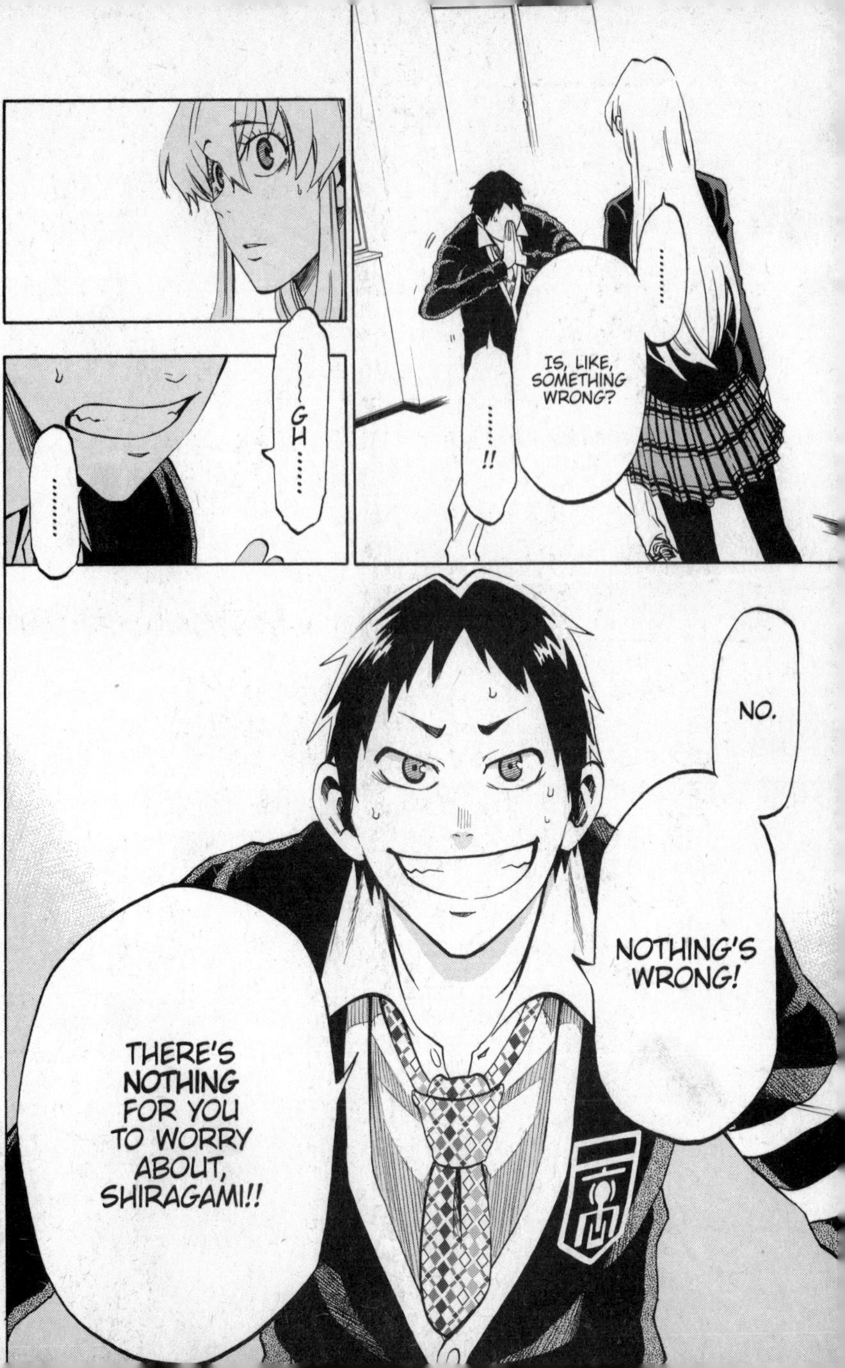
......
IS, LIKE, SOMETHING WRONG?
......!!
~~~GH......
......
NO.
NOTHING'S WRONG!
THERE'S NOTHING FOR YOU TO WORRY ABOUT, SHIRAGAMI!!
~~~

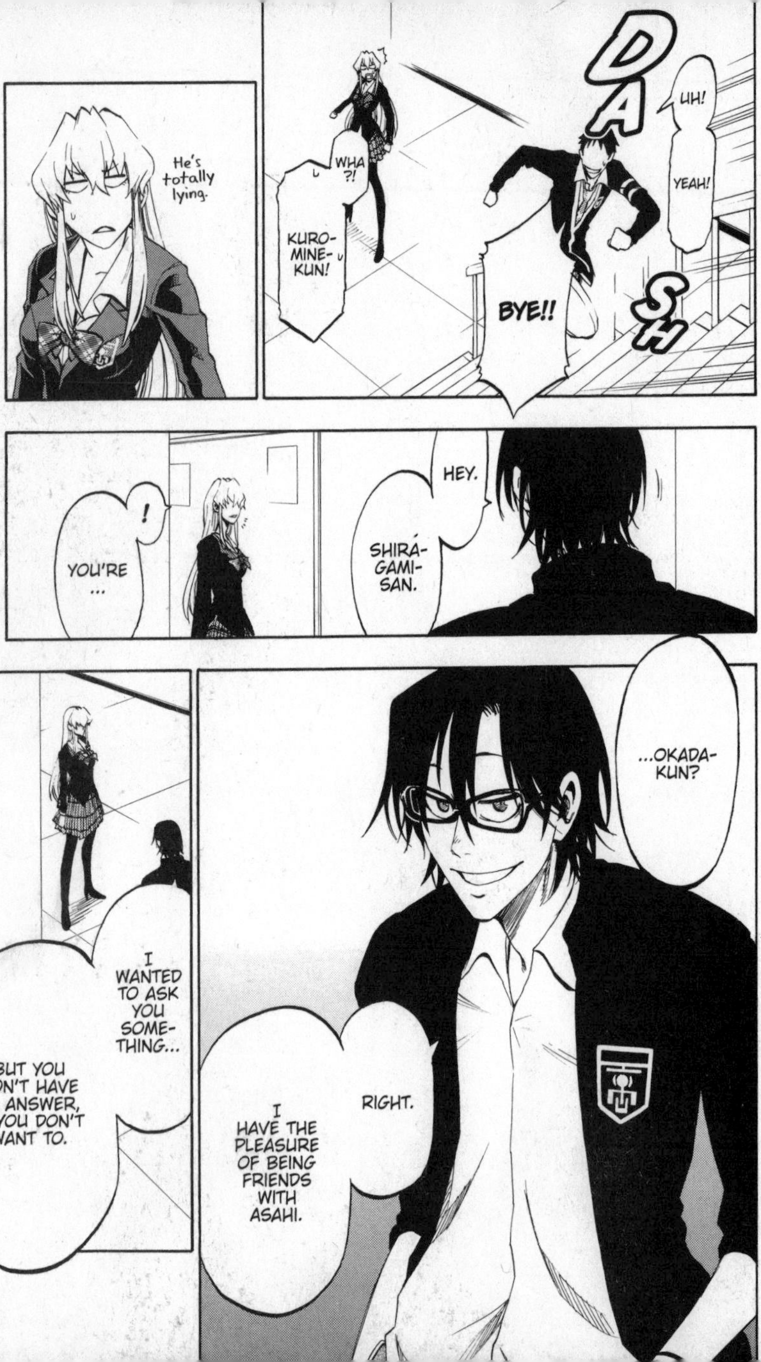
UH!
YEAH!
DASH
BYE!!
WHA?!
KUROMINE-KUN!
He's totally lying.
HEY.
SHIRAGAMI-SAN.
!
YOU'RE...
...OKADA-KUN?
RIGHT.
I HAVE THE PLEASURE OF BEING FRIENDS WITH ASAHI.
I WANTED TO ASK YOU SOMETHING...
BUT YOU DON'T HAVE TO ANSWER, IF YOU DON'T WANT TO.

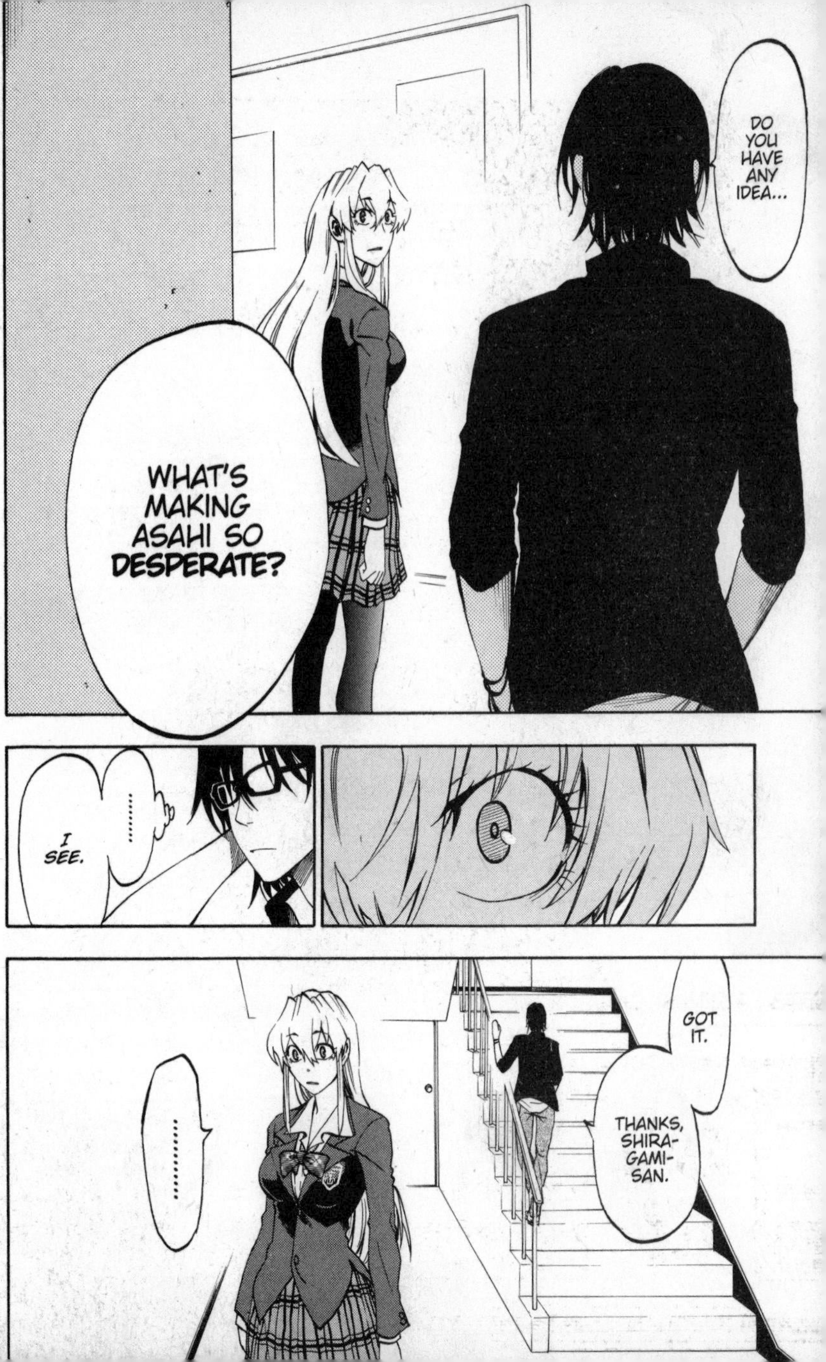
DO YOU HAVE ANY IDEA...
WHAT'S MAKING ASAHI SO **DESPERATE?**
......
I SEE.
GOT IT.
THANKS, SHIRA-GAMI-SAN.
......

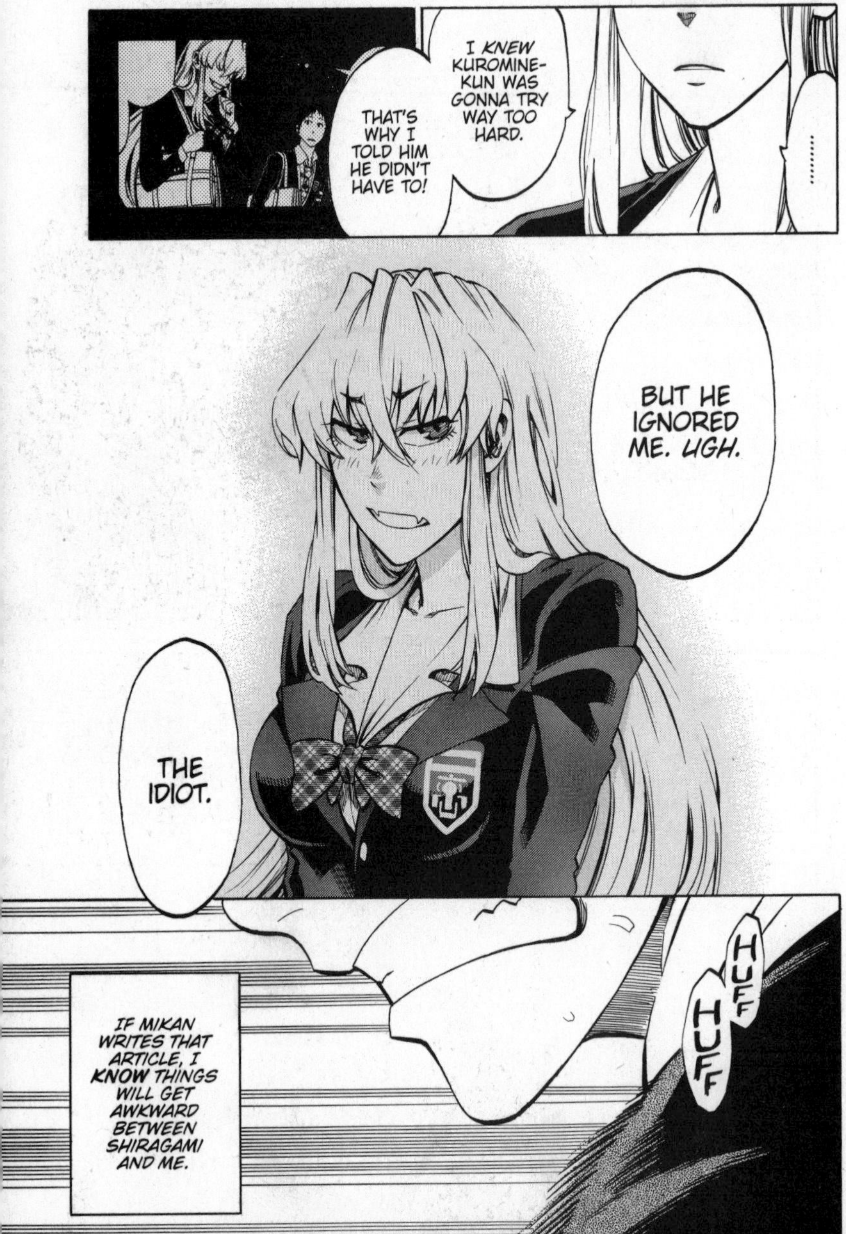
......
I KNEW KUROMINE-KUN WAS GONNA TRY WAY TOO HARD.
THAT'S WHY I TOLD HIM HE DIDN'T HAVE TO!
BUT HE IGNORED ME. UGH.
THE IDIOT.
HUFF
HUFF
IF MIKAN WRITES THAT ARTICLE, I KNOW THINGS WILL GET AWKWARD BETWEEN SHIRAGAMI AND ME.

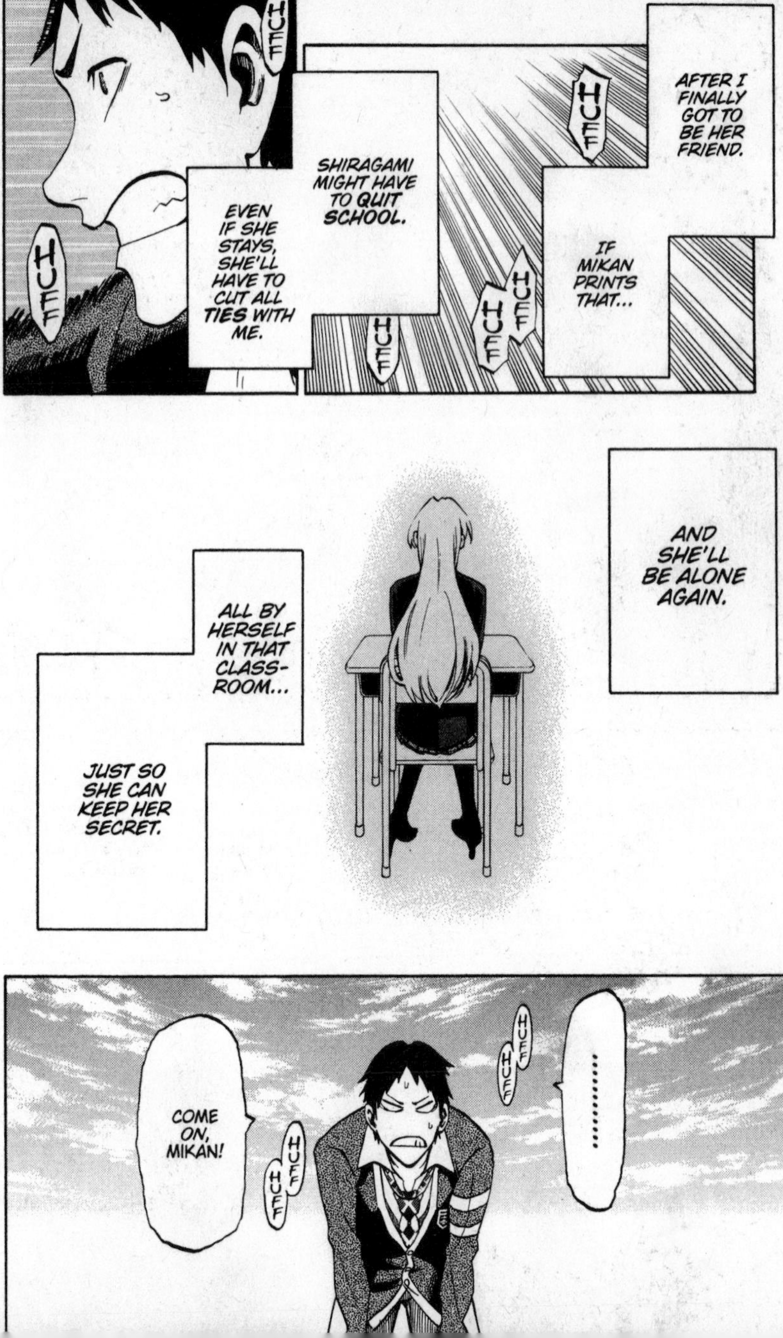
AFTER I FINALLY GOT TO BE HER FRIEND.
HUFF
IF MIKAN PRINTS THAT...
HUFF
HUFF
HUFF
SHIRAGAMI MIGHT HAVE TO QUIT SCHOOL.
EVEN IF SHE STAYS, SHE'LL HAVE TO CUT ALL TIES WITH ME.
HUFF
HUFF
AND SHE'LL BE ALONE AGAIN.
ALL BY HERSELF IN THAT CLASS-ROOM...
JUST SO SHE CAN KEEP HER SECRET.
....
HUFF
HUFF
COME ON, MIKAN!
HUFF
HUFF

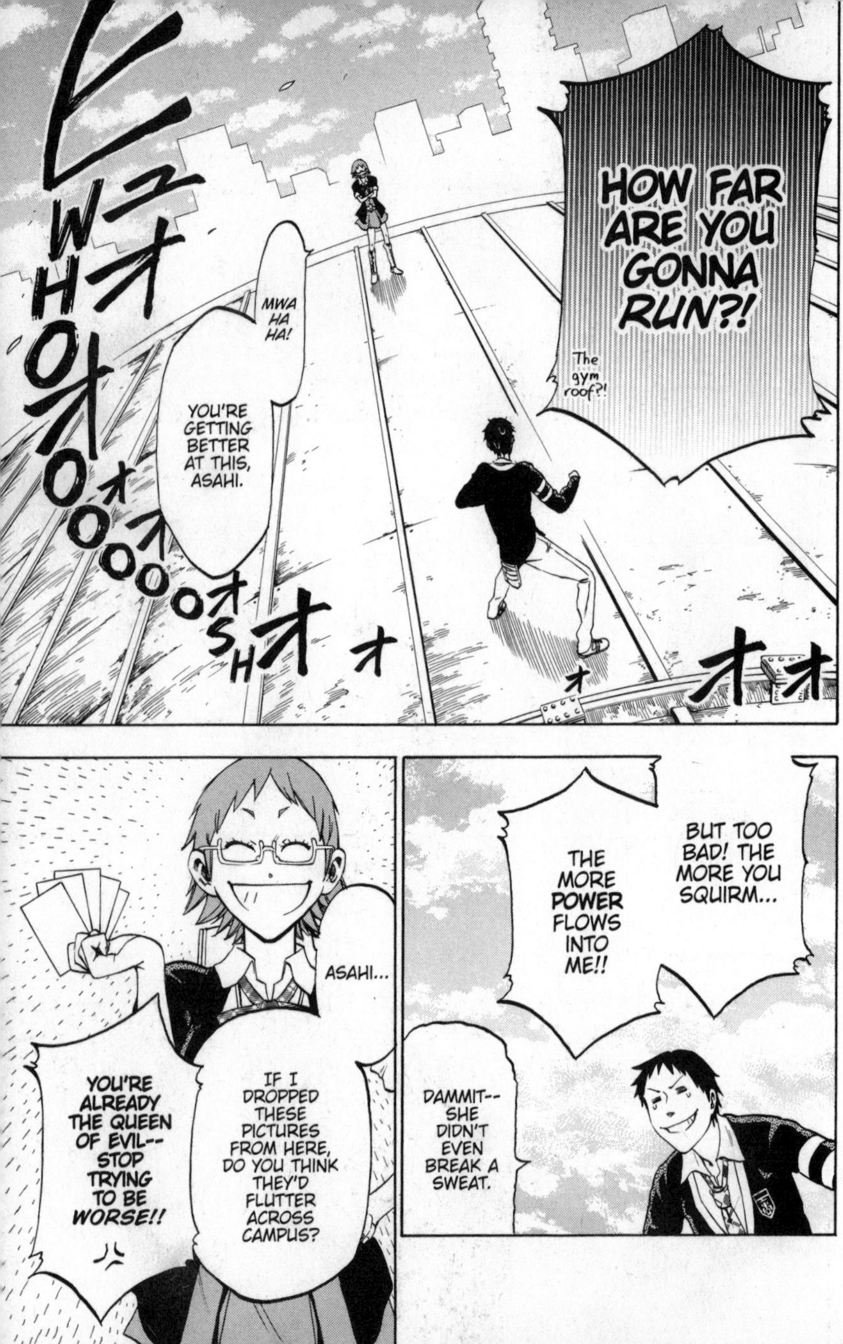
HOW FAR ARE YOU GONNA RUN?!
The gym roof?!
MWA HA HA!
YOU'RE GETTING BETTER AT THIS, ASAHI.
WHOOOOOOSH
BUT TOO BAD! THE MORE YOU SQUIRM...
THE MORE POWER FLOWS INTO ME!!
DAMMIT-- SHE DIDN'T EVEN BREAK A SWEAT.
ASAHI...
IF I DROPPED THESE PICTURES FROM HERE, DO YOU THINK THEY'D FLUTTER ACROSS CAMPUS?
YOU'RE ALREADY THE QUEEN OF EVIL-- STOP TRYING TO BE WORSE!!

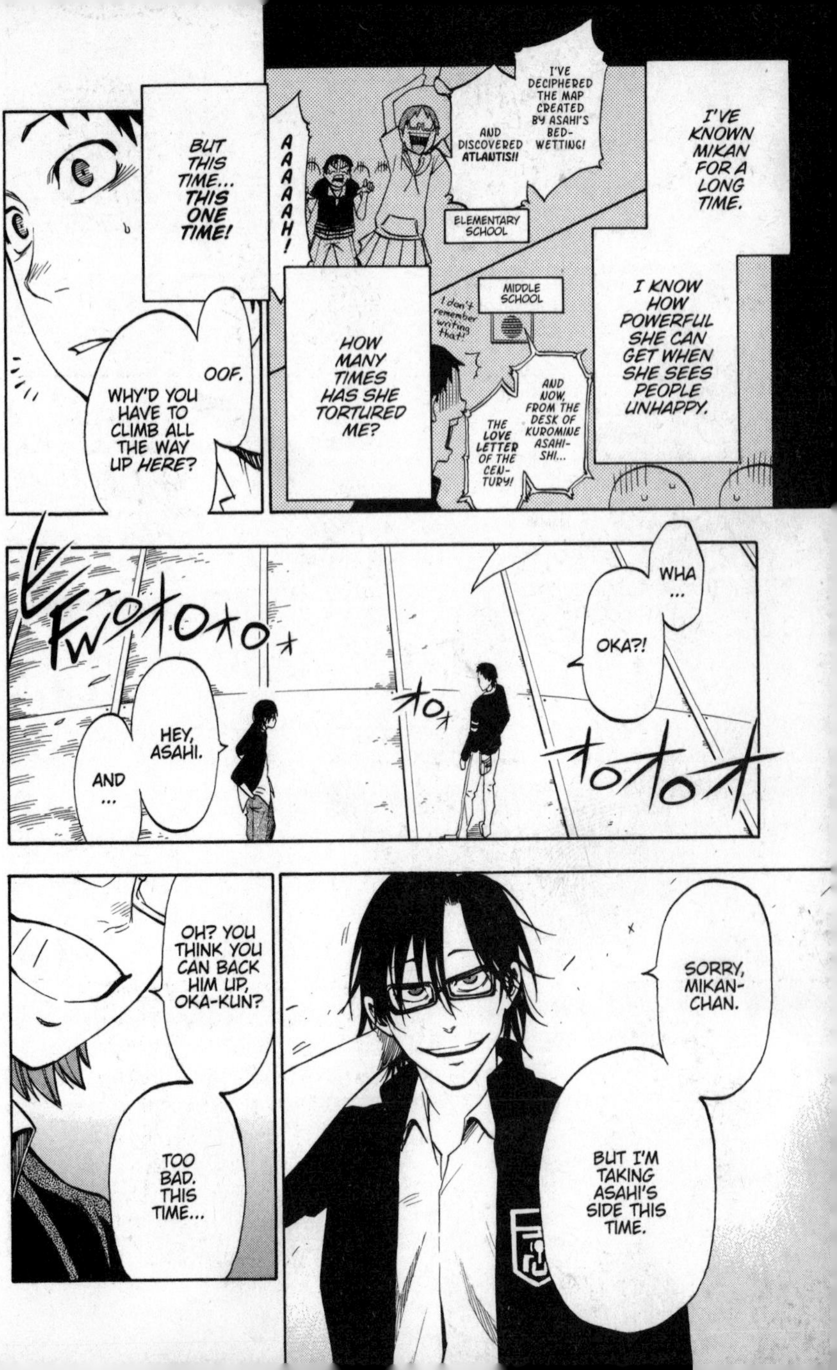
I'VE KNOWN MIKAN FOR A LONG TIME.
I'VE DECIPHERED THE MAP CREATED BY ASAHI'S BED-WETTING!
AND DISCOVERED ATLANTIS!!
ELEMENTARY SCHOOL
AAAAAH!
I KNOW HOW POWERFUL SHE CAN GET WHEN SHE SEES PEOPLE UNHAPPY.
MIDDLE SCHOOL
AND NOW, FROM THE DESK OF KUROMINE ASAHI-SHI...
THE LOVE LETTER OF THE CEN-TURY!
I don't remember writing that!
HOW MANY TIMES HAS SHE TORTURED ME?
BUT THIS TIME... THIS ONE TIME!
OOF.
WHY'D YOU HAVE TO CLIMB ALL THE WAY UP HERE?
WHA...
OKA?!
HEY, ASAHI.
AND...
SORRY, MIKAN-CHAN.
BUT I'M TAKING ASAHI'S SIDE THIS TIME.
OH? YOU THINK YOU CAN BACK HIM UP, OKA-KUN?
TOO BAD. THIS TIME...

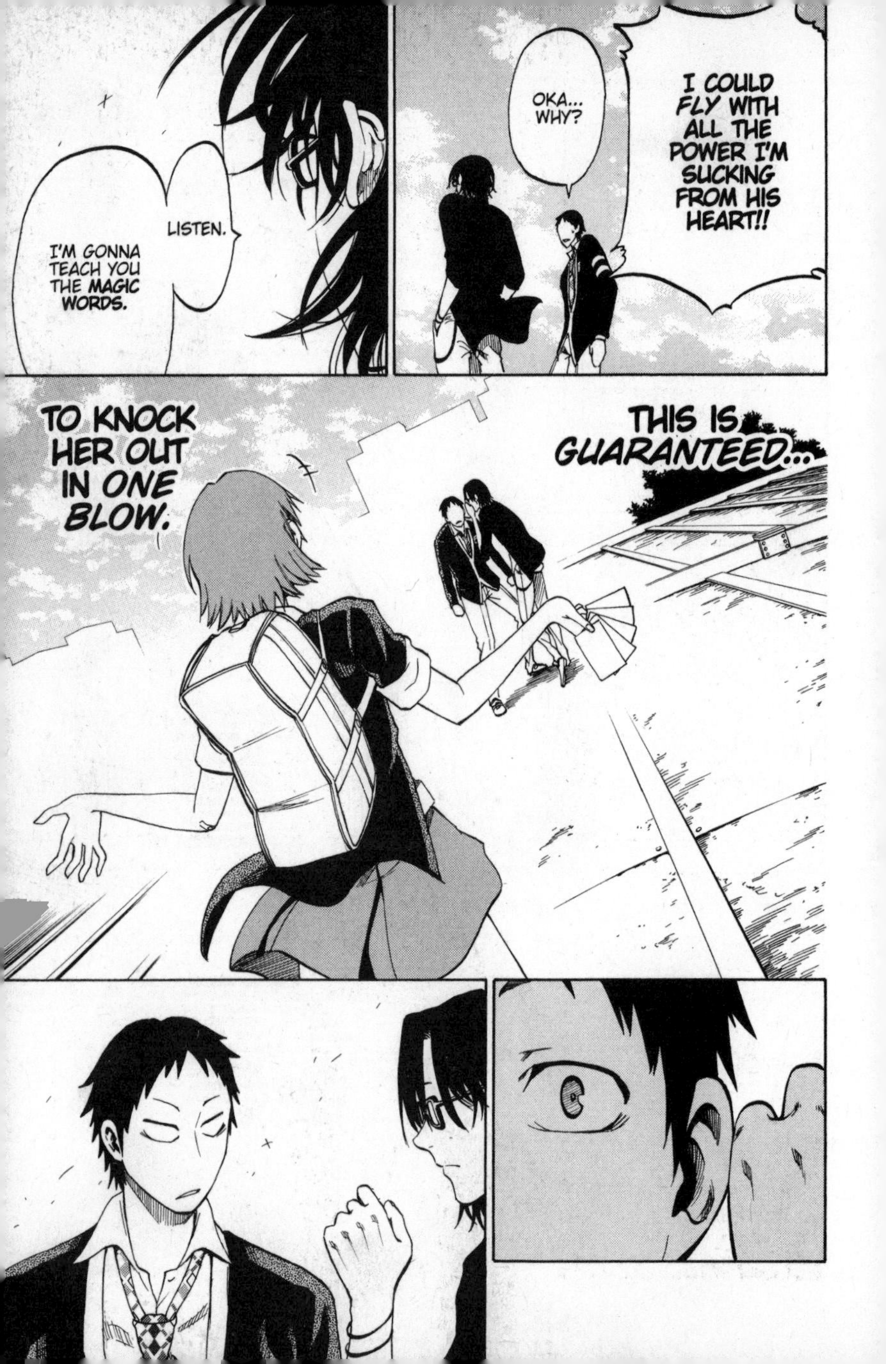
I COULD FLY WITH ALL THE POWER I'M SUCKING FROM HIS HEART!!
OKA... WHY?
LISTEN.
I'M GONNA TEACH YOU THE MAGIC WORDS.
THIS IS GUARANTEED...
TO KNOCK HER OUT IN ONE BLOW.

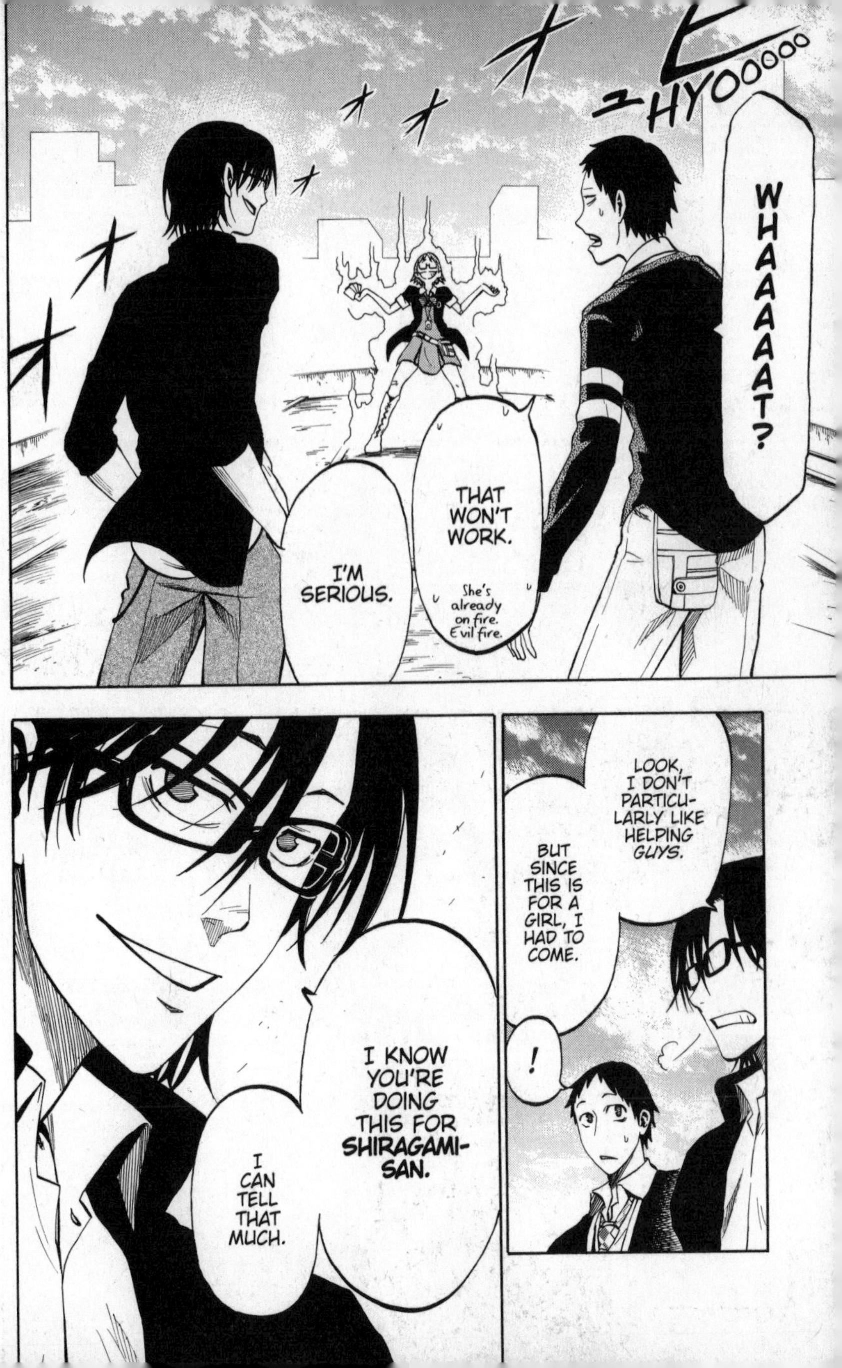
HYOOOOO
WHAAAAAT?
THAT WON'T WORK.
She's already on fire. Evil fire.
I'M SERIOUS.
LOOK, I DON'T PARTICULARLY LIKE HELPING GUYS.
BUT SINCE THIS IS FOR A GIRL, I HAD TO COME.
!
I KNOW YOU'RE DOING THIS FOR SHIRAGAMI-SAN.
I CAN TELL THAT MUCH.

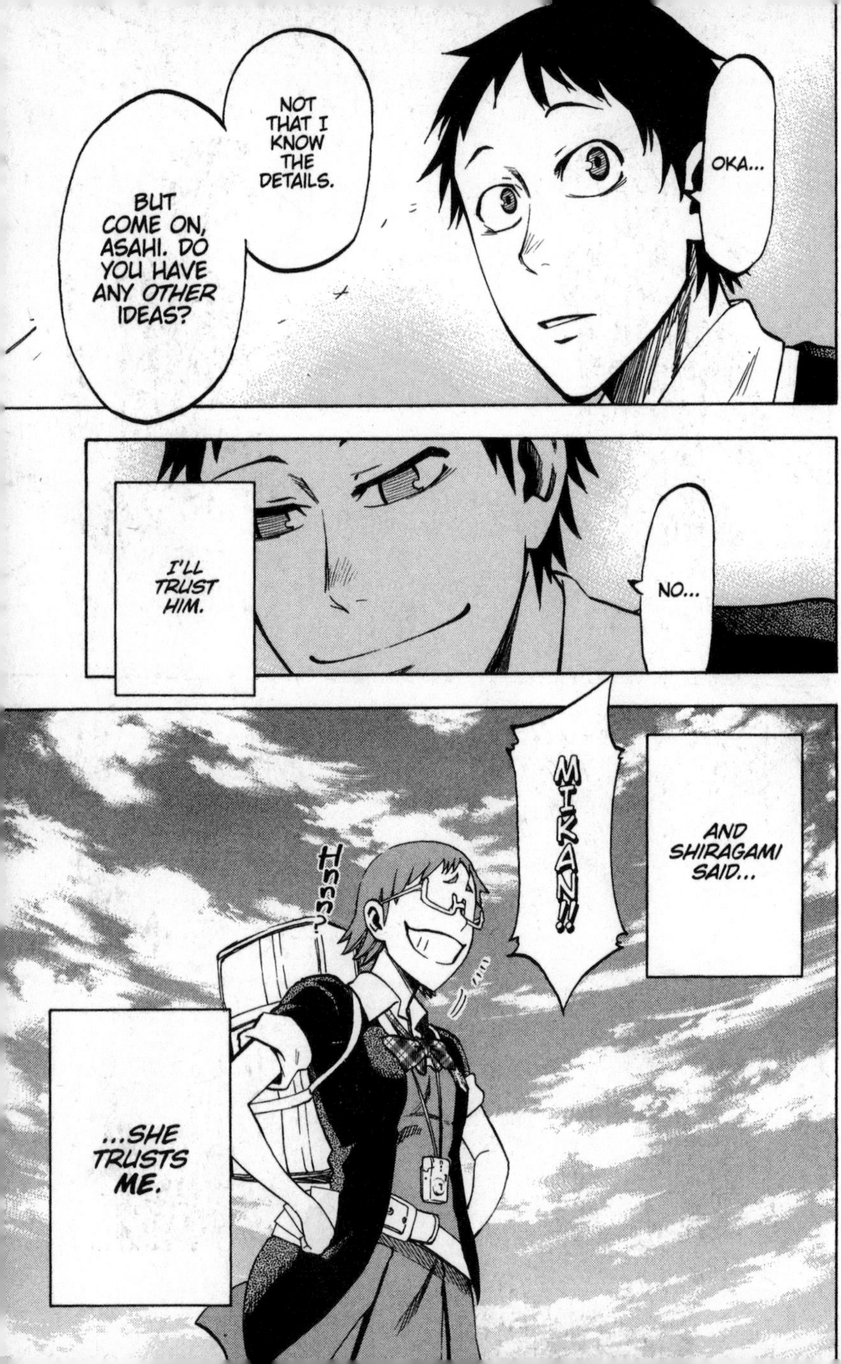
OKA...
NOT THAT I KNOW THE DETAILS.
BUT COME ON, ASAHI. DO YOU HAVE ANY OTHER IDEAS?
NO...
I'LL TRUST HIM.
AND SHIRAGAMI SAID...
MIRAN!!
Hnsss?
...SHE TRUSTS ME.

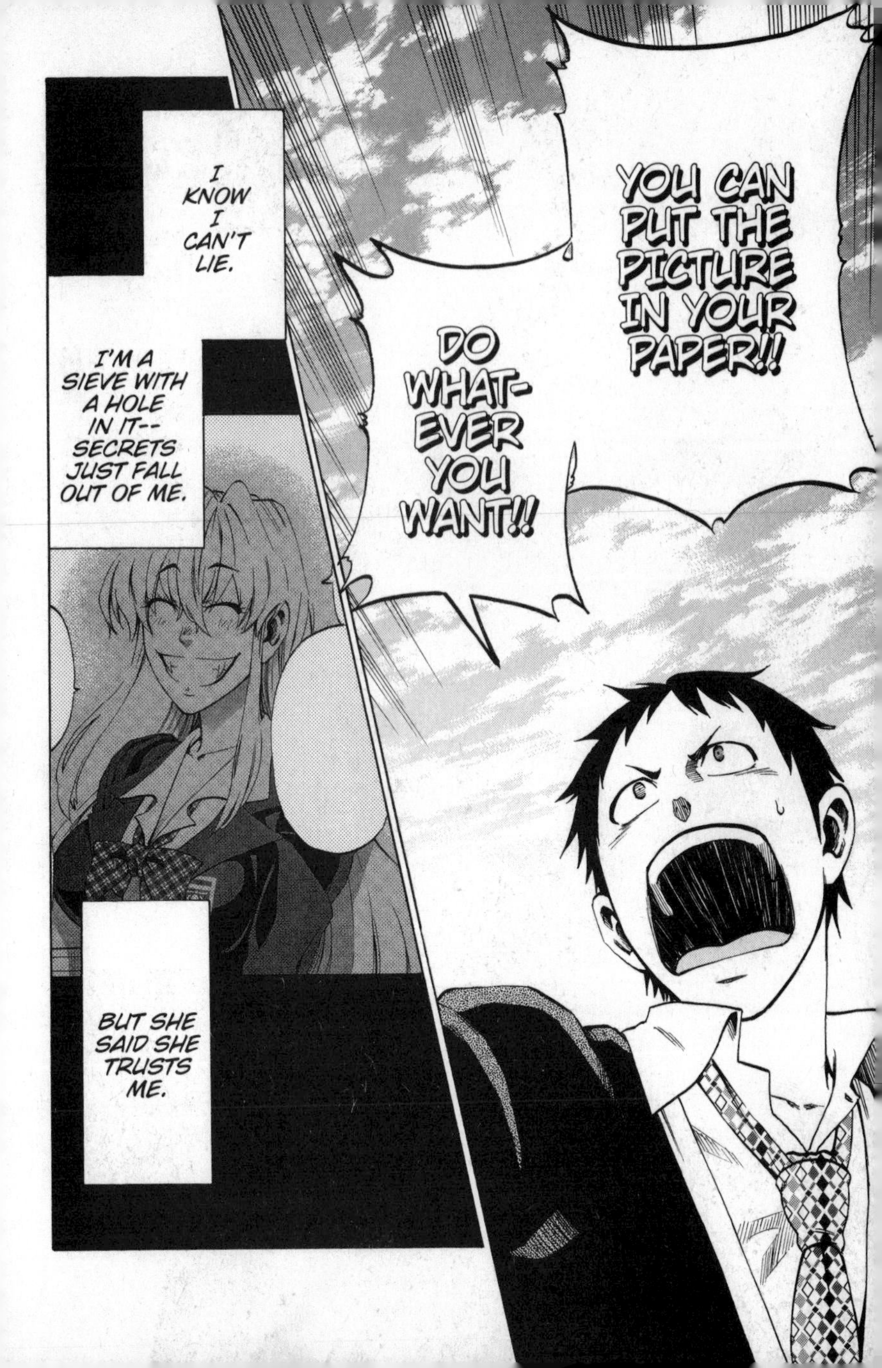
YOU CAN PUT THE PICTURE IN YOUR PAPER!!
DO WHAT-EVER YOU WANT!!
I KNOW I CAN'T LIE.
I'M A SIEVE WITH A HOLE IN IT-- SECRETS JUST FALL OUT OF ME.
BUT SHE SAID SHE TRUSTS ME.

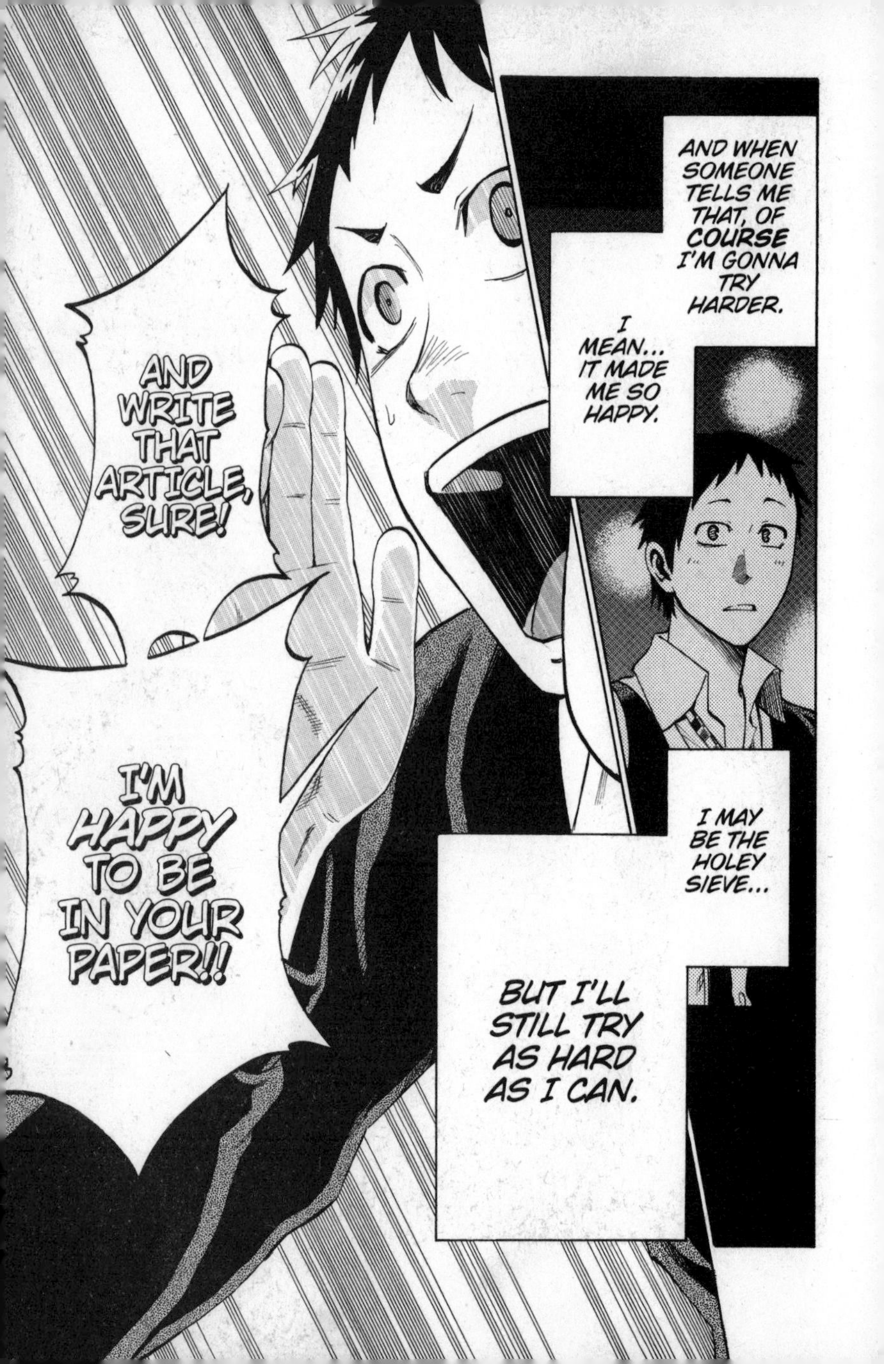
AND WHEN SOMEONE TELLS ME THAT, OF COURSE I'M GONNA TRY HARDER.
I MEAN... IT MADE ME SO HAPPY.
I MAY BE THE HOLEY SIEVE...
BUT I'LL STILL TRY AS HARD AS I CAN.
AND WRITE THAT ARTICLE, SURE!
I'M HAPPY TO BE IN YOUR PAPER!!

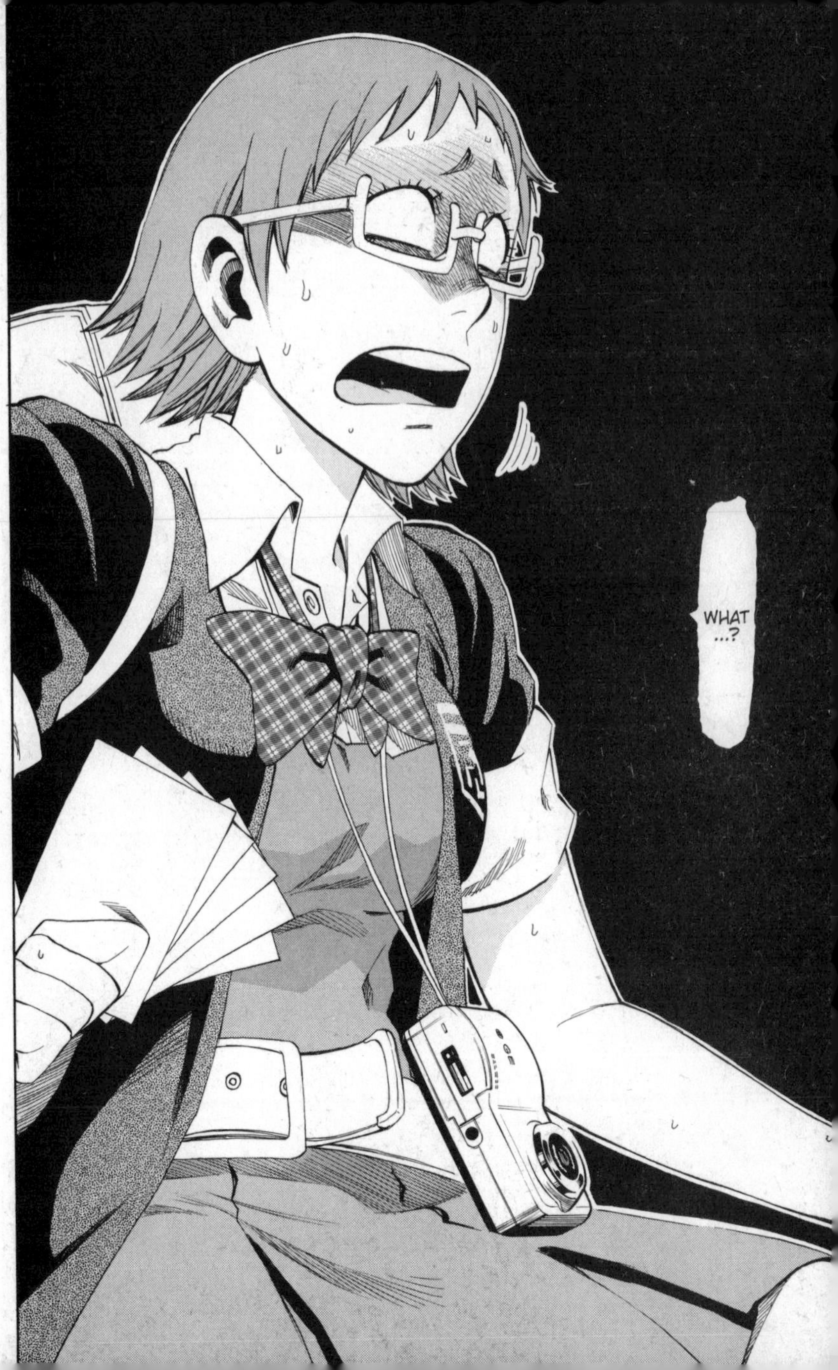
WHAT ...?

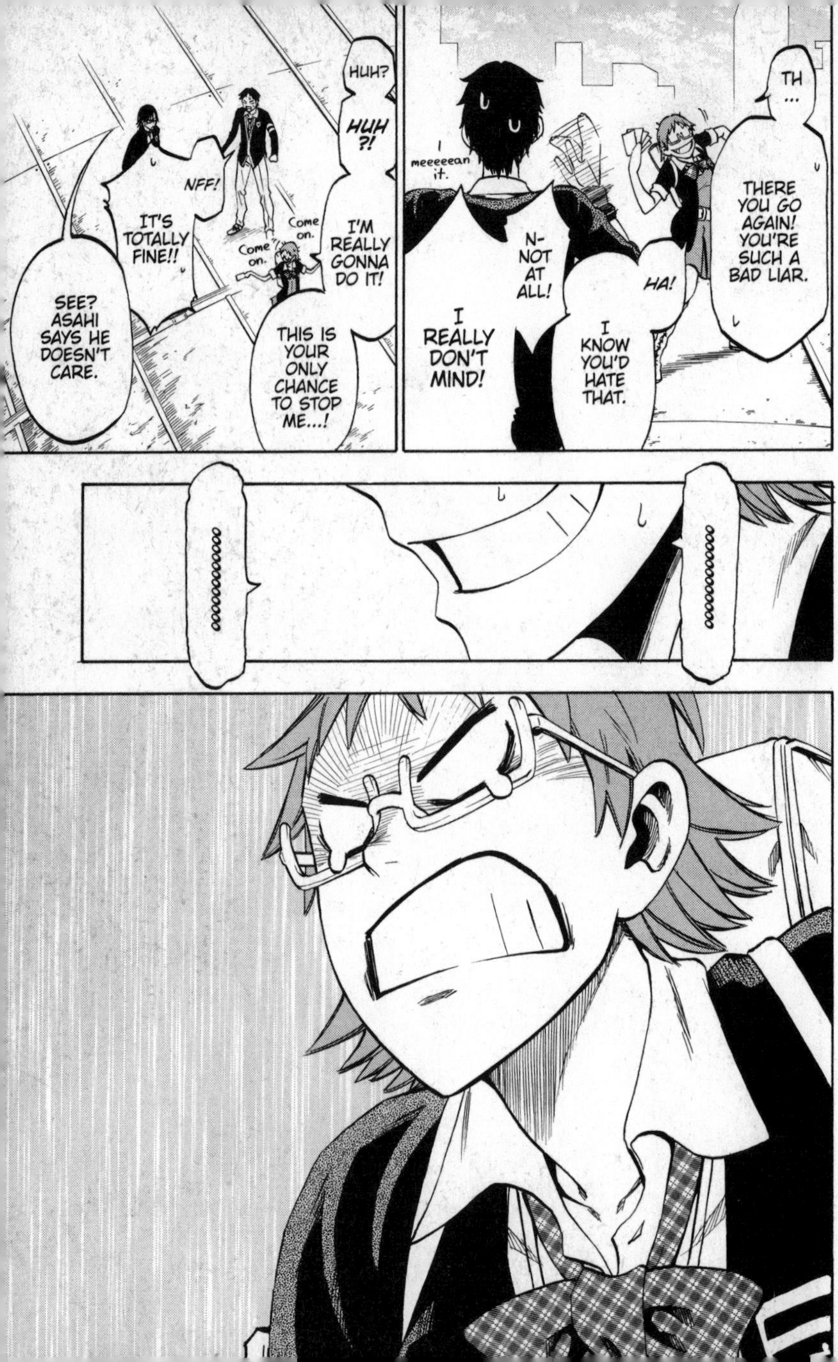
TH ...
THERE YOU GO AGAIN! YOU'RE SUCH A BAD LIAR.
HA!
I KNOW YOU'D HATE THAT.
N-NOT AT ALL!
I REALLY DON'T MIND!
I meeeeean it.
HUH?
HUH?!
I'M REALLY GONNA DO IT!
THIS IS YOUR ONLY CHANCE TO STOP ME...!
Come on.
Come on.
NFF!
IT'S TOTALLY FINE!!
SEE? ASAHI SAYS HE DOESN'T CARE.
ooooooooooo
ooooooooooo

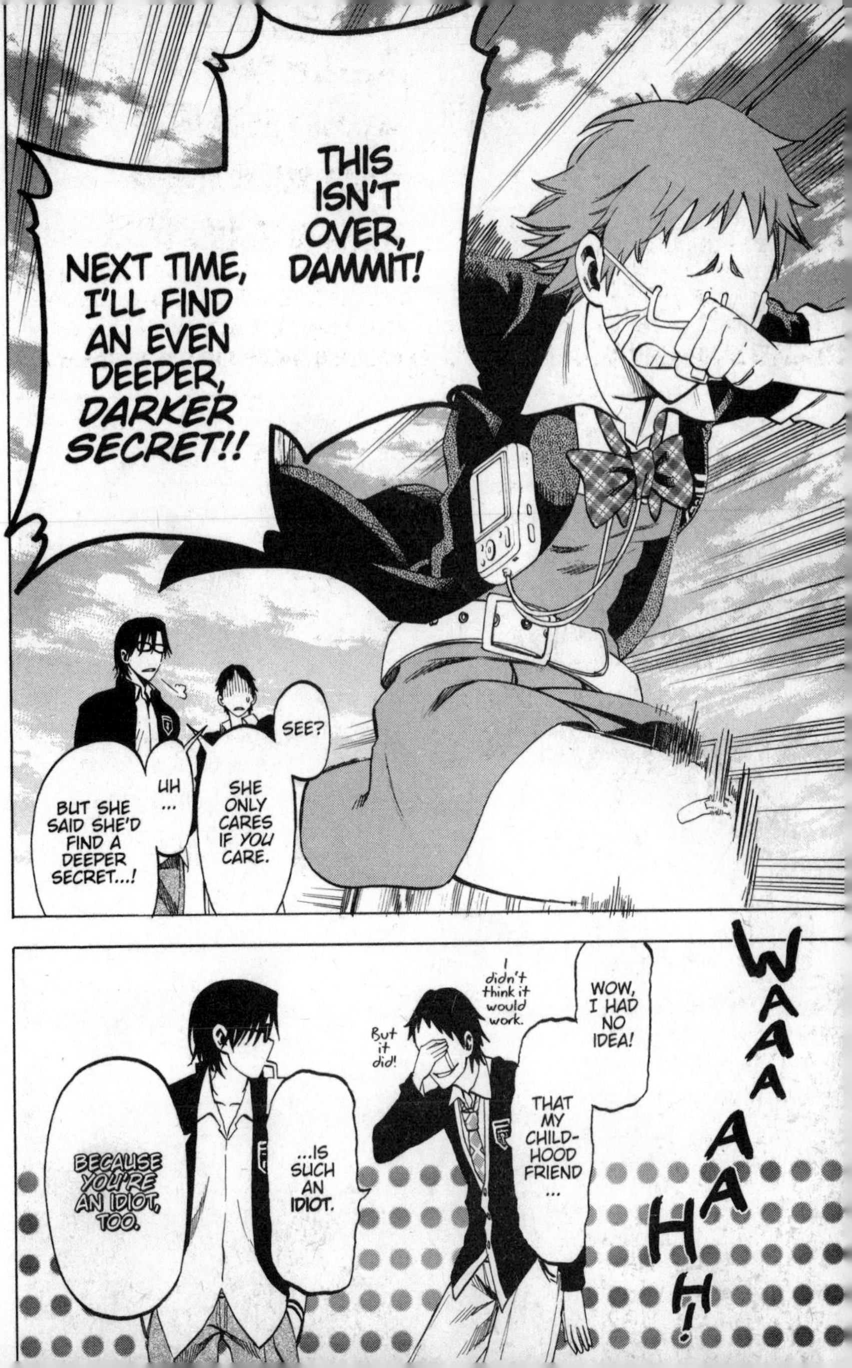
THIS ISN'T OVER, DAMMIT!
NEXT TIME, I'LL FIND AN EVEN DEEPER, DARKER SECRET!!
SEE?
SHE ONLY CARES IF YOU CARE.
UH ...
BUT SHE SAID SHE'D FIND A DEEPER SECRET...!
WAAAAAHH!
WOW, I HAD NO IDEA!
I didn't think it would work.
But it did!
THAT MY CHILD-HOOD FRIEND ...
...IS SUCH AN IDIOT.
BECAUSE YOU'RE AN IDIOT, TOO.

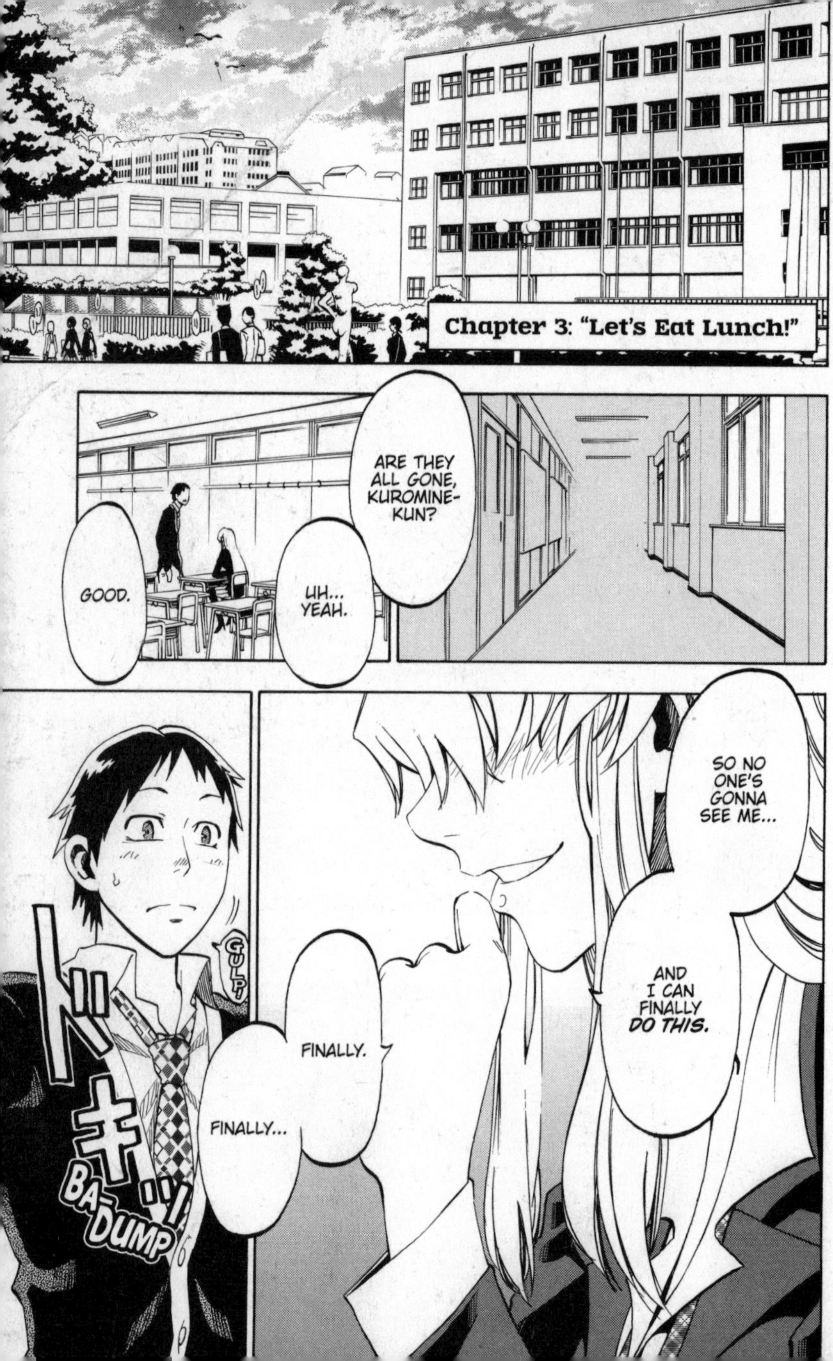
Chapter 3: "Let's Eat Lunch!"
ARE THEY ALL GONE, KUROMINE-KUN?
UH... YEAH.
GOOD.
SO NO ONE'S GONNA SEE ME...
AND I CAN FINALLY DO THIS.
FINALLY.
FINALLY...
GULP
BA-DUMP

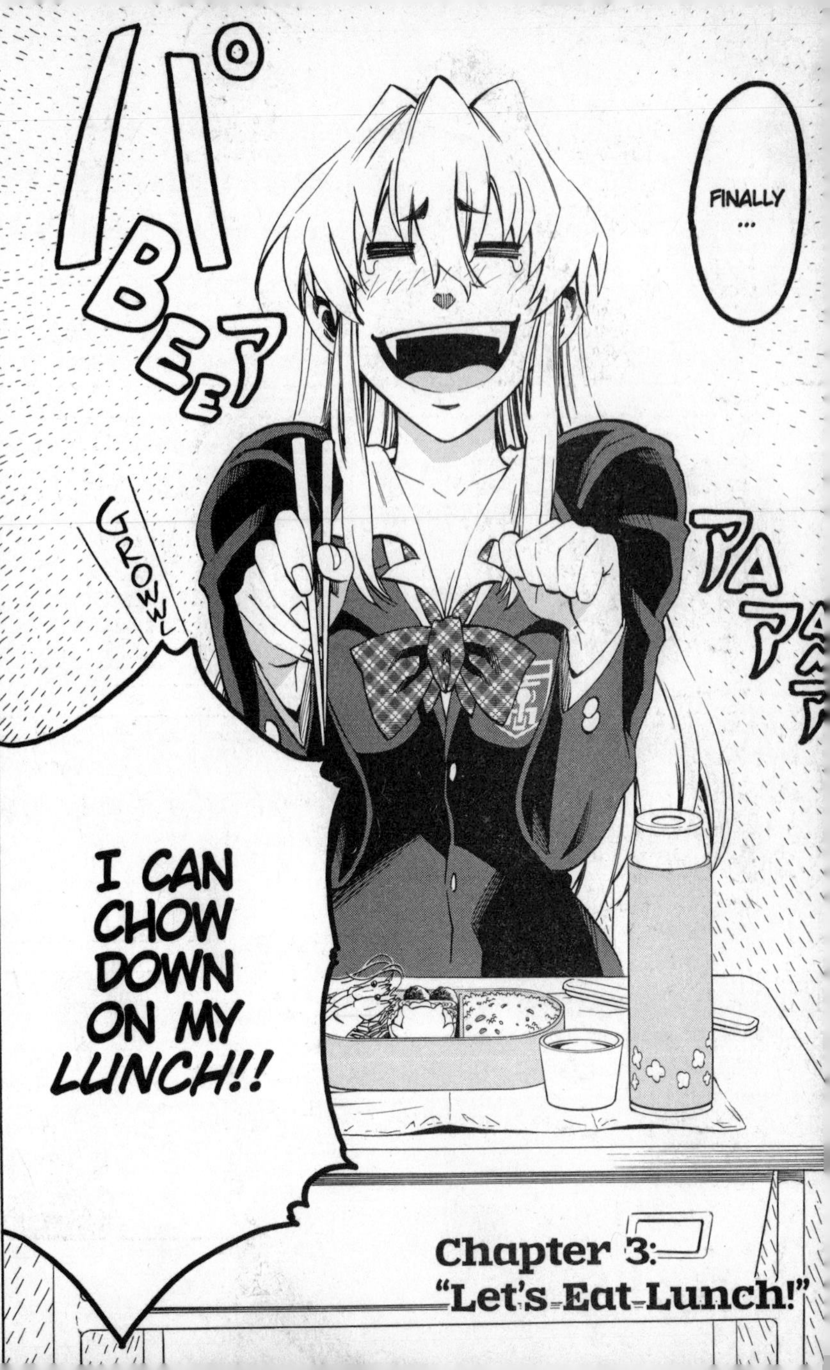
FINALLY ...
PAPAAT
BEEP!!
GROWWL
I CAN CHOW DOWN ON MY LUNCH!!

Chapter 3: "Let's Eat Lunch!"

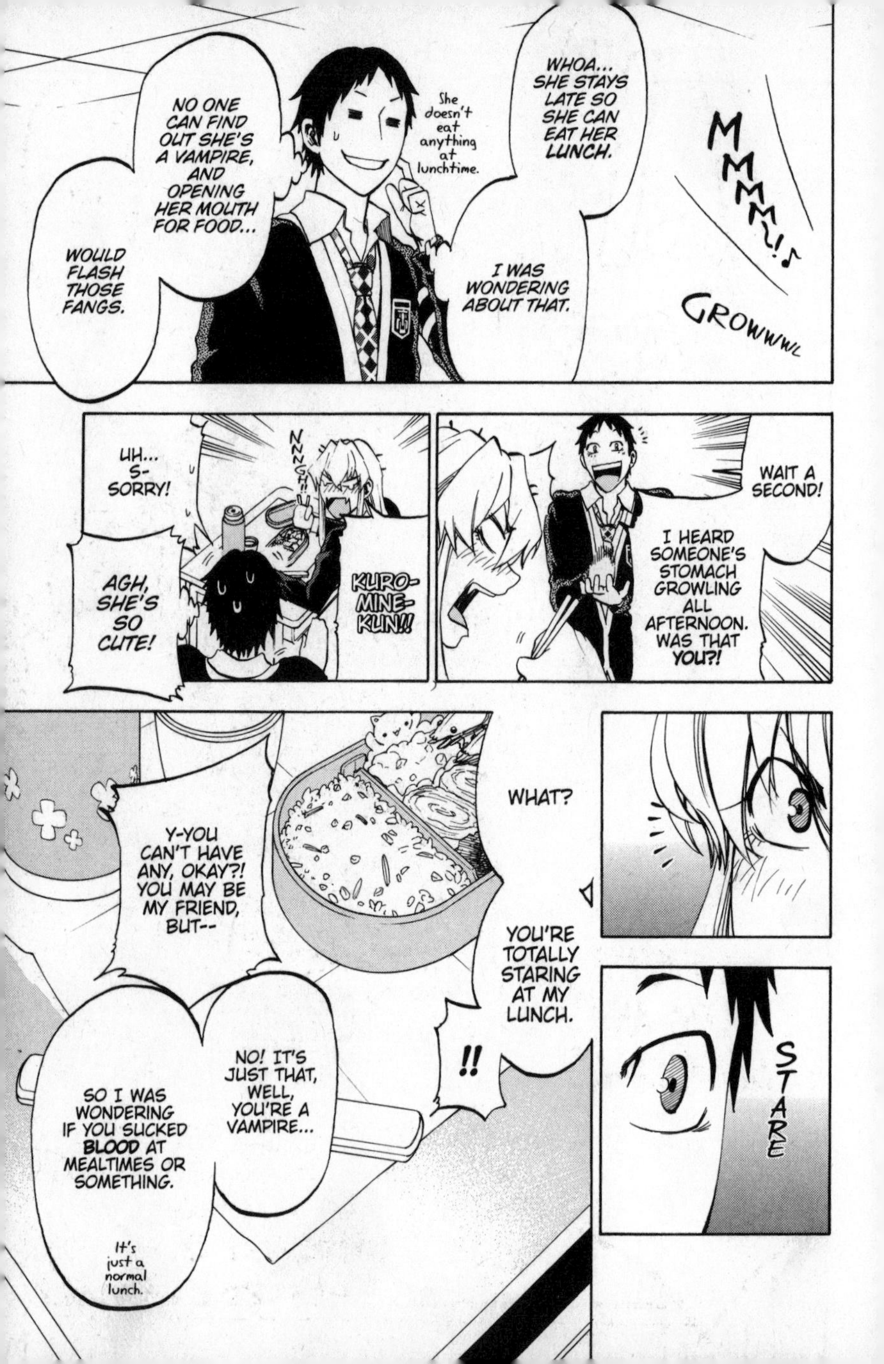
MMMM~!♪
GROWWWL
WHOA... SHE STAYS LATE SO SHE CAN EAT HER LUNCH.
I WAS WONDERING ABOUT THAT.
She doesn't eat anything at lunchtime.
NO ONE CAN FIND OUT SHE'S A VAMPIRE, AND OPENING HER MOUTH FOR FOOD...
WOULD FLASH THOSE FANGS.
WAIT A SECOND!
I HEARD SOMEONE'S STOMACH GROWLING ALL AFTERNOON. WAS THAT YOU?!
NNNGH!!
KURO-MINE-KUN!!
UH... S-SORRY!
AGH, SHE'S SO CUTE!
WHAT?
STARE
YOU'RE TOTALLY STARING AT MY LUNCH.
Y-YOU CAN'T HAVE ANY, OKAY?! YOU MAY BE MY FRIEND, BUT--
!!
NO! IT'S JUST THAT, WELL, YOU'RE A VAMPIRE...
SO I WAS WONDERING IF YOU SUCKED BLOOD AT MEALTIMES OR SOMETHING.
It's just a normal lunch.

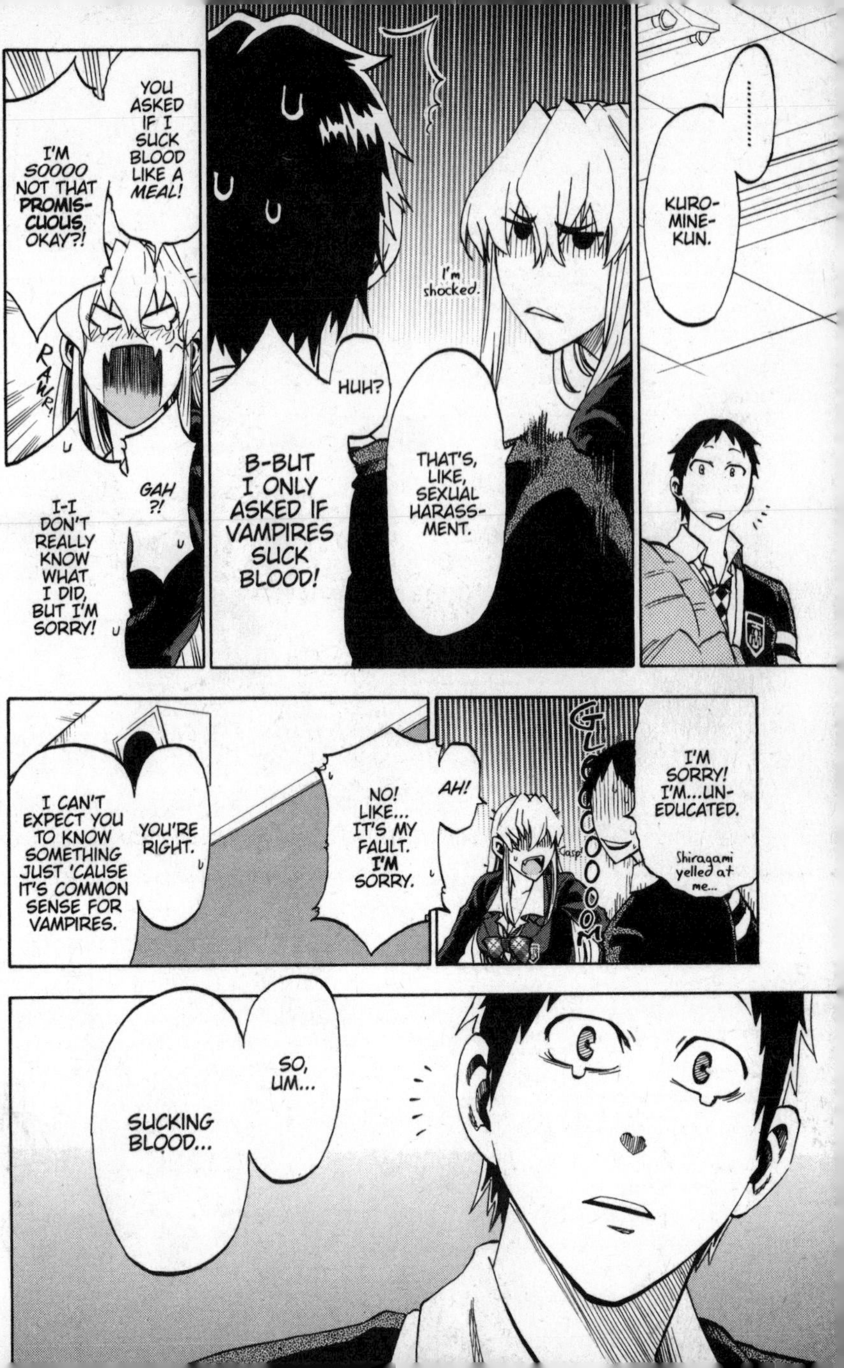
......
KURO-MINE-KUN.
I'm shocked.
THAT'S, LIKE, SEXUAL HARASSMENT.
HUH?
B-BUT I ONLY ASKED IF VAMPIRES SUCK BLOOD!
YOU ASKED IF I SUCK BLOOD LIKE A MEAL!
I'M SOOOO NOT THAT PROMISCUOUS, OKAY?!
RAWR!
GAH?!
I-I DON'T REALLY KNOW WHAT I DID, BUT I'M SORRY!
I'M SORRY! I'M...UNEDUCATED.
Shiragami yelled at me...
GLOOOOOOOM
Gasp!
AH!
NO! LIKE... IT'S MY FAULT. I'M SORRY.
YOU'RE RIGHT.
I CAN'T EXPECT YOU TO KNOW SOMETHING JUST 'CAUSE IT'S COMMON SENSE FOR VAMPIRES.
SO, UM...
SUCKING BLOOD...

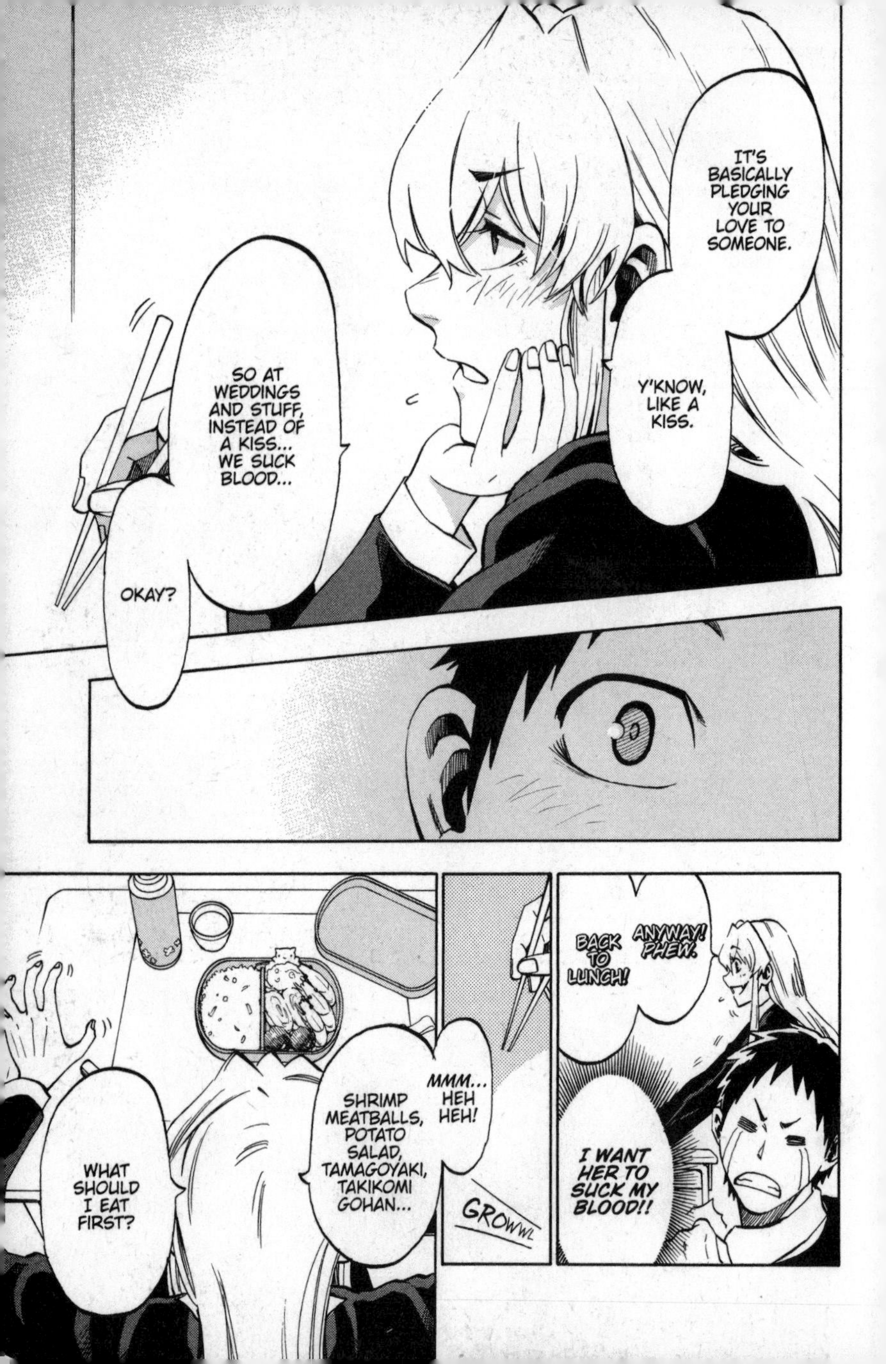
IT'S BASICALLY PLEDGING YOUR LOVE TO SOMEONE.
Y'KNOW, LIKE A KISS.
SO AT WEDDINGS AND STUFF, INSTEAD OF A KISS... WE SUCK BLOOD...
OKAY?
ANYWAY! PHEW.
BACK TO LUNCH!
I WANT HER TO SUCK MY BLOOD!!
GROWWL
MMM... HEH HEH!
SHRIMP MEATBALLS, POTATO SALAD, TAMAGOYAKI, TAKIKOMI GOHAN...
WHAT SHOULD I EAT FIRST?

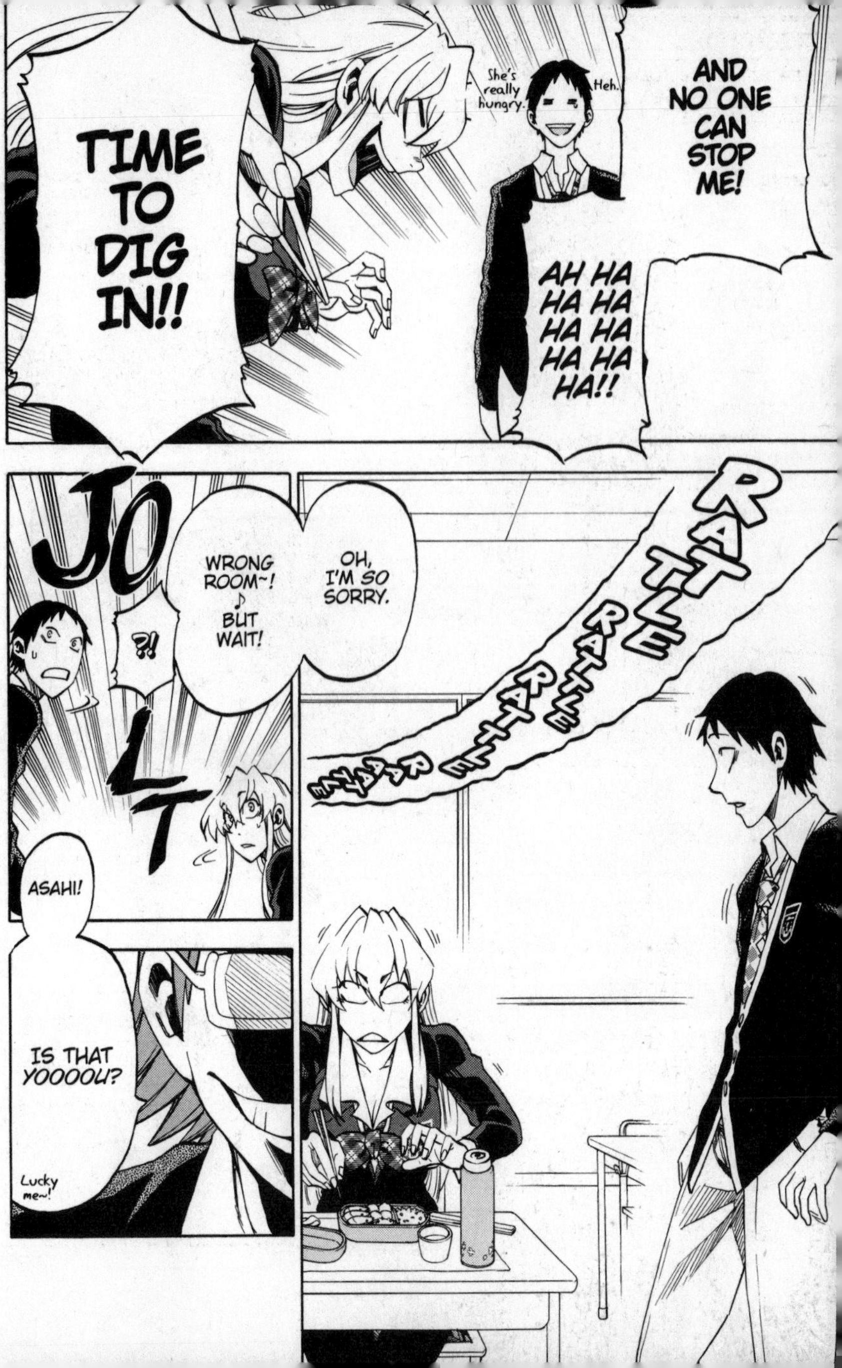
AND NO ONE CAN STOP ME!
AH HA HA HA HA HA HA HA HA!!
Heh.
She's really hungry.
TIME TO DIG IN!!
RATTLE RATTLE RATTLE RATTLE
JO
OH, I'M SO SORRY.
WRONG ROOM~! ♪ BUT WAIT!
?!
LT
ASAHI!
IS THAT YOOOOU?
Lucky me~!

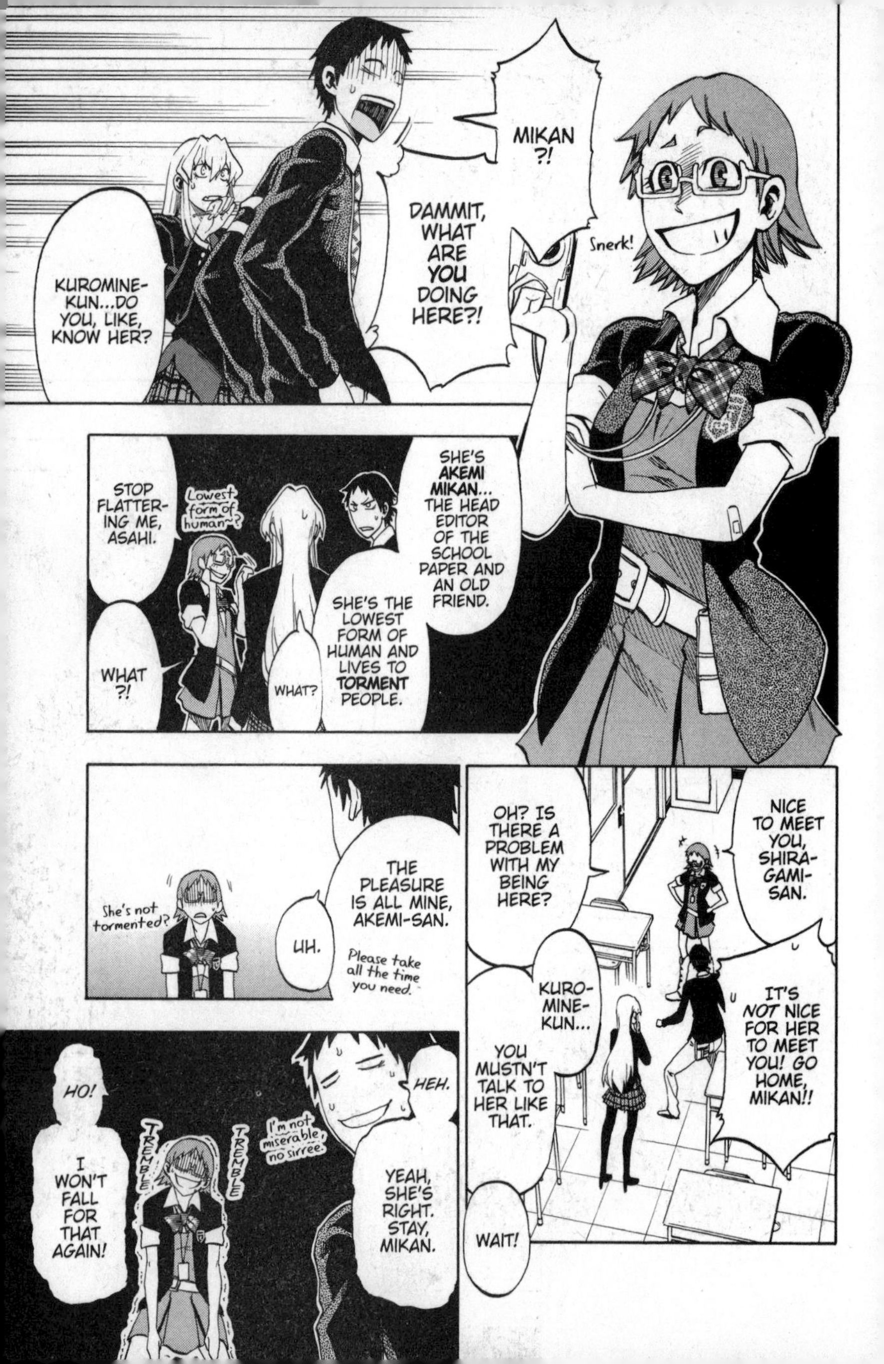
MIKAN ?!
Snerk!
DAMMIT, WHAT ARE YOU DOING HERE?!
KUROMINE-KUN...DO YOU, LIKE, KNOW HER?
SHE'S AKEMI MIKAN... THE HEAD EDITOR OF THE SCHOOL PAPER AND AN OLD FRIEND.
SHE'S THE LOWEST FORM OF HUMAN AND LIVES TO TORMENT PEOPLE.
WHAT?
STOP FLATTERING ME, ASAHI.
Lowest form of human~?
WHAT ?!
NICE TO MEET YOU, SHIRAGAMI-SAN.
OH? IS THERE A PROBLEM WITH MY BEING HERE?
IT'S NOT NICE FOR HER TO MEET YOU! GO HOME, MIKAN!!
KUROMINE-KUN...
YOU MUSTN'T TALK TO HER LIKE THAT.
WAIT!
THE PLEASURE IS ALL MINE, AKEMI-SAN.
UH.
Please take all the time you need.
She's not tormented?
HEH.
YEAH, SHE'S RIGHT. STAY, MIKAN.
I'm not miserable, no sirree.
TREMBLE
TREMBLE
HO!
I WON'T FALL FOR THAT AGAIN!

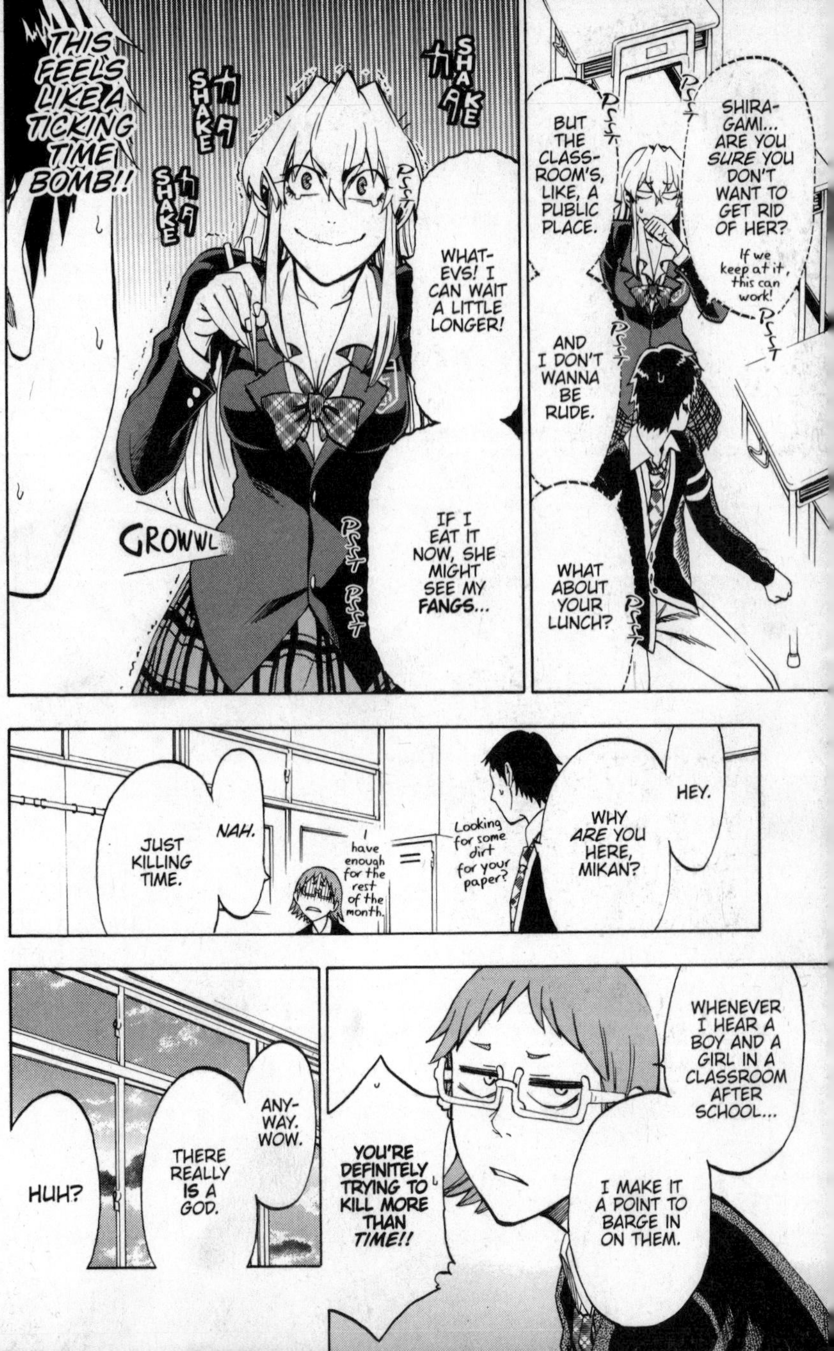
SHIRA-GAMI... ARE YOU SURE YOU DON'T WANT TO GET RID OF HER?
If we keep at it, this can work!
PSST
PSST
BUT THE CLASS-ROOM'S, LIKE, A PUBLIC PLACE.
PSST
AND I DON'T WANNA BE RUDE.
PSST
WHAT ABOUT YOUR LUNCH?
PSST
PSST
WHAT-EVS! I CAN WAIT A LITTLE LONGER!
IF I EAT IT NOW, SHE MIGHT SEE MY FANGS...
PSST PSST
GROWWL
SHAKE SHAKE
SHAKE SHAKE
SHAKE SHAKE
THIS FEELS LIKE A TICKING TIME BOMB!!
HEY.
WHY ARE YOU HERE, MIKAN?
Looking for some dirt for your paper?
I have enough for the rest of the month.
NAH.
JUST KILLING TIME.
WHENEVER I HEAR A BOY AND A GIRL IN A CLASSROOM AFTER SCHOOL...
I MAKE IT A POINT TO BARGE IN ON THEM.
YOU'RE DEFINITELY TRYING TO KILL MORE THAN TIME!!
ANY-WAY. WOW.
THERE REALLY IS A GOD.
HUH?

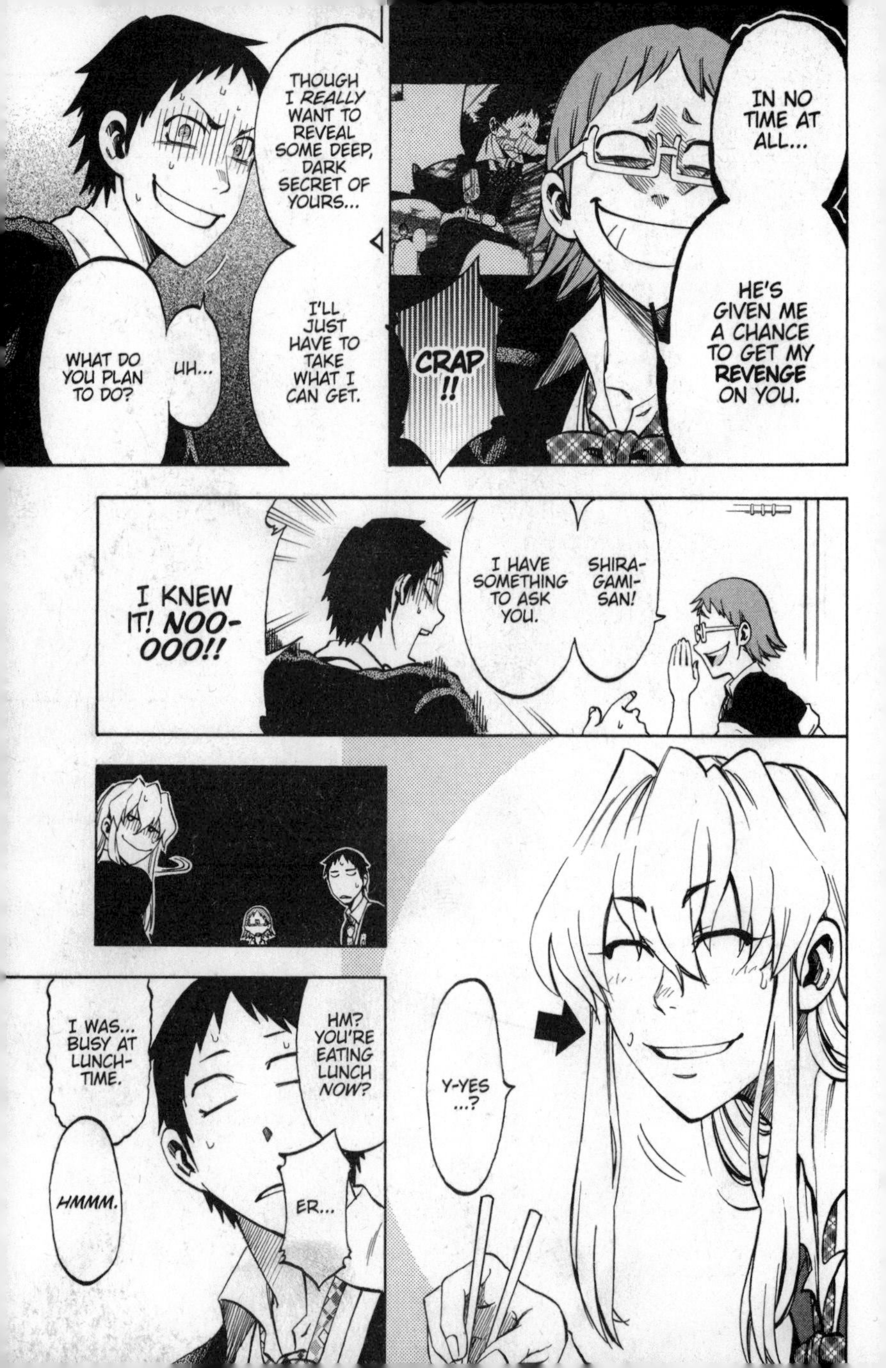
IN NO TIME AT ALL...
HE'S GIVEN ME A CHANCE TO GET MY REVENGE ON YOU.
CRAP!!
THOUGH I REALLY WANT TO REVEAL SOME DEEP, DARK SECRET OF YOURS...
I'LL JUST HAVE TO TAKE WHAT I CAN GET.
UH...
WHAT DO YOU PLAN TO DO?
SHIRA-GAMI-SAN!
I HAVE SOMETHING TO ASK YOU.
I KNEW IT! NOO-OOO!!
Y-YES ...?
HM? YOU'RE EATING LUNCH NOW?
I WAS... BUSY AT LUNCH-TIME.
ER...
HMMM.

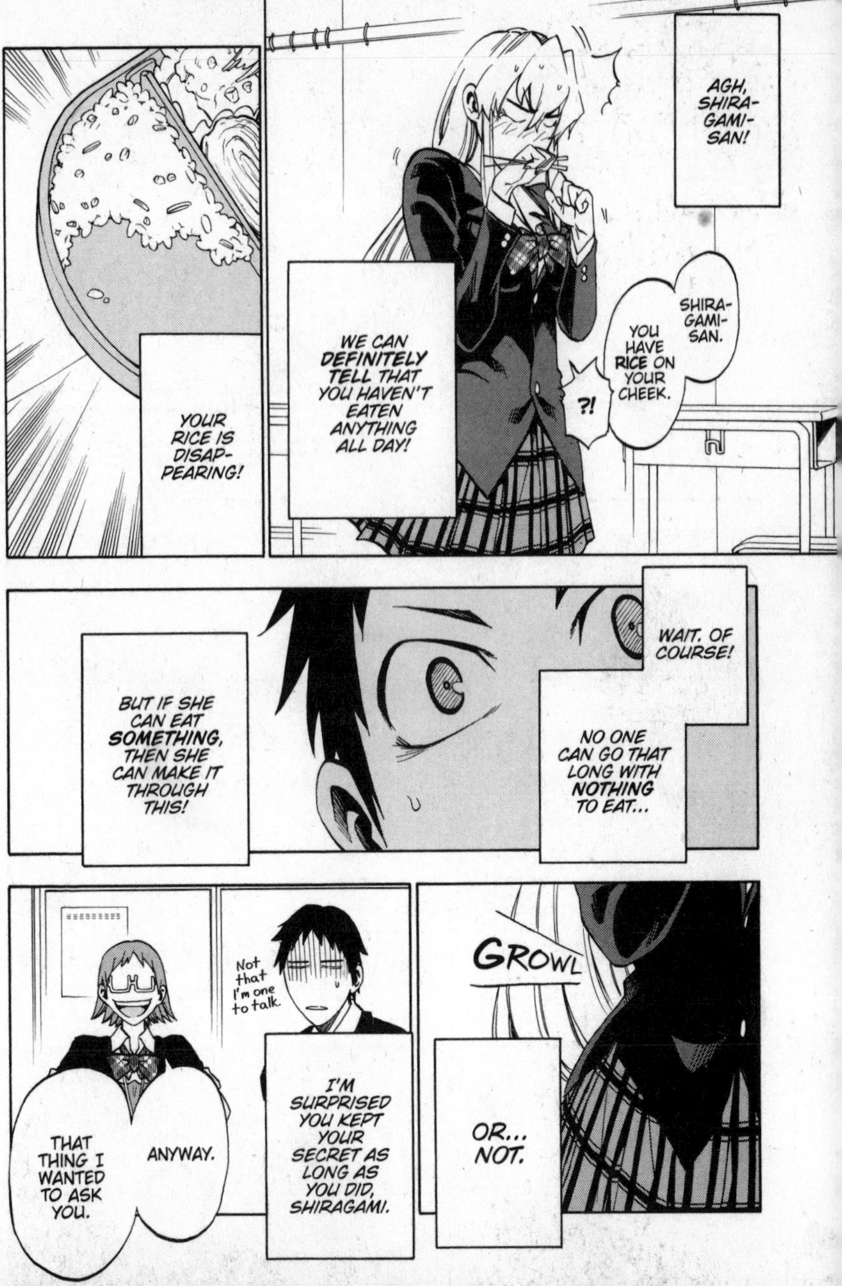
AGH, SHIRA-GAMI-SAN!
SHIRA-GAMI-SAN.
YOU HAVE RICE ON YOUR CHEEK.
?!
WE CAN DEFINITELY TELL THAT YOU HAVEN'T EATEN ANYTHING ALL DAY!
YOUR RICE IS DISAP-PEARING!
WAIT. OF COURSE!
NO ONE CAN GO THAT LONG WITH NOTHING TO EAT...
BUT IF SHE CAN EAT SOMETHING, THEN SHE CAN MAKE IT THROUGH THIS!
GROWL
OR... NOT.
I'M SURPRISED YOU KEPT YOUR SECRET AS LONG AS YOU DID, SHIRAGAMI.
Not that I'm one to talk.
ANYWAY.
THAT THING I WANTED TO ASK YOU.

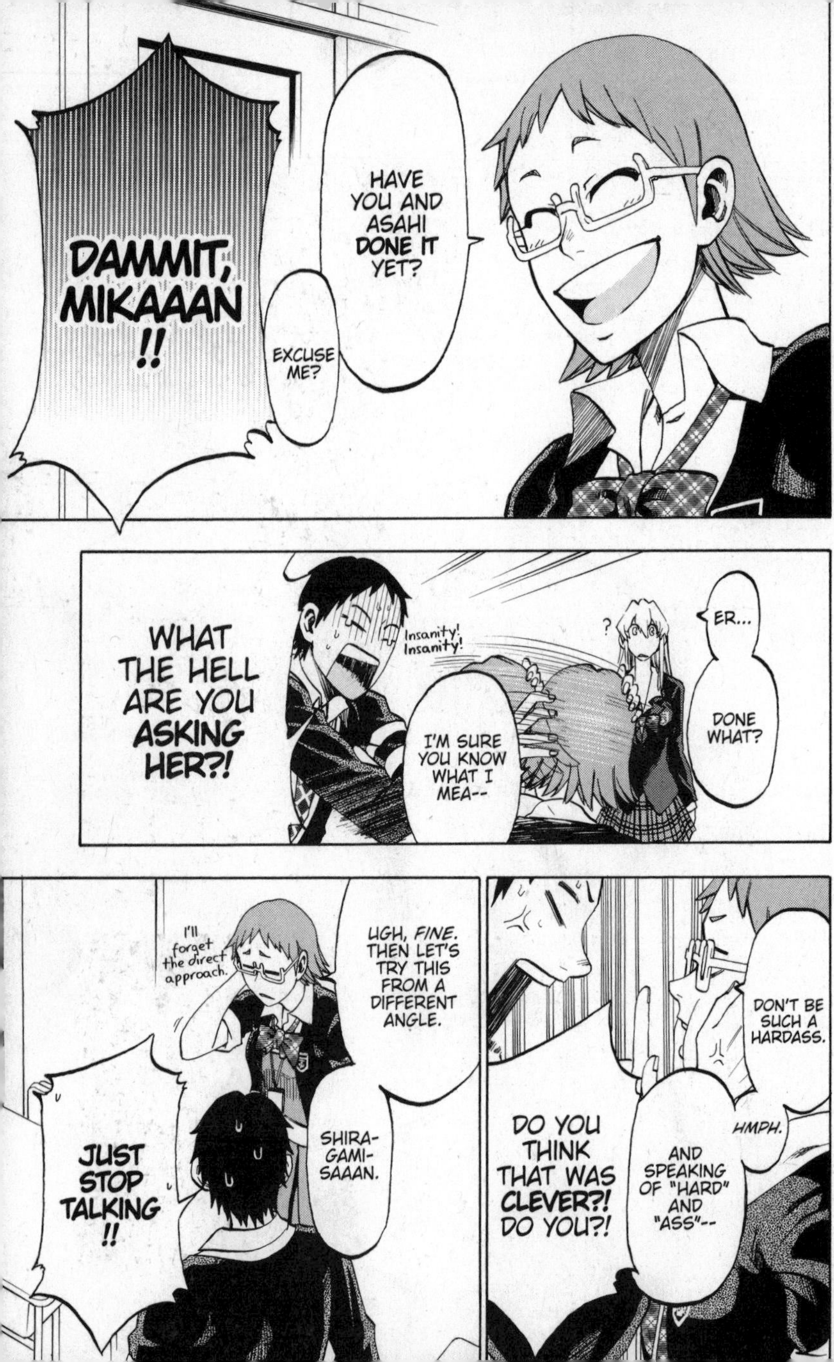
HAVE YOU AND ASAHI DONE IT YET?
EXCUSE ME?
DAMMIT, MIKAAAN !!
ER...
DONE WHAT?
I'M SURE YOU KNOW WHAT I MEA--
Insanity! Insanity!
WHAT THE HELL ARE YOU ASKING HER?!
DON'T BE SUCH A HARDASS.
HMPH.
AND SPEAKING OF "HARD" AND "ASS"--
DO YOU THINK THAT WAS CLEVER?! DO YOU?!
UGH, FINE. THEN LET'S TRY THIS FROM A DIFFERENT ANGLE.
I'll forget the direct approach.
SHIRA-GAMI-SAAAN.
JUST STOP TALKING !!

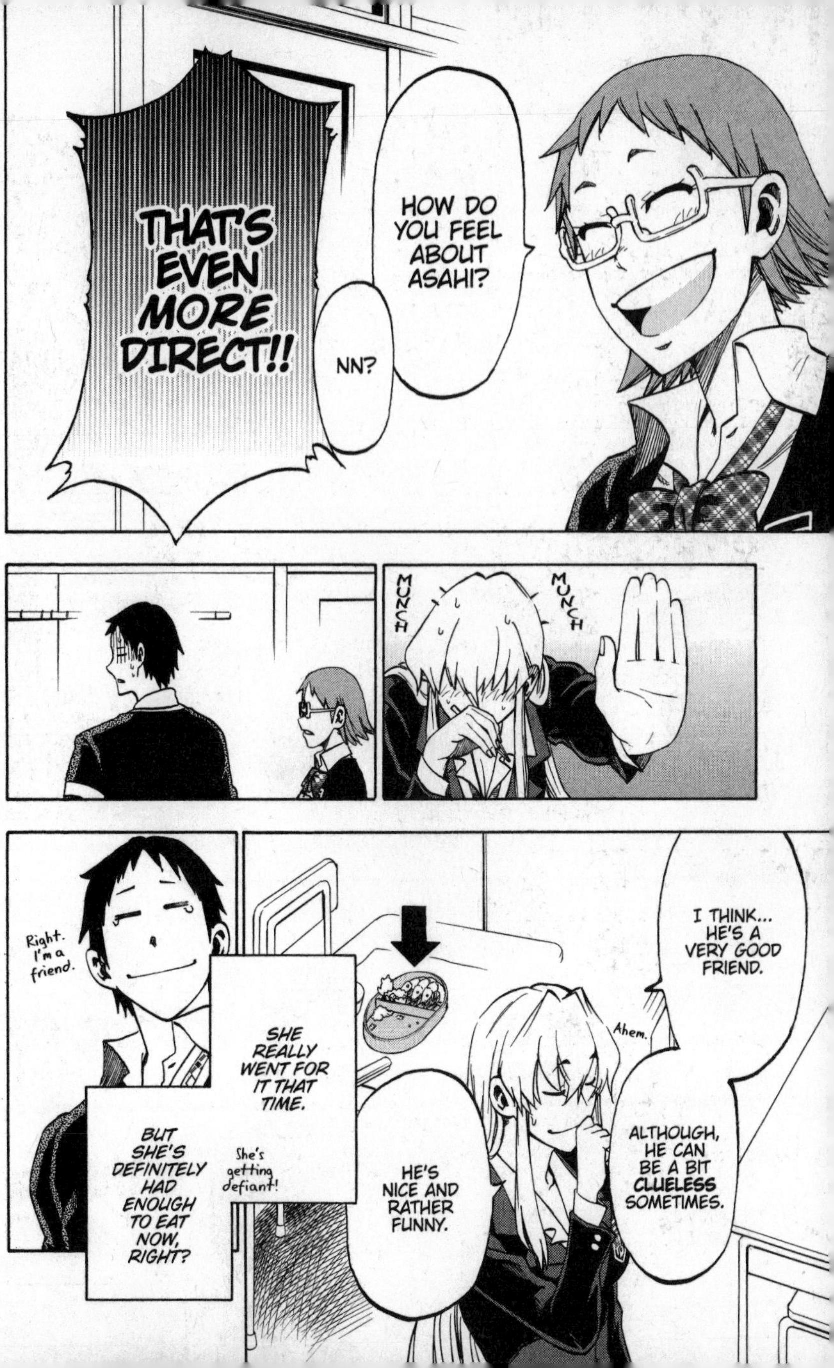
HOW DO YOU FEEL ABOUT ASAHI?
NN?
THAT'S EVEN MORE DIRECT!!
MUNCH
MUNCH
I THINK... HE'S A VERY GOOD FRIEND.
Ahem.
ALTHOUGH, HE CAN BE A BIT CLUELESS SOMETIMES.
HE'S NICE AND RATHER FUNNY.
SHE REALLY WENT FOR IT THAT TIME.
BUT SHE'S DEFINITELY HAD ENOUGH TO EAT NOW, RIGHT?
She's getting defiant!
Right. I'm a friend.

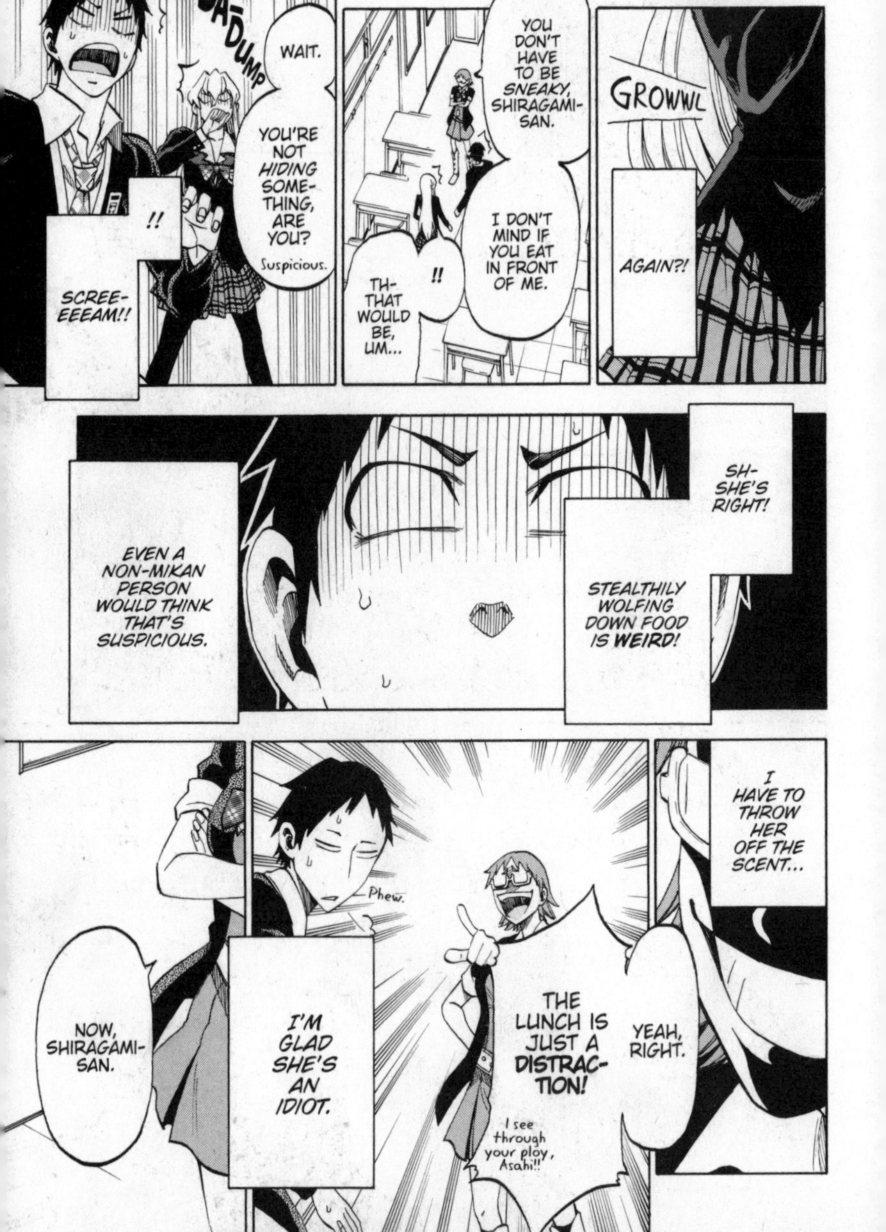
GROWWL
AGAIN?!
YOU DON'T HAVE TO BE SNEAKY, SHIRAGAMI-SAN.
I DON'T MIND IF YOU EAT IN FRONT OF ME.
!!
TH-THAT WOULD BE, UM...
WAIT.
BA-DUMP
YOU'RE NOT HIDING SOME-THING, ARE YOU?
Suspicious.
!!
SCREE-EEEAM!!
SH-SHE'S RIGHT!
STEALTHILY WOLFING DOWN FOOD IS WEIRD!
EVEN A NON-MIKAN PERSON WOULD THINK THAT'S SUSPICIOUS.
I HAVE TO THROW HER OFF THE SCENT...
YEAH, RIGHT.
THE LUNCH IS JUST A DISTRACTION!
I see through your ploy, Asahi!!
Phew.
I'M GLAD SHE'S AN IDIOT.
NOW, SHIRAGAMI-SAN.

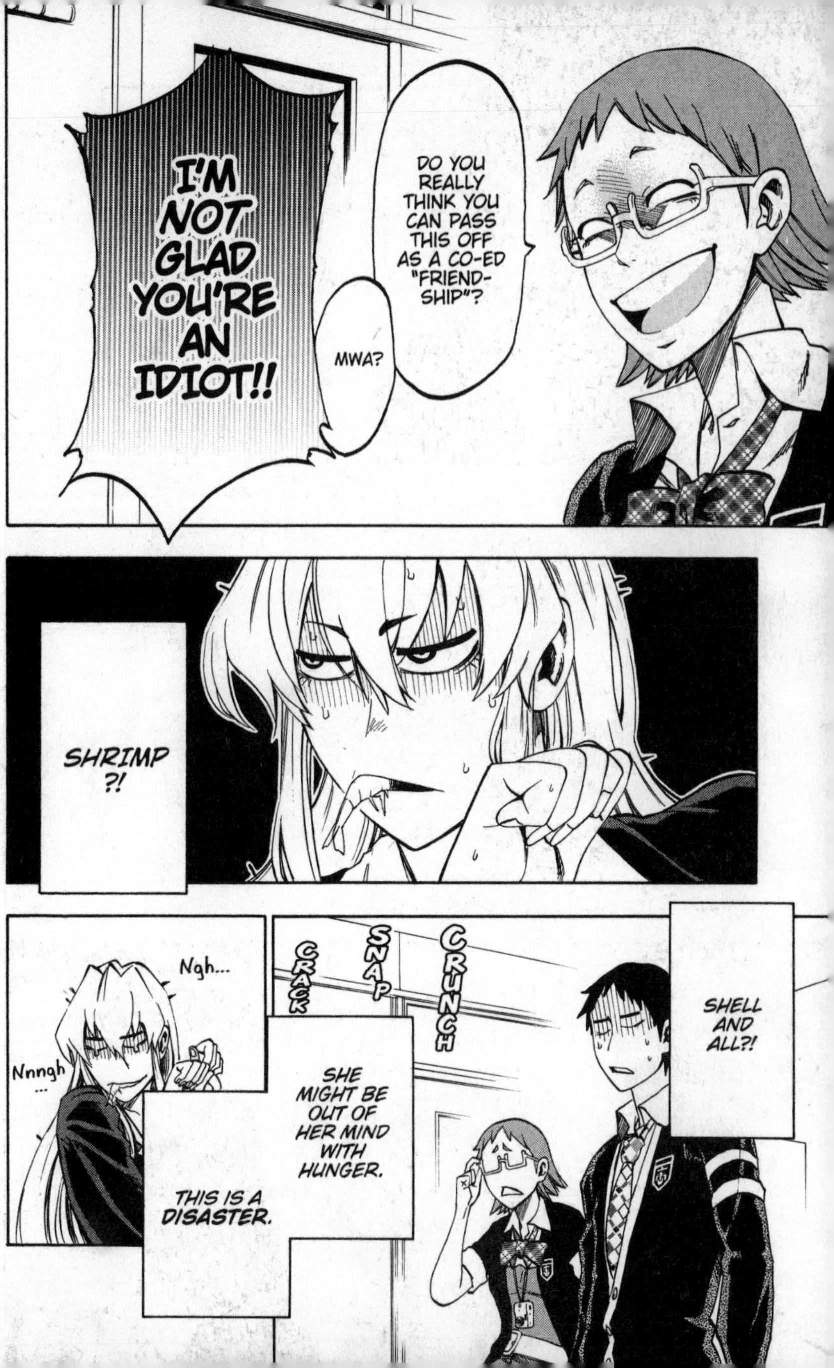
DO YOU REALLY THINK YOU CAN PASS THIS OFF AS A CO-ED "FRIEND-SHIP"?
MWA?
I'M NOT GLAD YOU'RE AN IDIOT!!
SHRIMP ?!
SHELL AND ALL?!
CRUNCH
SNAP
CRACK
SHE MIGHT BE OUT OF HER MIND WITH HUNGER.
THIS IS A DISASTER.
Ngh...
Nnngh ...

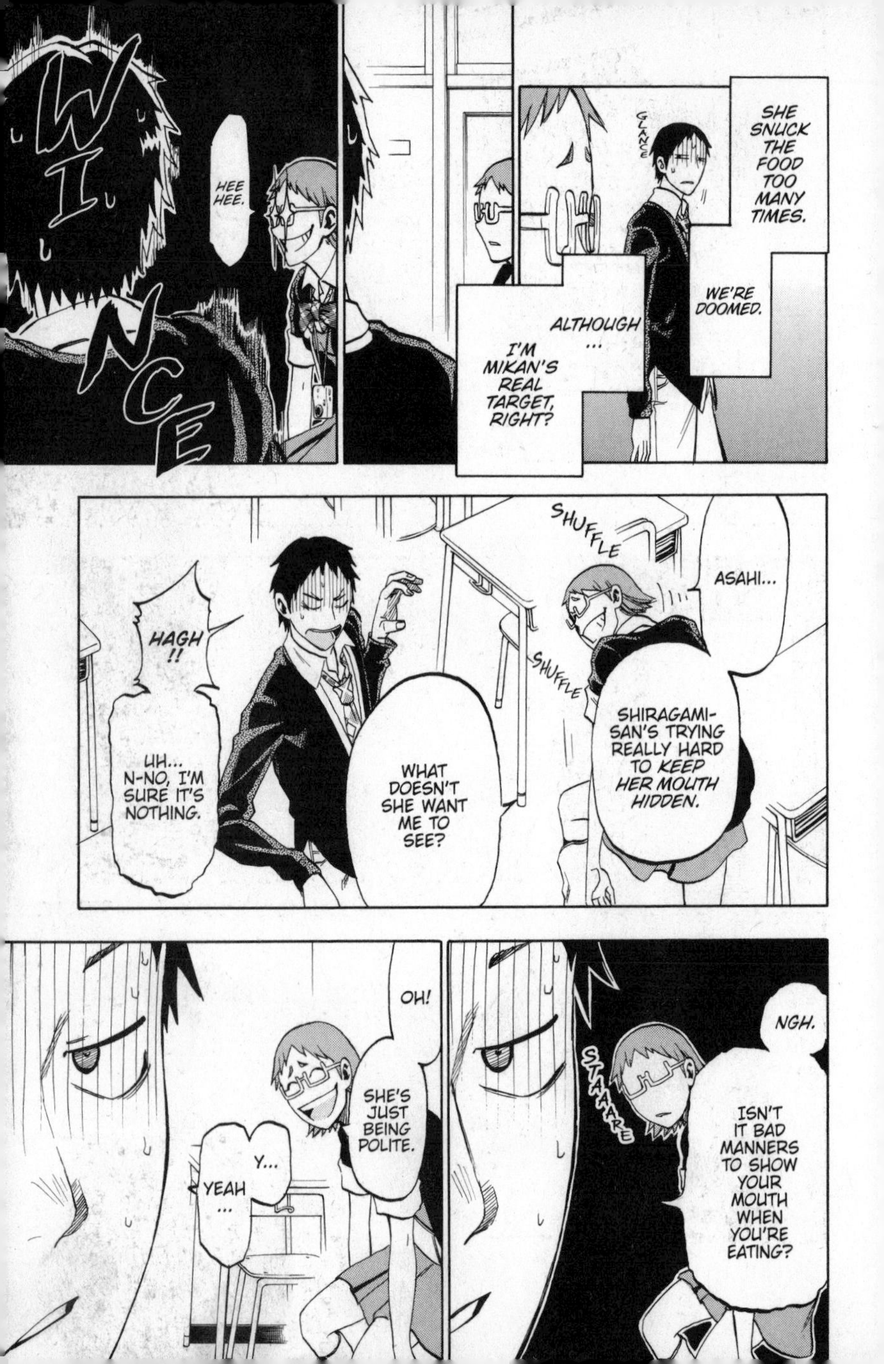
SHE SNUCK THE FOOD TOO MANY TIMES.
GLANCE
WE'RE DOOMED.
ALTHOUGH...
I'M MIKAN'S REAL TARGET, RIGHT?
HEE HEE.
WINCE
ASAHI...
SHUFFLE
SHUFFLE
SHIRAGAMI-SAN'S TRYING REALLY HARD TO KEEP HER MOUTH HIDDEN.
WHAT DOESN'T SHE WANT ME TO SEE?
HAGH!!
UH... N-NO, I'M SURE IT'S NOTHING.
NGH.
STAAARE
ISN'T IT BAD MANNERS TO SHOW YOUR MOUTH WHEN YOU'RE EATING?
OH!
SHE'S JUST BEING POLITE.
Y...
YEAH...

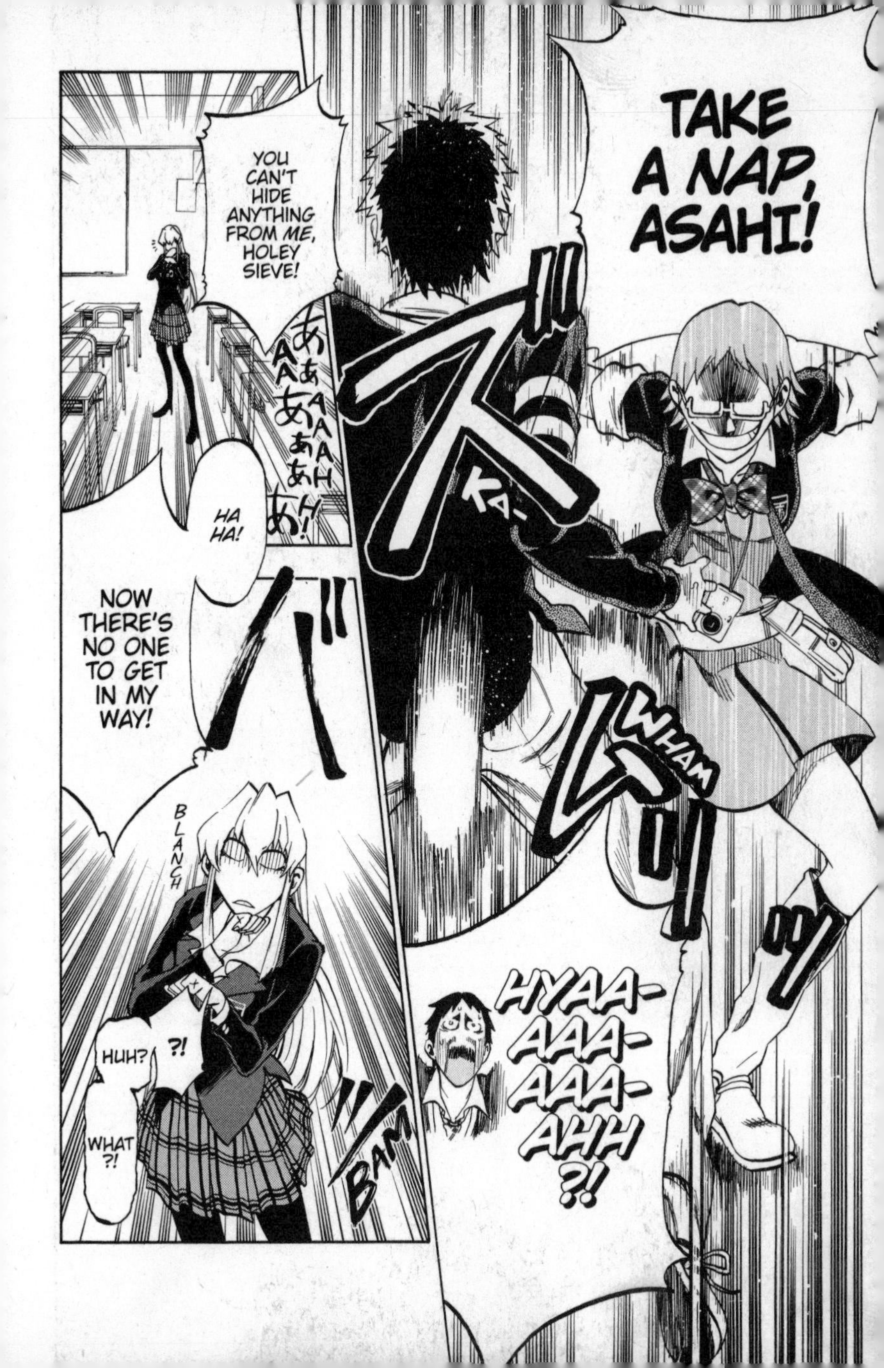
TAKE A NAP, ASAHI!
KA-
WHAM
HYAAA-AAA-AAA-AHH ?!
YOU CAN'T HIDE ANYTHING FROM ME, HOLEY SIEVE!
AAAAAH
HA HA!
NOW THERE'S NO ONE TO GET IN MY WAY!
BLANCH
HUH? ?!
WHAT ?!
BAM

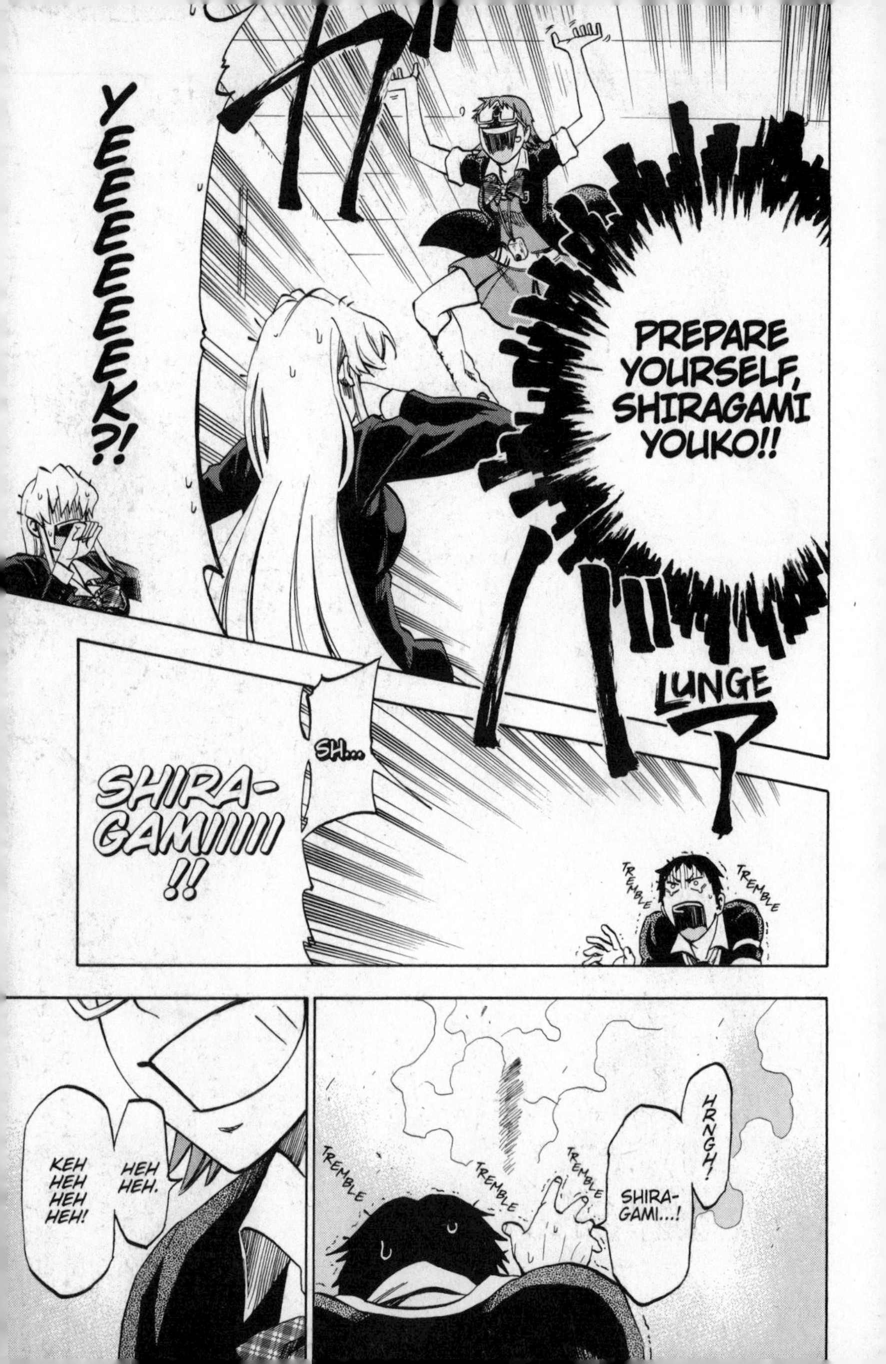
PREPARE YOURSELF, SHIRAGAMI YOUKO!!
LUNGE
YEEEEEEEK?!
TREMBLE TREMBLE
SH...
SHIRA-GAMIIIIII!!
HRNGH!
SHIRA-GAMI...!
TREMBLE TREMBLE TREMBLE
HEH HEH.
KEH HEH HEH HEH!

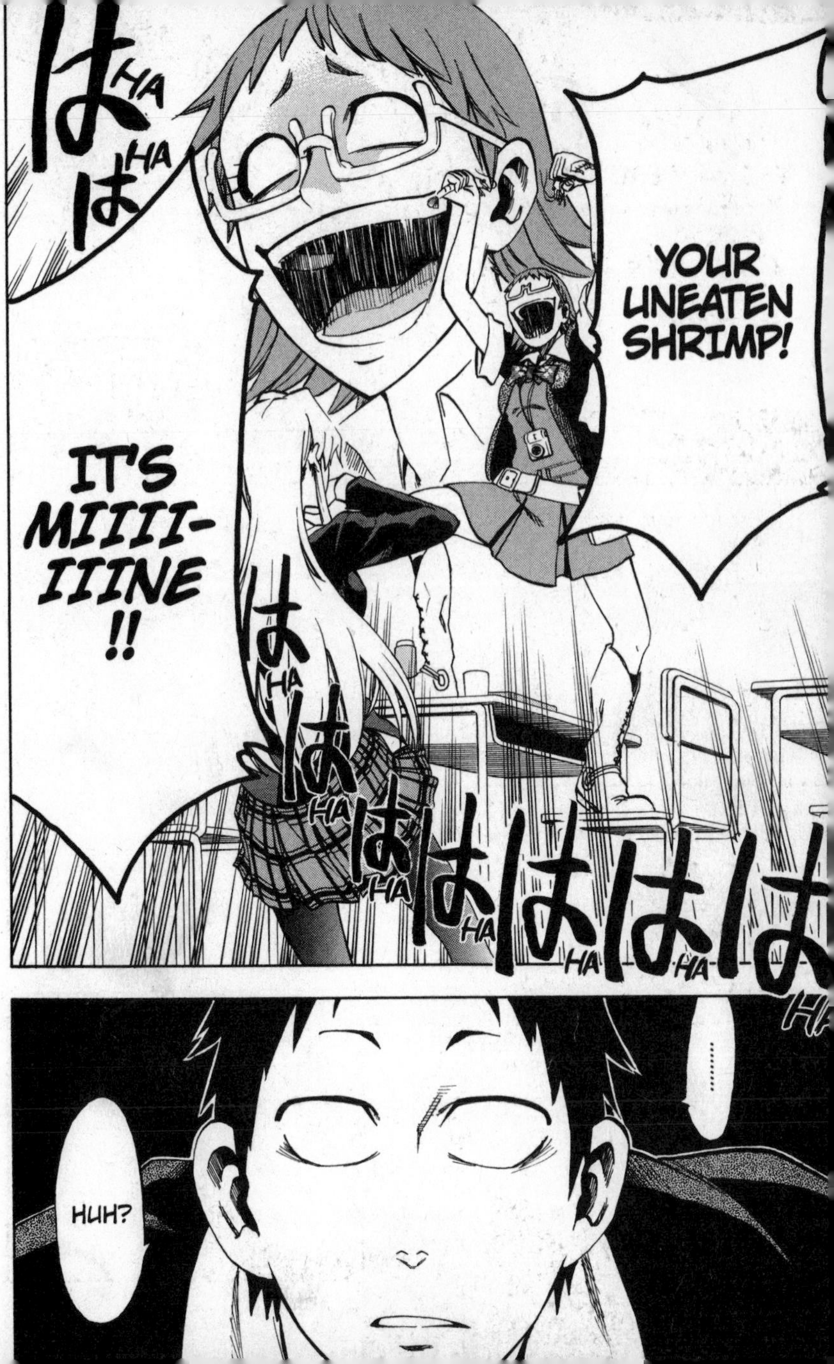
YOUR UNEATEN SHRIMP!
IT'S MIIII-IIINE!!
はHA はHA
はHA はHA はHA はHA はHA はHA はHA はHA
......
HUH?

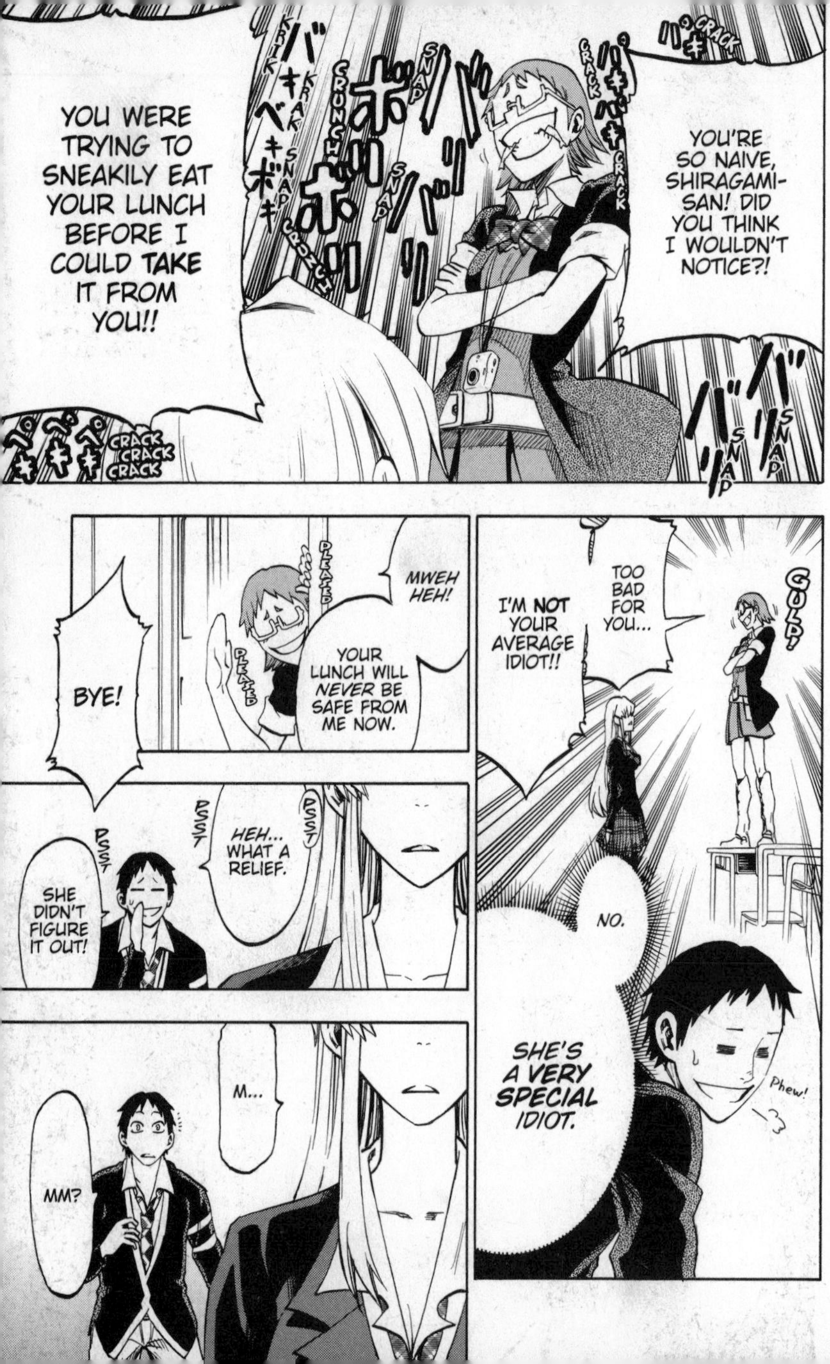
YOU'RE SO NAIVE, SHIRAGAMI-SAN! DID YOU THINK I WOULDN'T NOTICE?!
CRACK
CRACK
CRACK
SNAP
SNAP
CRUNCH
KRAK
KRIK
SNAP
CRUNCH
YOU WERE TRYING TO SNEAKILY EAT YOUR LUNCH BEFORE I COULD TAKE IT FROM YOU!!
SNAP
SNAP
SNAP
CRACK CRACK CRACK
GULP!
TOO BAD FOR YOU...
I'M NOT YOUR AVERAGE IDIOT!!
NO.
SHE'S A VERY SPECIAL IDIOT.
Phew!
MWEH HEH!
PLEASED
PLEASED
YOUR LUNCH WILL NEVER BE SAFE FROM ME NOW.
BYE!
PSST
HEH... WHAT A RELIEF.
PSST
SHE DIDN'T FIGURE IT OUT!
M...
MM?

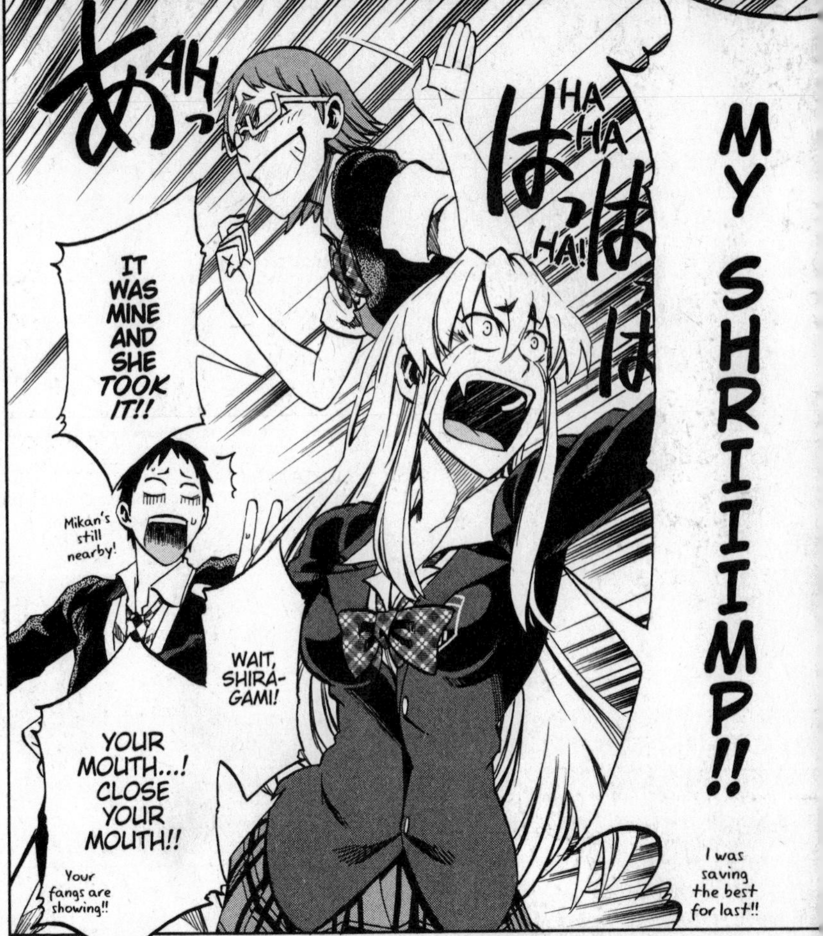
MY SHRIIIMP!!
I was saving the best for last!!
はっはは
HA HA HA!!
あっ
AH
IT WAS MINE AND SHE TOOK IT!!
Mikan's still nearby!
WAIT, SHIRA-GAMI!
YOUR MOUTH...! CLOSE YOUR MOUTH!!
Your fangs are showing!!
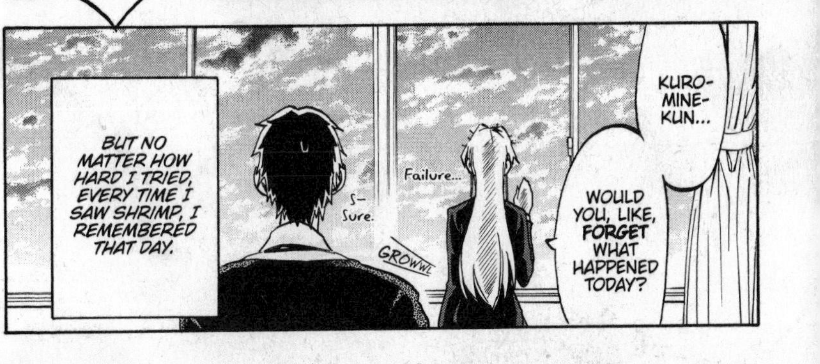
KURO-MINE-KUN...
WOULD YOU, LIKE, FORGET WHAT HAPPENED TODAY?
Failure...
GROWWL
S-Sure.
BUT NO MATTER HOW HARD I TRIED, EVERY TIME I SAW SHRIMP, I REMEMBERED THAT DAY.

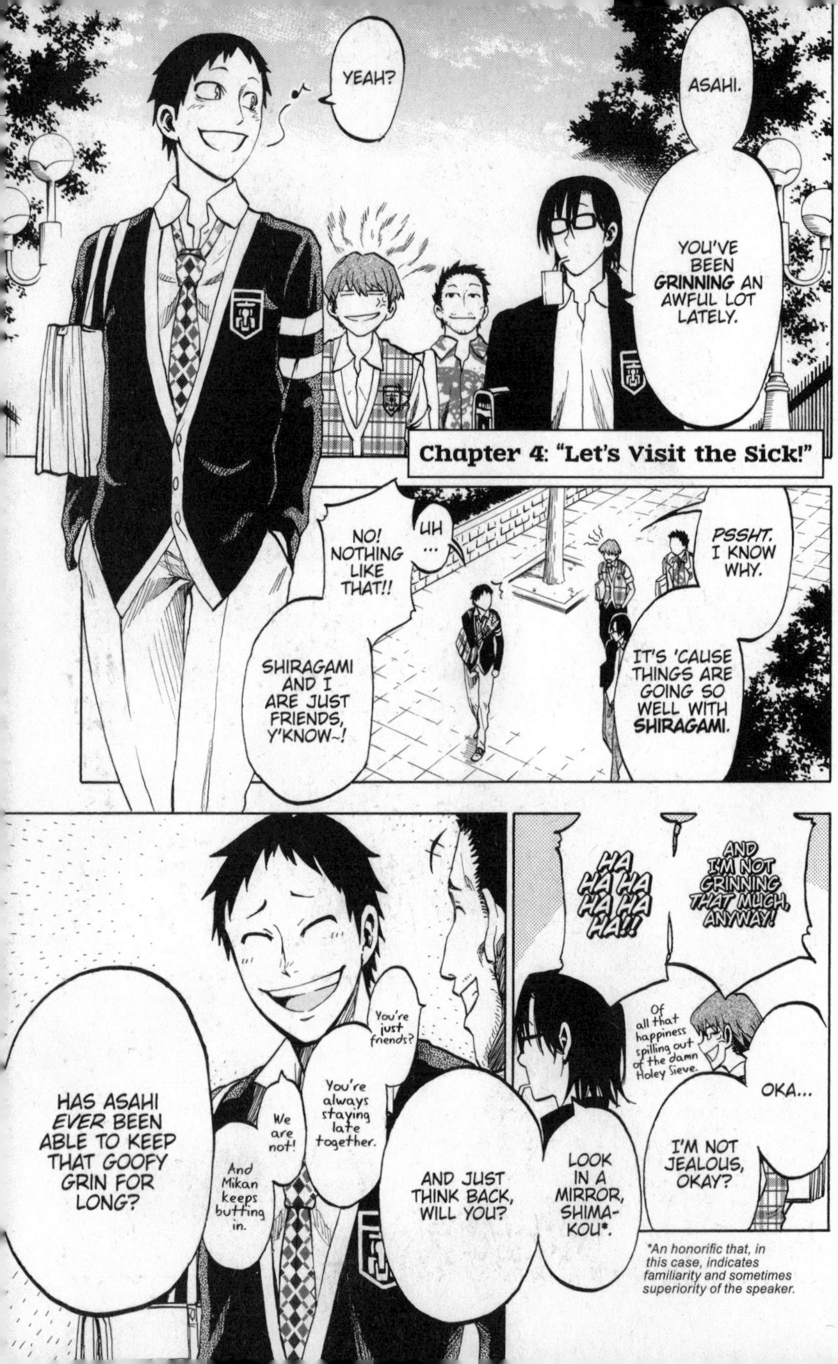
ASAHI.
YOU'VE BEEN GRINNING AN AWFUL LOT LATELY.
YEAH?
Chapter 4: "Let's Visit the Sick!"
PSSHT. I KNOW WHY.
IT'S 'CAUSE THINGS ARE GOING SO WELL WITH SHIRAGAMI.
UH ...
NO! NOTHING LIKE THAT!!
SHIRAGAMI AND I ARE JUST FRIENDS, Y'KNOW~!
AND I'M NOT GRINNING THAT MUCH, ANYWAY!
HA HA HA HA HA HA!!
Of all that happiness spilling out of the damn Holey Sieve.
OKA...
I'M NOT JEALOUS, OKAY?
LOOK IN A MIRROR, SHIMA-KOU*.
AND JUST THINK BACK, WILL YOU?
You're just friends?
You're always staying late together.
We are not!
And Mikan keeps butting in.
HAS ASAHI EVER BEEN ABLE TO KEEP THAT GOOFY GRIN FOR LONG?

*An honorific that, in this case, indicates familiarity and sometimes superiority of the speaker.

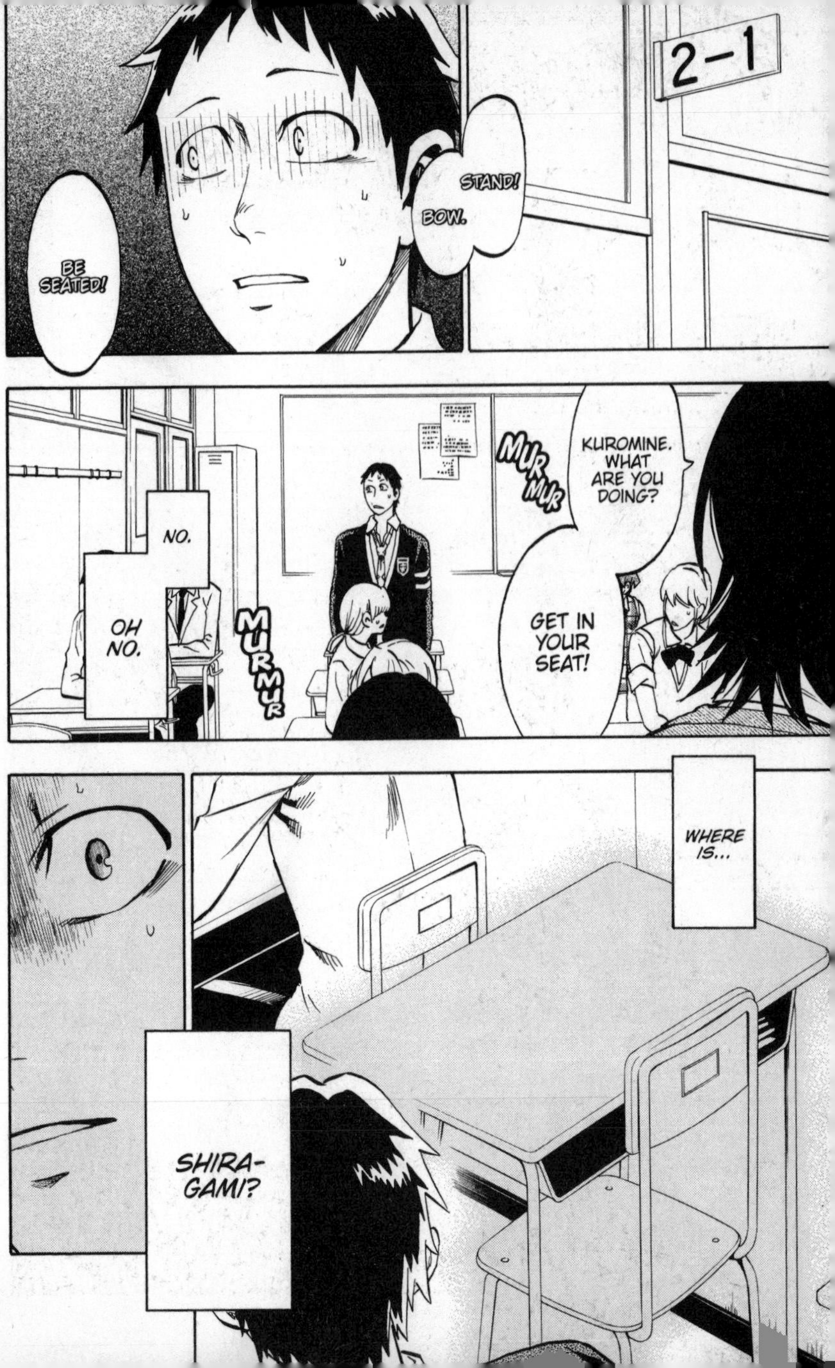
2-1
STAND!
BOW.
BE SEATED!
KUROMINE. WHAT ARE YOU DOING?
GET IN YOUR SEAT!
MUR MUR
MURMUR
NO.
OH NO.
WHERE IS...
SHIRA-GAMI?

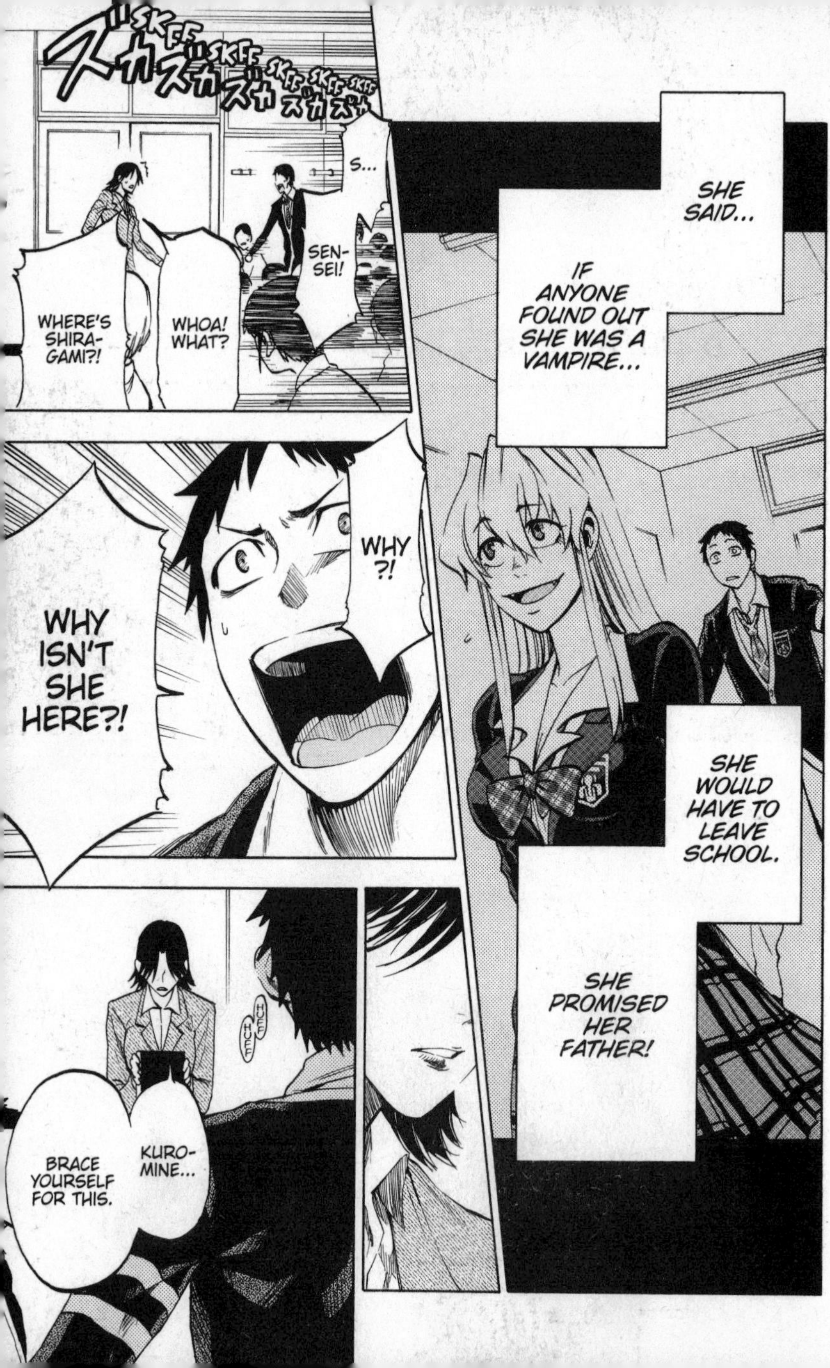
SHE SAID...
IF ANYONE FOUND OUT SHE WAS A VAMPIRE...
SHE WOULD HAVE TO LEAVE SCHOOL.
SHE PROMISED HER FATHER!
SKFF SKFF SKFF SKFF SKFF
S...
SEN-SEI!
WHOA! WHAT?
WHERE'S SHIRA-GAMI?!
WHY ?!
WHY ISN'T SHE HERE?!
HUFF HUFF
KURO-MINE...
BRACE YOURSELF FOR THIS.

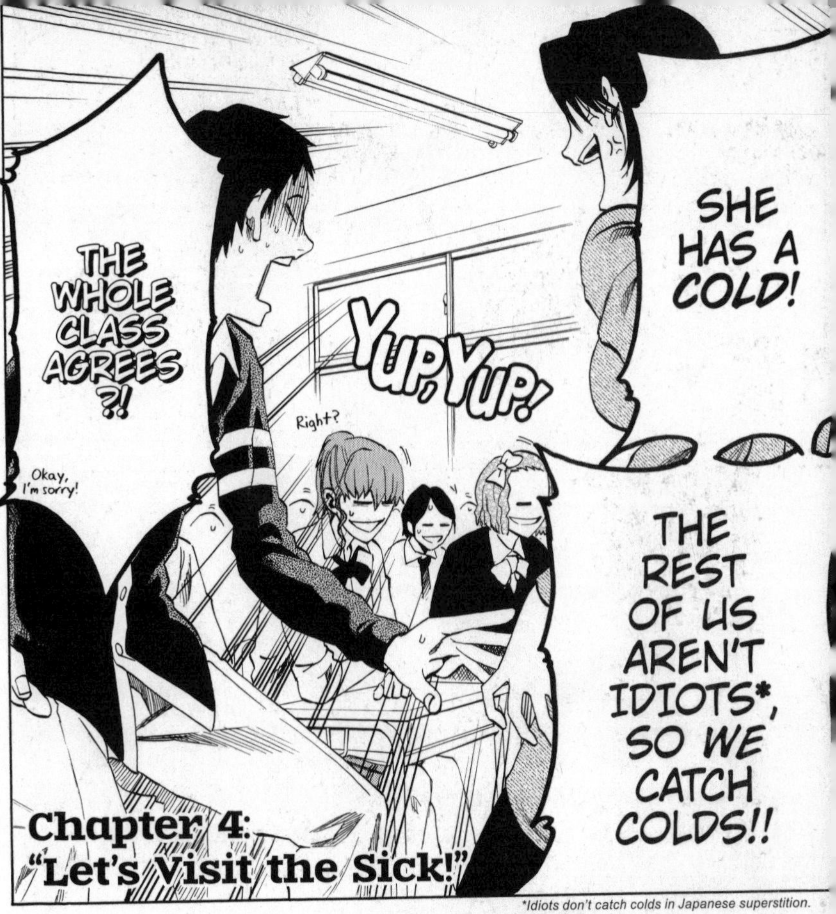
SHE HAS A COLD!
THE REST OF US AREN'T IDIOTS*, SO WE CATCH COLDS!!
YUP, YUP!
Right?
THE WHOLE CLASS AGREES ?!
Okay, I'm sorry!
Chapter 4: "Let's Visit the Sick!"

*Idiots don't catch colds in Japanese superstition.

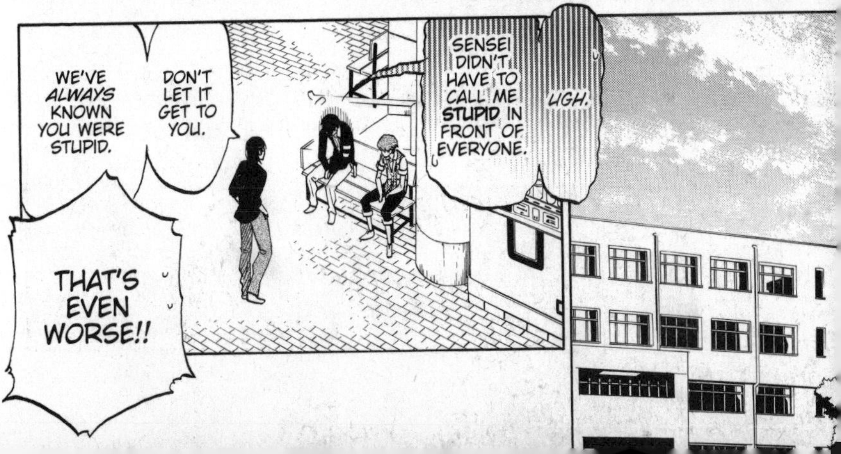
UGH.
SENSEI DIDN'T HAVE TO CALL ME STUPID IN FRONT OF EVERYONE.
DON'T LET IT GET TO YOU.
WE'VE ALWAYS KNOWN YOU WERE STUPID.
THAT'S EVEN WORSE!!

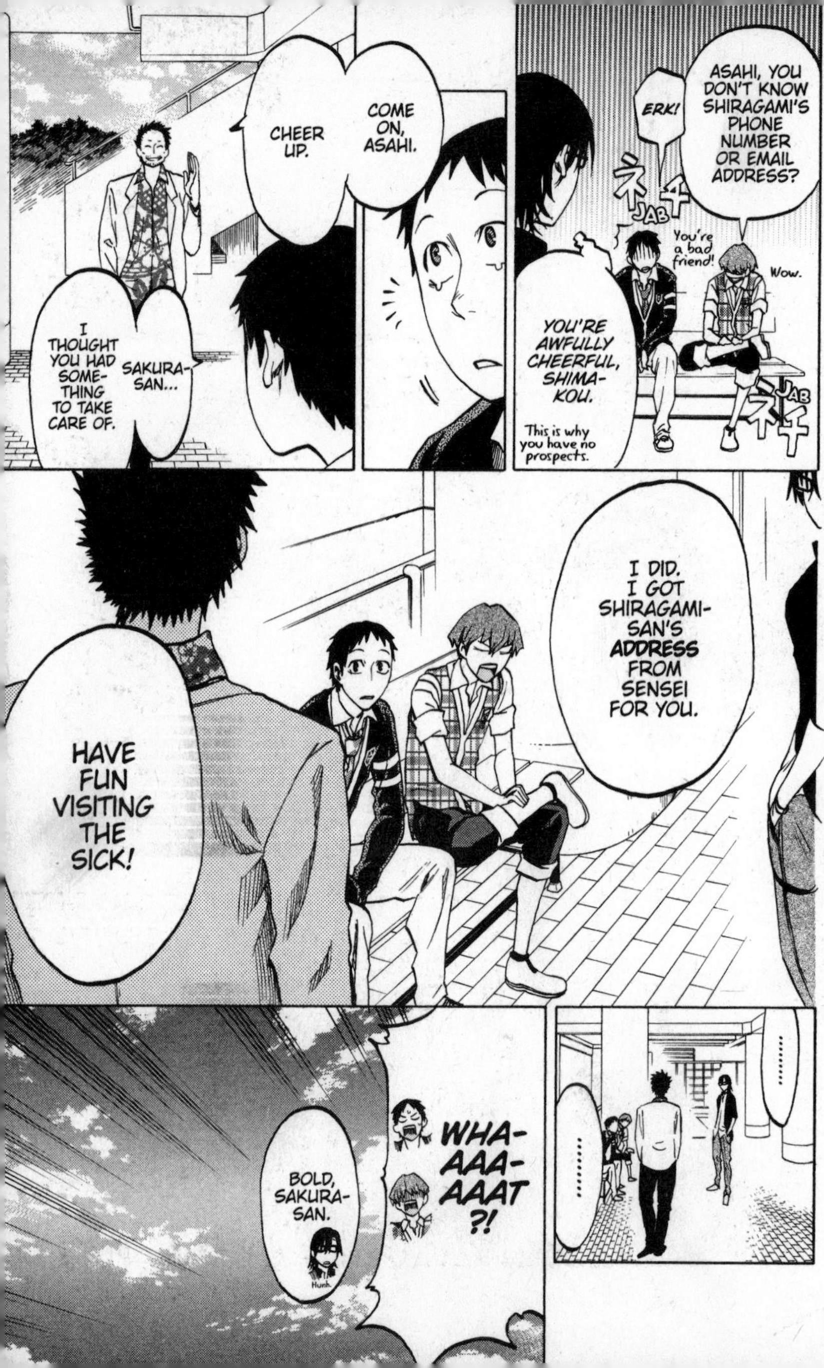
ASAHI, YOU DON'T KNOW SHIRAGAMI'S PHONE NUMBER OR EMAIL ADDRESS?
ERK!
JAB
JAB
You're a bad friend!
Wow.
YOU'RE AWFULLY CHEERFUL, SHIMA-KOU.
This is why you have no prospects.
COME ON, ASAHI.
CHEER UP.
SAKURA-SAN...
I THOUGHT YOU HAD SOME-THING TO TAKE CARE OF.
I DID. I GOT SHIRAGAMI-SAN'S ADDRESS FROM SENSEI FOR YOU.
HAVE FUN VISITING THE SICK!
......
......
WHA-AAA-AAAT?!
BOLD, SAKURA-SAN.
Hunh.

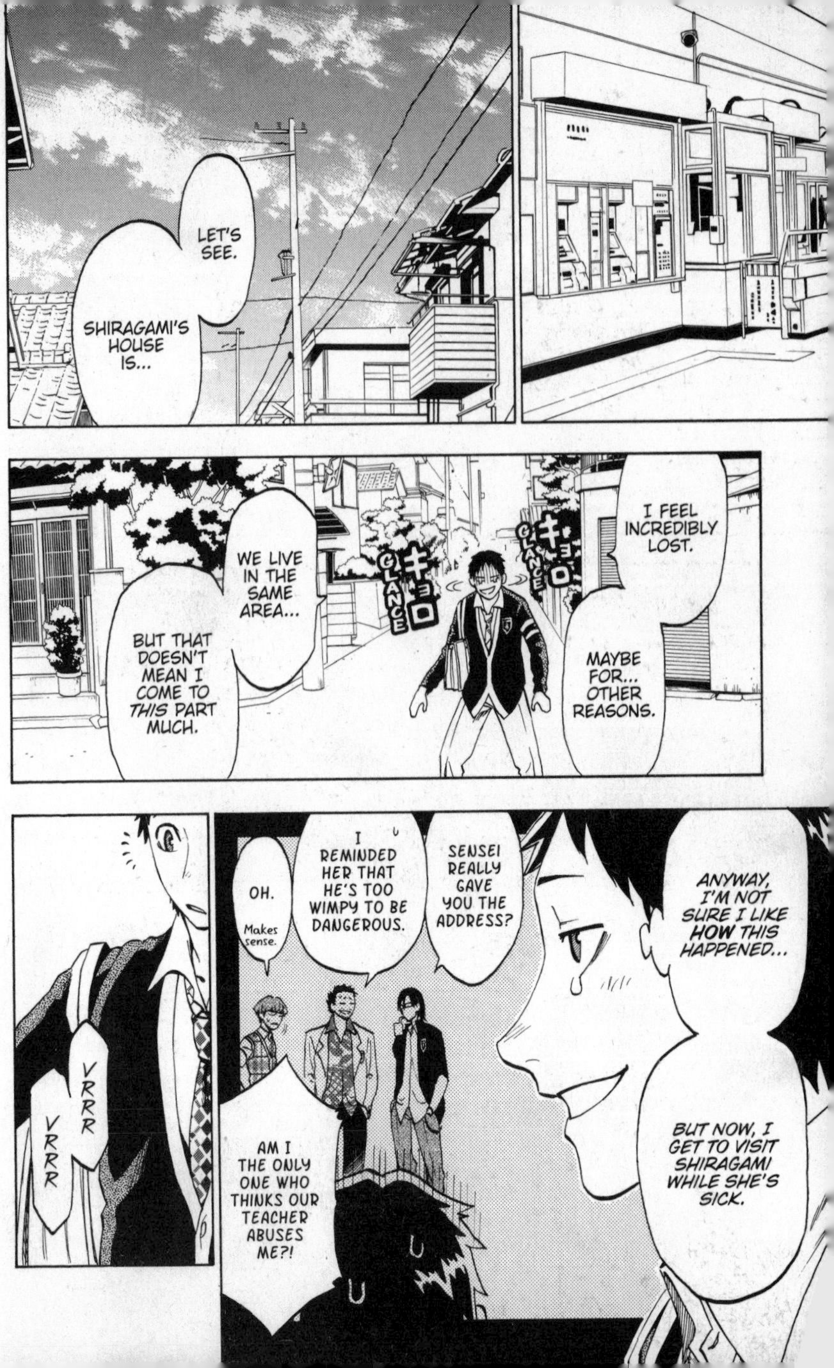
LET'S SEE.
SHIRAGAMI'S HOUSE IS...
I FEEL INCREDIBLY LOST.
キョロ GLANCE
キョロ GLANCE
MAYBE FOR... OTHER REASONS.
WE LIVE IN THE SAME AREA...
BUT THAT DOESN'T MEAN I COME TO *THIS* PART MUCH.
ANYWAY, I'M NOT SURE I LIKE ***HOW*** *THIS HAPPENED...*
BUT NOW, I GET TO VISIT SHIRAGAMI WHILE SHE'S SICK.
SENSEI REALLY GAVE YOU THE ADDRESS?
I REMINDED HER THAT HE'S TOO WIMPY TO BE DANGEROUS.
OH.
Makes sense.
AM I THE ONLY ONE WHO THINKS OUR TEACHER ABUSES ME?!
VRRR
VRRR

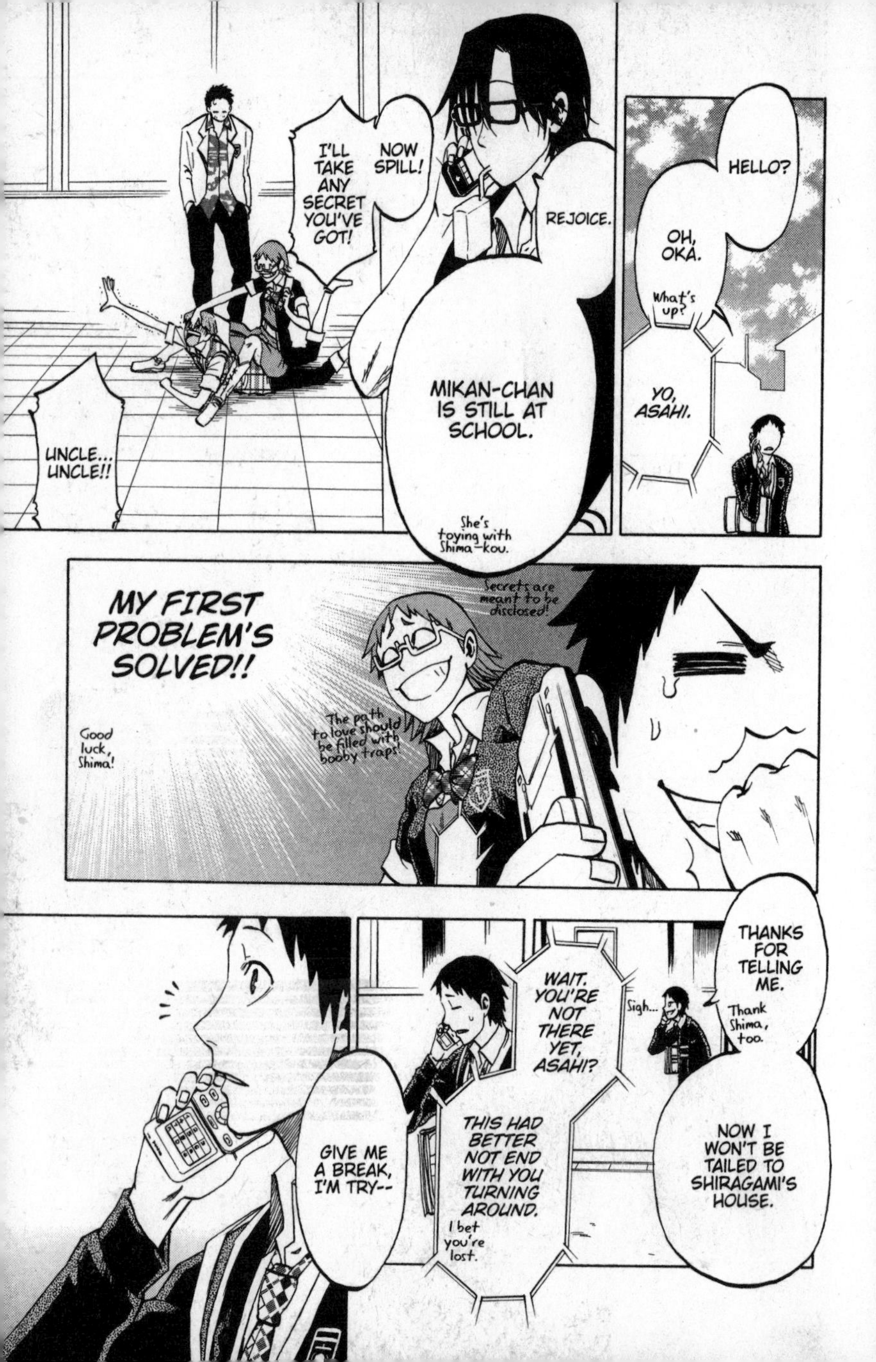
HELLO?
OH, OKA.
What's up?
YO, ASAHI.
REJOICE.
MIKAN-CHAN IS STILL AT SCHOOL.
She's toying with Shima-kou.
NOW SPILL!
I'LL TAKE ANY SECRET YOU'VE GOT!
UNCLE... UNCLE!!
Secrets are meant to be disclosed!
MY FIRST PROBLEM'S SOLVED!!
The path to love should be filled with booby traps!
Good luck, Shima!
THANKS FOR TELLING ME.
Thank Shima, too.
Sigh...
NOW I WON'T BE TAILED TO SHIRAGAMI'S HOUSE.
WAIT. YOU'RE NOT THERE YET, ASAHI?
THIS HAD BETTER NOT END WITH YOU TURNING AROUND.
I bet you're lost.
GIVE ME A BREAK, I'M TRY--

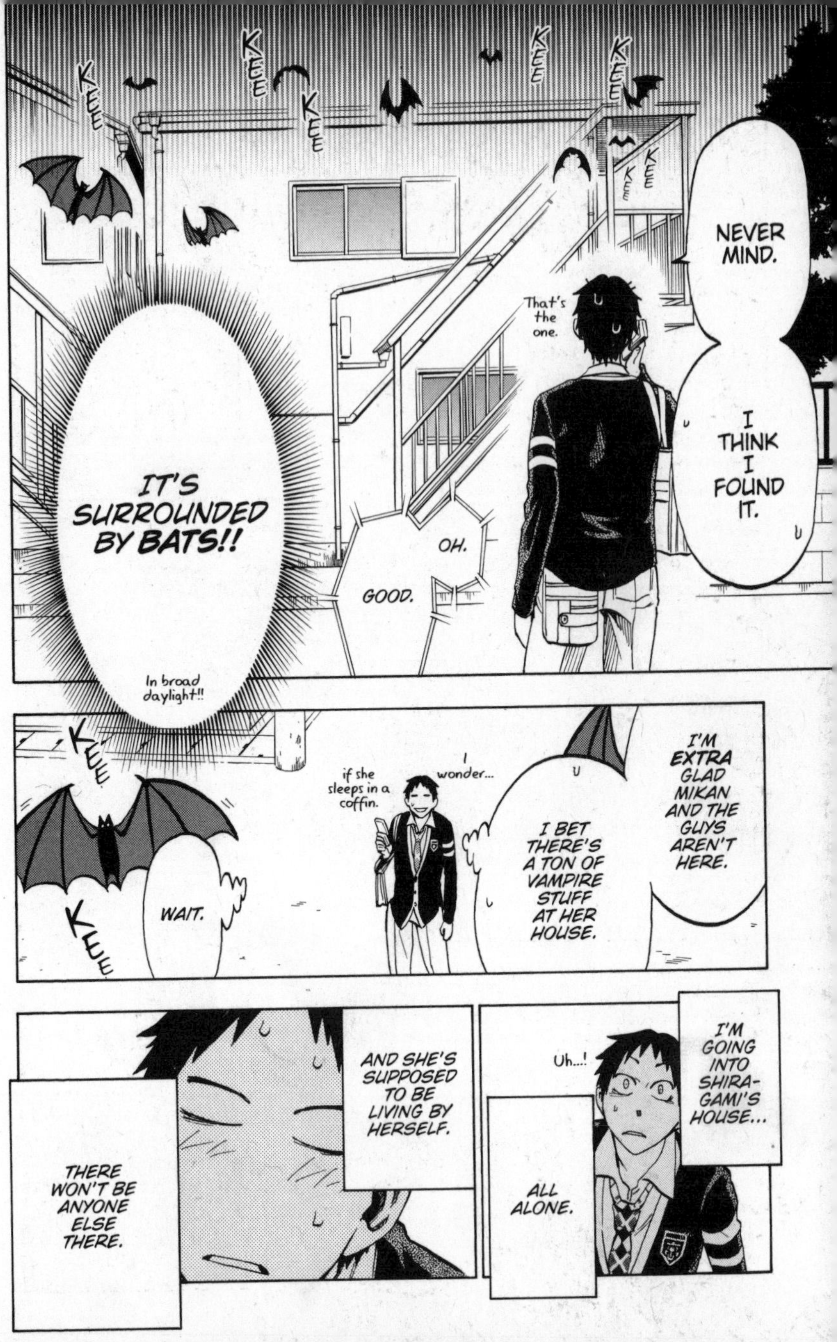
KEE
KEE
KEE
KEE
KEE
KEE
NEVER MIND.
That's the one.
I THINK I FOUND IT.
OH.
GOOD.
IT'S SURROUNDED BY BATS!!
In broad daylight!!
KEE
KEE
I'M EXTRA GLAD MIKAN AND THE GUYS AREN'T HERE.
I BET THERE'S A TON OF VAMPIRE STUFF AT HER HOUSE.
I wonder...
if she sleeps in a coffin.
WAIT.
I'M GOING INTO SHIRA-GAMI'S HOUSE...
Uh...!
ALL ALONE.
AND SHE'S SUPPOSED TO BE LIVING BY HERSELF.
THERE WON'T BE ANYONE ELSE THERE.

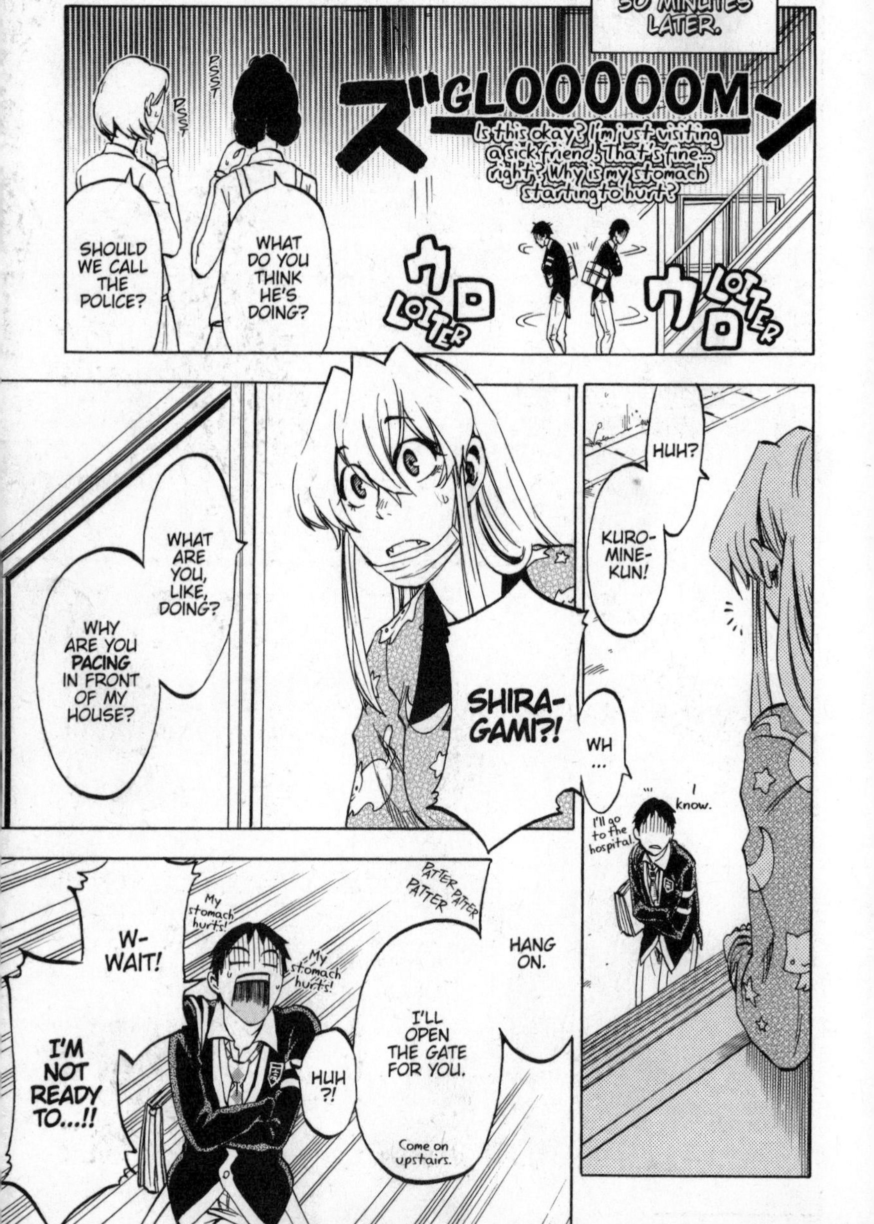
30 MINUTES LATER.
ズGLOOOOOM
Is this okay? I'm just visiting a sick friend. That's fine... right? Why is my stomach starting to hurt?
ウロ LOITER
ウロ LOITER
PSST
PSST
WHAT DO YOU THINK HE'S DOING?
SHOULD WE CALL THE POLICE?
HUH?
KURO-MINE-KUN!
WH...
...
I know.
I'll go to the hospital.
SHIRA-GAMI?!
WHAT ARE YOU, LIKE, DOING?
WHY ARE YOU PACING IN FRONT OF MY HOUSE?
PATTER PATTER PATTER
HANG ON.
I'LL OPEN THE GATE FOR YOU.
Come on upstairs.
HUH?!
My stomach hurts!
My stomach hurts!
W-WAIT!
I'M NOT READY TO...!!

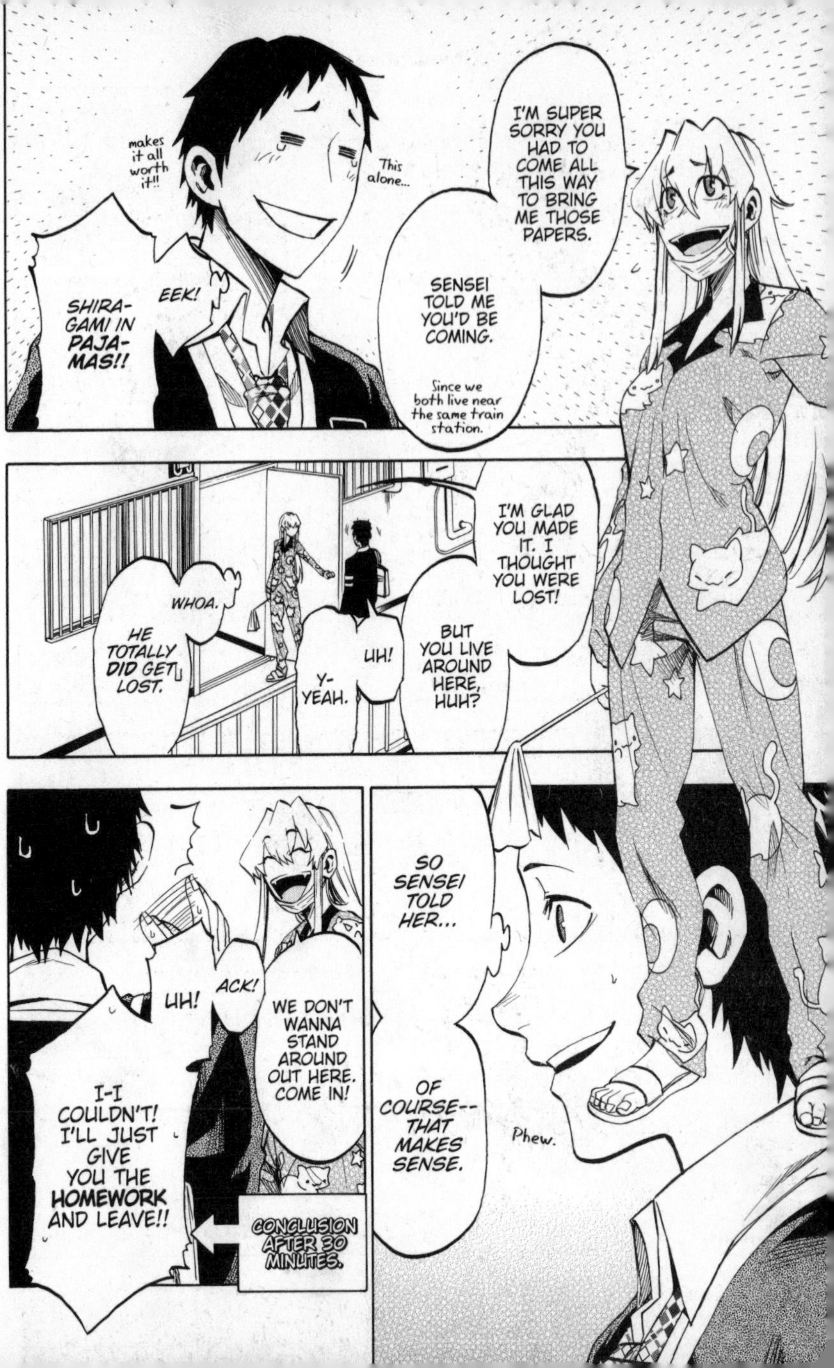
I'M SUPER SORRY YOU HAD TO COME ALL THIS WAY TO BRING ME THOSE PAPERS.
SENSEI TOLD ME YOU'D BE COMING.
Since we both live near the same train station.
This alone...
makes it all worth it!!
EEK!
SHIRAGAMI IN PAJAMAS!!
I'M GLAD YOU MADE IT. I THOUGHT YOU WERE LOST!
BUT YOU LIVE AROUND HERE, HUH?
UH!
Y-YEAH.
WHOA.
HE TOTALLY DID GET LOST.
SO SENSEI TOLD HER...
OF COURSE--THAT MAKES SENSE.
Phew.
WE DON'T WANNA STAND AROUND OUT HERE. COME IN!
ACK!
UH!
I-I COULDN'T! I'LL JUST GIVE YOU THE HOMEWORK AND LEAVE!!
CONCLUSION AFTER 30 MINUTES.

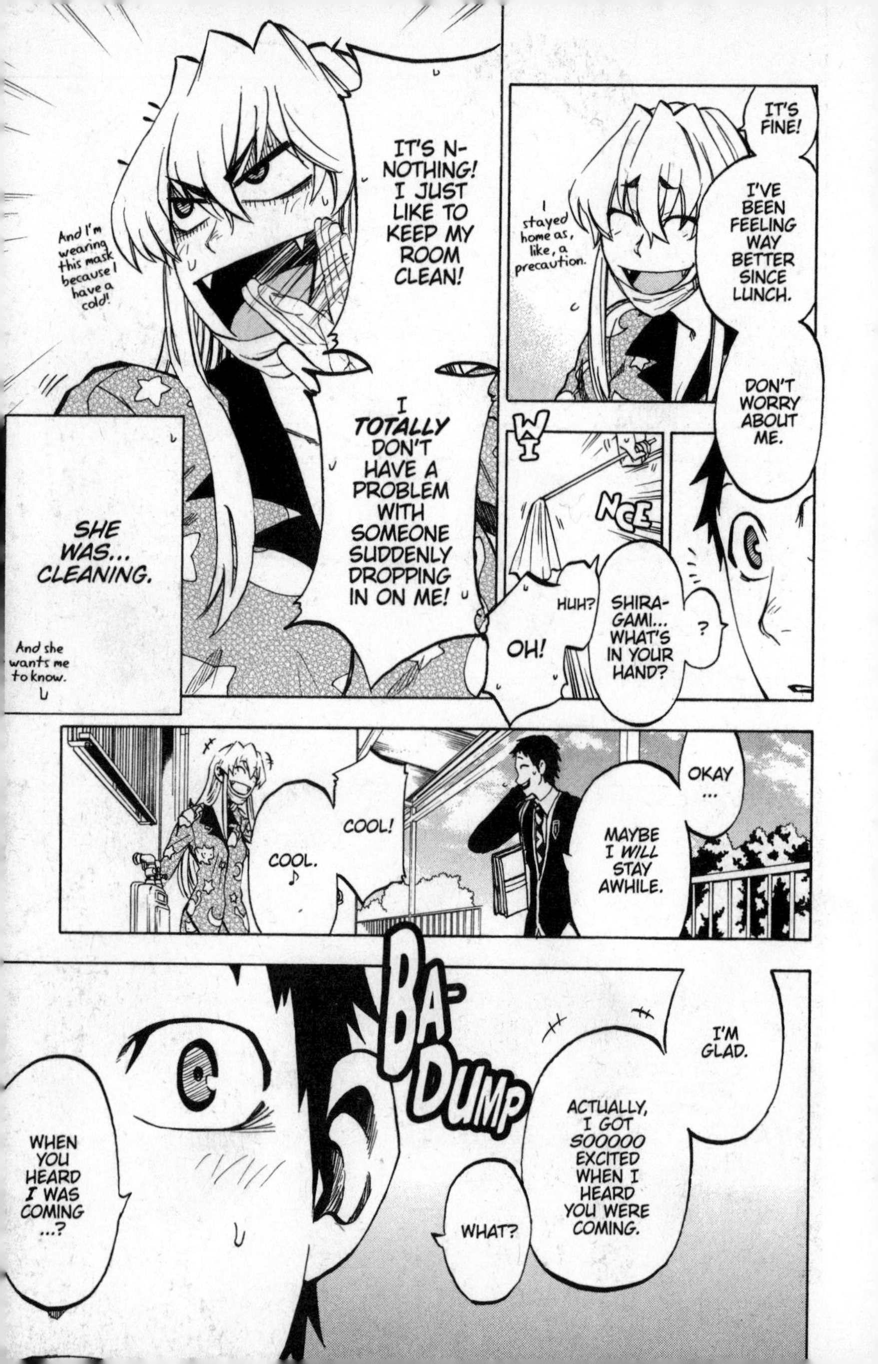
IT'S FINE!
I'VE BEEN FEELING WAY BETTER SINCE LUNCH.
I stayed home as, like, a precaution.
DON'T WORRY ABOUT ME.
WAI
NCE
SHIRA-GAMI... WHAT'S IN YOUR HAND?
?
HUH?
OH!
IT'S N-NOTHING! I JUST LIKE TO KEEP MY ROOM CLEAN!
And I'm wearing this mask because I have a cold!
I TOTALLY DON'T HAVE A PROBLEM WITH SOMEONE SUDDENLY DROPPING IN ON ME!
SHE WAS... CLEANING.
And she wants me to know.
OKAY ...
MAYBE I WILL STAY AWHILE.
COOL!
COOL. ♪
BA-DUMP
I'M GLAD.
ACTUALLY, I GOT SOOOOO EXCITED WHEN I HEARD YOU WERE COMING.
WHAT?
WHEN YOU HEARD I WAS COMING ...?

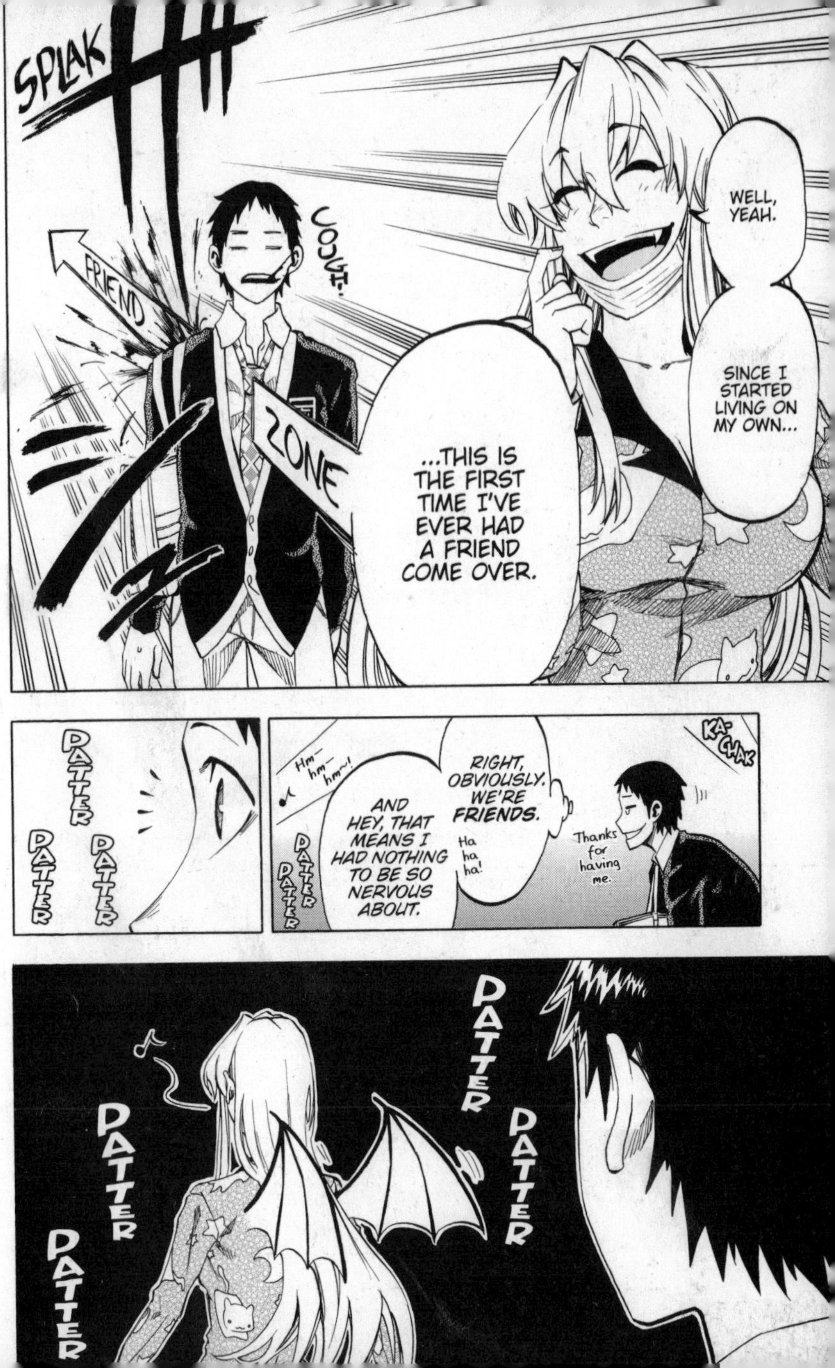
WELL, YEAH.
SINCE I STARTED LIVING ON MY OWN...
...THIS IS THE FIRST TIME I'VE EVER HAD A FRIEND COME OVER.
COUGH!
FRIEND
ZONE
SPLAK
KA-CHAK
RIGHT, OBVIOUSLY. WE'RE FRIENDS.
Thanks for having me.
Ha ha ha!
AND HEY, THAT MEANS I HAD NOTHING TO BE SO NERVOUS ABOUT.
Hm-hm-hm~!
PATTER PATTER
PATTER PATTER PATTER
PATTER PATTER
PATTER PATTER

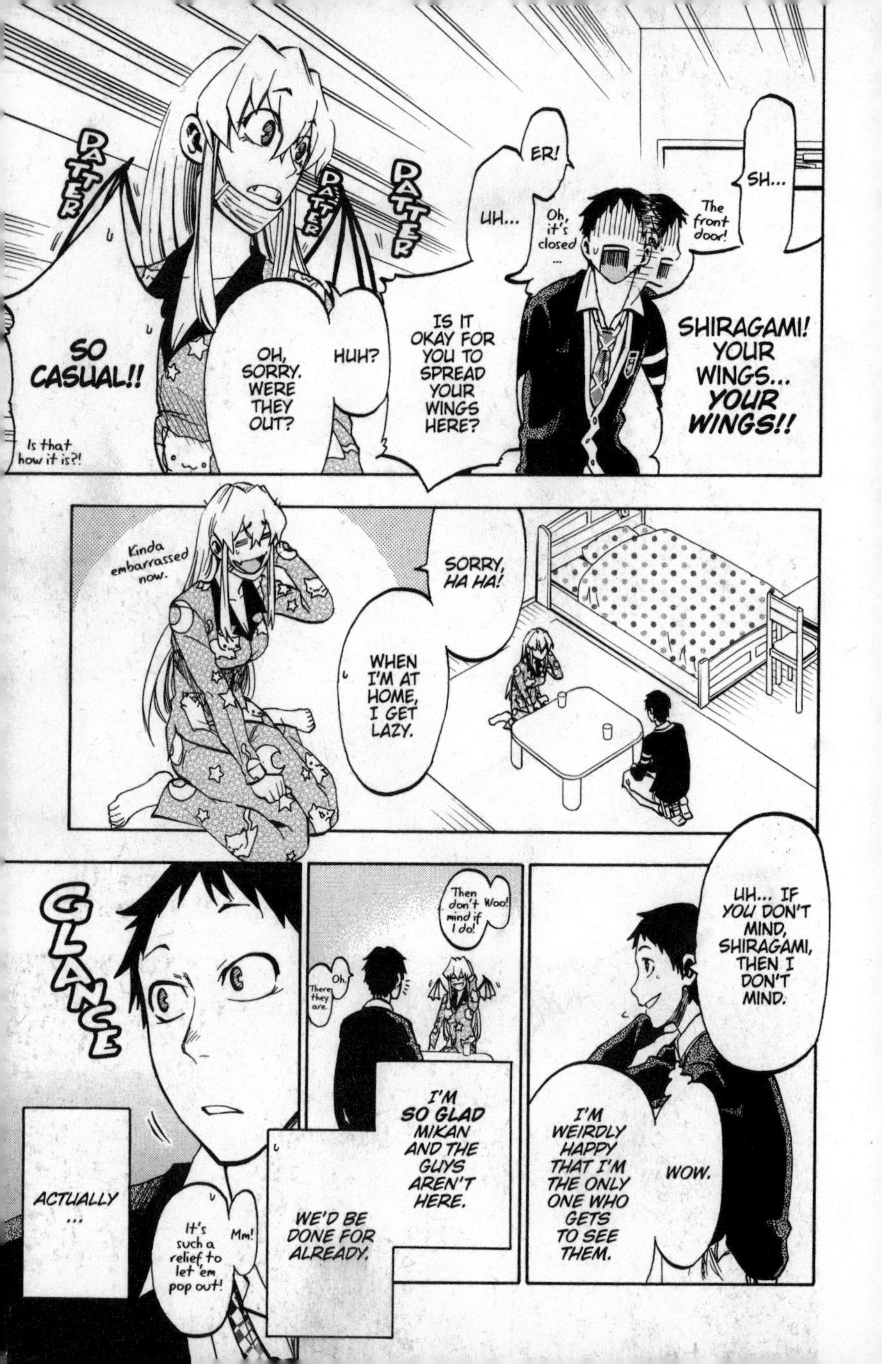
SH...
The front door!
ER!
Oh, it's closed ...
UH...
SHIRAGAMI! YOUR WINGS... YOUR WINGS!!
IS IT OKAY FOR YOU TO SPREAD YOUR WINGS HERE?
HUH?
OH, SORRY. WERE THEY OUT?
DATTER
DATTER
DATTER
SO CASUAL!!
Is that how it is?!
WHEN I'M AT HOME, I GET LAZY.
SORRY, HA HA!
Kinda embarrassed now.
UH... IF YOU DON'T MIND, SHIRAGAMI, THEN I DON'T MIND.
WOW.
I'M WEIRDLY HAPPY THAT I'M THE ONLY ONE WHO GETS TO SEE THEM.
Then don't mind if I do!
Woo!
Oh. There they are.
I'M SO GLAD MIKAN AND THE GUYS AREN'T HERE.
WE'D BE DONE FOR ALREADY.
GLANCE
Mm!
It's such a relief to let 'em pop out!
ACTUALLY ...

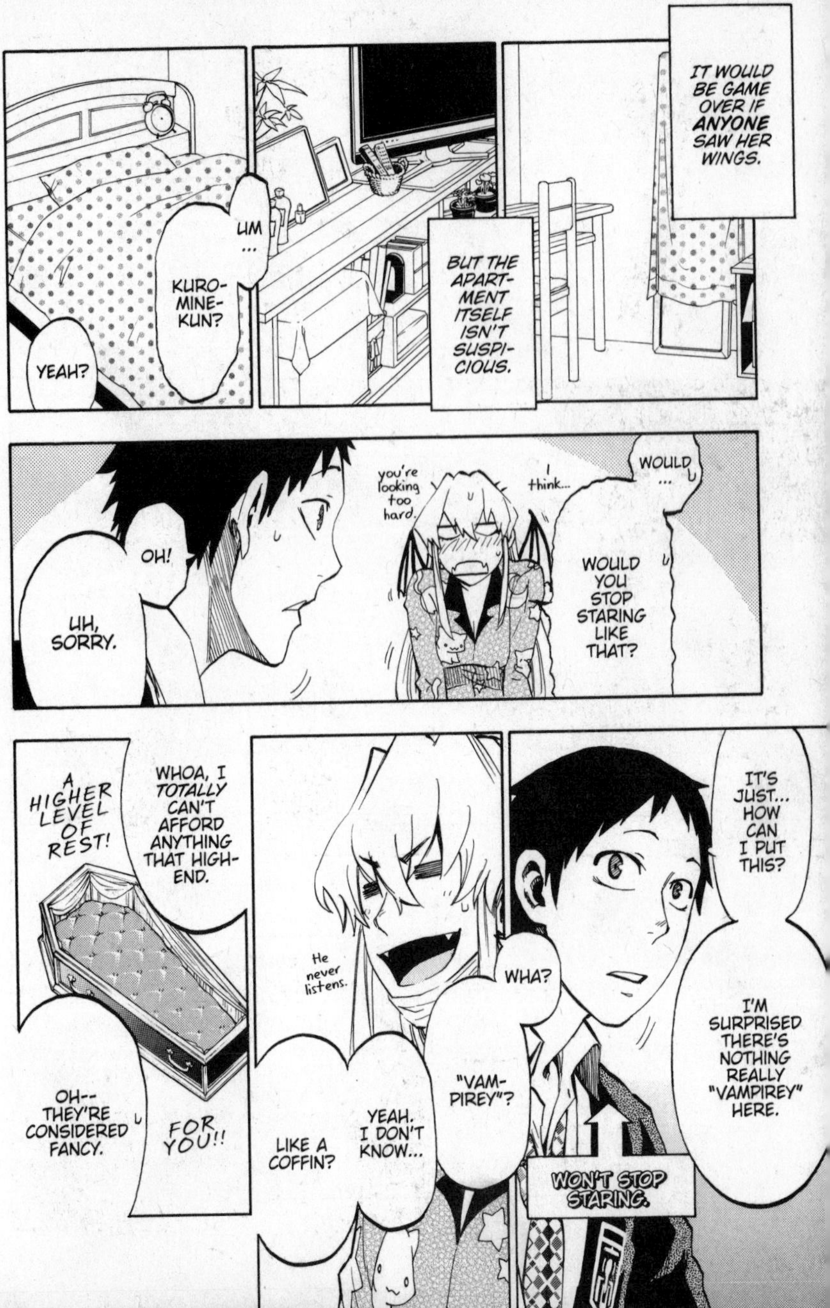
IT WOULD BE GAME OVER IF ANYONE SAW HER WINGS.
BUT THE APARTMENT ITSELF ISN'T SUSPICIOUS.
UM...
KURO-MINE-KUN?
YEAH?
WOULD...
WOULD YOU STOP STARING LIKE THAT?
I think...
you're looking too hard.
OH!
UH, SORRY.
IT'S JUST... HOW CAN I PUT THIS?
I'M SURPRISED THERE'S NOTHING REALLY "VAMPIREY" HERE.
WON'T STOP STARING.
WHA?
"VAM-PIREY"?
YEAH. I DON'T KNOW...
LIKE A COFFIN?
He never listens.
WHOA, I TOTALLY CAN'T AFFORD ANYTHING THAT HIGH-END.
A HIGHER LEVEL OF REST!
FOR YOU!!
OH-- THEY'RE CONSIDERED FANCY.

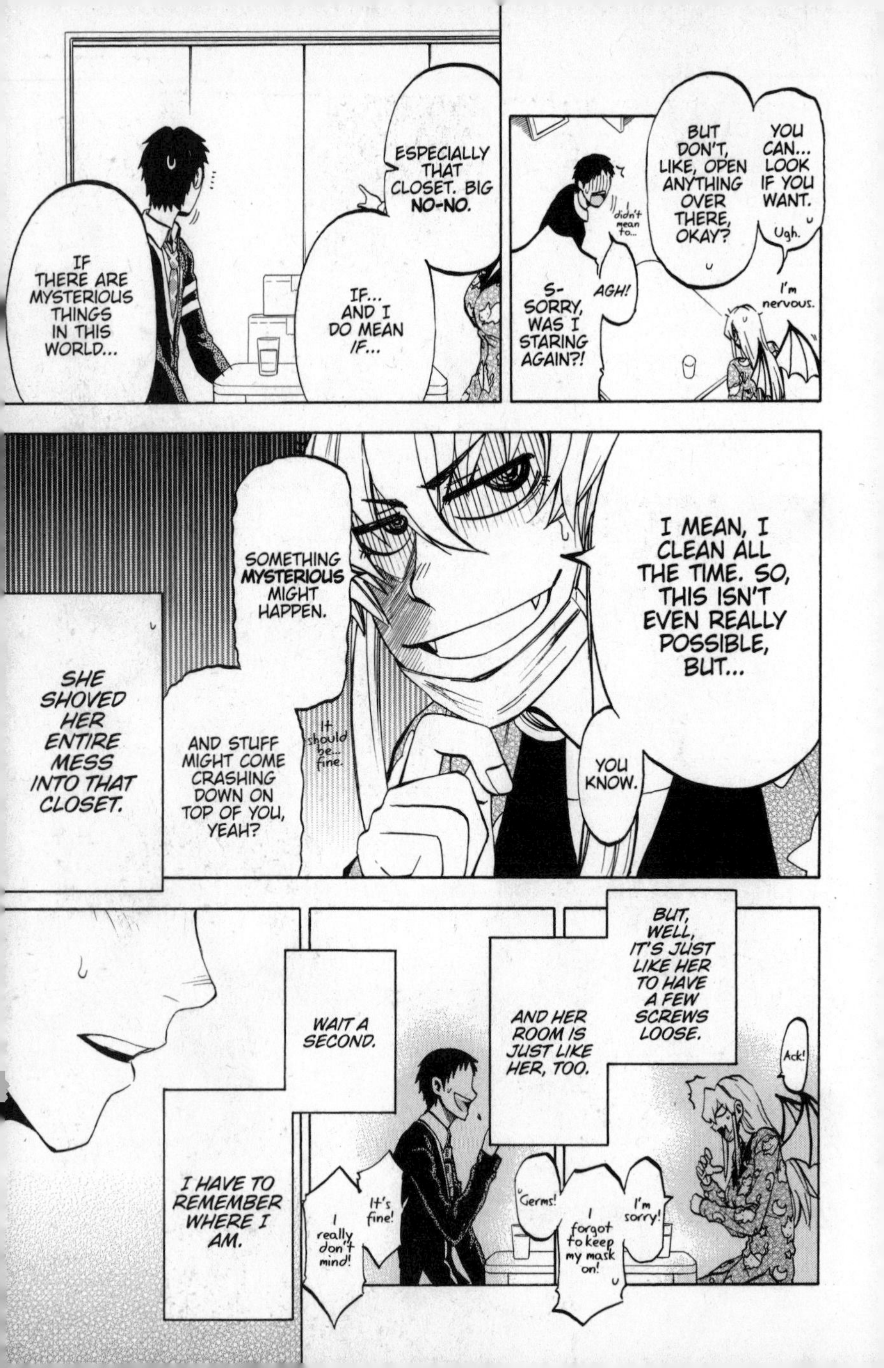
YOU CAN... LOOK IF YOU WANT.
BUT DON'T, LIKE, OPEN ANYTHING OVER THERE, OKAY?
Ugh.
I'm nervous.
AGH!
S-SORRY, WAS I STARING AGAIN?!
I didn't mean to...
ESPECIALLY THAT CLOSET. BIG NO-NO.
IF... AND I DO MEAN IF...
IF THERE ARE MYSTERIOUS THINGS IN THIS WORLD...
I MEAN, I CLEAN ALL THE TIME. SO, THIS ISN'T EVEN REALLY POSSIBLE, BUT...
YOU KNOW.
SOMETHING MYSTERIOUS MIGHT HAPPEN.
It should be... fine.
AND STUFF MIGHT COME CRASHING DOWN ON TOP OF YOU, YEAH?
SHE SHOVED HER ENTIRE MESS INTO THAT CLOSET.
BUT, WELL, IT'S JUST LIKE HER TO HAVE A FEW SCREWS LOOSE.
AND HER ROOM IS JUST LIKE HER, TOO.
Ack!
I'm sorry!
I forgot to keep my mask on!
Germs!
It's fine!
I really don't mind!
WAIT A SECOND.
I HAVE TO REMEMBER WHERE I AM.

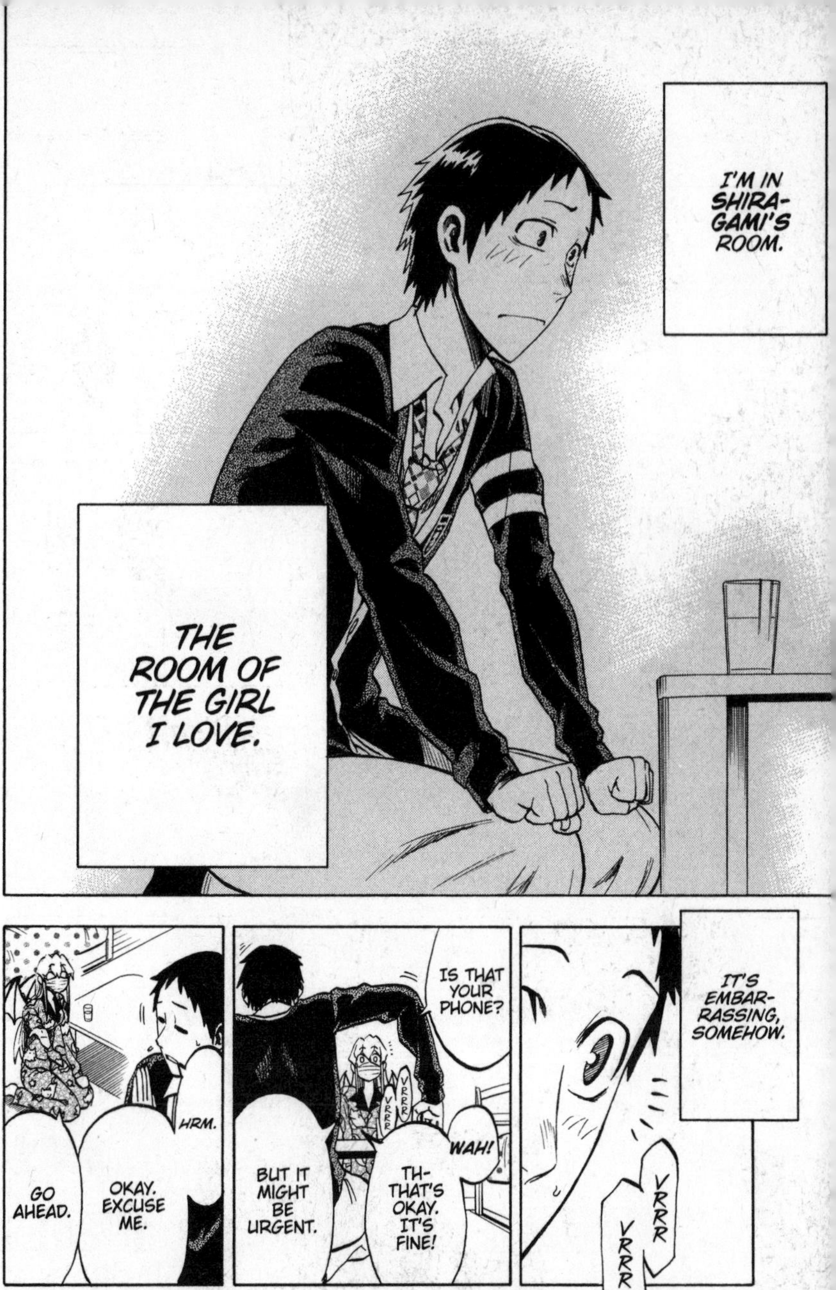
I'M IN SHIRA-GAMI'S ROOM.
THE ROOM OF THE GIRL I LOVE.
IT'S EMBAR-RASSING, SOMEHOW.
VRRR
VRRR
IS THAT YOUR PHONE?
VRRR
VRRR
WAH!
TH-THAT'S OKAY. IT'S FINE!
BUT IT MIGHT BE URGENT.
HRM.
OKAY. EXCUSE ME.
GO AHEAD.

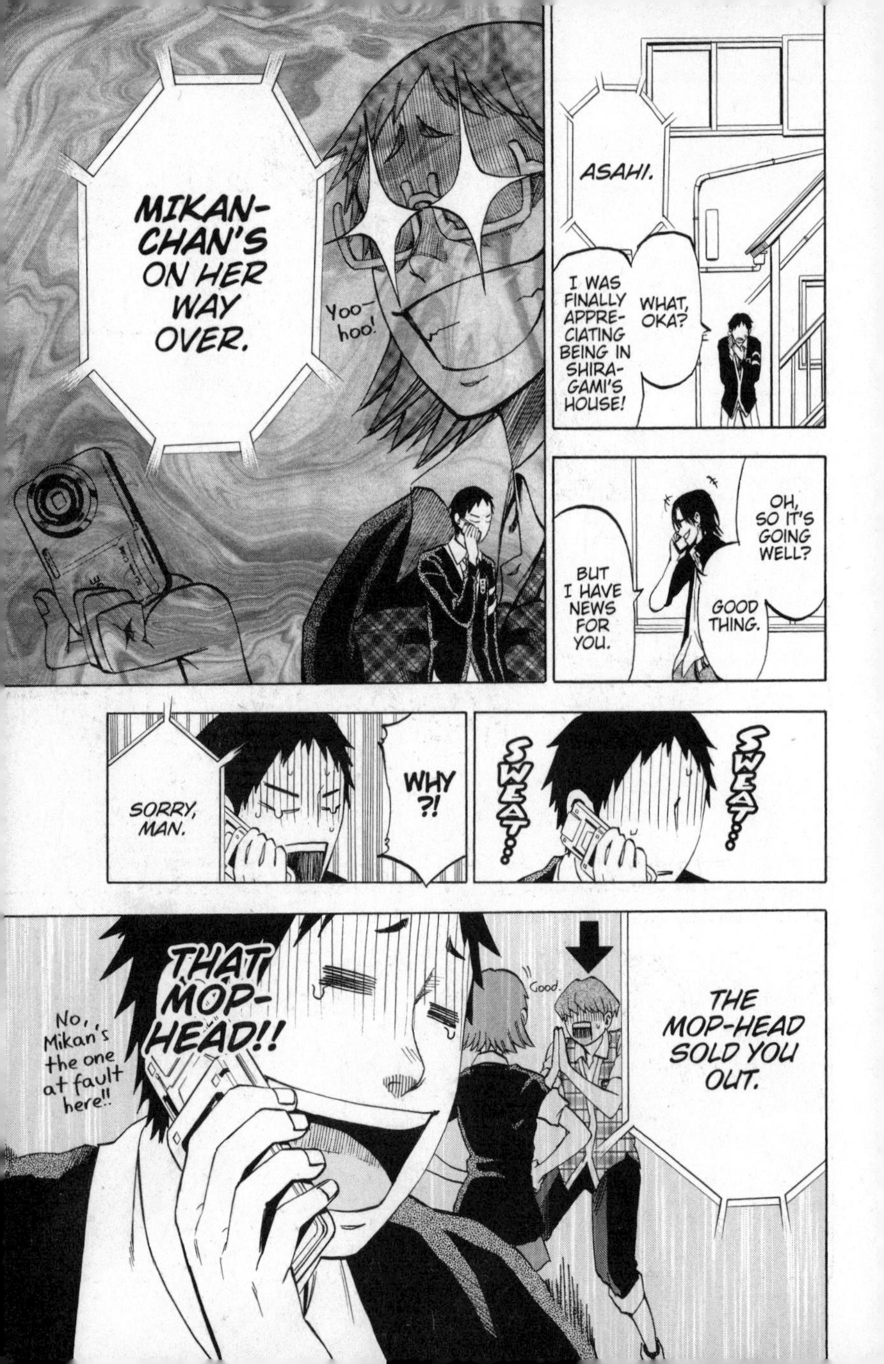
ASAHI.
WHAT, OKA?
I WAS FINALLY APPRECIATING BEING IN SHIRAGAMI'S HOUSE!
OH, SO IT'S GOING WELL?
GOOD THING.
BUT I HAVE NEWS FOR YOU.
MIKAN-CHAN'S ON HER WAY OVER.
Yoo-hoo!
SWEAT...
SWEAT...
WHY?!
SORRY, MAN.
THE MOP-HEAD SOLD YOU OUT.
Good.
THAT MOP-HEAD!!
No, Mikan's the one at fault here!!

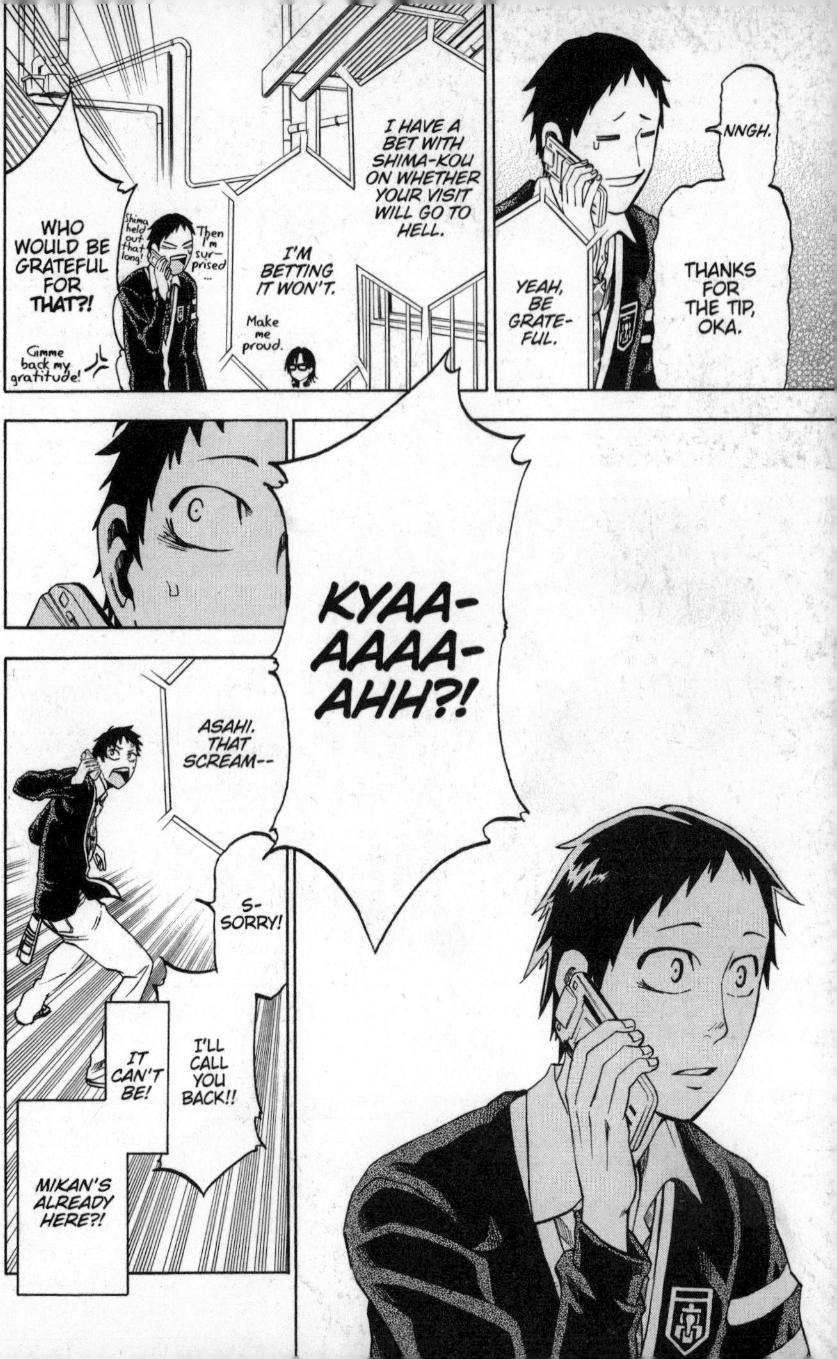
NNGH.
THANKS FOR THE TIP, OKA.
YEAH, BE GRATE-FUL.
I HAVE A BET WITH SHIMA-KOU ON WHETHER YOUR VISIT WILL GO TO HELL.
I'M BETTING IT WON'T.
Make me proud.
WHO WOULD BE GRATEFUL FOR THAT?!
Then I'm sur-prised...
Shima held out that long!
Gimme back my gratitude!
KYAA-AAAA-AHH?!
ASAHI. THAT SCREAM--
S-SORRY!
I'LL CALL YOU BACK!!
IT CAN'T BE!
MIKAN'S ALREADY HERE?!

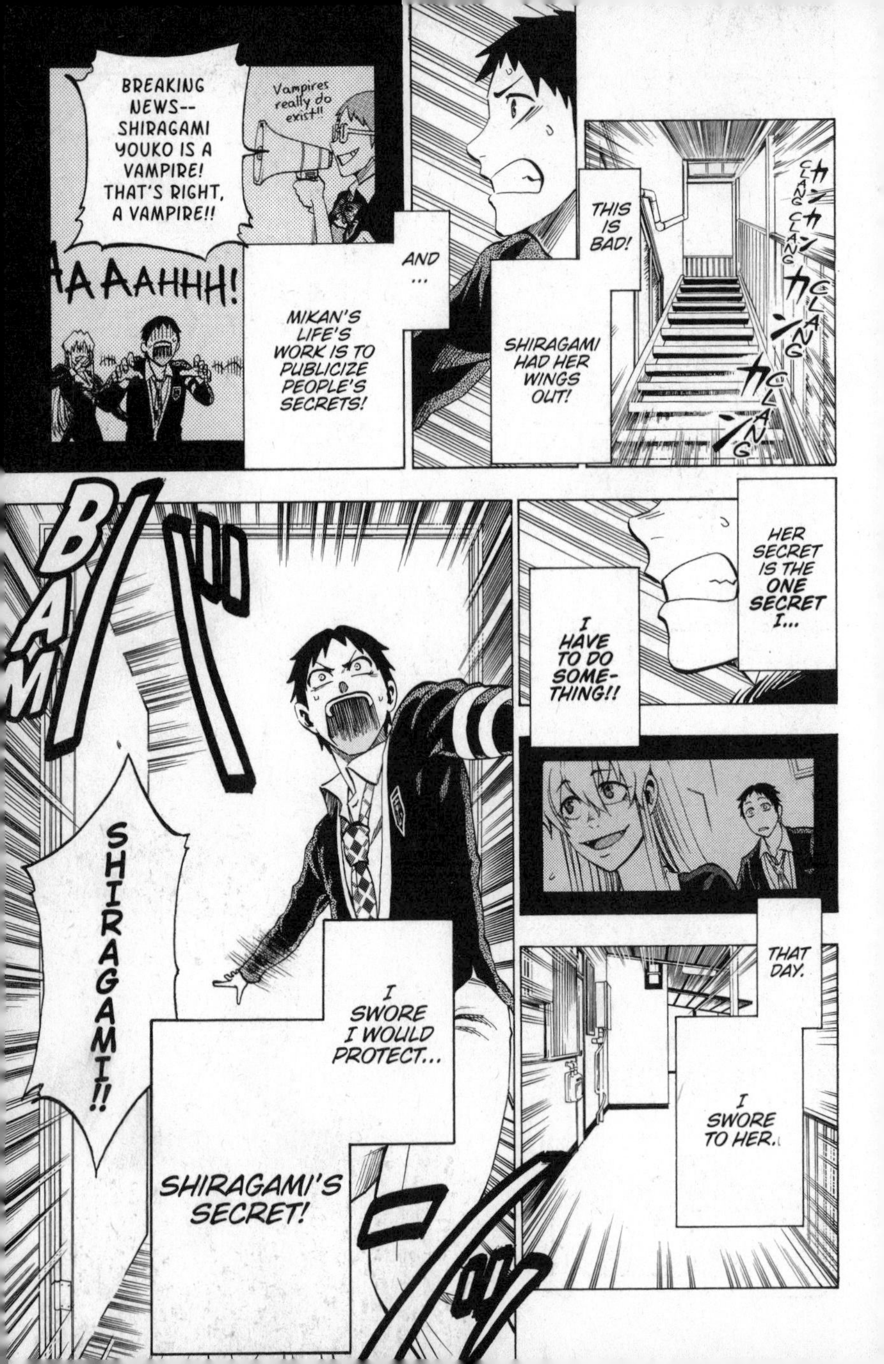
CLANG CLANG CLANG CLANG
THIS IS BAD!
SHIRAGAMI HAD HER WINGS OUT!
AND ...
MIKAN'S LIFE'S WORK IS TO PUBLICIZE PEOPLE'S SECRETS!
BREAKING NEWS-- SHIRAGAMI YOUKO IS A VAMPIRE! THAT'S RIGHT, A VAMPIRE!!
Vampires really do exist!!
AAAAHHH!
HER SECRET IS THE ONE SECRET I...
I HAVE TO DO SOME-THING!!
THAT DAY.
I SWORE TO HER.
BAM
I SWORE I WOULD PROTECT...
SHIRAGAMI'S SECRET!
SHIRAGAMI!!

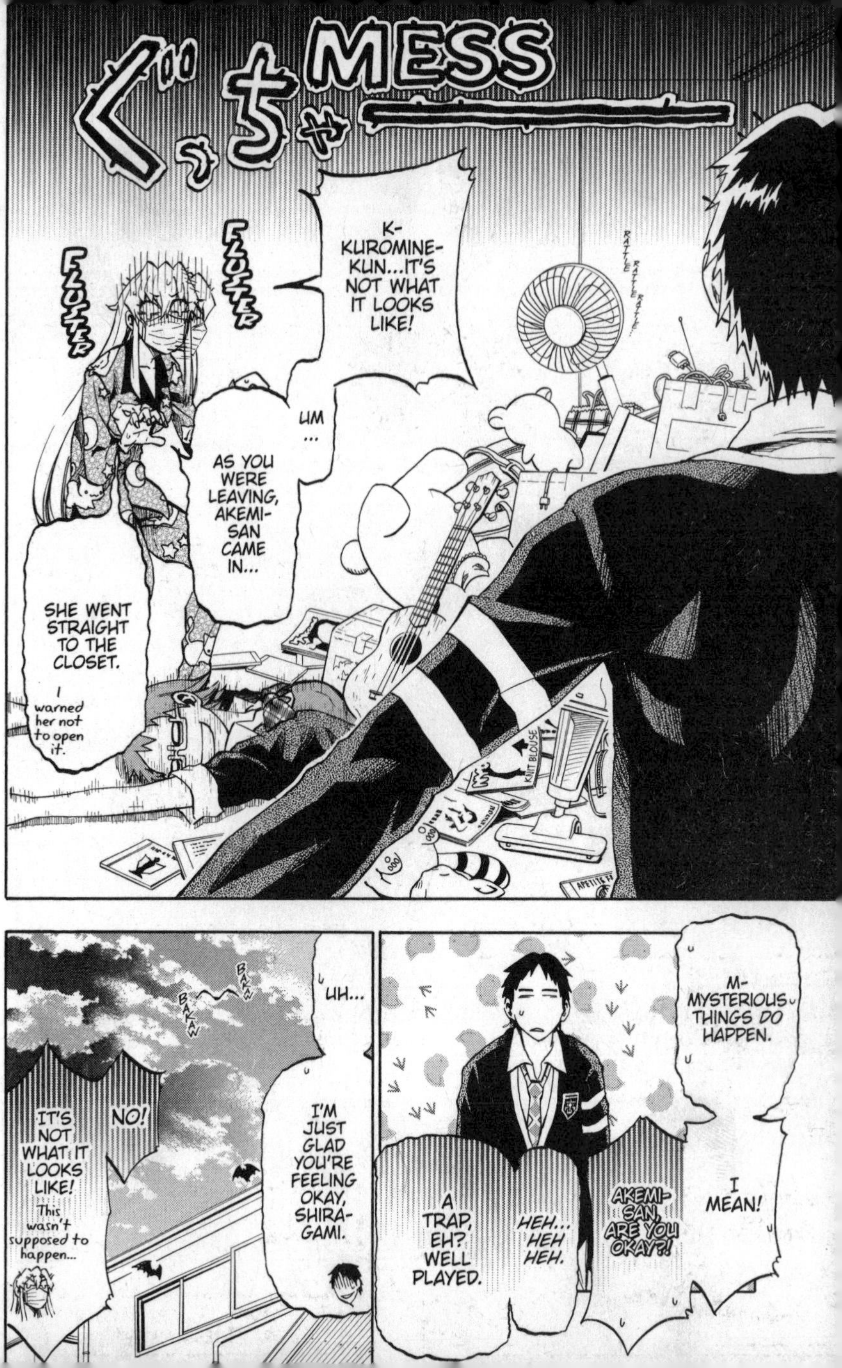
MESS
RATTLE RATTLE RATTLE...
K-KUROMINE-KUN...IT'S NOT WHAT IT LOOKS LIKE!
FLUTTER FLUTTER
UM...
AS YOU WERE LEAVING, AKEMI-SAN CAME IN...
SHE WENT STRAIGHT TO THE CLOSET.
I warned her not to open it.
M-MYSTERIOUS THINGS DO HAPPEN.
I MEAN!
AKEMI-SAN, ARE YOU OKAY?!
HEH... HEH HEH.
A TRAP, EH? WELL PLAYED.
UH...
I'M JUST GLAD YOU'RE FEELING OKAY, SHIRA-GAMI.
BAKAW BAKAW
NO!
IT'S NOT WHAT IT LOOKS LIKE!
This wasn't supposed to happen...

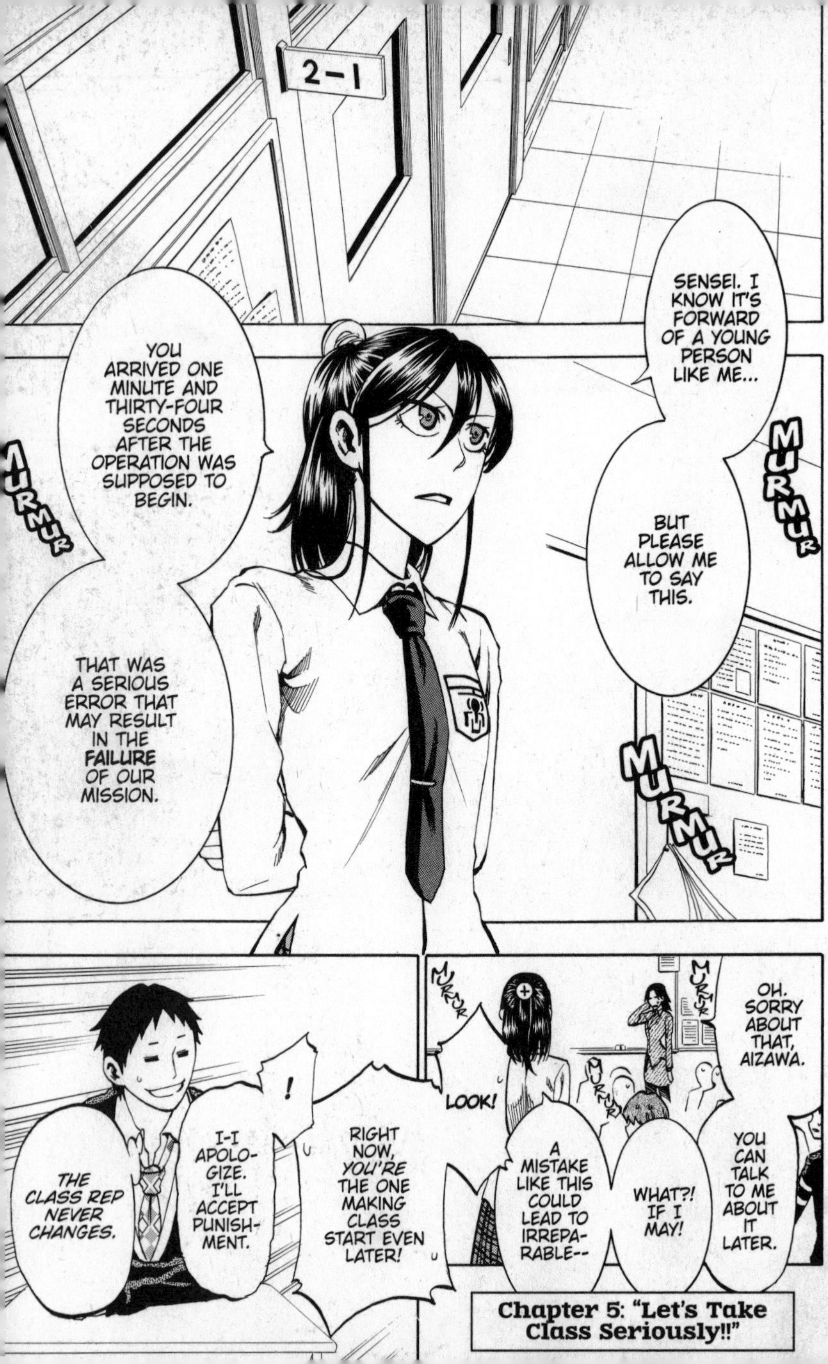
SENSEI. I KNOW IT'S FORWARD OF A YOUNG PERSON LIKE ME...
BUT PLEASE ALLOW ME TO SAY THIS.
MURMUR
MURMUR
YOU ARRIVED ONE MINUTE AND THIRTY-FOUR SECONDS AFTER THE OPERATION WAS SUPPOSED TO BEGIN.
MURMUR
THAT WAS A SERIOUS ERROR THAT MAY RESULT IN THE **FAILURE** OF OUR MISSION.
OH. SORRY ABOUT THAT, AIZAWA.
MURMUR
YOU CAN TALK TO ME ABOUT IT LATER.
WHAT?! IF I MAY!
MURMUR
MURMUR
A MISTAKE LIKE THIS COULD LEAD TO IRREPARABLE--
LOOK!
RIGHT NOW, *YOU'RE* THE ONE MAKING CLASS START EVEN LATER!
!
I-I APOLOGIZE. I'LL ACCEPT PUNISHMENT.
THE CLASS REP NEVER CHANGES.

Chapter 5: "Let's Take Class Seriously!!"

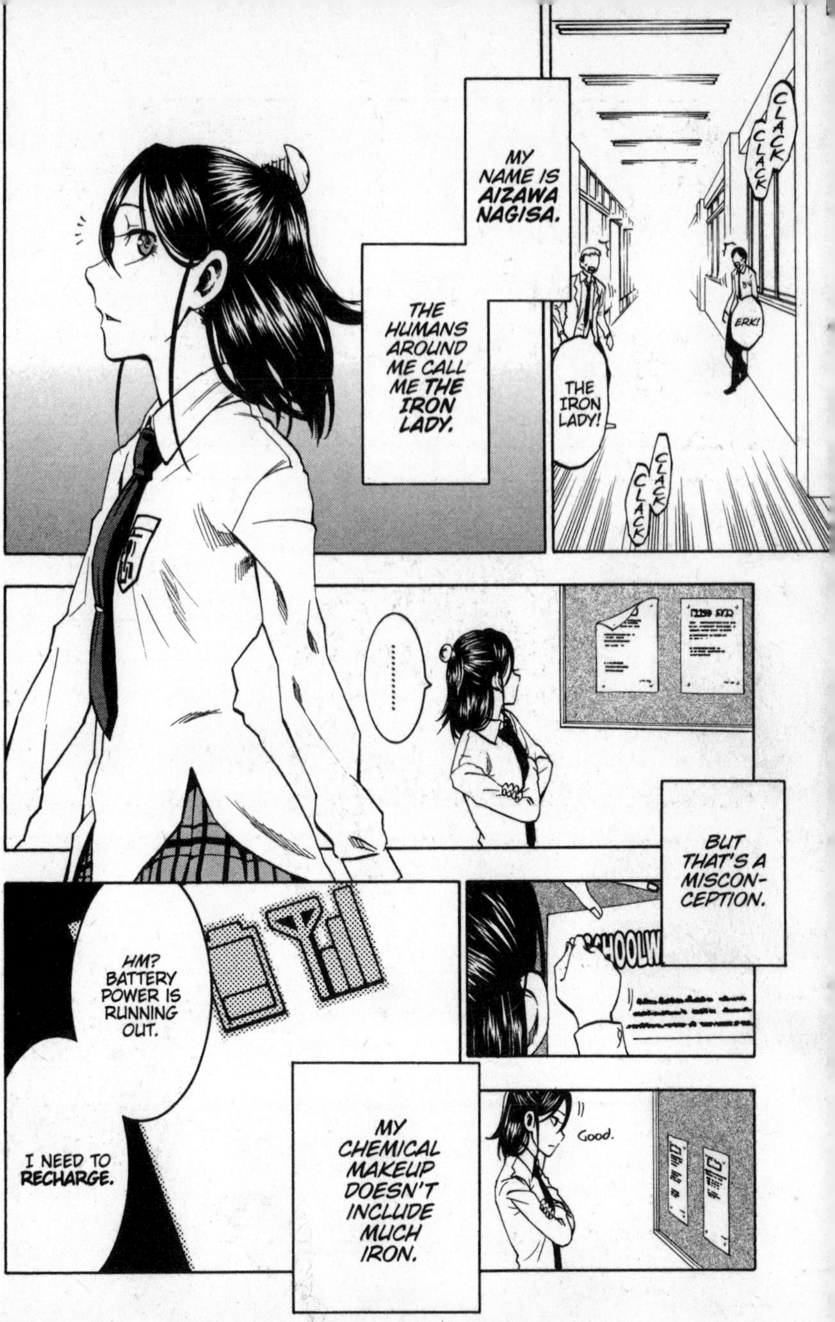
CLACK CLACK
ERK!
THE IRON LADY!
CLACK CLACK
MY NAME IS AIZAWA NAGISA.
THE HUMANS AROUND ME CALL ME THE IRON LADY.
......
BUT THAT'S A MISCONCEPTION.
SCHOOLW
HM? BATTERY POWER IS RUNNING OUT.
Good.
MY CHEMICAL MAKEUP DOESN'T INCLUDE MUCH IRON.
I NEED TO RECHARGE.

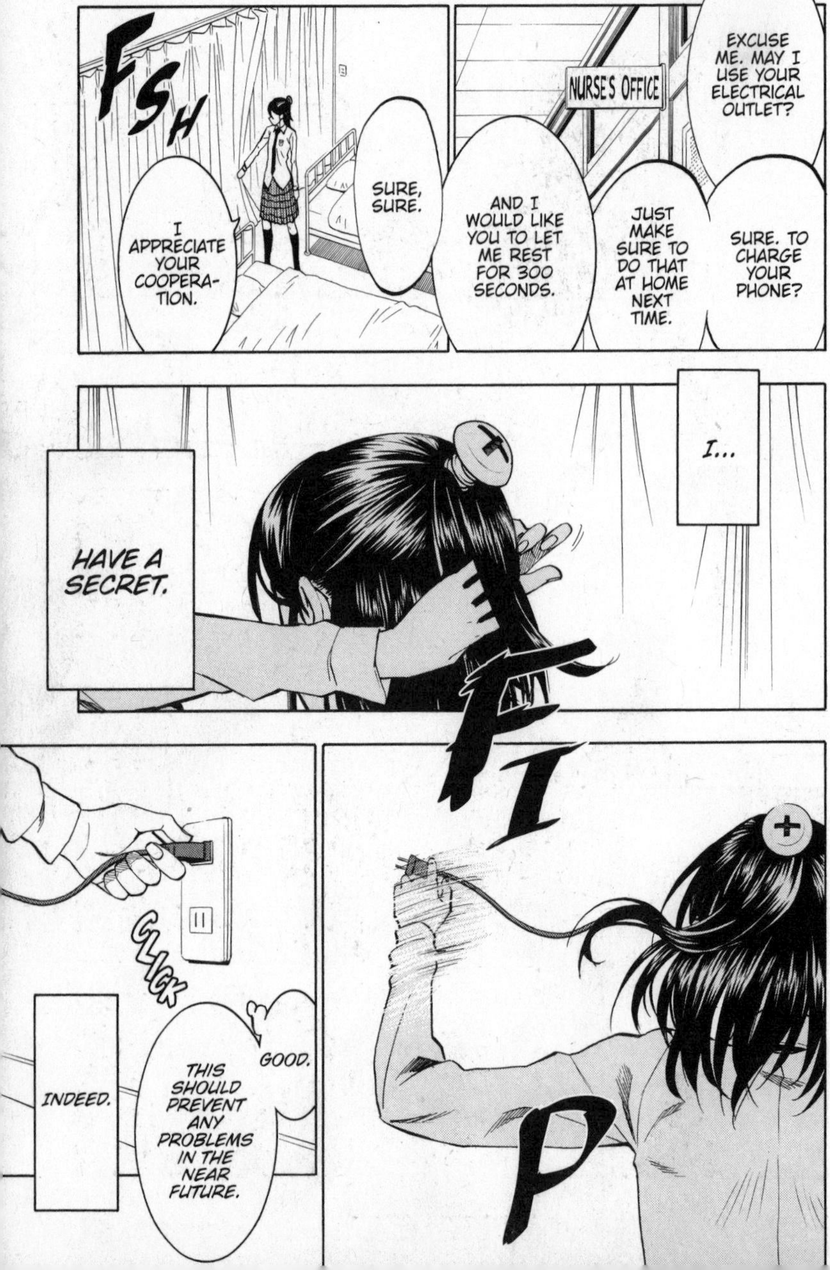
EXCUSE ME. MAY I USE YOUR ELECTRICAL OUTLET?
NURSE'S OFFICE
SURE. TO CHARGE YOUR PHONE?
JUST MAKE SURE TO DO THAT AT HOME NEXT TIME.
AND I WOULD LIKE YOU TO LET ME REST FOR 300 SECONDS.
SURE, SURE.
FSH
I APPRECIATE YOUR COOPERA-TION.
I...
HAVE A SECRET.
FTIP
CLICK
GOOD.
THIS SHOULD PREVENT ANY PROBLEMS IN THE NEAR FUTURE.
INDEED.

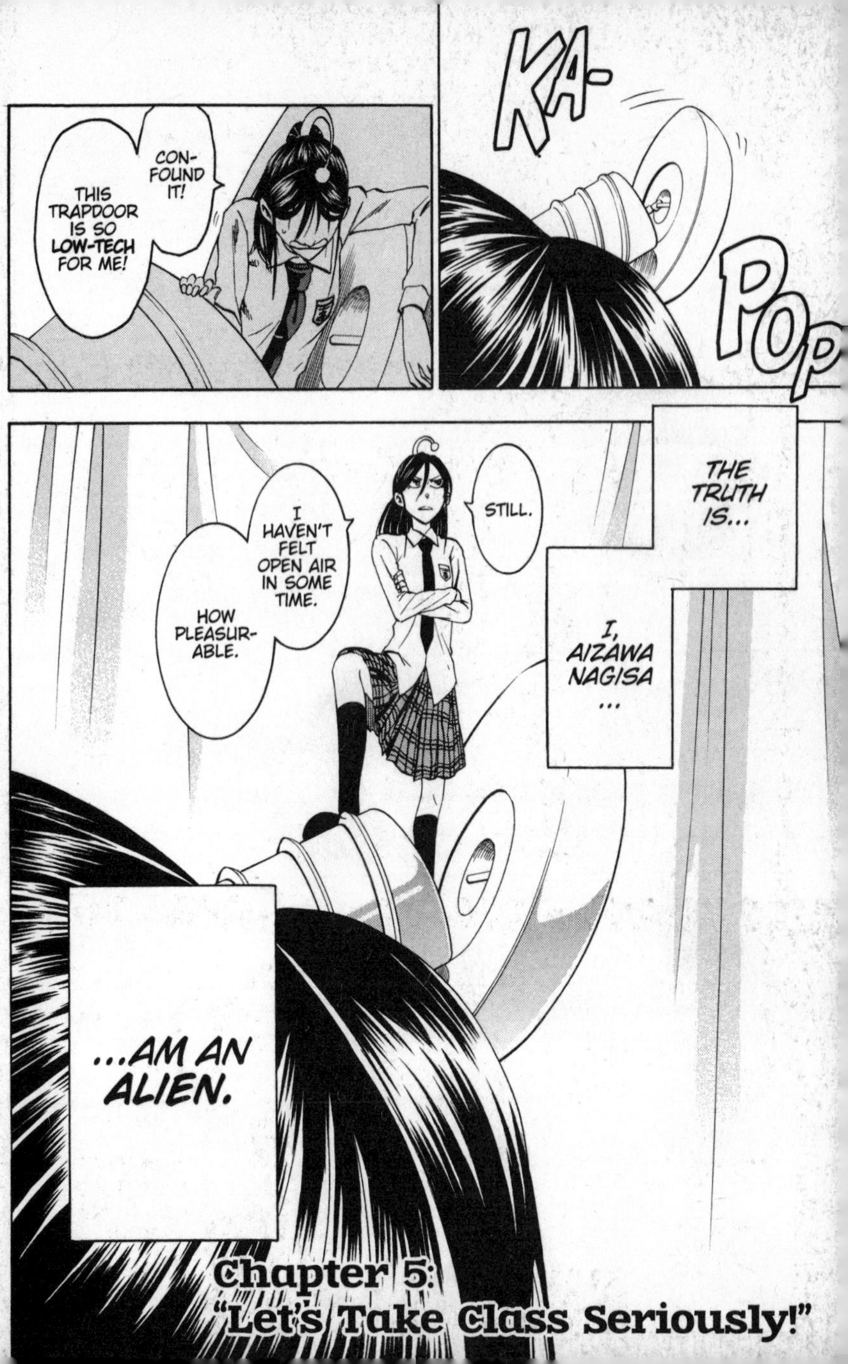
KA-POP
CON-FOUND IT!
THIS TRAPDOOR IS SO LOW-TECH FOR ME!
THE TRUTH IS...
STILL.
I HAVEN'T FELT OPEN AIR IN SOME TIME.
HOW PLEASUR-ABLE.
I, AIZAWA NAGISA ...
...AM AN ALIEN.

Chapter 5: "Let's Take Class Seriously!"

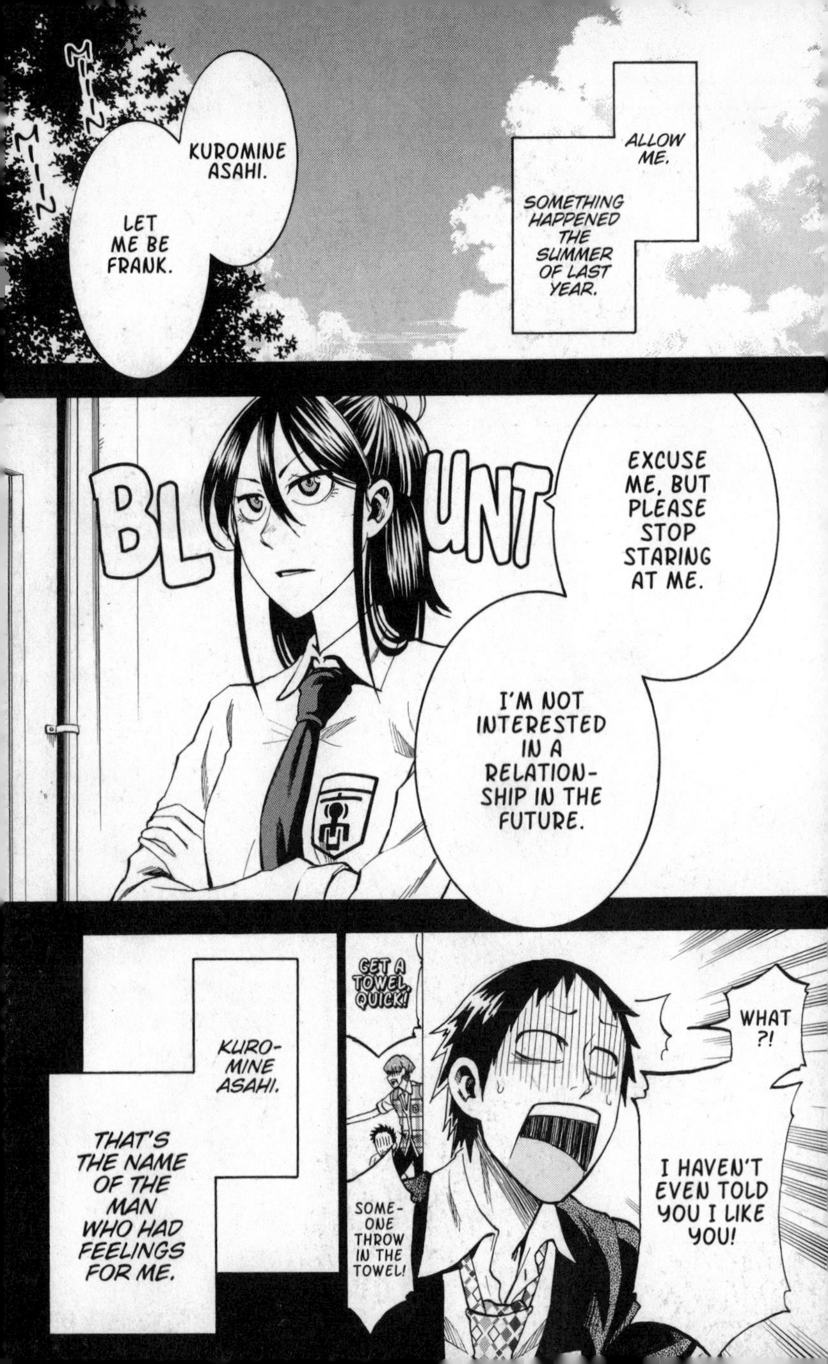
ALLOW ME.
SOMETHING HAPPENED THE SUMMER OF LAST YEAR.
KUROMINE ASAHI.
LET ME BE FRANK.
M-I-I-N M-I-I-N
EXCUSE ME, BUT PLEASE STOP STARING AT ME.
I'M NOT INTERESTED IN A RELATIONSHIP IN THE FUTURE.
BLUNT
WHAT ?!
I HAVEN'T EVEN TOLD YOU I LIKE YOU!
GET A TOWEL, QUICK!
SOME-ONE THROW IN THE TOWEL!
KURO-MINE ASAHI.
THAT'S THE NAME OF THE MAN WHO HAD FEELINGS FOR ME.

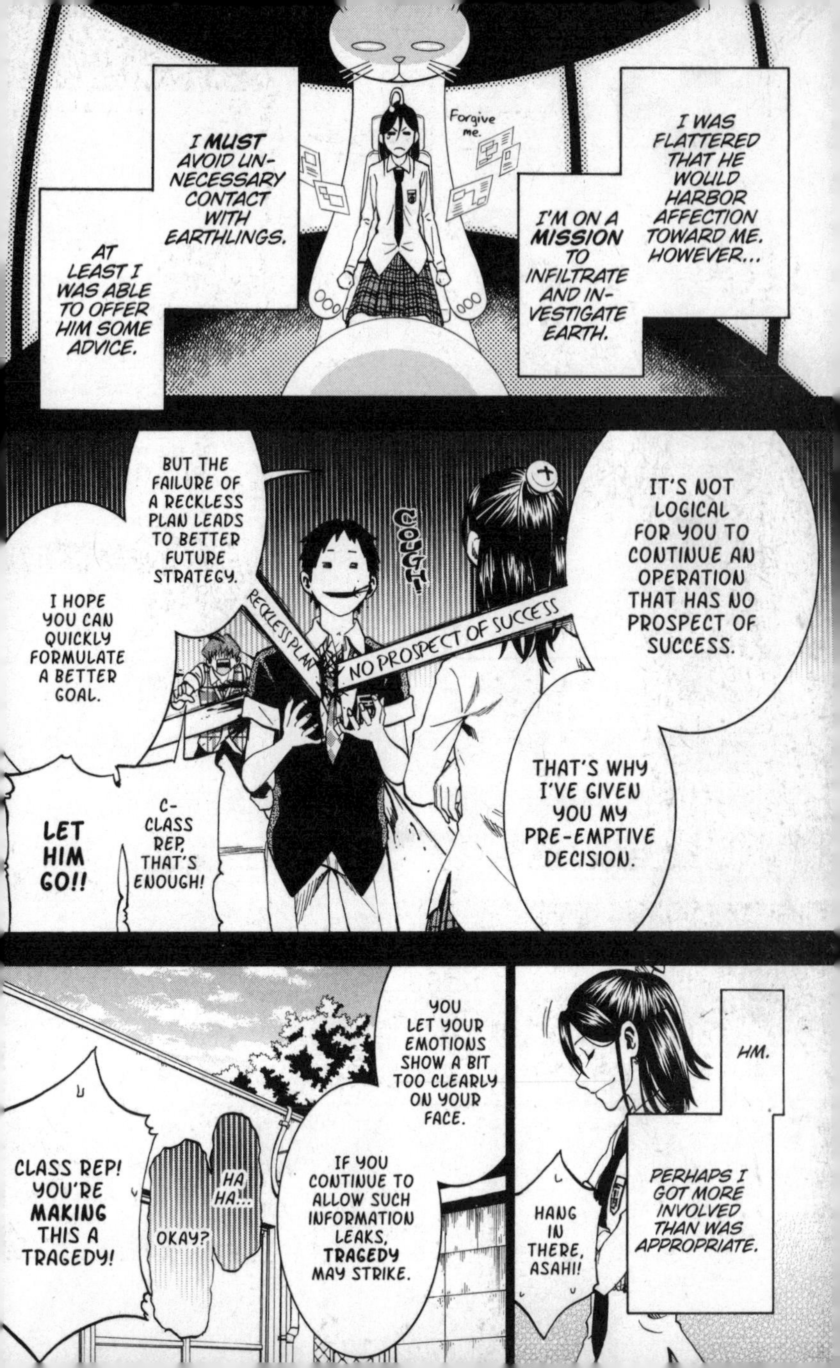
I WAS FLATTERED THAT HE WOULD HARBOR AFFECTION TOWARD ME. HOWEVER...
I'M ON A MISSION TO INFILTRATE AND INVESTIGATE EARTH.
Forgive me.
I MUST AVOID UNNECESSARY CONTACT WITH EARTHLINGS.
AT LEAST I WAS ABLE TO OFFER HIM SOME ADVICE.
IT'S NOT LOGICAL FOR YOU TO CONTINUE AN OPERATION THAT HAS NO PROSPECT OF SUCCESS.
NO PROSPECT OF SUCCESS
COUGH!
RECKLESS PLAN
BUT THE FAILURE OF A RECKLESS PLAN LEADS TO BETTER FUTURE STRATEGY.
I HOPE YOU CAN QUICKLY FORMULATE A BETTER GOAL.
THAT'S WHY I'VE GIVEN YOU MY PRE-EMPTIVE DECISION.
C-CLASS REP, THAT'S ENOUGH!
LET HIM GO!!
HM.
PERHAPS I GOT MORE INVOLVED THAN WAS APPROPRIATE.
HANG IN THERE, ASAHI!
YOU LET YOUR EMOTIONS SHOW A BIT TOO CLEARLY ON YOUR FACE.
IF YOU CONTINUE TO ALLOW SUCH INFORMATION LEAKS, TRAGEDY MAY STRIKE.
HA HA...
OKAY?
CLASS REP! YOU'RE MAKING THIS A TRAGEDY!

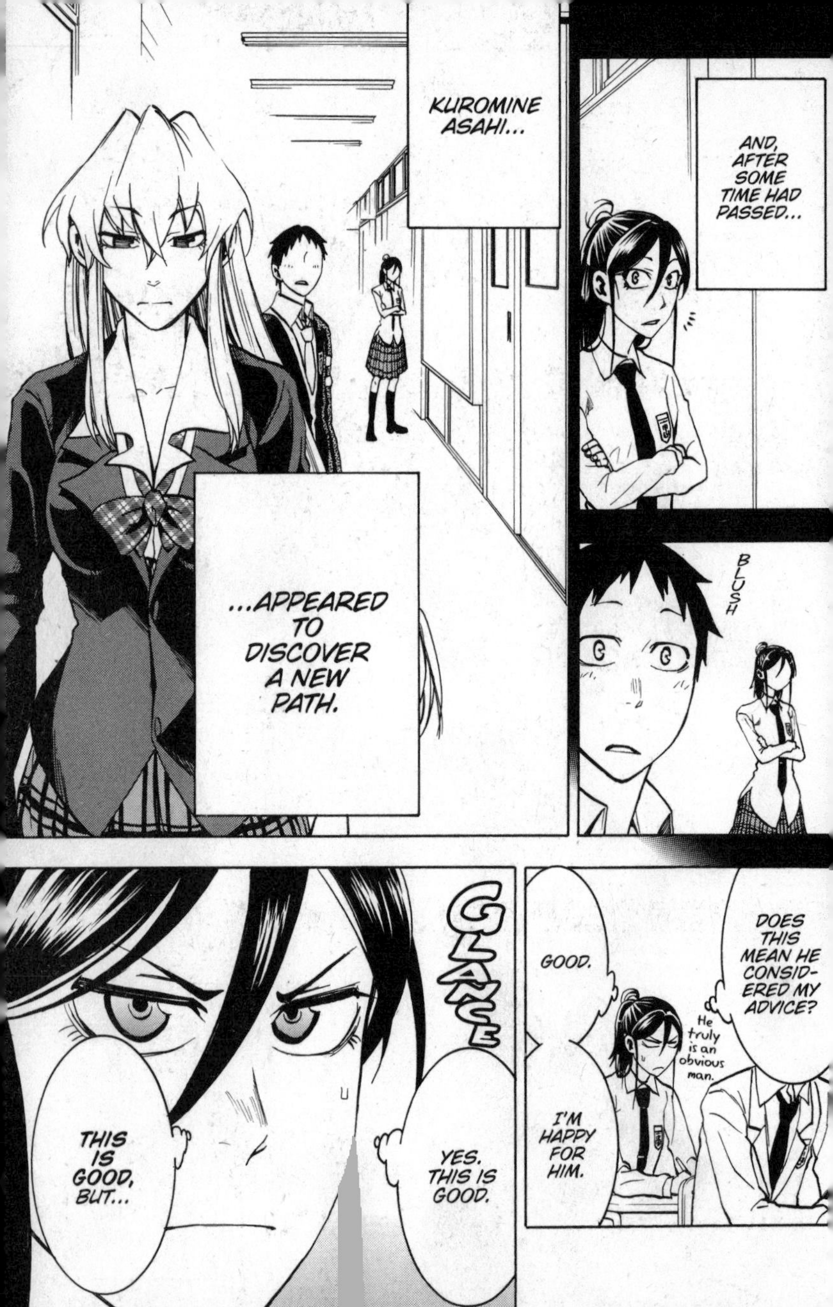
AND, AFTER SOME TIME HAD PASSED...
BLUSH
KUROMINE ASAHI...
...APPEARED TO DISCOVER A NEW PATH.
DOES THIS MEAN HE CONSID-ERED MY ADVICE?
GOOD.
He truly is an obvious man.
I'M HAPPY FOR HIM.
GLANCE
YES. THIS IS GOOD.
THIS IS GOOD, BUT...

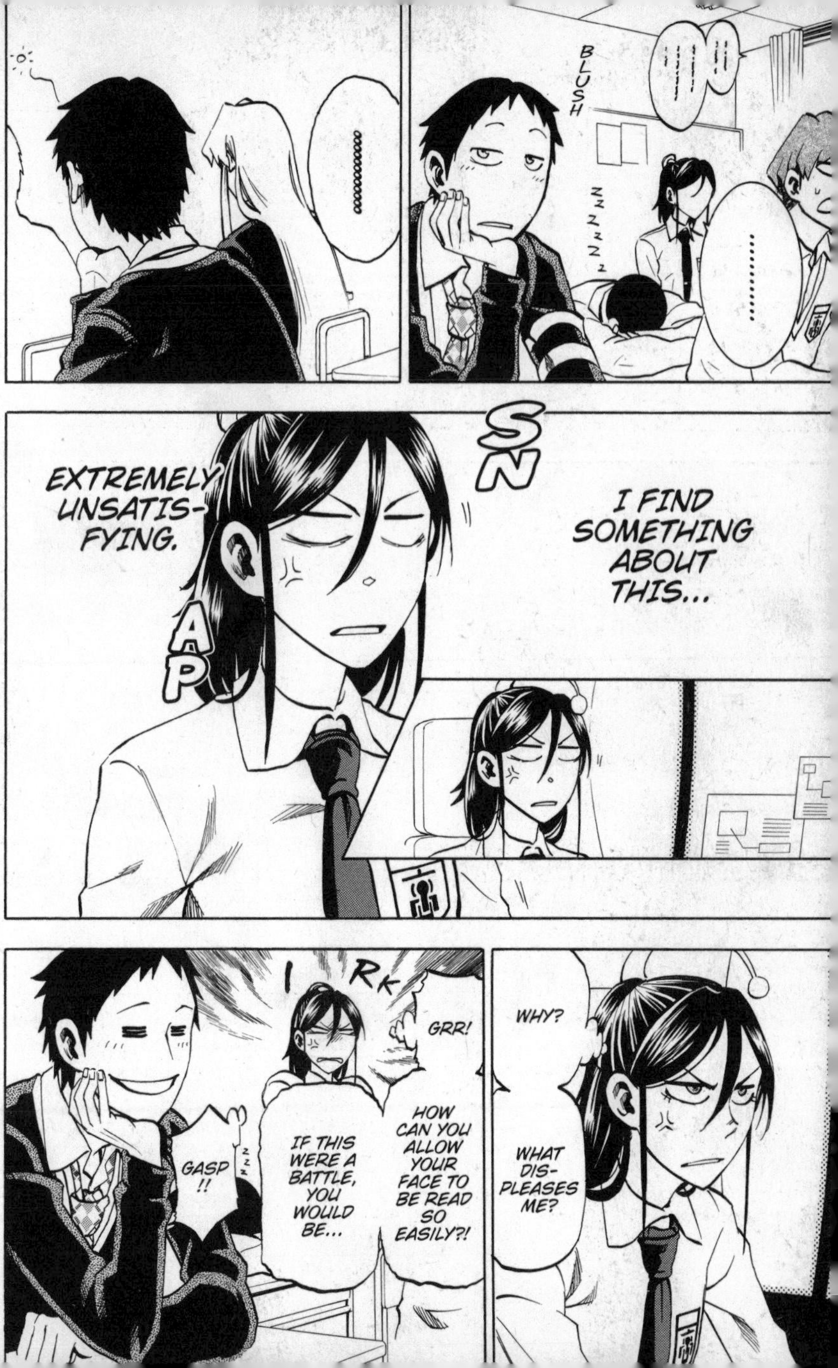
....
ZZZZZZ
BLUSH
......!!
.......!!
....
SN
I FIND SOMETHING ABOUT THIS...
EXTREMELY UNSATIS-FYING.
AP
WHY?
WHAT DIS-PLEASES ME?
GRR!
IRK
HOW CAN YOU ALLOW YOUR FACE TO BE READ SO EASILY?!
IF THIS WERE A BATTLE, YOU WOULD BE...
ZZZ
GASP !!

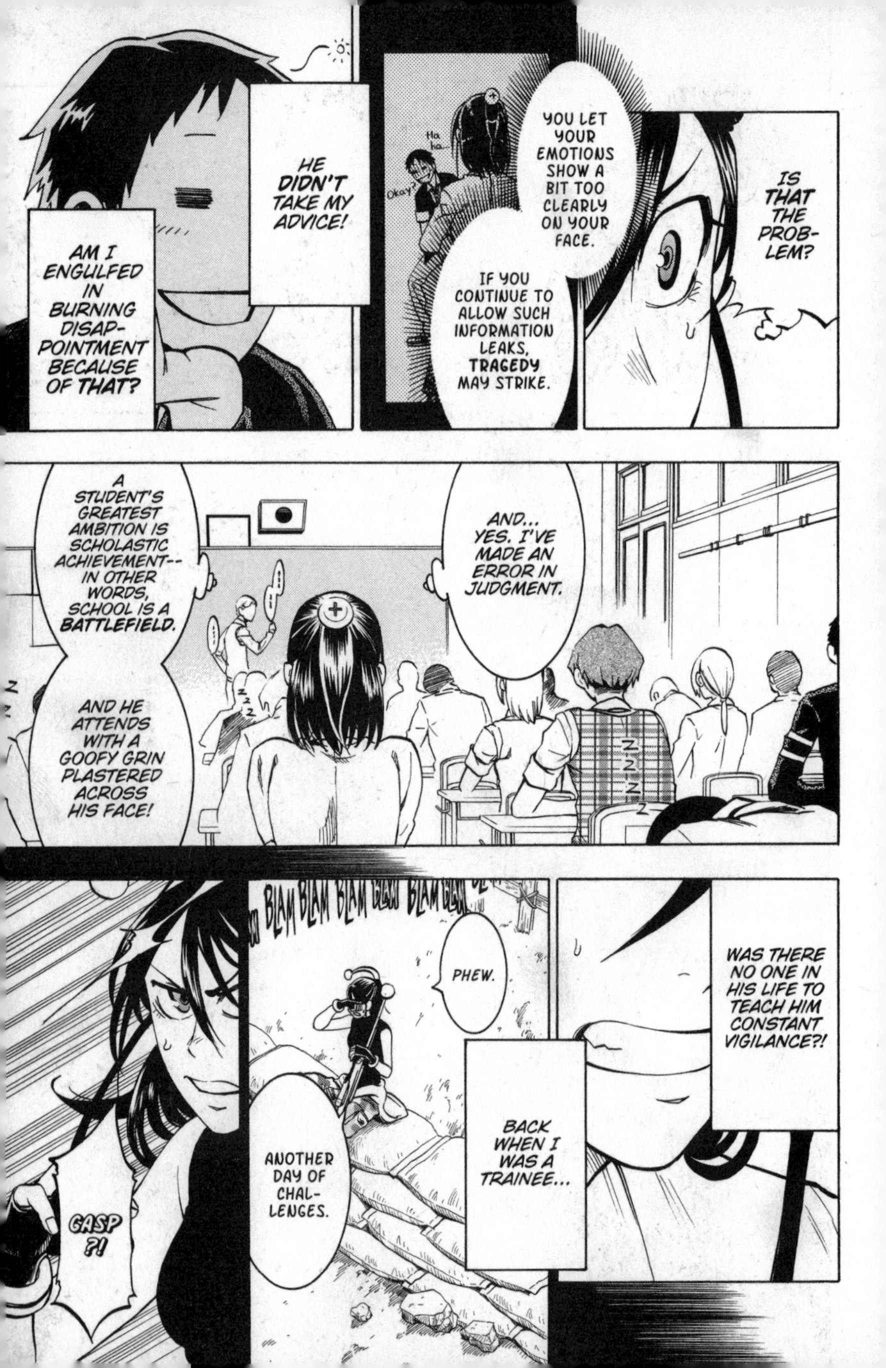
IS THAT THE PROB-LEM?
YOU LET YOUR EMOTIONS SHOW A BIT TOO CLEARLY ON YOUR FACE.
IF YOU CONTINUE TO ALLOW SUCH INFORMATION LEAKS, TRAGEDY MAY STRIKE.
Ha ha...
Okay?
HE DIDN'T TAKE MY ADVICE!
AM I ENGULFED IN BURNING DISAP-POINTMENT BECAUSE OF THAT?
AND... YES. I'VE MADE AN ERROR IN JUDGMENT.
A STUDENT'S GREATEST AMBITION IS SCHOLASTIC ACHIEVEMENT-- IN OTHER WORDS, SCHOOL IS A BATTLEFIELD.
AND HE ATTENDS WITH A GOOFY GRIN PLASTERED ACROSS HIS FACE!
WAS THERE NO ONE IN HIS LIFE TO TEACH HIM CONSTANT VIGILANCE?!
BACK WHEN I WAS A TRAINEE...
BLAM BLAM BLAM BLAM BLAM
PHEW.
ANOTHER DAY OF CHAL-LENGES.
GASP ?!

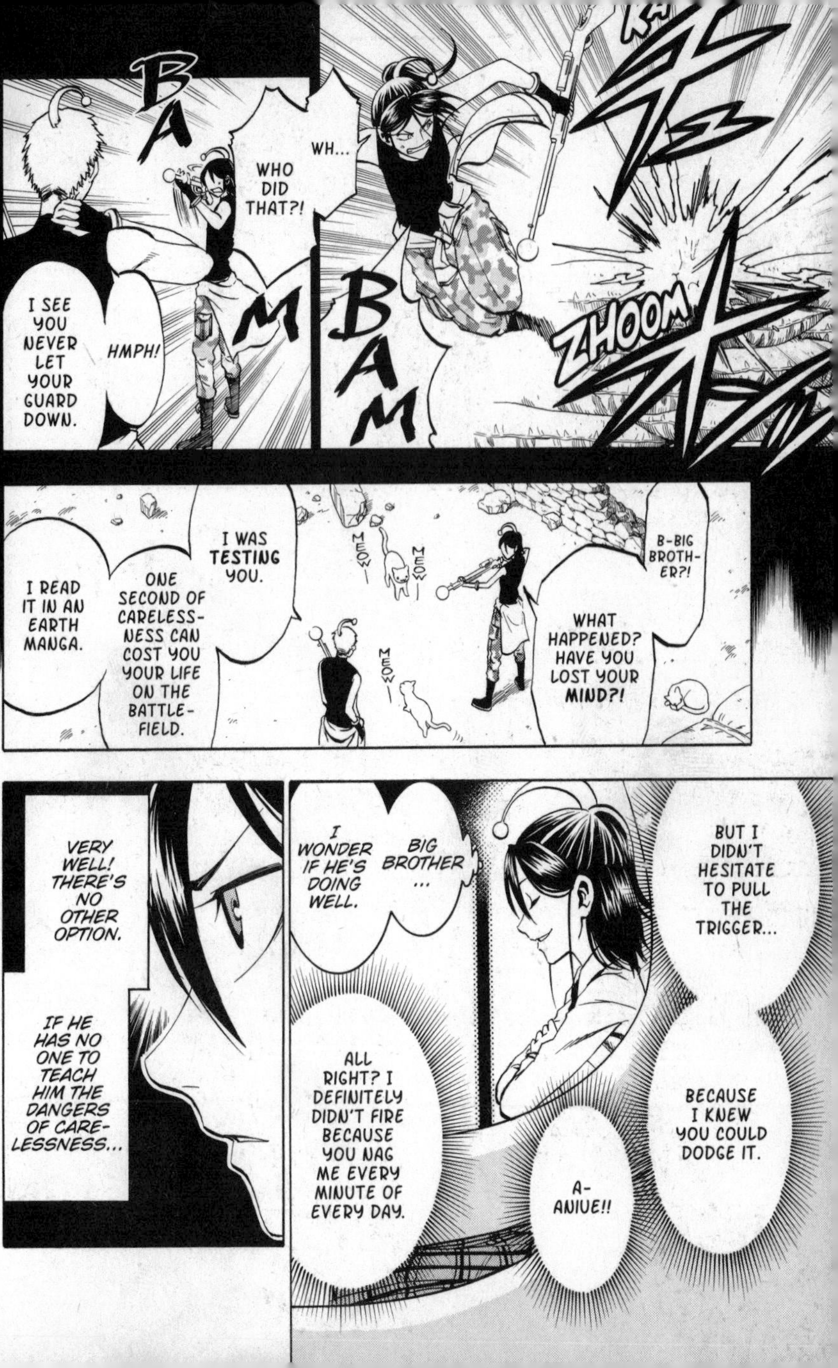
ZHOOM
BAM
WH...
WHO DID THAT?!
BAM
HMPH!
I SEE YOU NEVER LET YOUR GUARD DOWN.
B-BIG BROTH-ER?!
WHAT HAPPENED? HAVE YOU LOST YOUR MIND?!
MEOW
MEOW
MEOW
I WAS TESTING YOU.
ONE SECOND OF CARELESS-NESS CAN COST YOU YOUR LIFE ON THE BATTLE-FIELD.
I READ IT IN AN EARTH MANGA.
BUT I DIDN'T HESITATE TO PULL THE TRIGGER...
BECAUSE I KNEW YOU COULD DODGE IT.
A-ANIUE!!
ALL RIGHT? I DEFINITELY DIDN'T FIRE BECAUSE YOU NAG ME EVERY MINUTE OF EVERY DAY.
BIG BROTHER...
I WONDER IF HE'S DOING WELL.
VERY WELL! THERE'S NO OTHER OPTION.
IF HE HAS NO ONE TO TEACH HIM THE DANGERS OF CARE-LESSNESS...

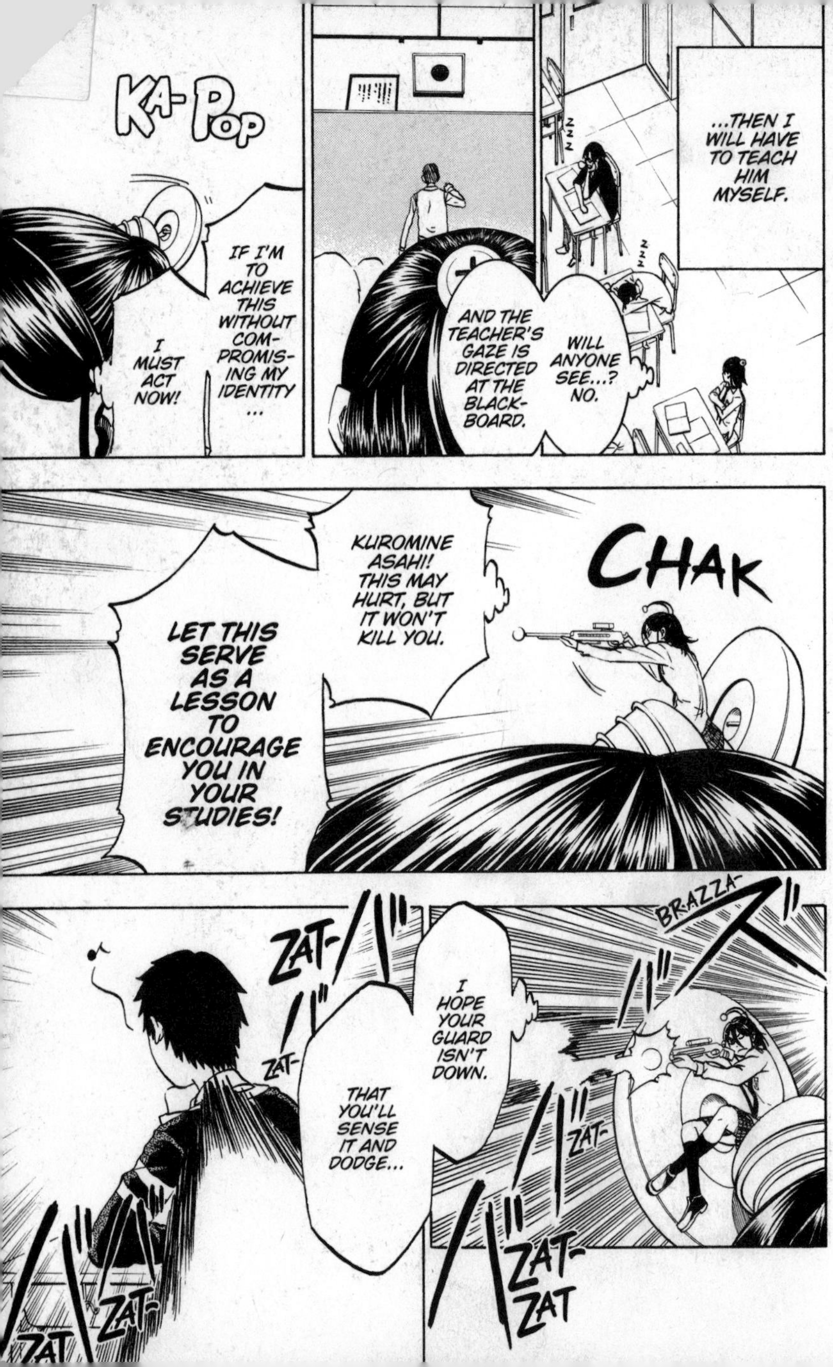
...THEN I WILL HAVE TO TEACH HIM MYSELF.
ZZZ
ZZZ
AND THE TEACHER'S GAZE IS DIRECTED AT THE BLACKBOARD.
WILL ANYONE SEE...? NO.
KA-POP
IF I'M TO ACHIEVE THIS WITHOUT COMPROMISING MY IDENTITY...
I MUST ACT NOW!
CHAK
KUROMINE ASAHI! THIS MAY HURT, BUT IT WON'T KILL YOU.
LET THIS SERVE AS A LESSON TO ENCOURAGE YOU IN YOUR STUDIES!
BRAZZA-
I HOPE YOUR GUARD ISN'T DOWN.
THAT YOU'LL SENSE IT AND DODGE...
ZAT-
ZAT-ZAT
ZAT-
ZAT-
ZAT-
ZAT

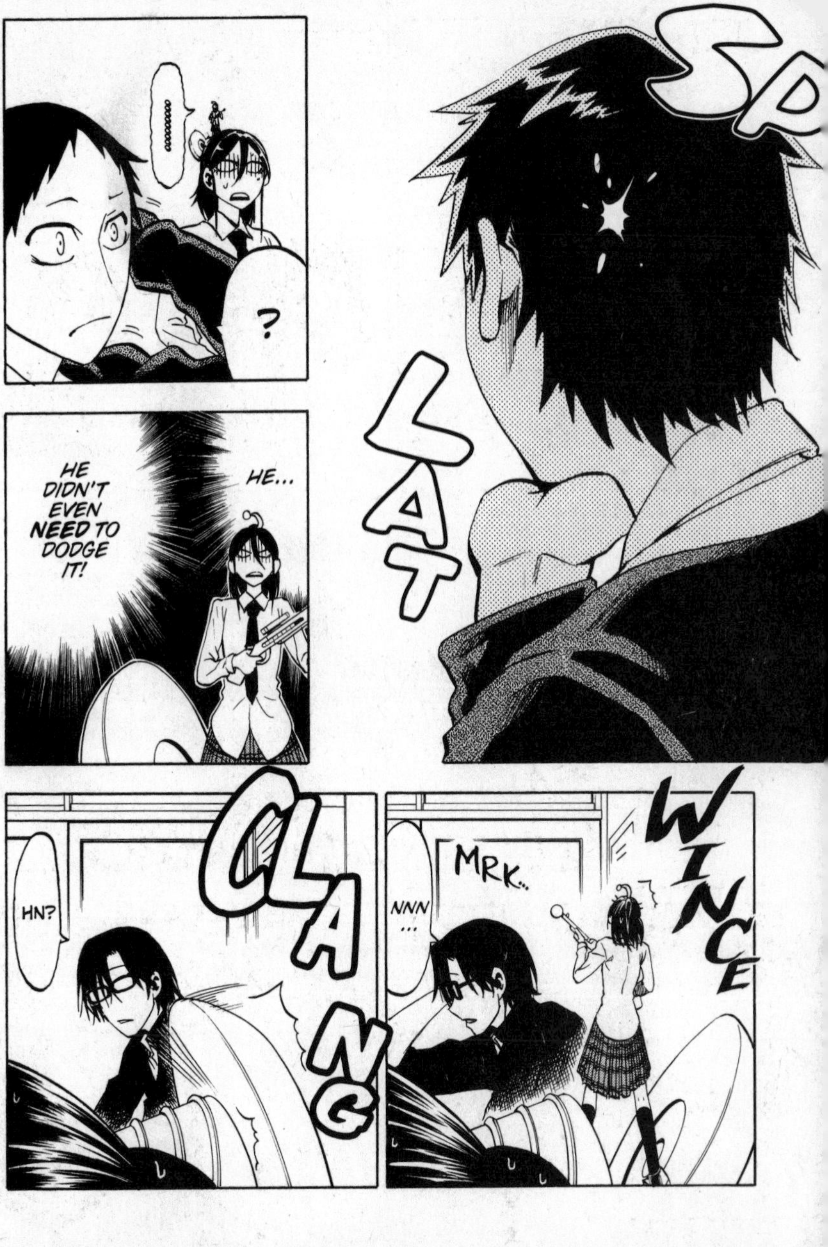
SPLAT
....
?
HE...
HE DIDN'T EVEN NEED TO DODGE IT!
WINCE
MRK...
NNN...
CLANG
HN?

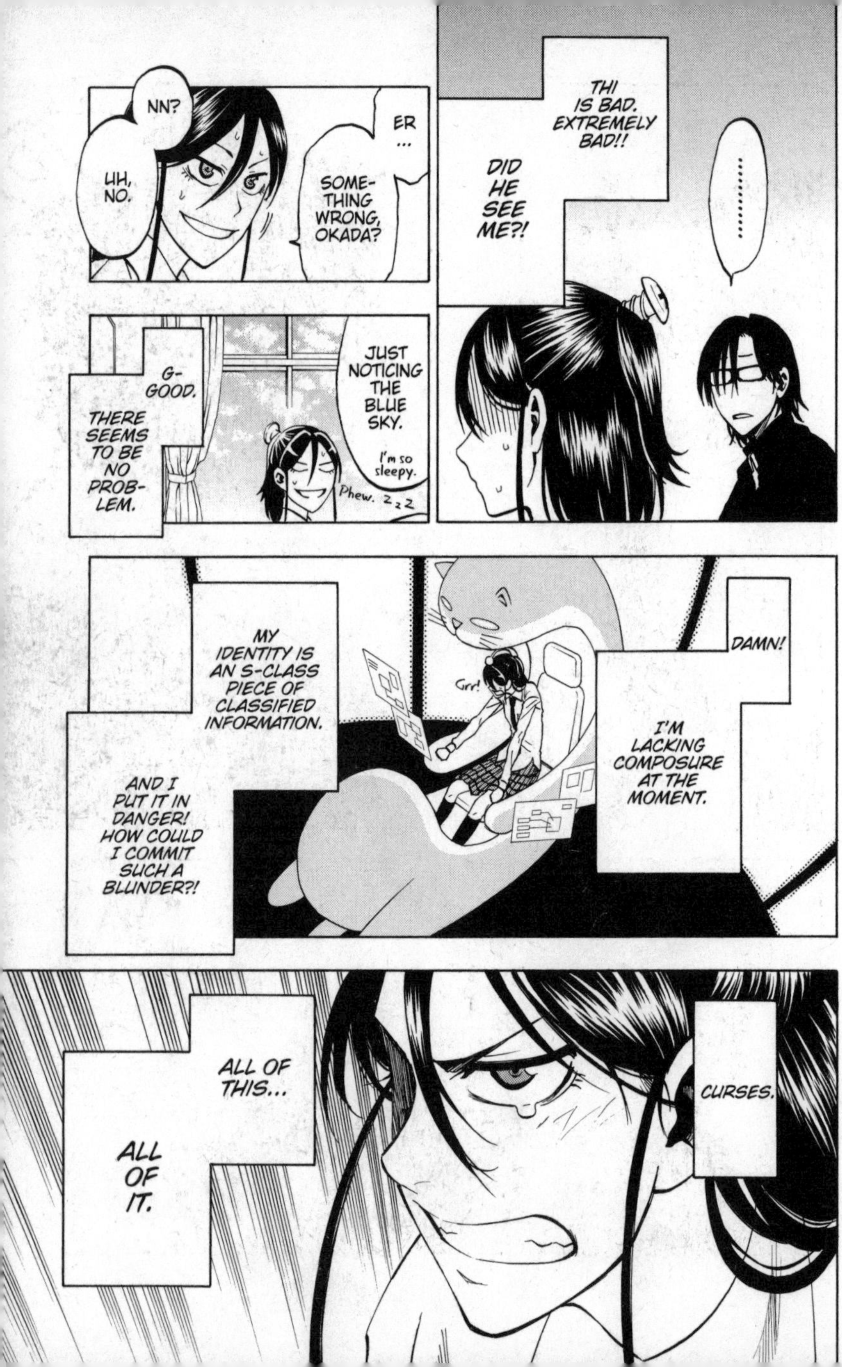
......
THI IS BAD. EXTREMELY BAD!!
DID HE SEE ME?!
ER ...
SOMETHING WRONG, OKADA?
NN?
UH, NO.
JUST NOTICING THE BLUE SKY.
I'm so sleepy.
Phew. zzz
G-GOOD.
THERE SEEMS TO BE NO PROBLEM.
DAMN!
I'M LACKING COMPOSURE AT THE MOMENT.
Grr!
MY IDENTITY IS AN S-CLASS PIECE OF CLASSIFIED INFORMATION.
AND I PUT IT IN DANGER! HOW COULD I COMMIT SUCH A BLUNDER?!
CURSES.
ALL OF THIS...
ALL OF IT.

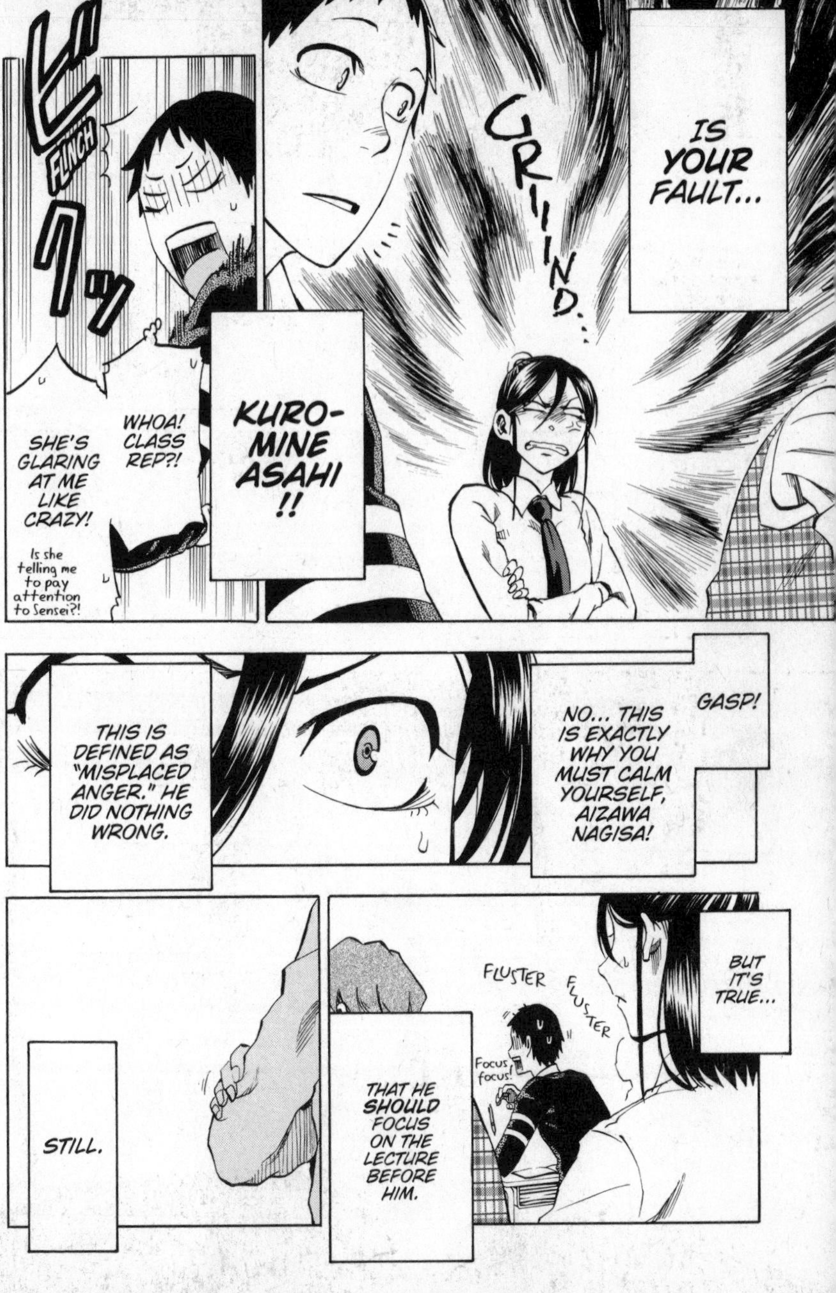
IS YOUR FAULT...
GRIIIND...
KURO-MINE ASAHI!!
FLINCH
WHOA! CLASS REP?!
SHE'S GLARING AT ME LIKE CRAZY!
Is she telling me to pay attention to Sensei?!
GASP!
NO... THIS IS EXACTLY WHY YOU MUST CALM YOURSELF, AIZAWA NAGISA!
THIS IS DEFINED AS "MISPLACED ANGER." HE DID NOTHING WRONG.
BUT IT'S TRUE...
FLUSTER
FLUSTER
Focus focus!
THAT HE SHOULD FOCUS ON THE LECTURE BEFORE HIM.
STILL.

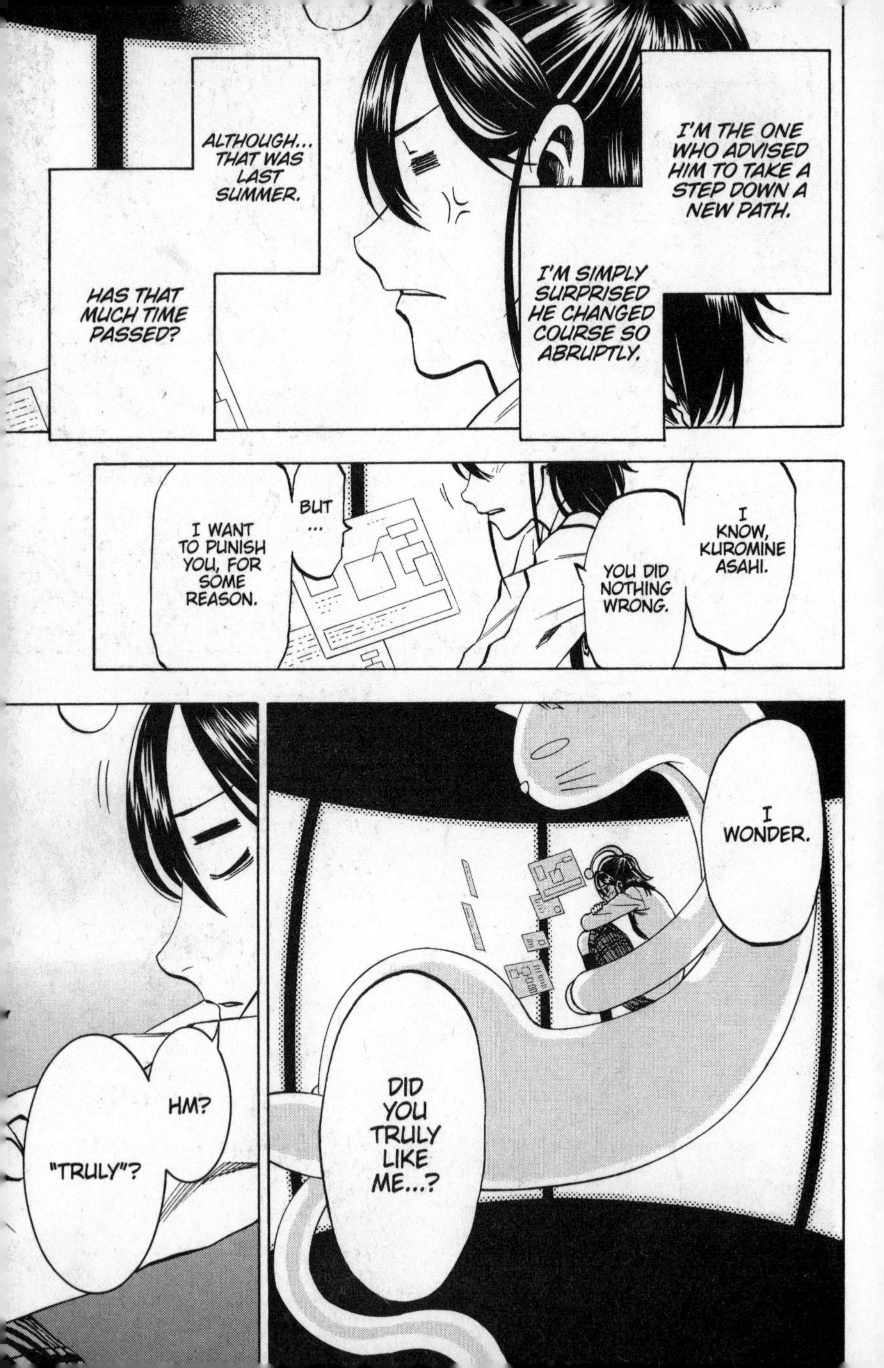
I'M THE ONE WHO ADVISED HIM TO TAKE A STEP DOWN A NEW PATH.
I'M SIMPLY SURPRISED HE CHANGED COURSE SO ABRUPTLY.
ALTHOUGH... THAT WAS LAST SUMMER.
HAS THAT MUCH TIME PASSED?
I KNOW, KUROMINE ASAHI.
YOU DID NOTHING WRONG.
BUT ...
I WANT TO PUNISH YOU, FOR SOME REASON.
I WONDER.
DID YOU TRULY LIKE ME...?
HM?
"TRULY"?

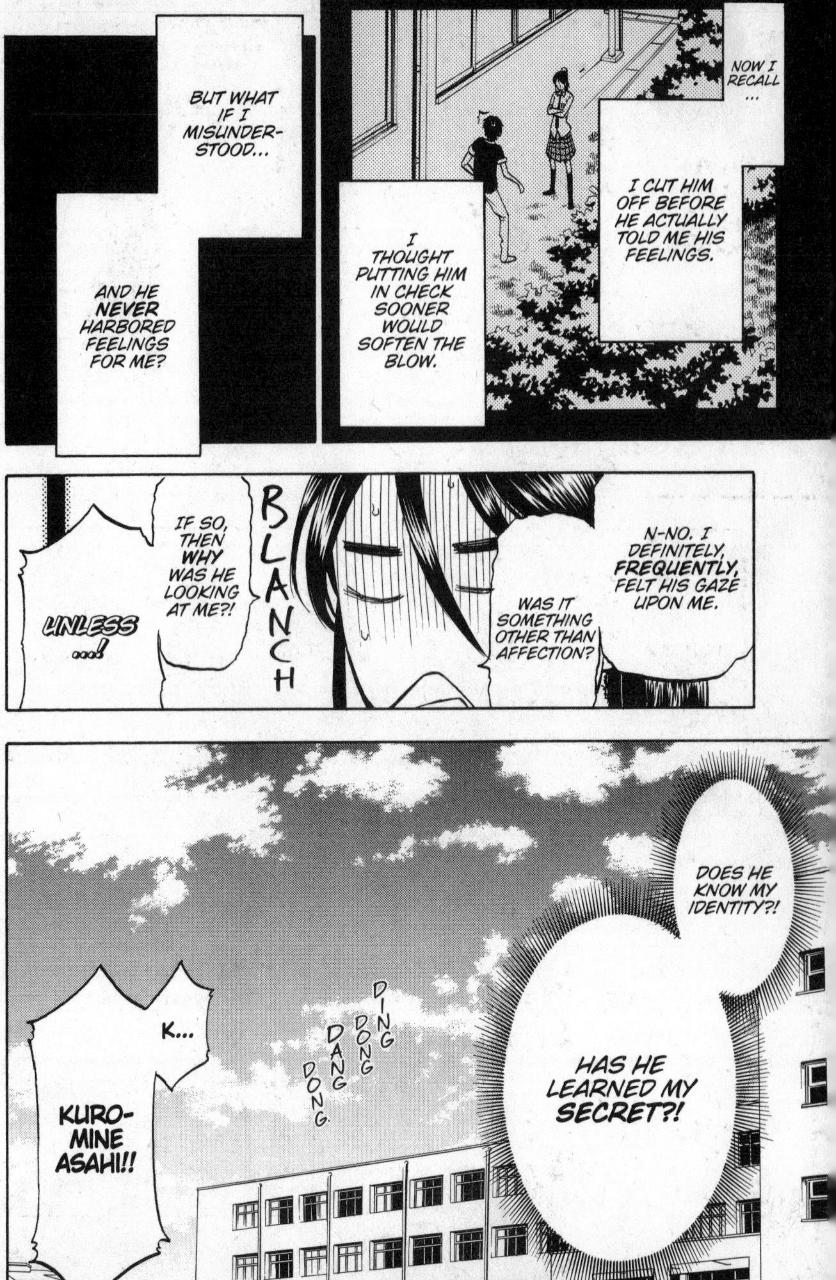
NOW I RECALL ...
I CUT HIM OFF BEFORE HE ACTUALLY TOLD ME HIS FEELINGS.
I THOUGHT PUTTING HIM IN CHECK SOONER WOULD SOFTEN THE BLOW.
BUT WHAT IF I MISUNDER-STOOD...
AND HE NEVER HARBORED FEELINGS FOR ME?
N-NO. I DEFINITELY, FREQUENTLY, FELT HIS GAZE UPON ME.
WAS IT SOMETHING OTHER THAN AFFECTION?
BLANCH
IF SO, THEN WHY WAS HE LOOKING AT ME?!
UNLESS ...!
DOES HE KNOW MY IDENTITY?!
HAS HE LEARNED MY SECRET?!
DING DONG DANG DONG
K...
KURO-MINE ASAHI!!

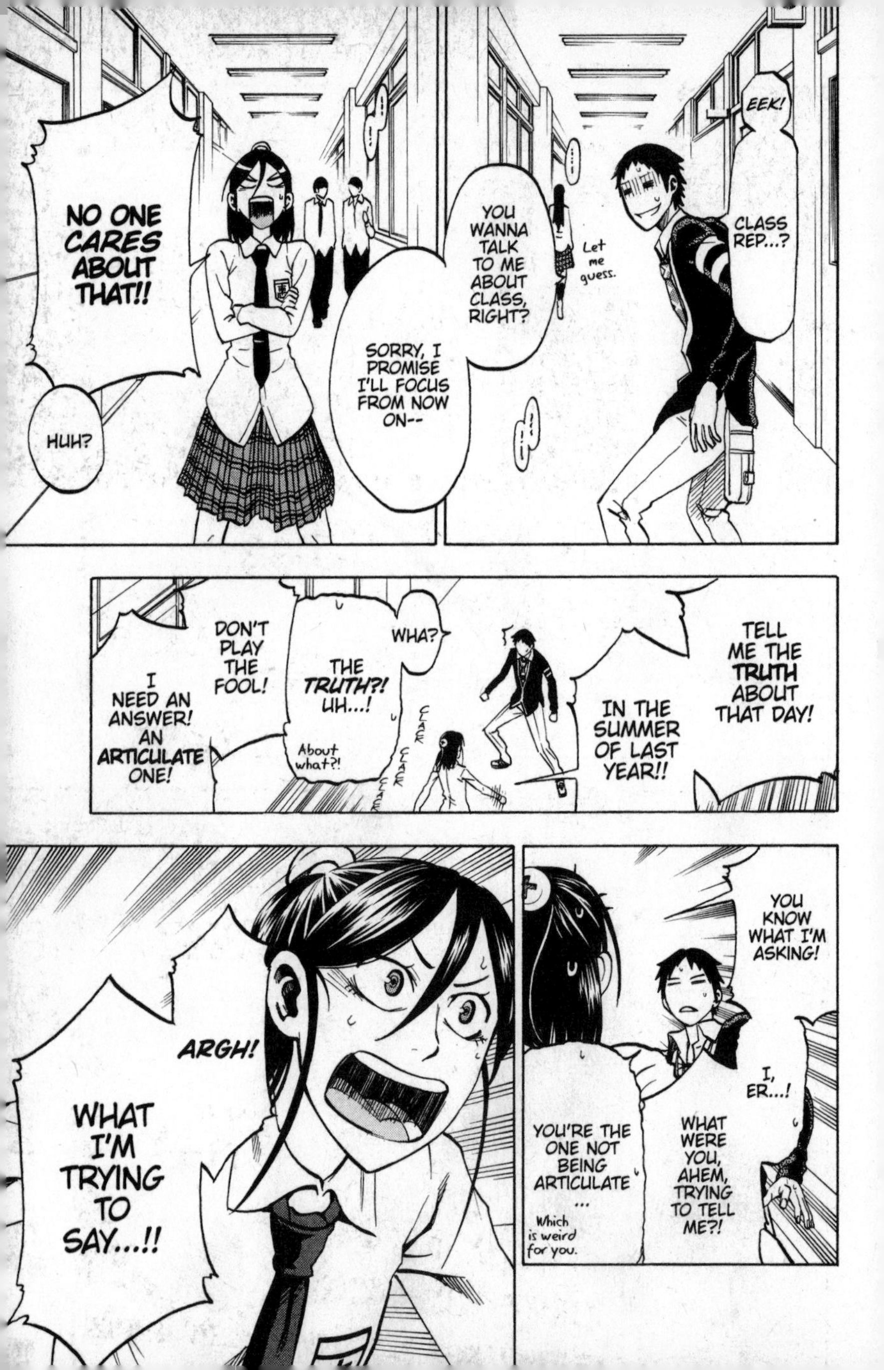
EEK!
CLASS REP...?
...!
Let me guess.
YOU WANNA TALK TO ME ABOUT CLASS, RIGHT?
SORRY, I PROMISE I'LL FOCUS FROM NOW ON--
...!!
...!
NO ONE CARES ABOUT THAT!!
HUH?
TELL ME THE TRUTH ABOUT THAT DAY!
IN THE SUMMER OF LAST YEAR!!
CLACK CLACK CLACK
WHA?
THE TRUTH?! UH...!
About what?!
DON'T PLAY THE FOOL!
I NEED AN ANSWER! AN ARTICULATE ONE!
YOU KNOW WHAT I'M ASKING!
I, ER...!
WHAT WERE YOU, AHEM, TRYING TO TELL ME?!
YOU'RE THE ONE NOT BEING ARTICULATE ...
Which is weird for you.
ARGH!
WHAT I'M TRYING TO SAY...!!

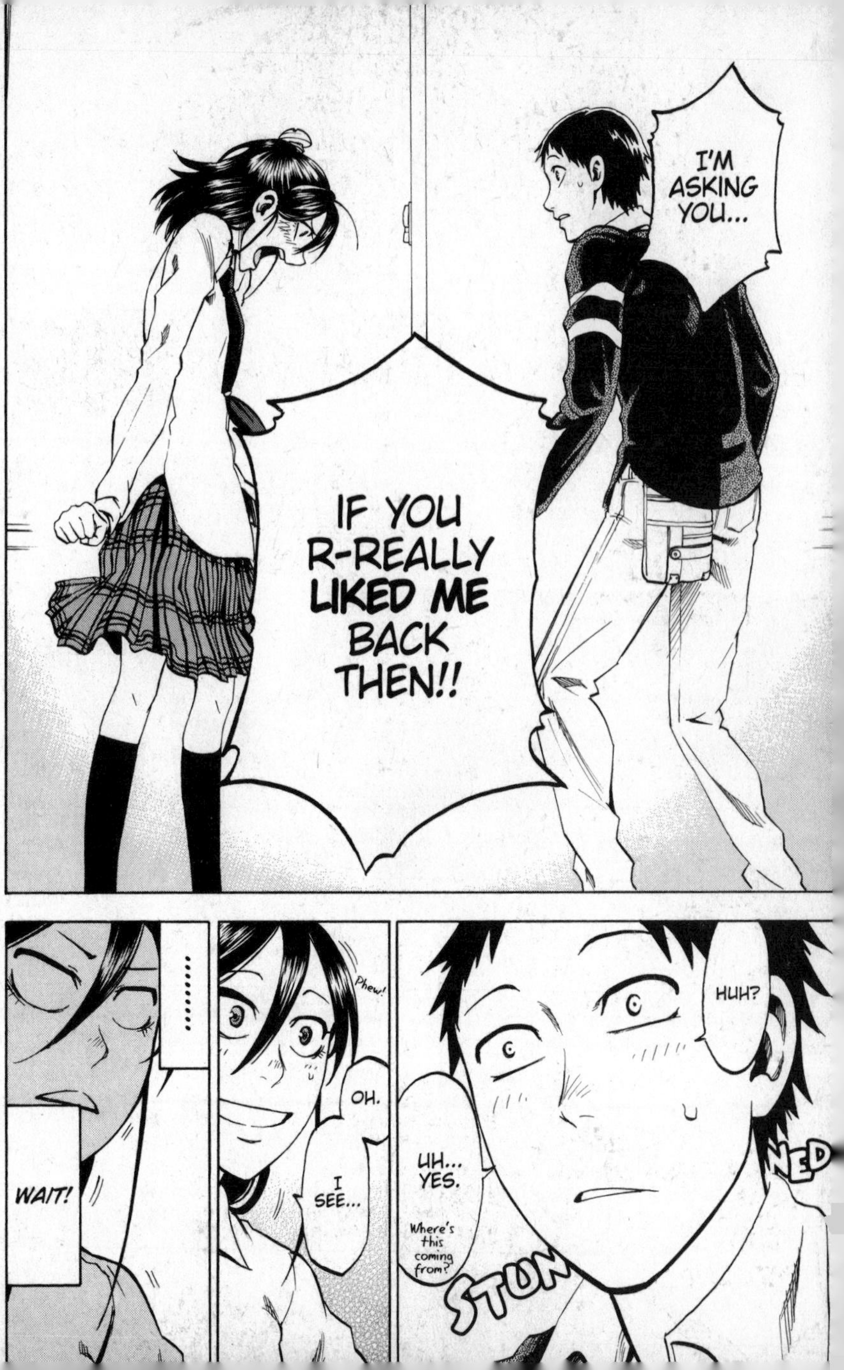
I'M ASKING YOU...
IF YOU R-REALLY LIKED ME BACK THEN!!
HUH?
UH... YES.
Where's this coming from?
STUN
NED
OH.
I SEE...
Phew!
....
WAIT!

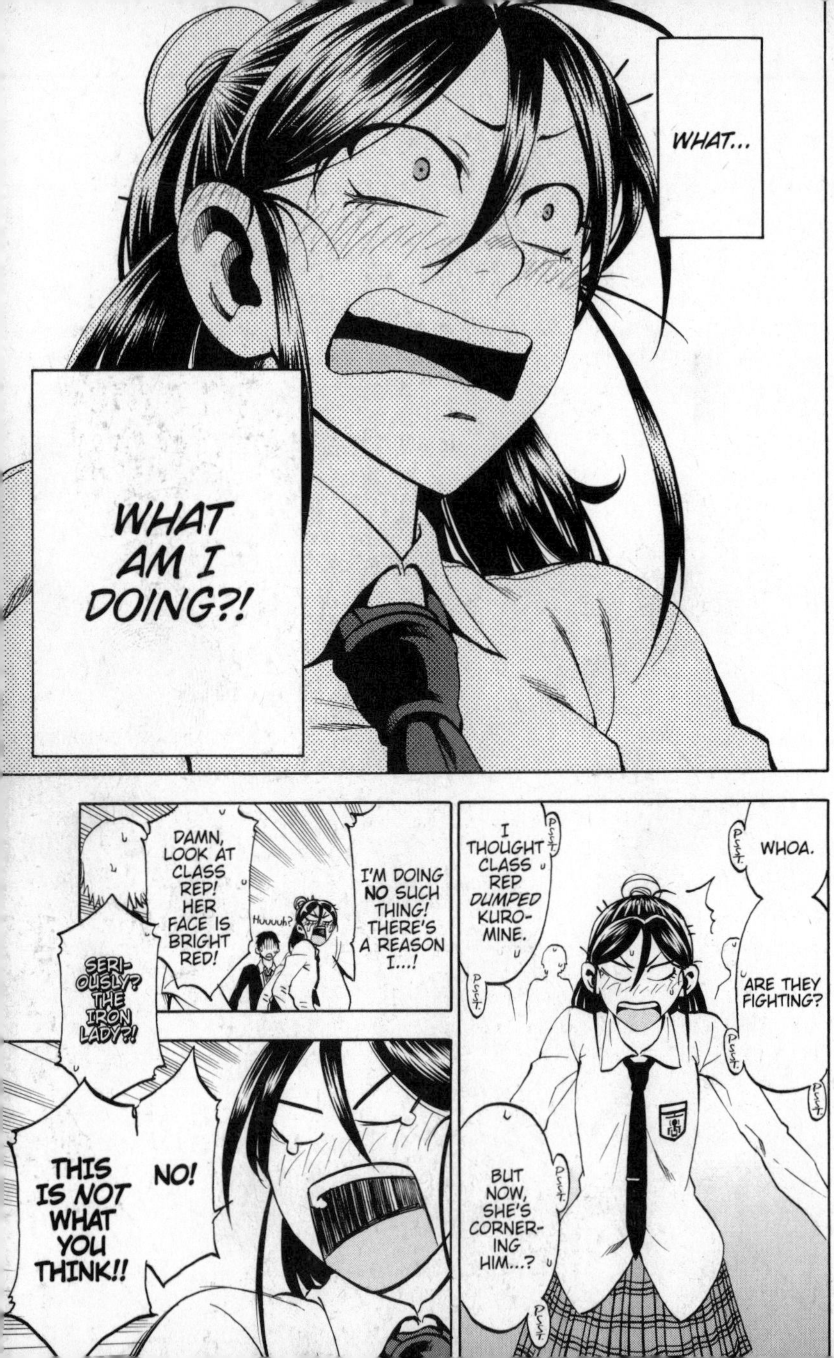
WHAT...
WHAT AM I DOING?!
WHOA.
I THOUGHT CLASS REP DUMPED KUROMINE.
ARE THEY FIGHTING?
BUT NOW, SHE'S CORNERING HIM...?
Psst.
I'M DOING NO SUCH THING! THERE'S A REASON I...!
Huuuuh?
DAMN, LOOK AT CLASS REP! HER FACE IS BRIGHT RED!
SERIOUSLY? THE IRON LADY?!
NO!
THIS IS NOT WHAT YOU THINK!!

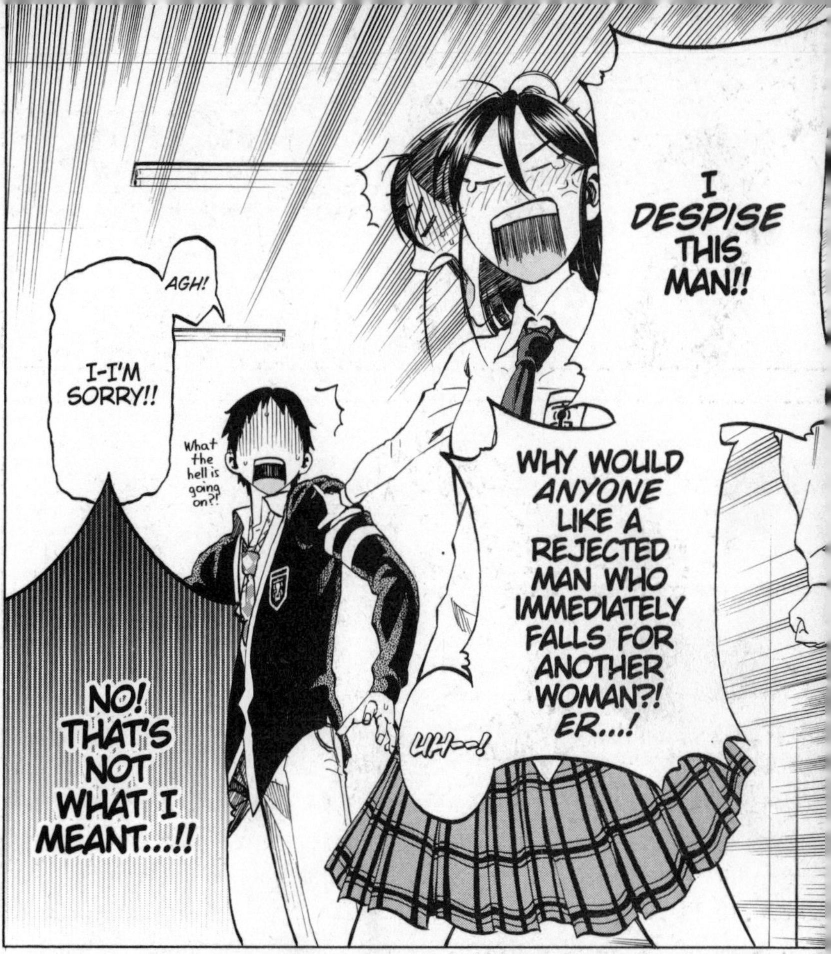
I DESPISE THIS MAN!!
WHY WOULD ANYONE LIKE A REJECTED MAN WHO IMMEDIATELY FALLS FOR ANOTHER WOMAN?! ER...!
UH--!
AGH!
I-I'M SORRY!!
What the hell is going on?!
NO! THAT'S NOT WHAT I MEANT...!!

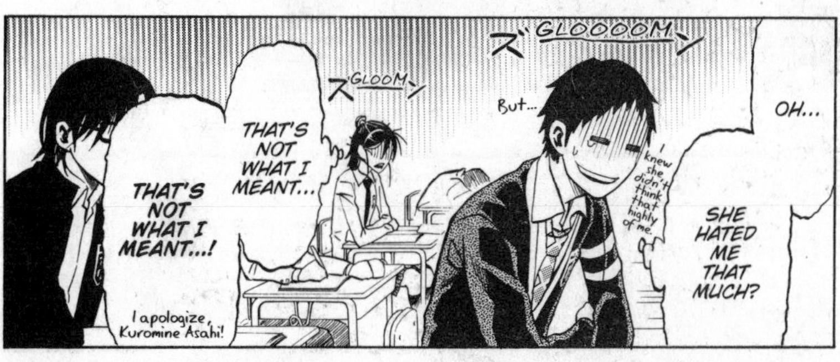
OH...
SHE HATED ME THAT MUCH?
I knew she didn't think that highly of me.
GLOOOOM
But...
GLOOM
THAT'S NOT WHAT I MEANT...
THAT'S NOT WHAT I MEANT...!
I apologize, Kuromine Asahi!

Chapter 6: "Let's Prove Who's Worse!"

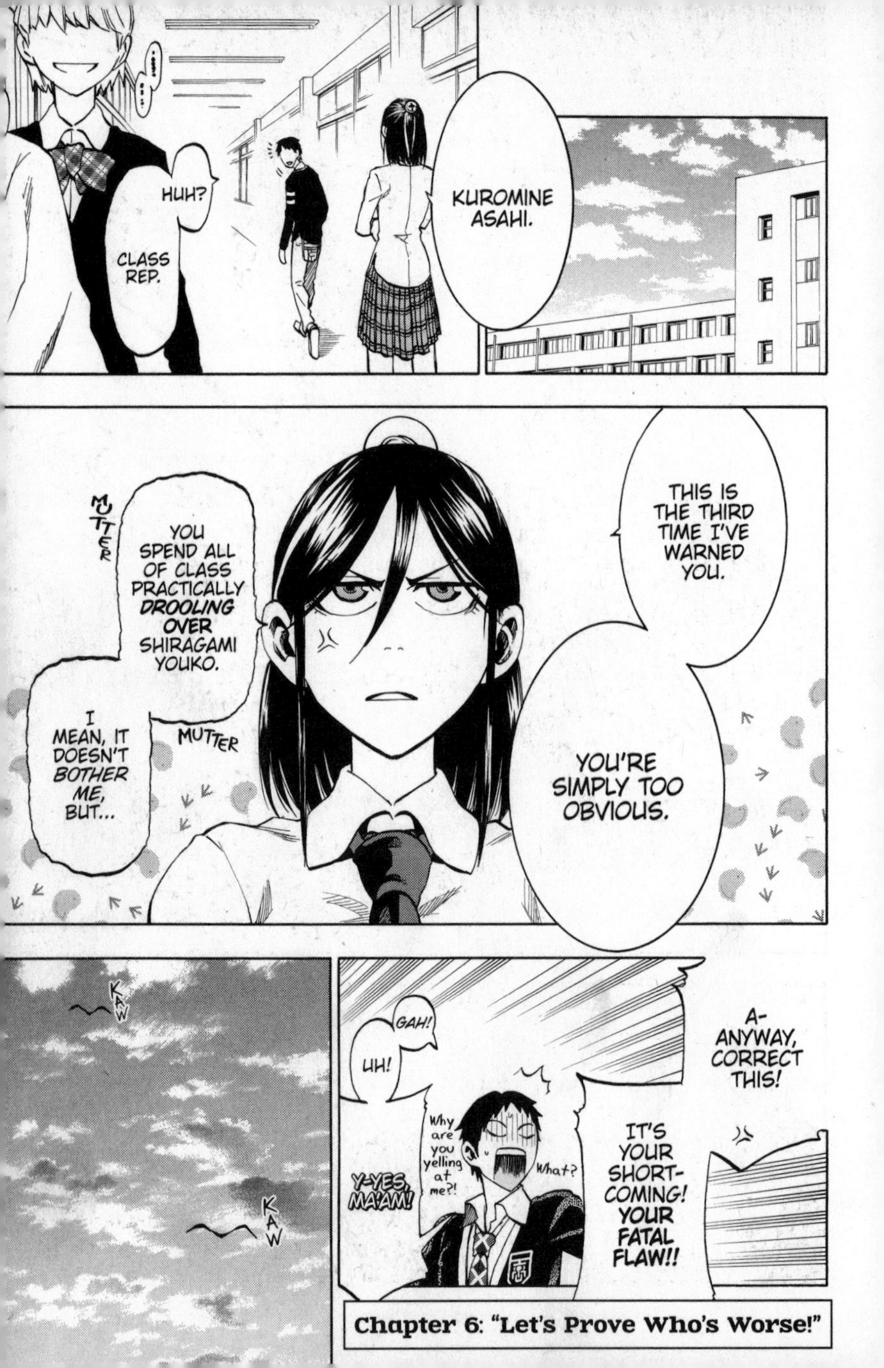
KUROMINE ASAHI.
HUH?
CLASS REP.
THIS IS THE THIRD TIME I'VE WARNED YOU.
YOU'RE SIMPLY TOO OBVIOUS.
YOU SPEND ALL OF CLASS PRACTICALLY DROOLING OVER SHIRAGAMI YOUKO.
MUTTER
I MEAN, IT DOESN'T BOTHER ME, BUT...
MUTTER
A- ANYWAY, CORRECT THIS!
IT'S YOUR SHORT-COMING! YOUR FATAL FLAW!!
GAH!
UH!
Why are you yelling at me?!
What?
Y-YES, MA'AM!
KAW
KAW

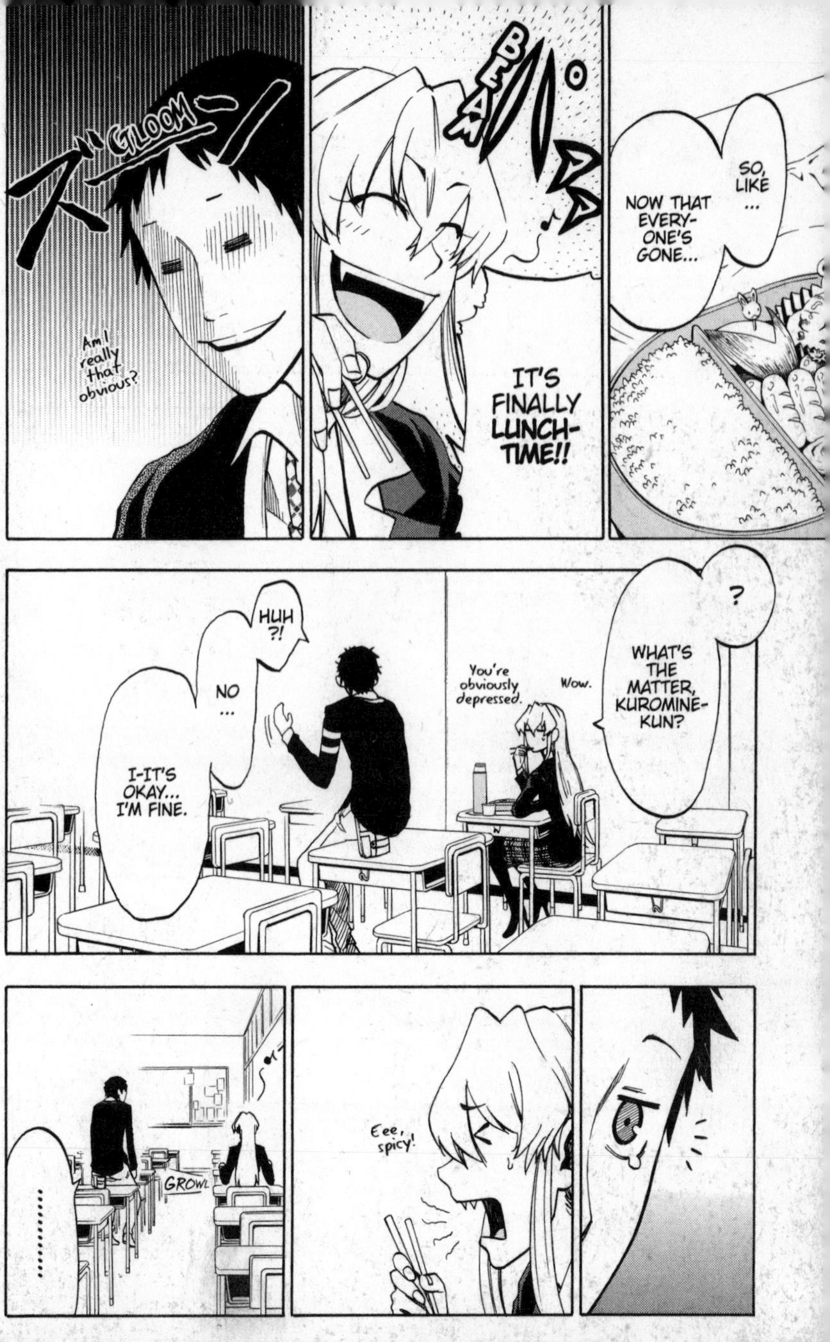
SO, LIKE ...
NOW THAT EVERY-ONE'S GONE...
IT'S FINALLY LUNCH-TIME!!
BEAM
Am I really that obvious?
GLOOM
?
WHAT'S THE MATTER, KUROMINE-KUN?
Wow.
You're obviously depressed.
HUH ?!
NO ...
I-IT'S OKAY... I'M FINE.
Eee, spicy!
GROWL
....

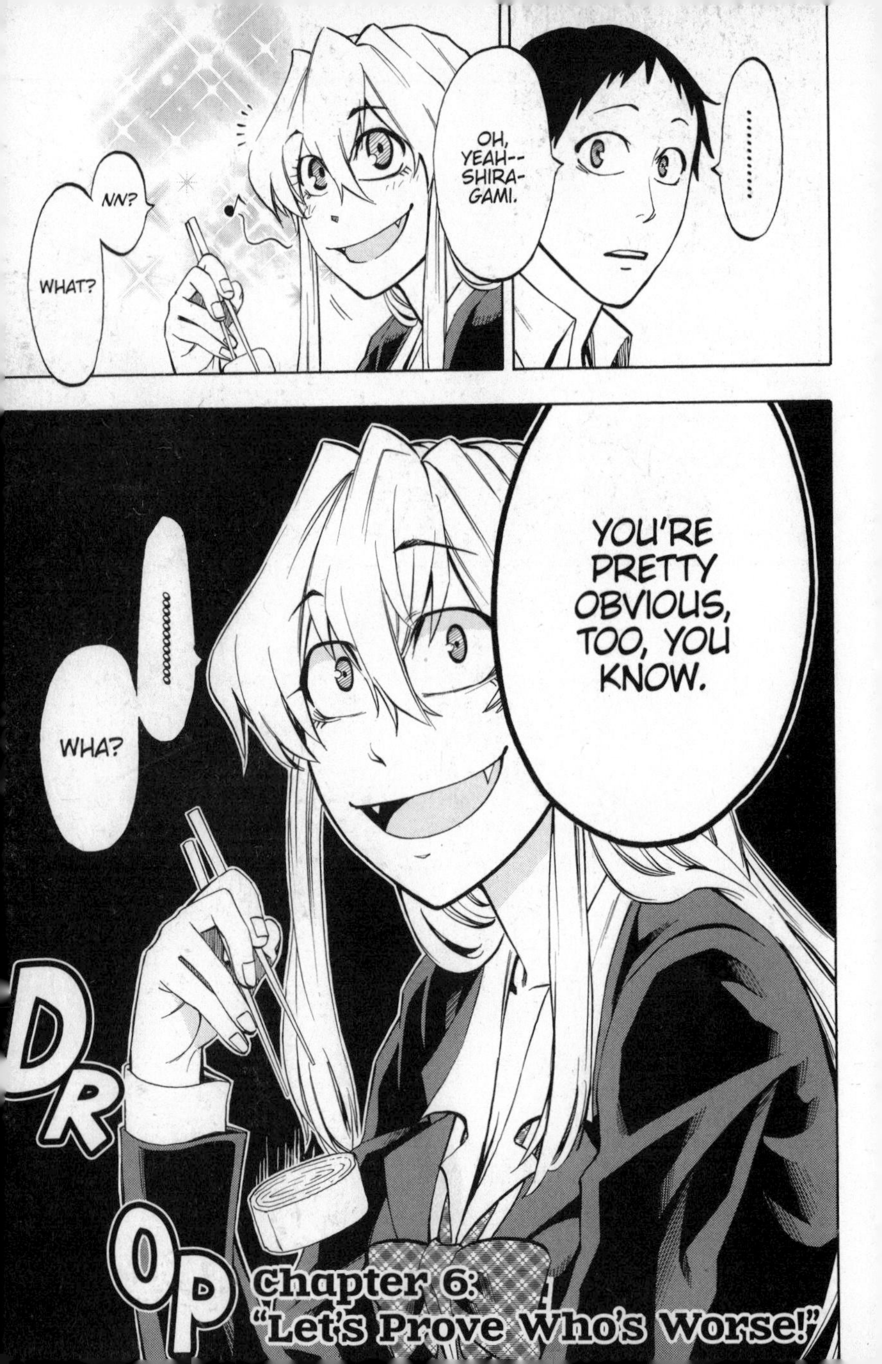
......
OH, YEAH-- SHIRA- GAMI.
NN?
WHAT?
YOU'RE PRETTY OBVIOUS, TOO, YOU KNOW.
......
WHA?
DROP
Chapter 6: "Let's Prove Who's Worse!"

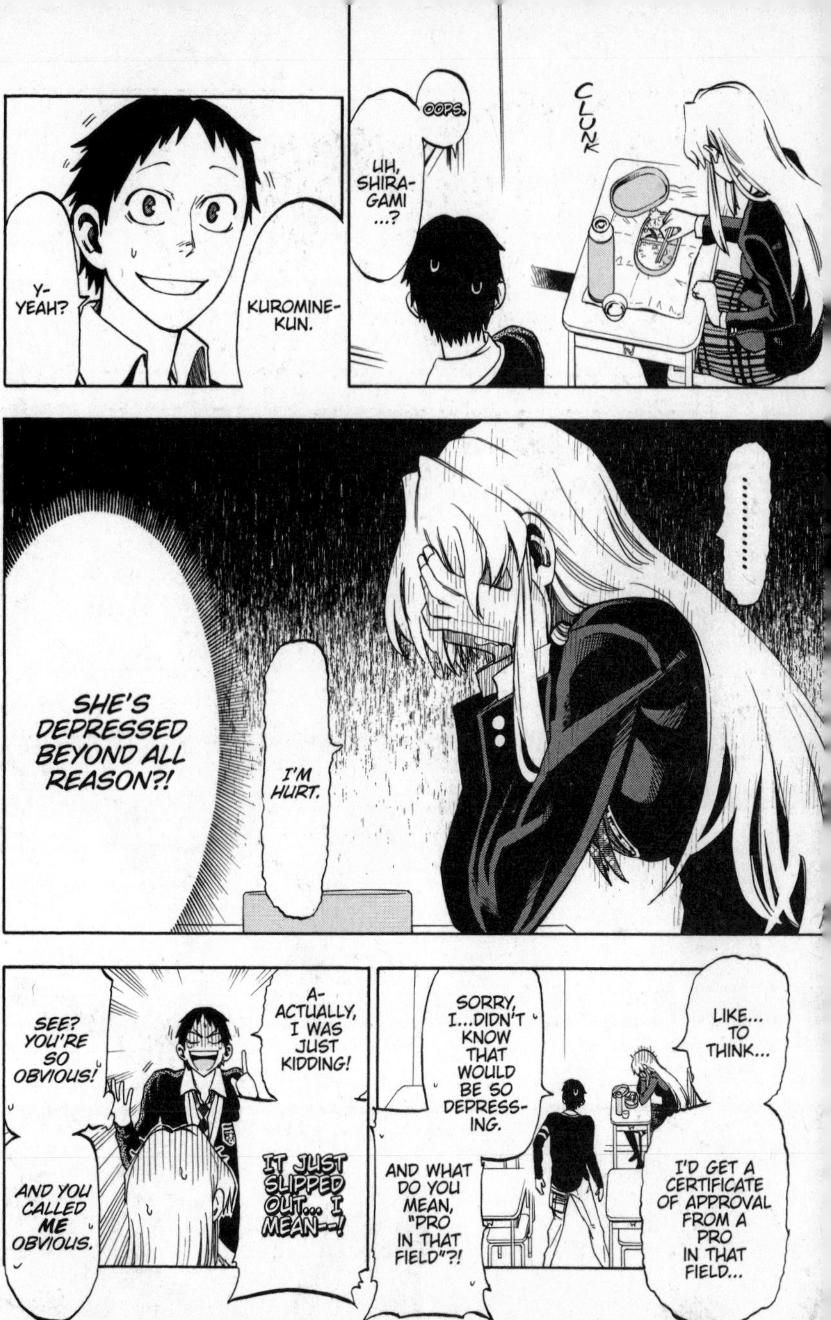
CLUNK
OOPS.
UH, SHIRAGAMI ...?
KUROMINE-KUN.
Y-YEAH?
......
I'M HURT.
SHE'S DEPRESSED BEYOND ALL REASON?!
LIKE... TO THINK...
I'D GET A CERTIFICATE OF APPROVAL FROM A PRO IN THAT FIELD...
SORRY, I...DIDN'T KNOW THAT WOULD BE SO DEPRESSING.
AND WHAT DO YOU MEAN, "PRO IN THAT FIELD"?!
A-ACTUALLY, I WAS JUST KIDDING!
IT JUST SLIPPED OUT... I MEAN--!
SEE? YOU'RE SO OBVIOUS!
AND YOU CALLED ME OBVIOUS.

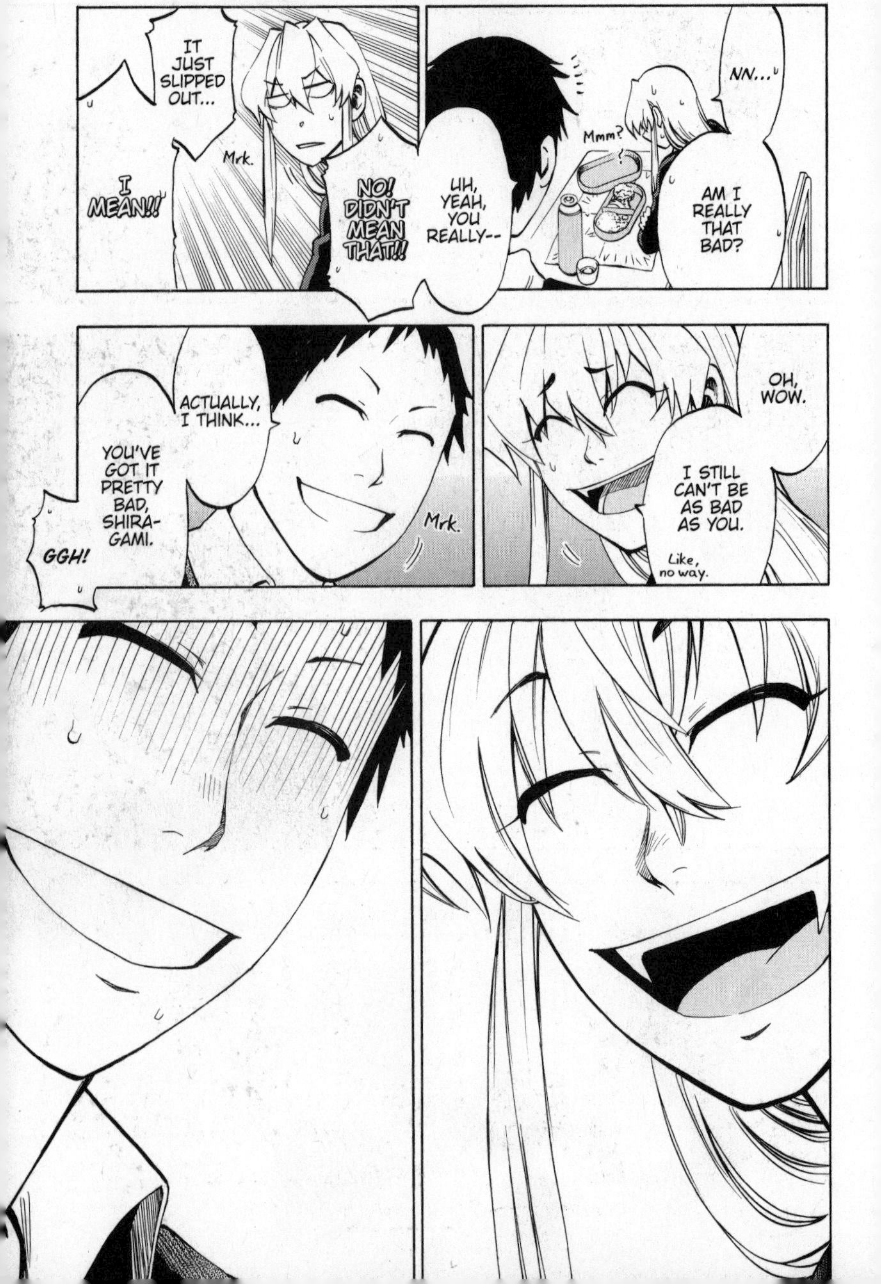
NN...
AM I REALLY THAT BAD?
Mmm?
UH, YEAH, YOU REALLY--
NO! DIDN'T MEAN THAT!!
Mrk.
IT JUST SLIPPED OUT...
I MEAN!!
OH, WOW.
I STILL CAN'T BE AS BAD AS YOU.
Like, no way.
Mrk.
ACTUALLY, I THINK...
YOU'VE GOT IT PRETTY BAD, SHIRA-GAMI.
GGH!

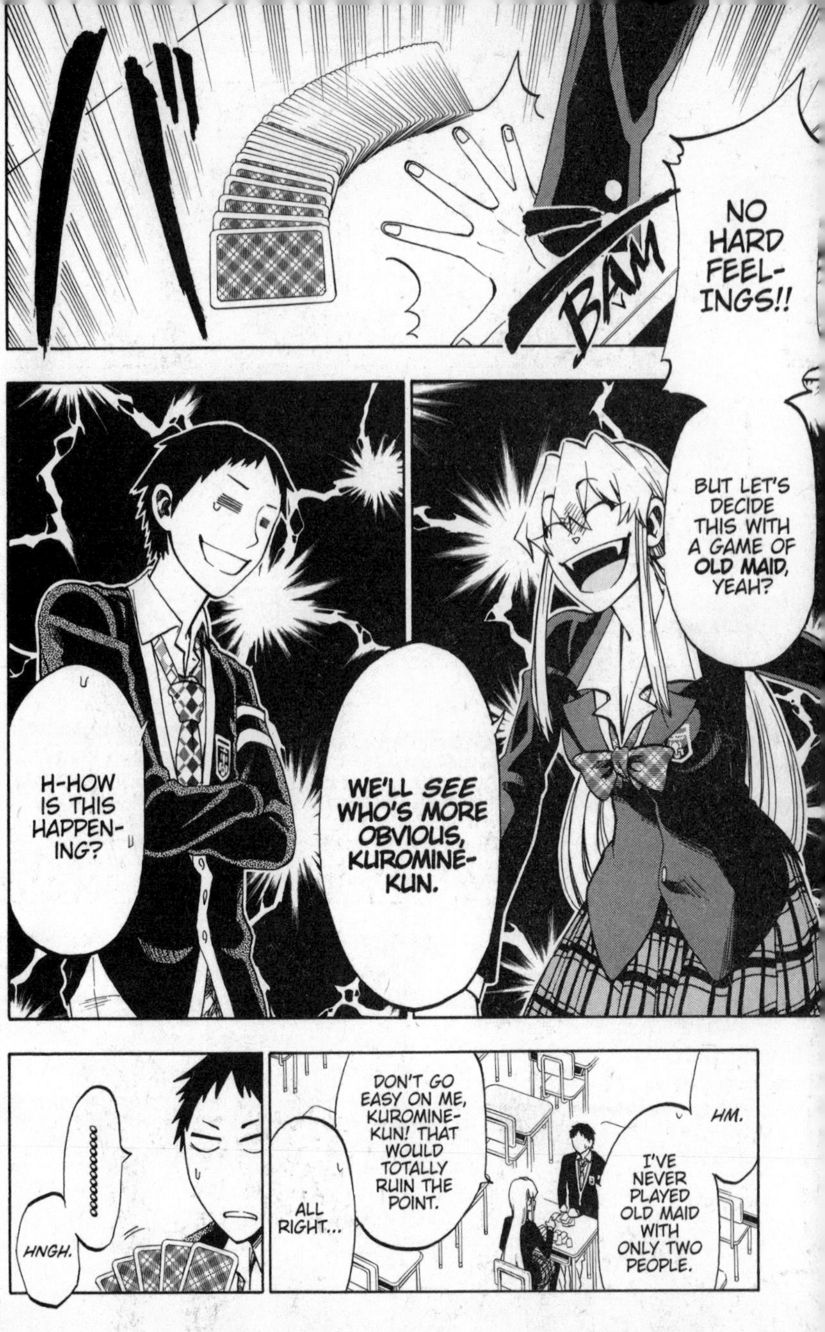
NO HARD FEEL-INGS!!
BAM
BUT LET'S DECIDE THIS WITH A GAME OF OLD MAID, YEAH?
WE'LL SEE WHO'S MORE OBVIOUS, KUROMINE-KUN.
H-HOW IS THIS HAPPEN-ING?
HM.
I'VE NEVER PLAYED OLD MAID WITH ONLY TWO PEOPLE.
DON'T GO EASY ON ME, KUROMINE-KUN! THAT WOULD TOTALLY RUIN THE POINT.
ALL RIGHT...
....
HNGH.

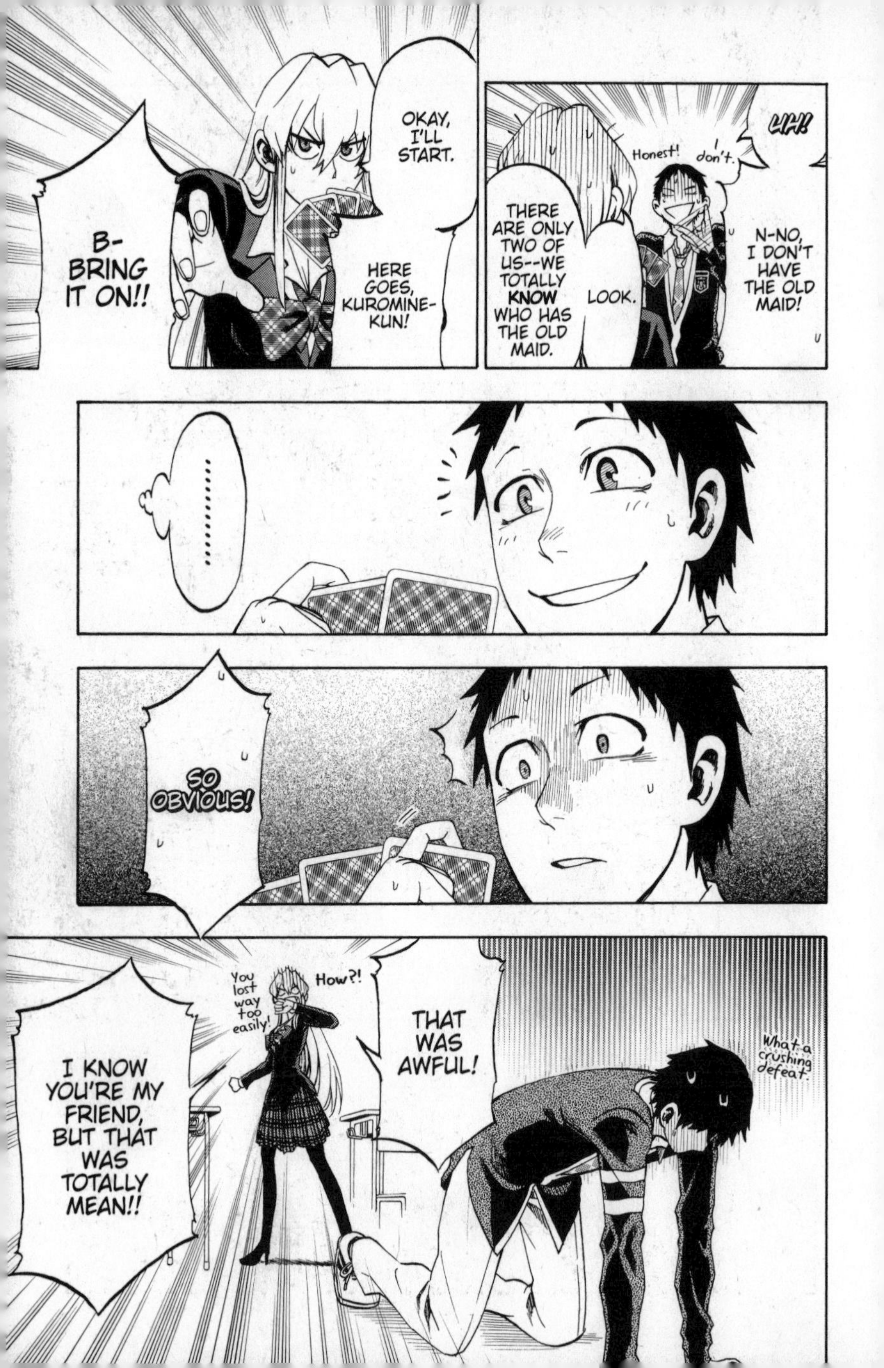
UH!
N-NO, I DON'T HAVE THE OLD MAID!
I don't. Honest!
LOOK.
THERE ARE ONLY TWO OF US--WE TOTALLY **KNOW** WHO HAS THE OLD MAID.
OKAY, I'LL START.
HERE GOES, KUROMINE-KUN!
B-BRING IT ON!!
....
SO OBVIOUS!
What a crushing defeat.
THAT WAS AWFUL!
How?!
You lost way too easily!
I KNOW YOU'RE MY FRIEND, BUT THAT WAS TOTALLY MEAN!!

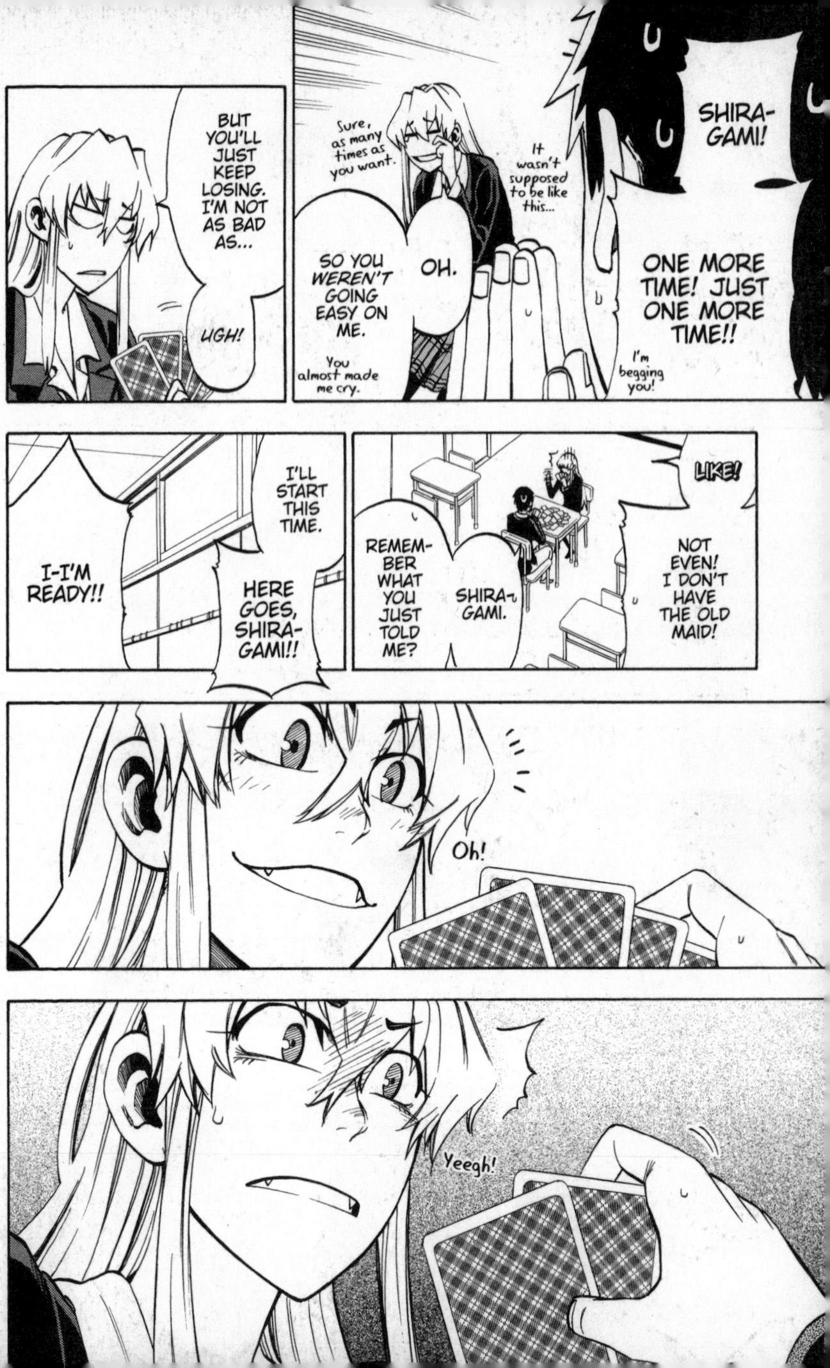
SHIRA-GAMI!
ONE MORE TIME! JUST ONE MORE TIME!!
I'm begging you!
It wasn't supposed to be like this...
Sure, as many times as you want.
OH.
SO YOU WEREN'T GOING EASY ON ME.
You almost made me cry.
BUT YOU'LL JUST KEEP LOSING. I'M NOT AS BAD AS...
UGH!
LIKE!
NOT EVEN! I DON'T HAVE THE OLD MAID!
SHIRA-GAMI.
REMEMBER WHAT YOU JUST TOLD ME?
I'LL START THIS TIME.
HERE GOES, SHIRA-GAMI!!
I-I'M READY!!
Oh!
Yeegh!

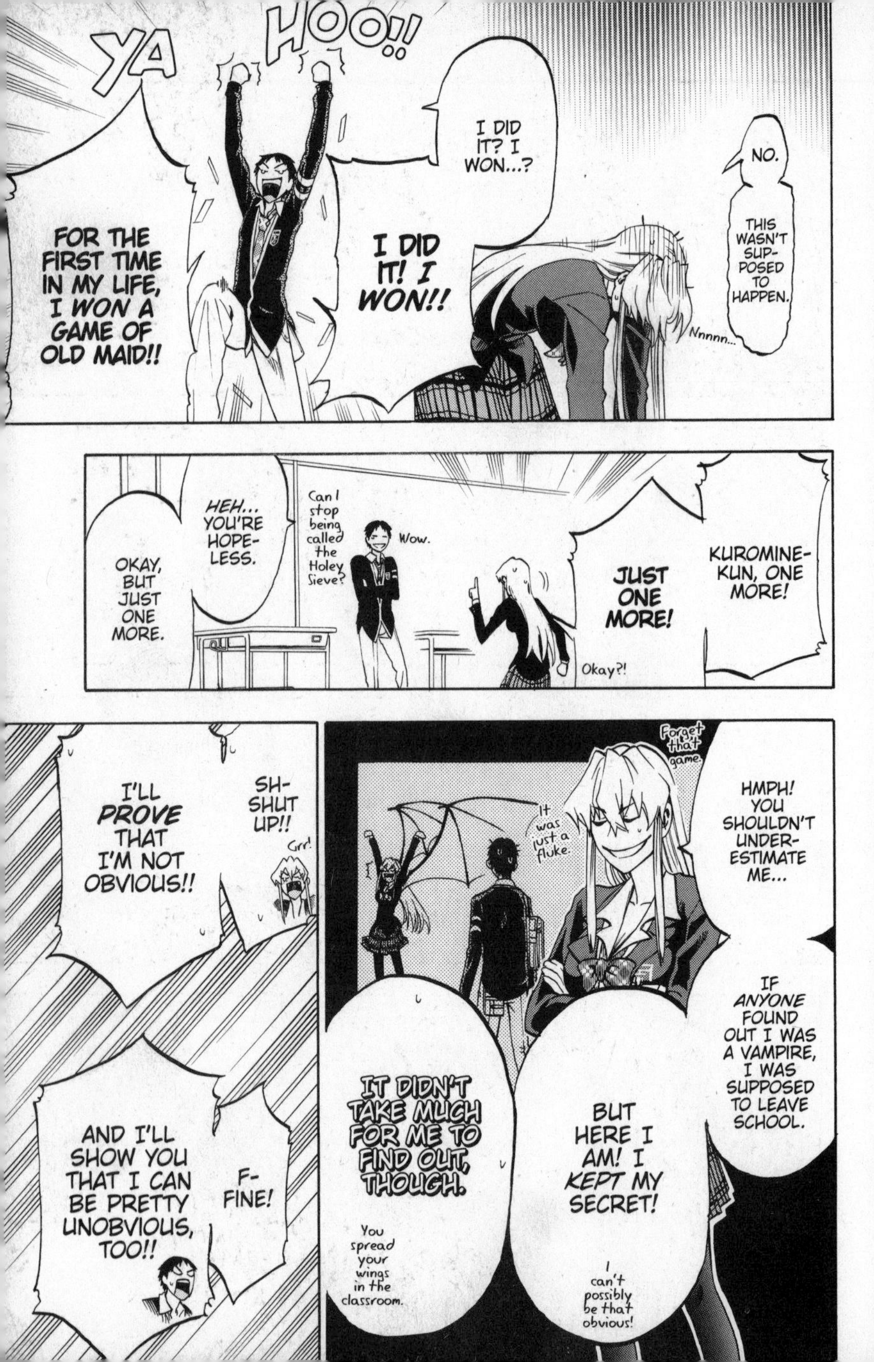
NO.
THIS WASN'T SUP-POSED TO HAPPEN.
Nnnnn...
I DID IT? I WON...?
YA HOO!!
I DID IT! I WON!!
FOR THE FIRST TIME IN MY LIFE, I WON A GAME OF OLD MAID!!
KUROMINE-KUN, ONE MORE!
JUST ONE MORE!
Okay?!
Can I stop being called the Holey Sieve?
Wow.
HEH... YOU'RE HOPE-LESS.
OKAY, BUT JUST ONE MORE.
HMPH! YOU SHOULDN'T UNDER-ESTIMATE ME...
Forget that game.
It was just a fluke.
IF ANYONE FOUND OUT I WAS A VAMPIRE, I WAS SUPPOSED TO LEAVE SCHOOL.
BUT HERE I AM! I KEPT MY SECRET!
I can't possibly be that obvious!
IT DIDN'T TAKE MUCH FOR ME TO FIND OUT, THOUGH.
You spread your wings in the classroom.
SH-SHUT UP!!
Grr!
I'LL PROVE THAT I'M NOT OBVIOUS!!
F-FINE!
AND I'LL SHOW YOU THAT I CAN BE PRETTY UNOBVIOUS, TOO!!

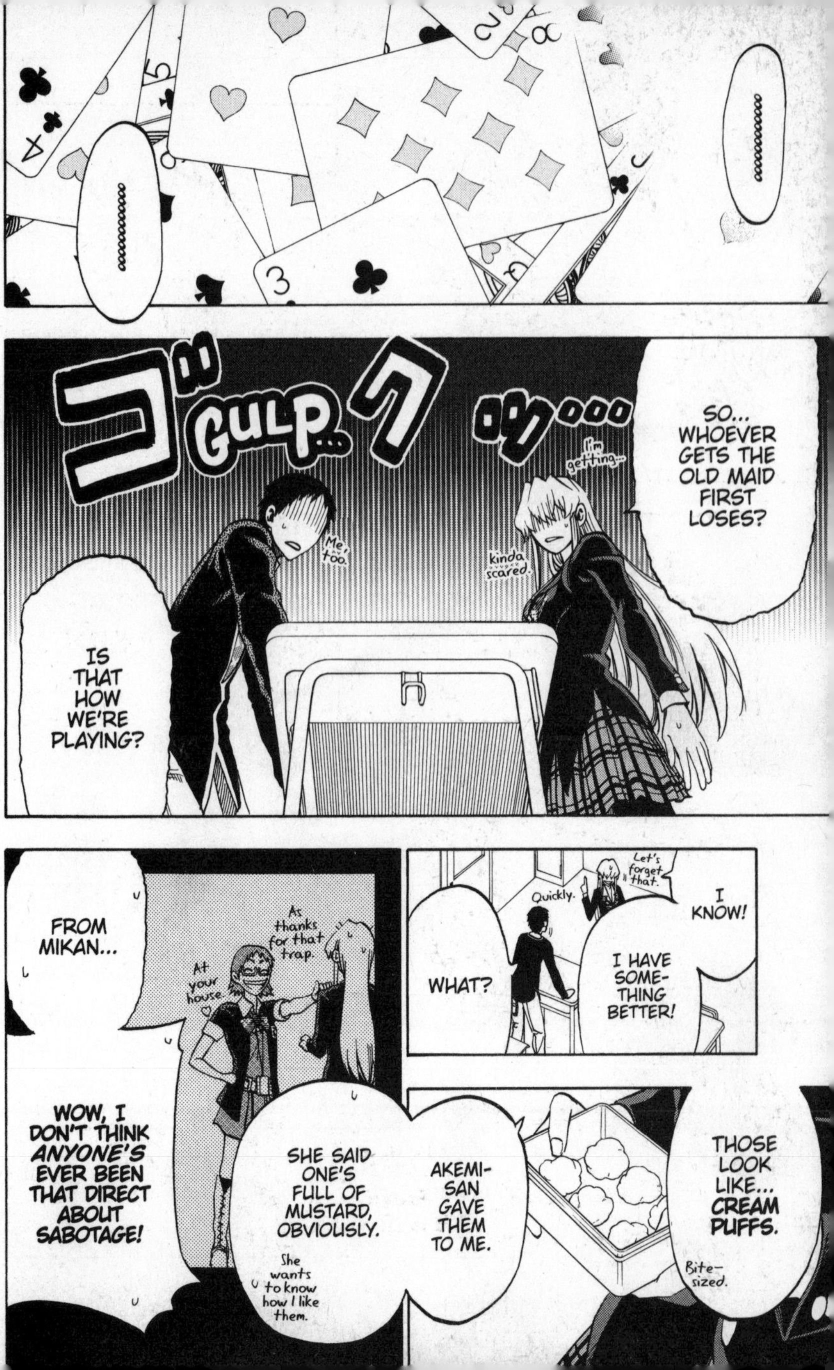
....
....
SO... WHOEVER GETS THE OLD MAID FIRST LOSES?
I'm getting...
kinda scared.
GULP...
Me, too.
IS THAT HOW WE'RE PLAYING?
I KNOW!
Let's forget that.
Quickly.
I HAVE SOMETHING BETTER!
WHAT?
FROM MIKAN...
As thanks for that trap.
At your house.
THOSE LOOK LIKE... CREAM PUFFS.
Bite-sized.
AKEMI-SAN GAVE THEM TO ME.
SHE SAID ONE'S FULL OF MUSTARD, OBVIOUSLY.
She wants to know how I like them.
WOW, I DON'T THINK ANYONE'S EVER BEEN THAT DIRECT ABOUT SABOTAGE!

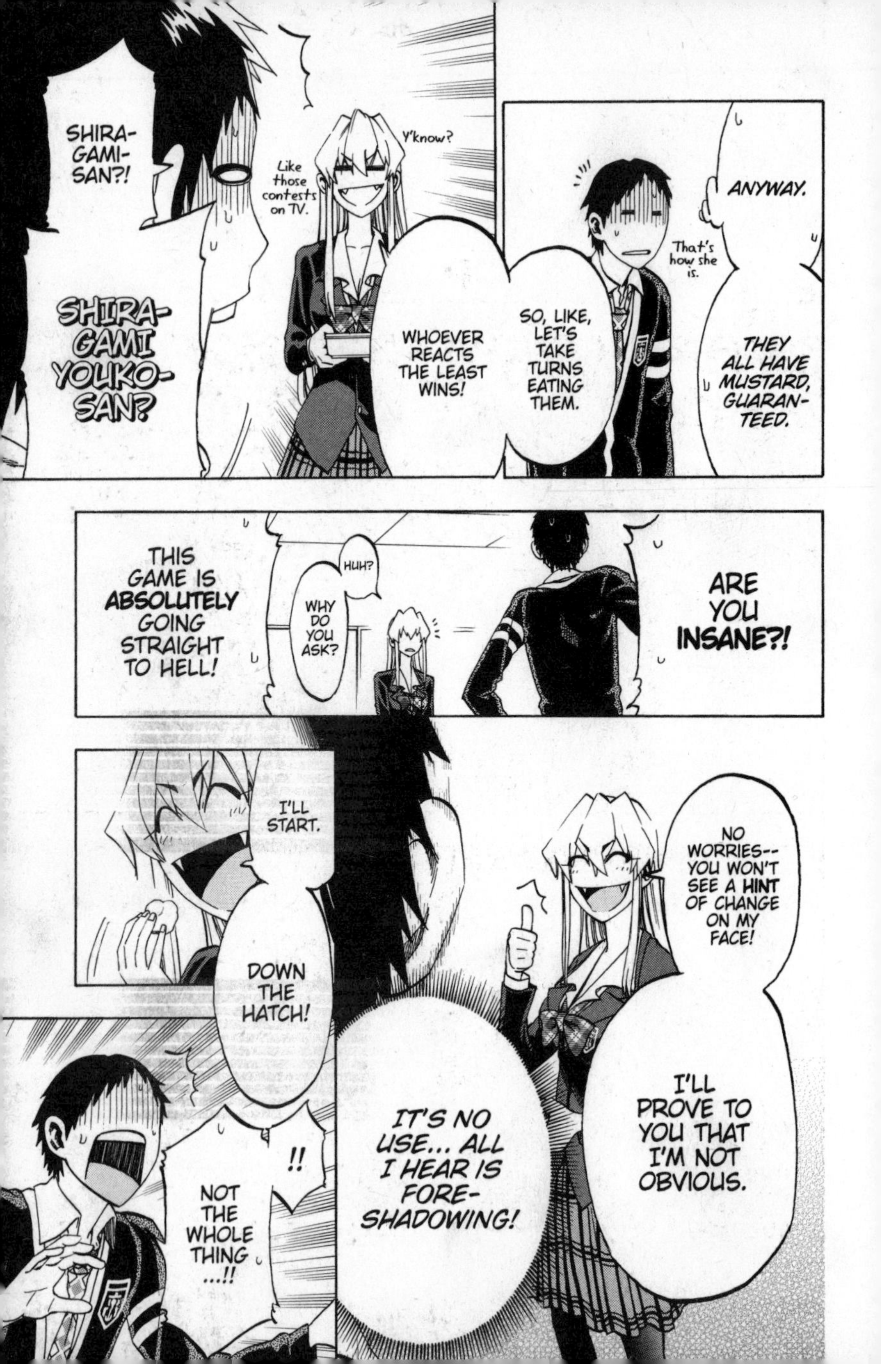
ANYWAY.
THEY ALL HAVE MUSTARD, GUARANTEED.
That's how she is.
SO, LIKE, LET'S TAKE TURNS EATING THEM.
WHOEVER REACTS THE LEAST WINS!
Y'know?
Like those contests on TV.
SHIRA-GAMI-SAN?!
SHIRA-GAMI YOUKO-SAN?
ARE YOU INSANE?!
HUH?
WHY DO YOU ASK?
THIS GAME IS ABSOLUTELY GOING STRAIGHT TO HELL!
NO WORRIES--YOU WON'T SEE A HINT OF CHANGE ON MY FACE!
I'LL PROVE TO YOU THAT I'M NOT OBVIOUS.
IT'S NO USE... ALL I HEAR IS FORE-SHADOWING!
I'LL START.
DOWN THE HATCH!
!!
NOT THE WHOLE THING ...!!

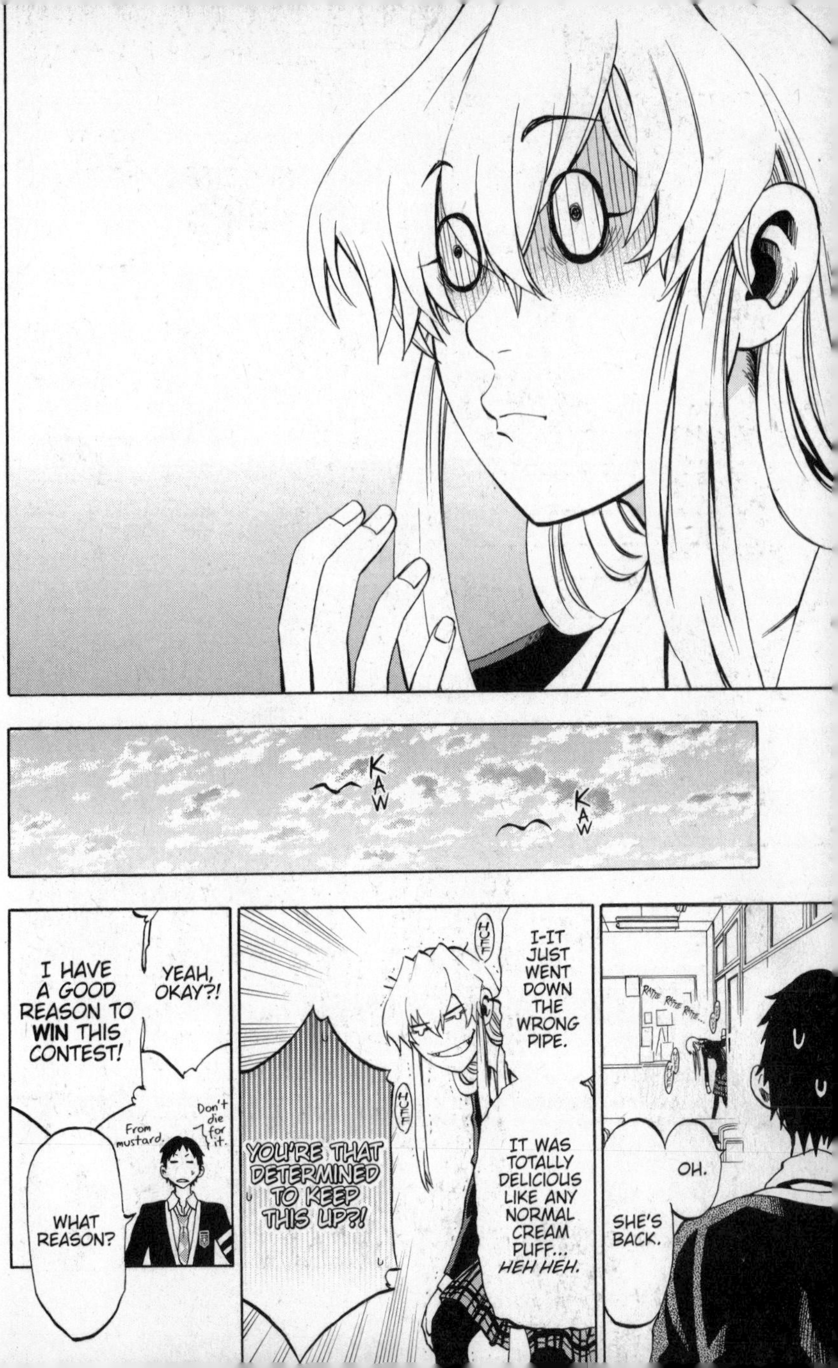
KAW
KAW
RATTLE RATTLE RATTLE...
HUFF HUFF
OH.
SHE'S BACK.
HUFF
I-IT JUST WENT DOWN THE WRONG PIPE.
HUFF
IT WAS TOTALLY DELICIOUS LIKE ANY NORMAL CREAM PUFF... HEH HEH.
YOU'RE THAT DETERMINED TO KEEP THIS UP?!
I HAVE A GOOD REASON TO WIN THIS CONTEST!
YEAH, OKAY?!
WHAT REASON?
Don't die for it.
From mustard.

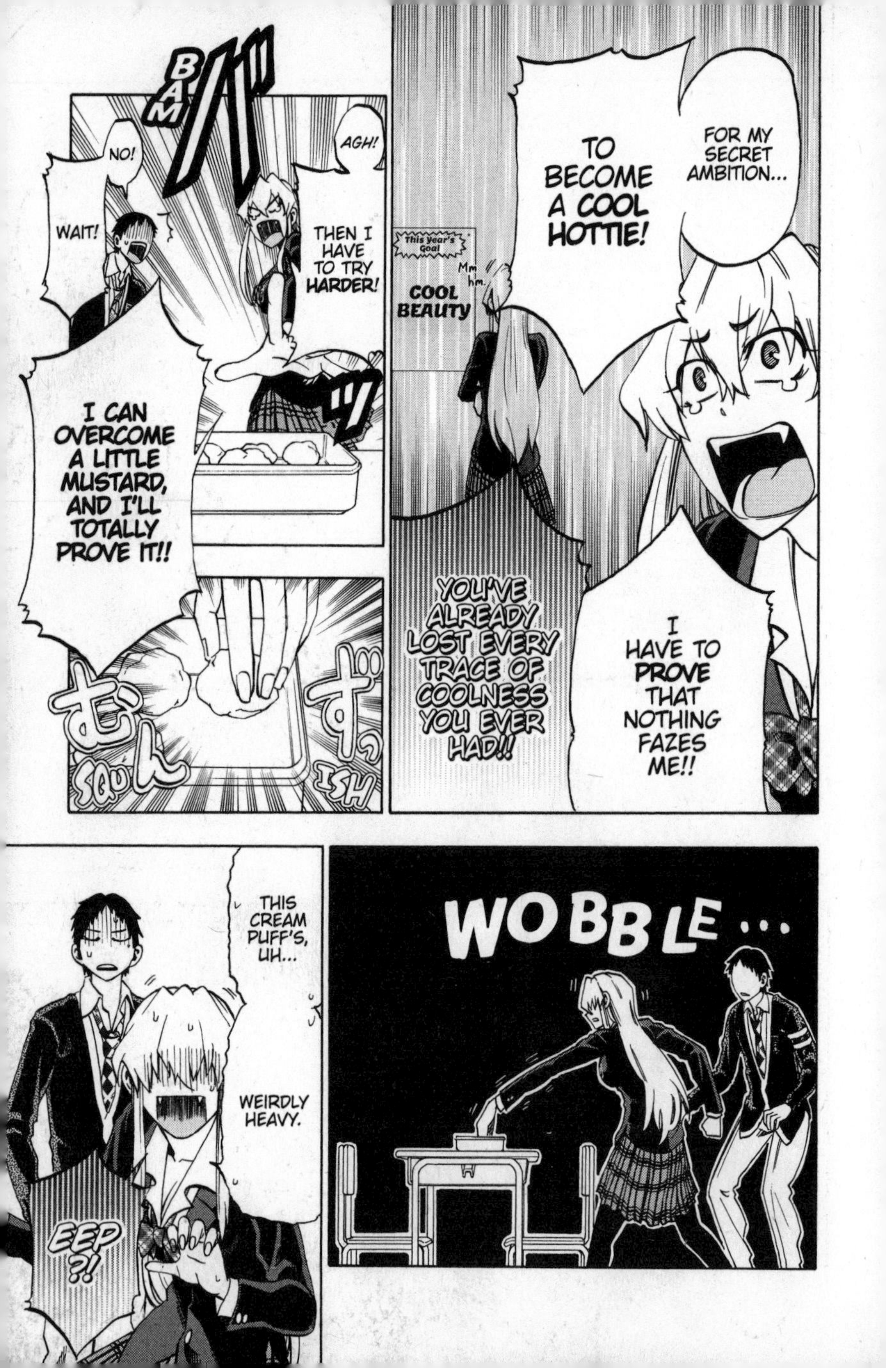
FOR MY SECRET AMBITION...
TO BECOME A COOL HOTTIE!
This year's Goal
COOL BEAUTY
Mm hm.
I HAVE TO PROVE THAT NOTHING FAZES ME!!
YOU'VE ALREADY LOST EVERY TRACE OF COOLNESS YOU EVER HAD!!
AGH!
THEN I HAVE TO TRY HARDER!
BAM
NO!
WAIT!
I CAN OVERCOME A LITTLE MUSTARD, AND I'LL TOTALLY PROVE IT!!
ISH
SQU
WOBBLE...
THIS CREAM PUFF'S, UH...
WEIRDLY HEAVY.
EEP ?!

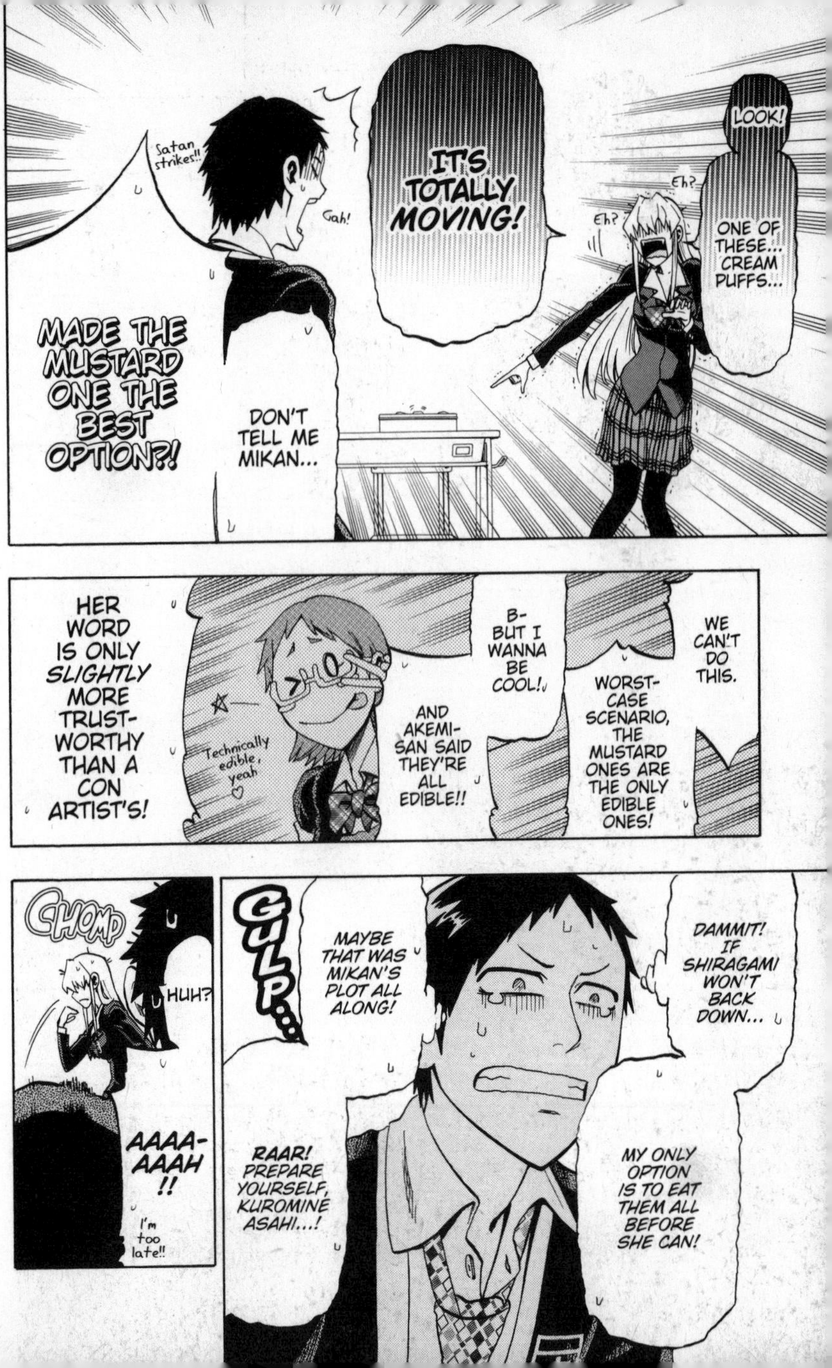
LOOK!
ONE OF THESE... CREAM PUFFS...
Eh?
Eh?
IT'S TOTALLY MOVING!
Gah!
Satan strikes!!
DON'T TELL ME MIKAN...
MADE THE MUSTARD ONE THE BEST OPTION?!
WE CAN'T DO THIS.
WORST-CASE SCENARIO, THE MUSTARD ONES ARE THE ONLY EDIBLE ONES!
B-BUT I WANNA BE COOL!
AND AKEMI-SAN SAID THEY'RE ALL EDIBLE!!
Technically edible, yeah
HER WORD IS ONLY SLIGHTLY MORE TRUST-WORTHY THAN A CON ARTIST'S!
DAMMIT! IF SHIRAGAMI WON'T BACK DOWN...
MY ONLY OPTION IS TO EAT THEM ALL BEFORE SHE CAN!
MAYBE THAT WAS MIKAN'S PLOT ALL ALONG!
GULP...
RAAR! PREPARE YOURSELF, KUROMINE ASAHI...!
CHOMP
HUH?
AAAA-AAAH!!
I'm too late!!

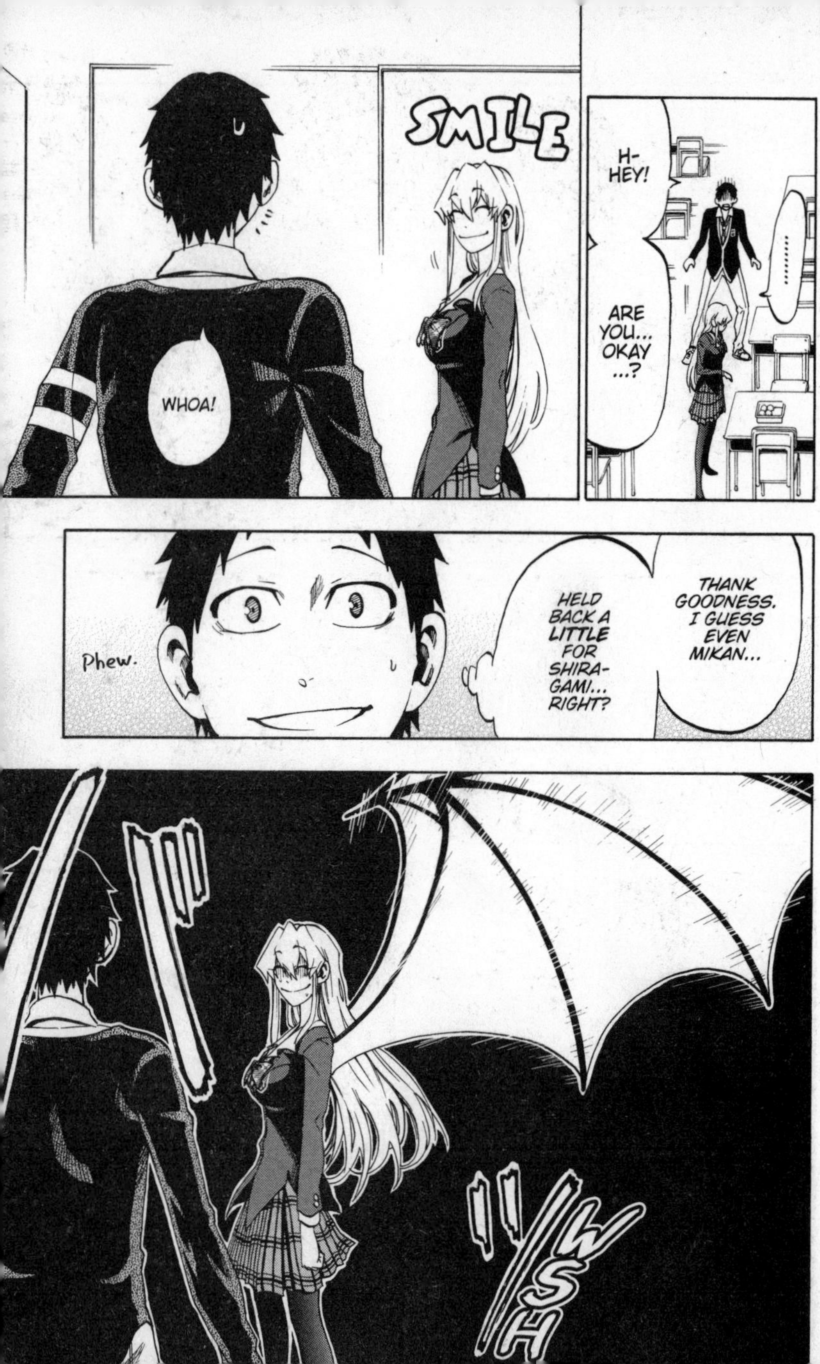
H-HEY!
ARE YOU... OKAY ...?
......
SMILE
WHOA!
THANK GOODNESS. I GUESS EVEN MIKAN...
HELD BACK A LITTLE FOR SHIRAGAMI... RIGHT?
Phew.
WSH

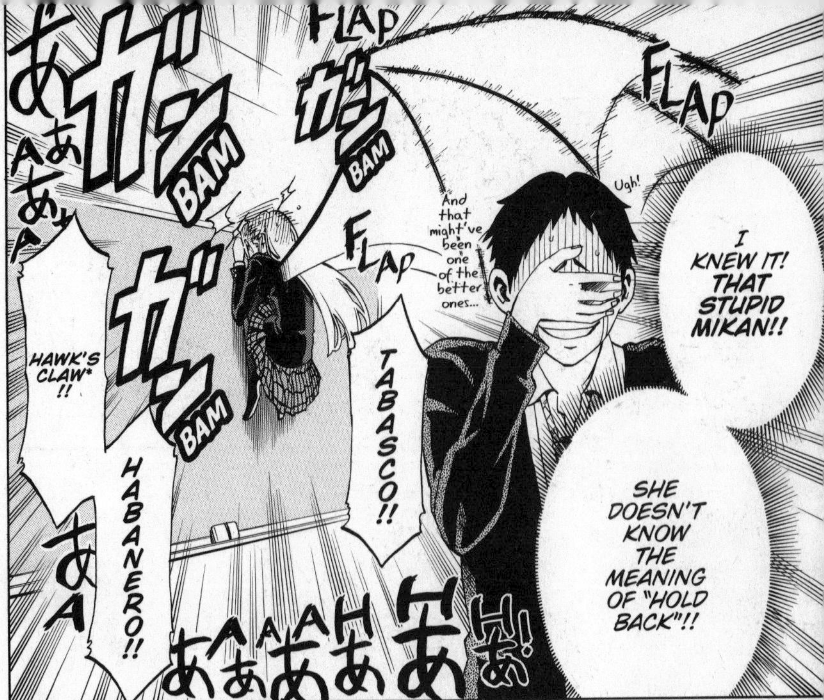
FLAP
I KNEW IT! THAT STUPID MIKAN!!
Ugh!
And that might've been one of the better ones...
FLAP
FLAP
BAM
BAM
BAM
SHE DOESN'T KNOW THE MEANING OF "HOLD BACK"!!
TABASCO!!
HAWK'S CLAW*!!
HABANERO!!
AAAAH

*ALSO KNOWN AS TAKANOTSUME, A TYPE OF CHILI PEPPER FROM JAPAN.

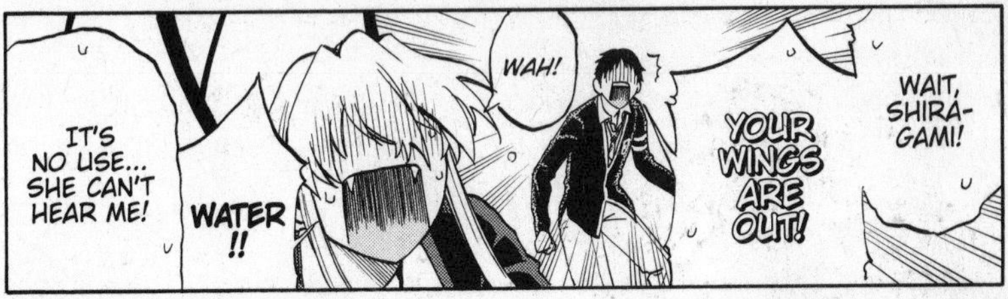
WAIT, SHIRA-GAMI!
YOUR WINGS ARE OUT!
WAH!
WATER!!
IT'S NO USE... SHE CAN'T HEAR ME!

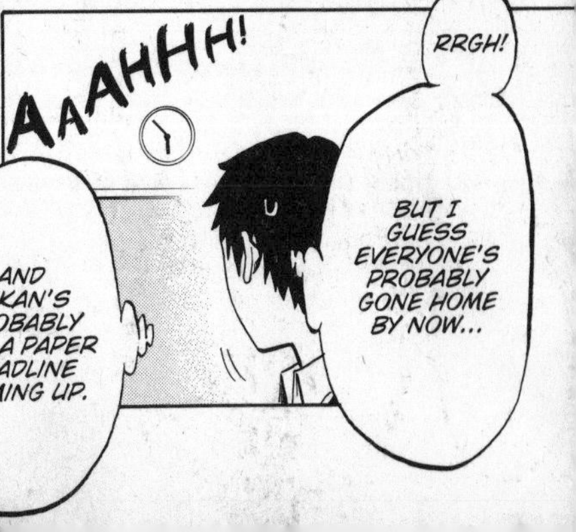
RRGH!
AAAHHH!
BUT I GUESS EVERYONE'S PROBABLY GONE HOME BY NOW...
AND MIKAN'S PROBABLY GOT A PAPER DEADLINE COMING UP.

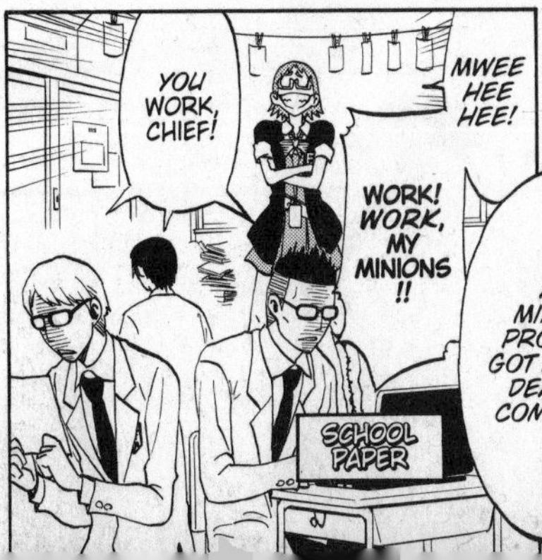
MWEE HEE HEE!
YOU WORK, CHIEF!
WORK! WORK, MY MINIONS!!
SCHOOL PAPER

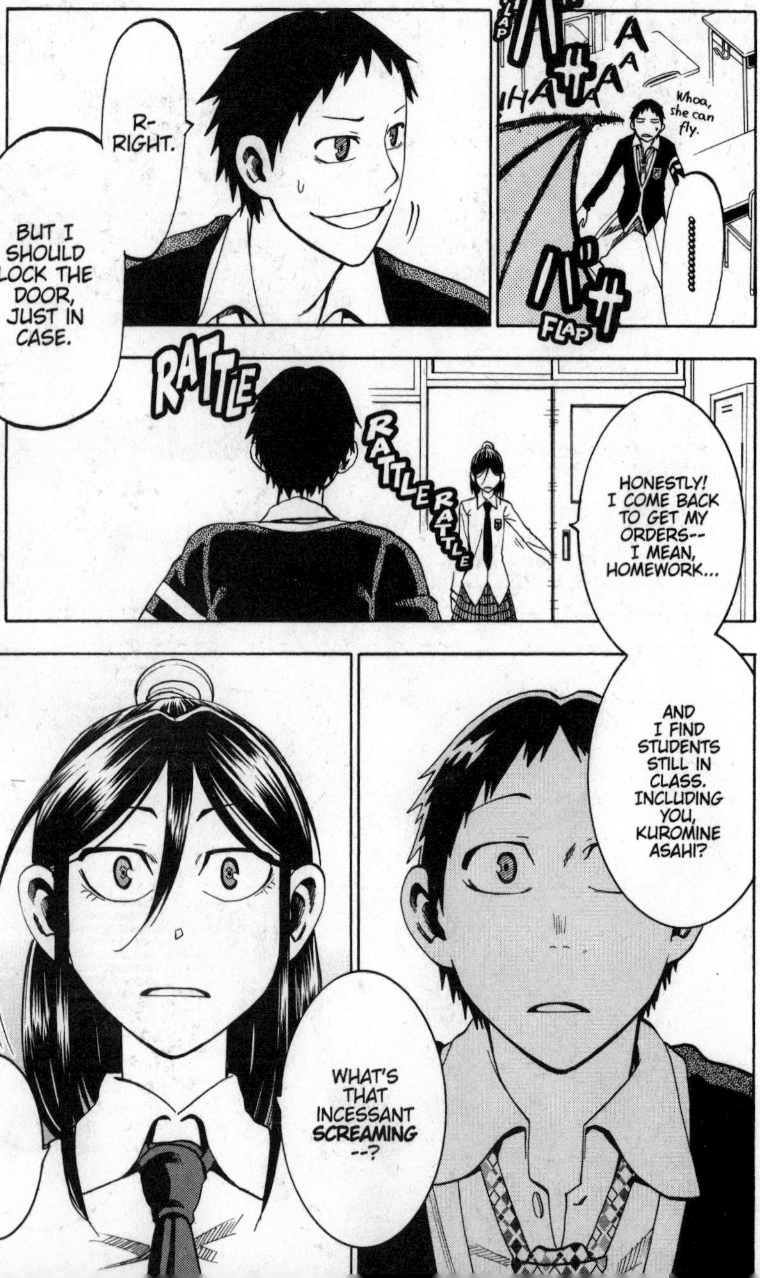
FLAP
HAAAAA
Whoa, she can fly.
FLAP
R-RIGHT.
BUT I SHOULD LOCK THE DOOR, JUST IN CASE.
RATTLE
RATTLE RATTLE
HONESTLY! I COME BACK TO GET MY ORDERS-- I MEAN, HOMEWORK...
AND I FIND STUDENTS STILL IN CLASS. INCLUDING YOU, KUROMINE ASAHI?
WHAT'S THAT INCESSANT SCREAMING --?
....

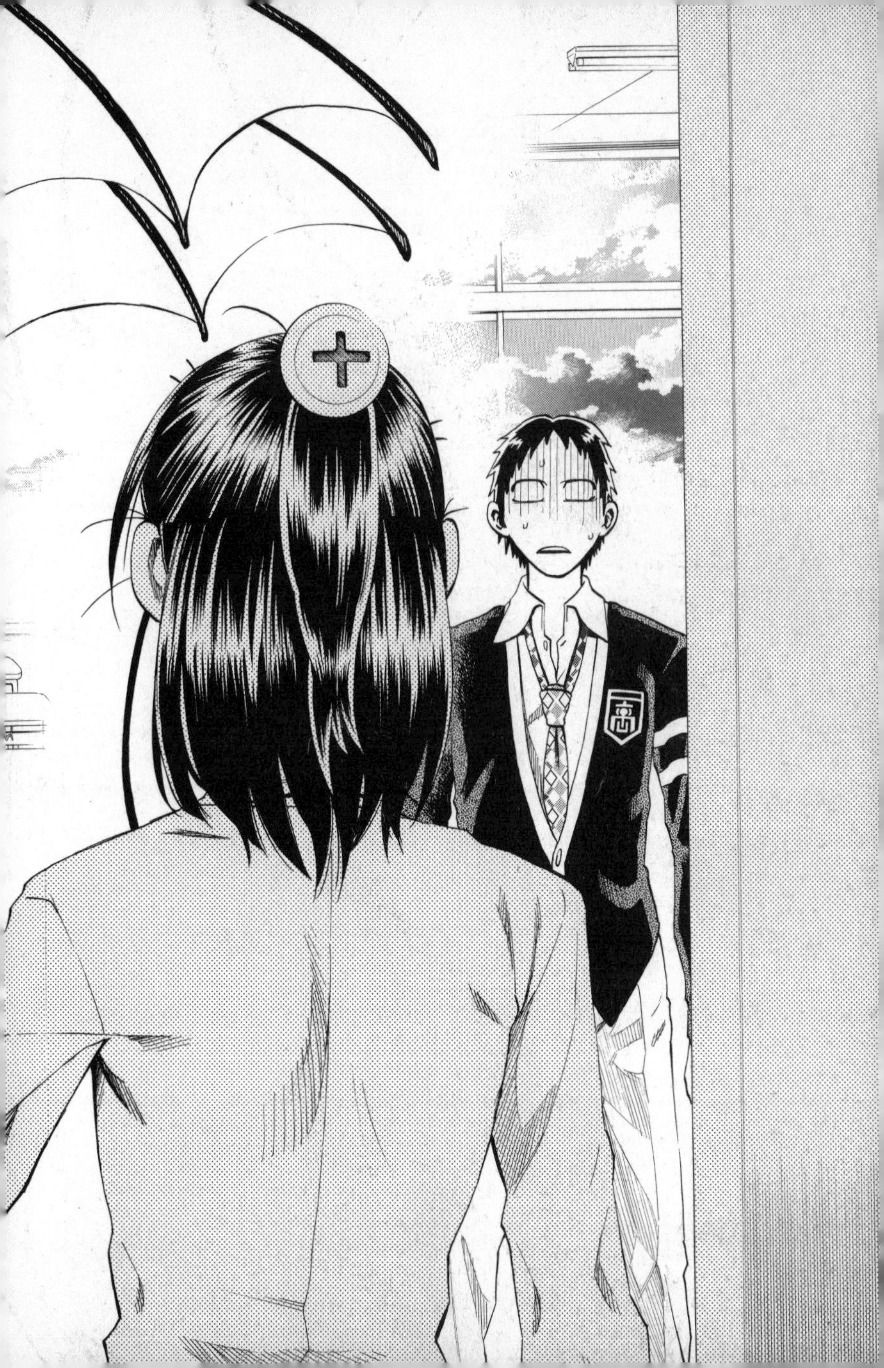

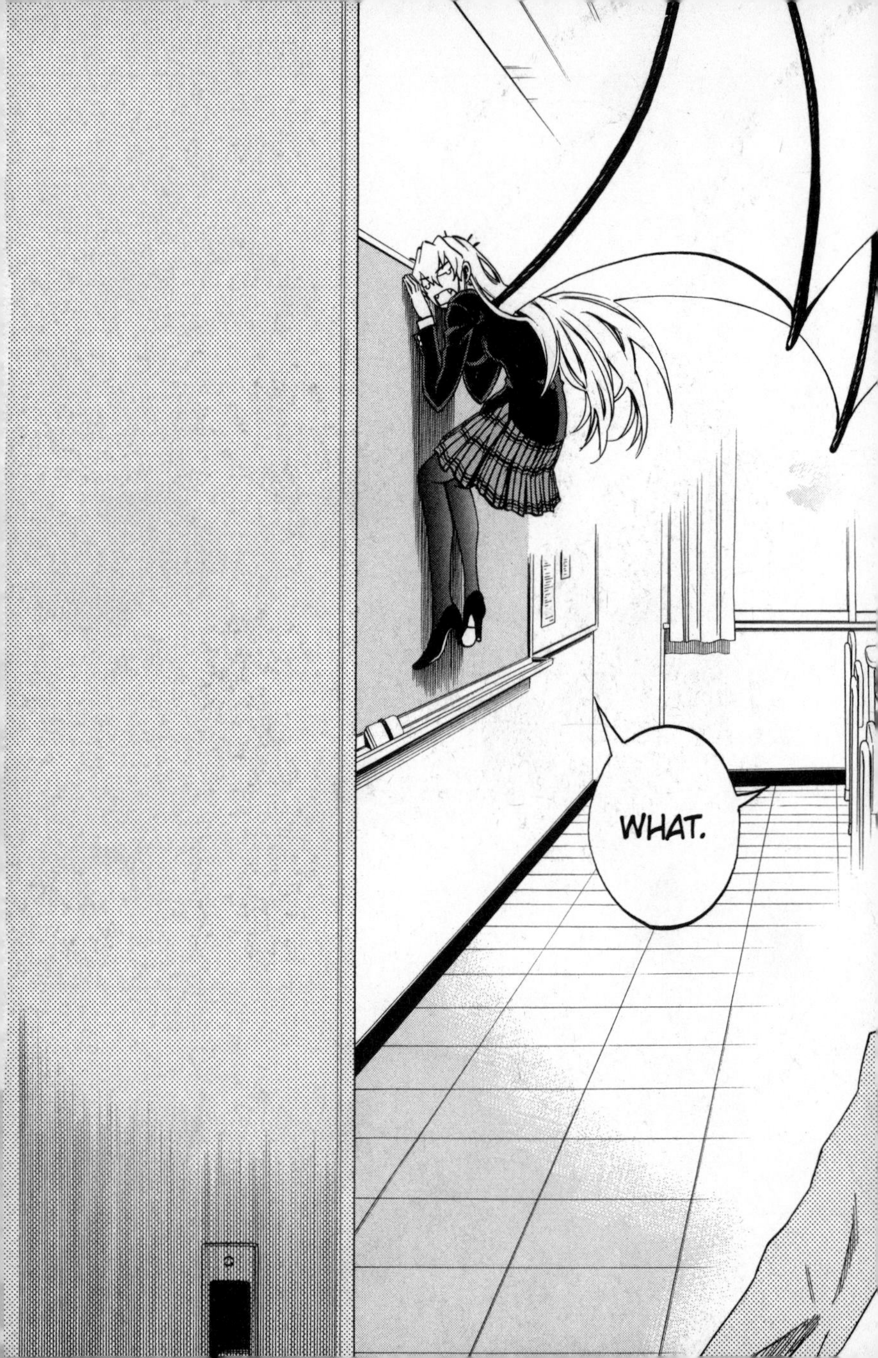
WHAT.

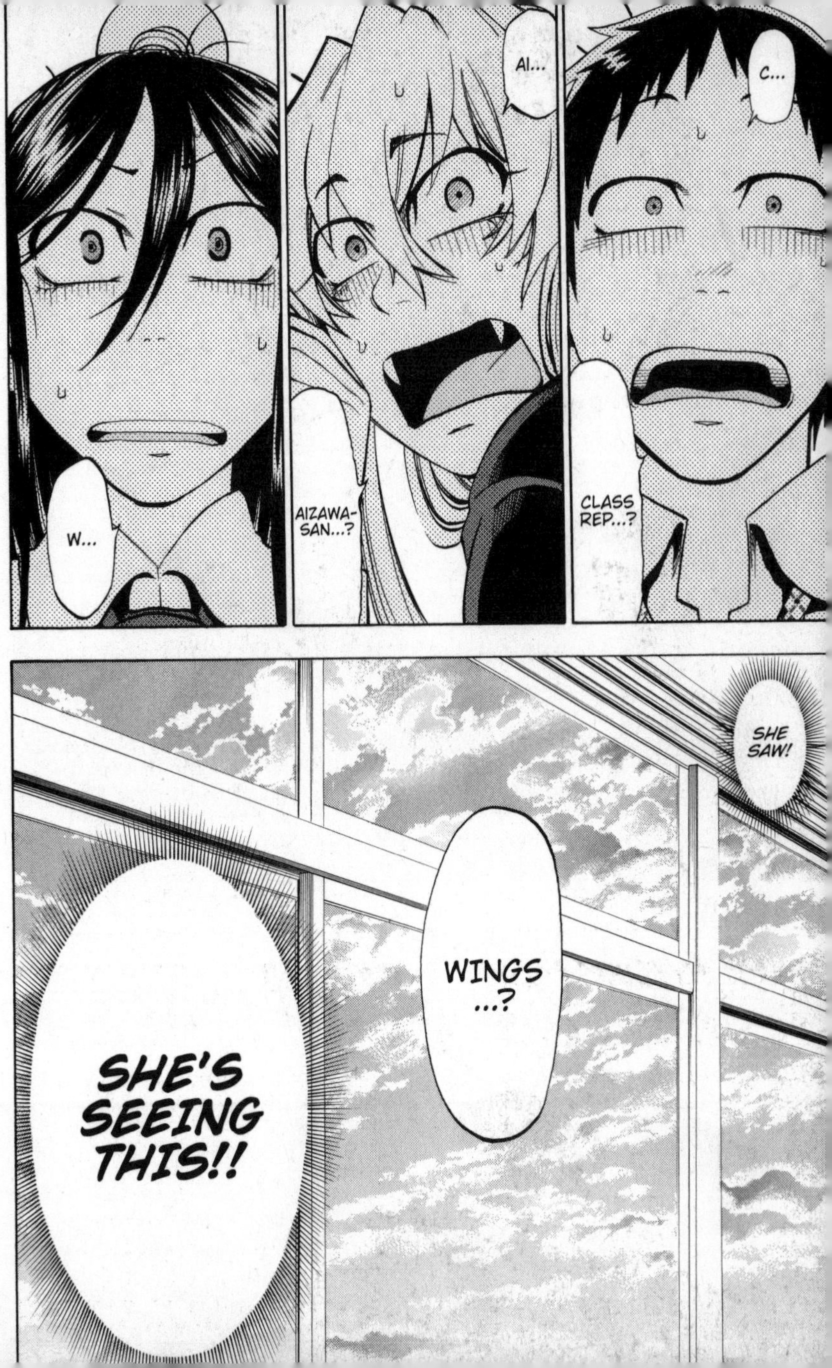
C...
CLASS REP...?
AI...
AIZAWA-SAN...?
W...
SHE SAW!
WINGS ...?
SHE'S SEEING THIS!!

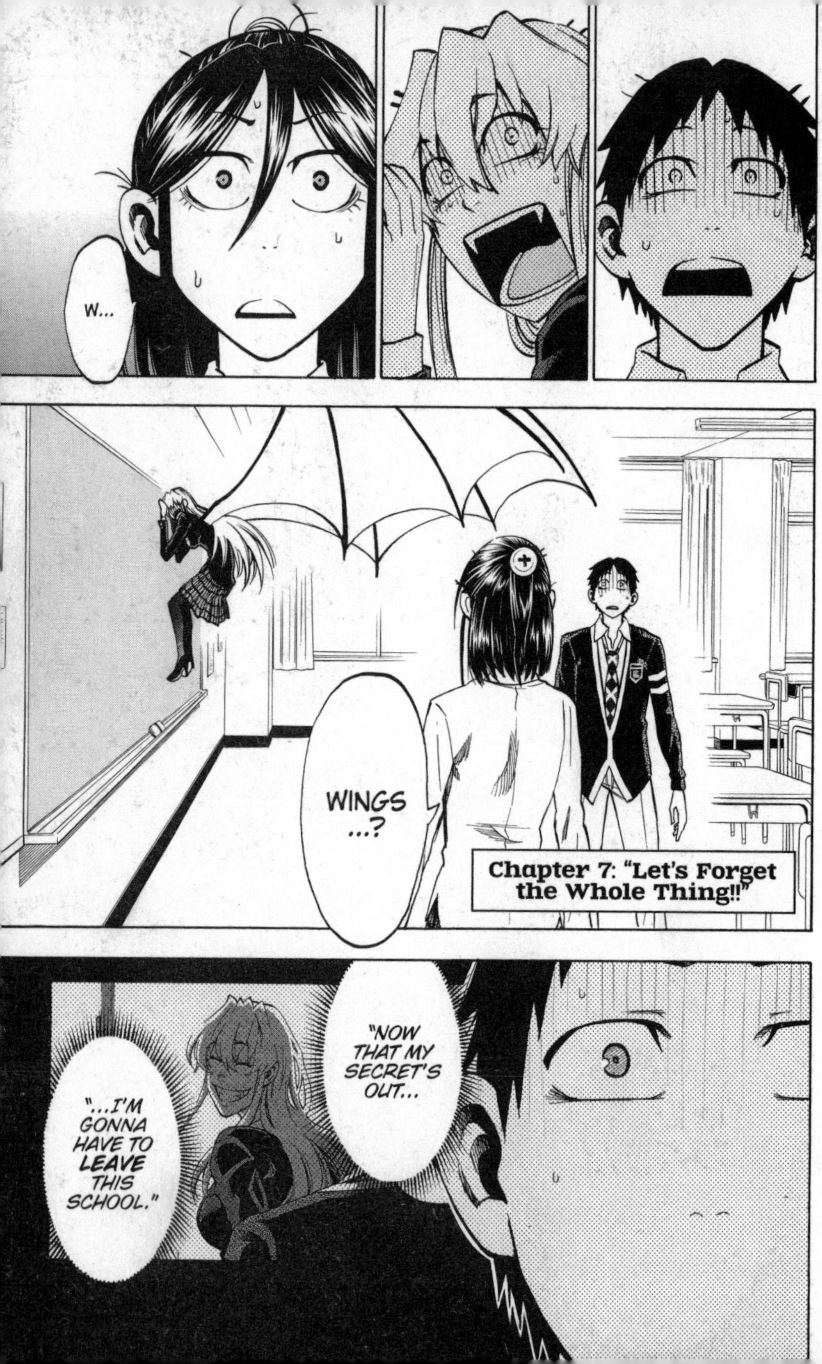
W...
WINGS ...?
Chapter 7: "Let's Forget the Whole Thing!!"
"NOW THAT MY SECRET'S OUT...
"...I'M GONNA HAVE TO LEAVE THIS SCHOOL."

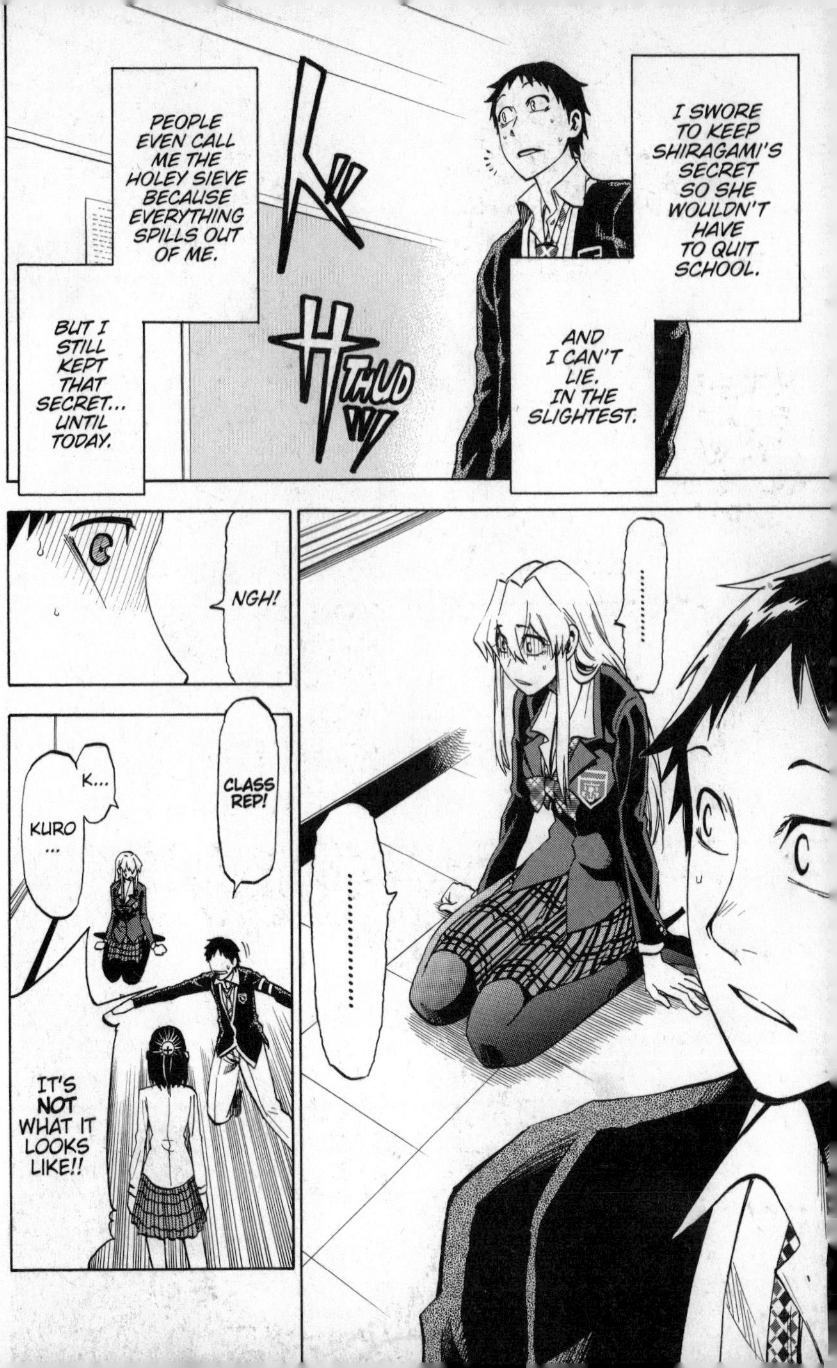
I SWORE TO KEEP SHIRAGAMI'S SECRET SO SHE WOULDN'T HAVE TO QUIT SCHOOL.
AND I CAN'T LIE. IN THE SLIGHTEST.
PEOPLE EVEN CALL ME THE HOLEY SIEVE BECAUSE EVERYTHING SPILLS OUT OF ME.
THUD
BUT I STILL KEPT THAT SECRET... UNTIL TODAY.
....
....
NGH!
CLASS REP!
K... KURO ...
IT'S NOT WHAT IT LOOKS LIKE!!

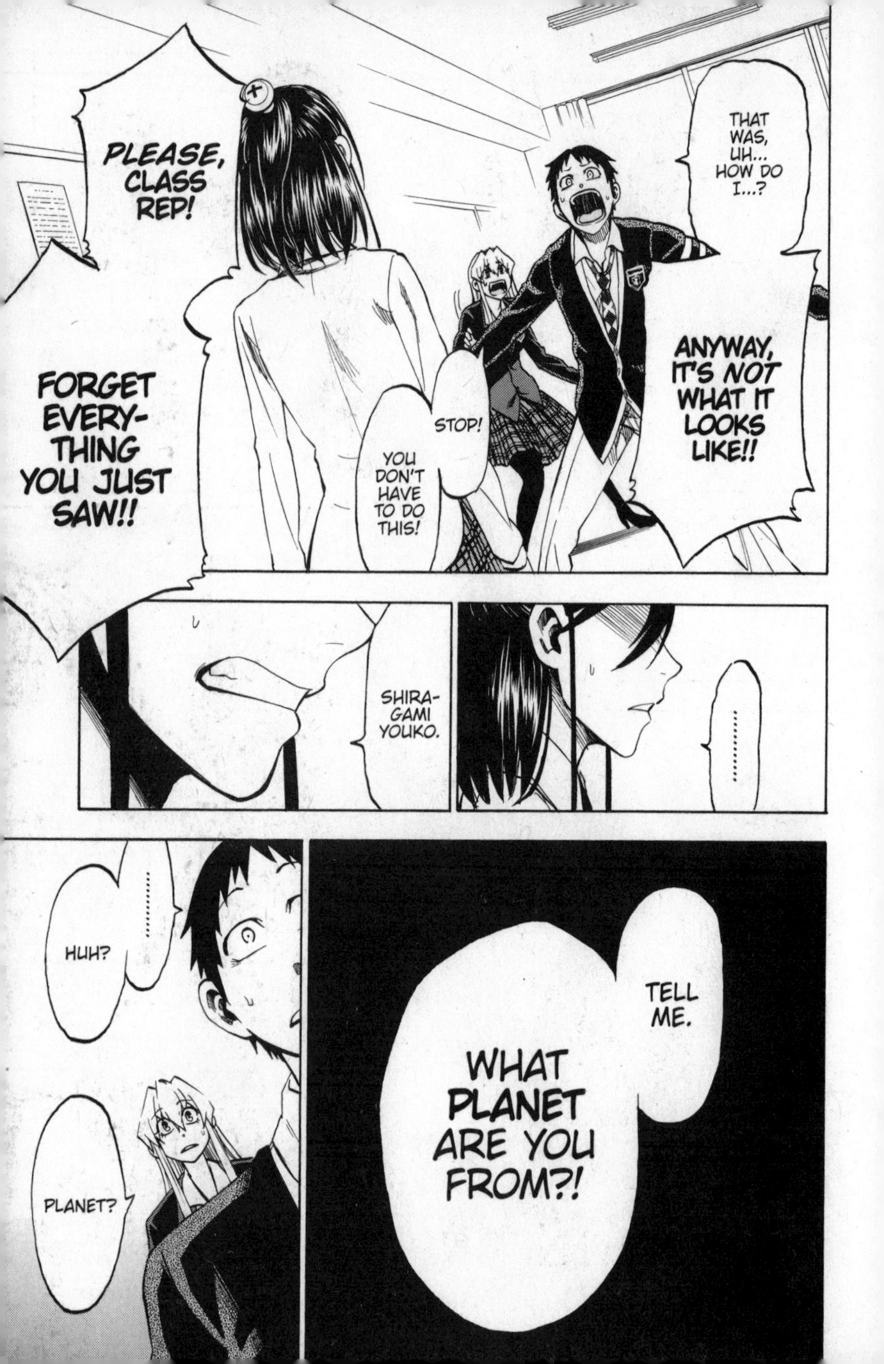
THAT WAS, UH... HOW DO I...?
ANYWAY, IT'S NOT WHAT IT LOOKS LIKE!!
STOP!
YOU DON'T HAVE TO DO THIS!
PLEASE, CLASS REP!
FORGET EVERYTHING YOU JUST SAW!!
......
SHIRAGAMI YOUKO.
TELL ME.
WHAT PLANET ARE YOU FROM?!
......
HUH?
PLANET?

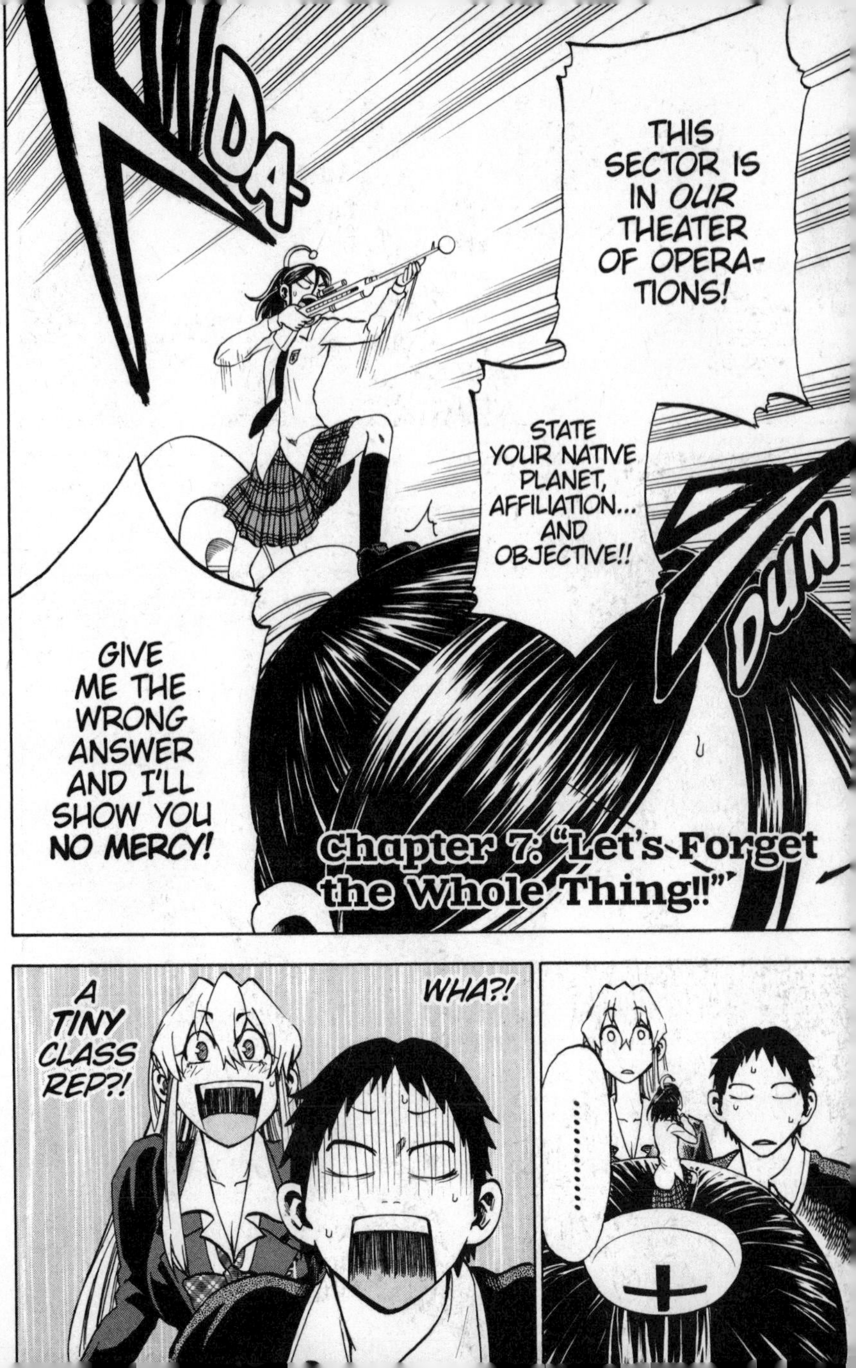
THIS SECTOR IS IN OUR THEATER OF OPERATIONS!
DUN
STATE YOUR NATIVE PLANET, AFFILIATION... AND OBJECTIVE!!
WHADA-
GIVE ME THE WRONG ANSWER AND I'LL SHOW YOU NO MERCY!
Chapter 7: "Let's Forget the Whole Thing!!"
......
WHA?!
A TINY CLASS REP?!

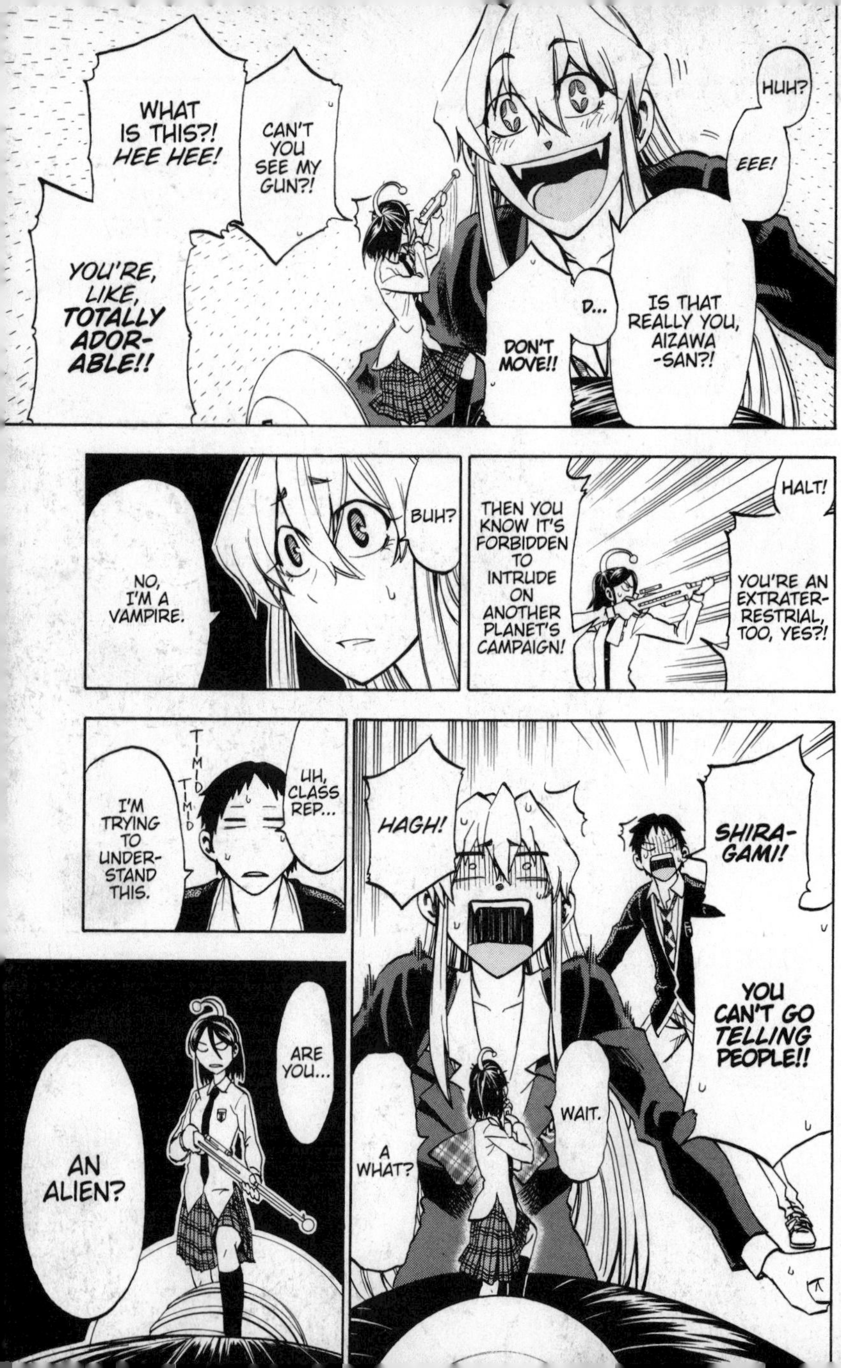
HUH?
EEE!
IS THAT REALLY YOU, AIZAWA-SAN?!
D...
DON'T MOVE!!
CAN'T YOU SEE MY GUN?!
WHAT IS THIS?! HEE HEE!
YOU'RE, LIKE, TOTALLY ADOR-ABLE!!
HALT!
YOU'RE AN EXTRATER-RESTRIAL, TOO, YES?!
THEN YOU KNOW IT'S FORBIDDEN TO INTRUDE ON ANOTHER PLANET'S CAMPAIGN!
BUH?
NO, I'M A VAMPIRE.
SHIRA-GAMI!
HAGH!
YOU CAN'T GO TELLING PEOPLE!!
WAIT.
A WHAT?
UH, CLASS REP...
TIMID TIMID
I'M TRYING TO UNDER-STAND THIS.
ARE YOU...
AN ALIEN?

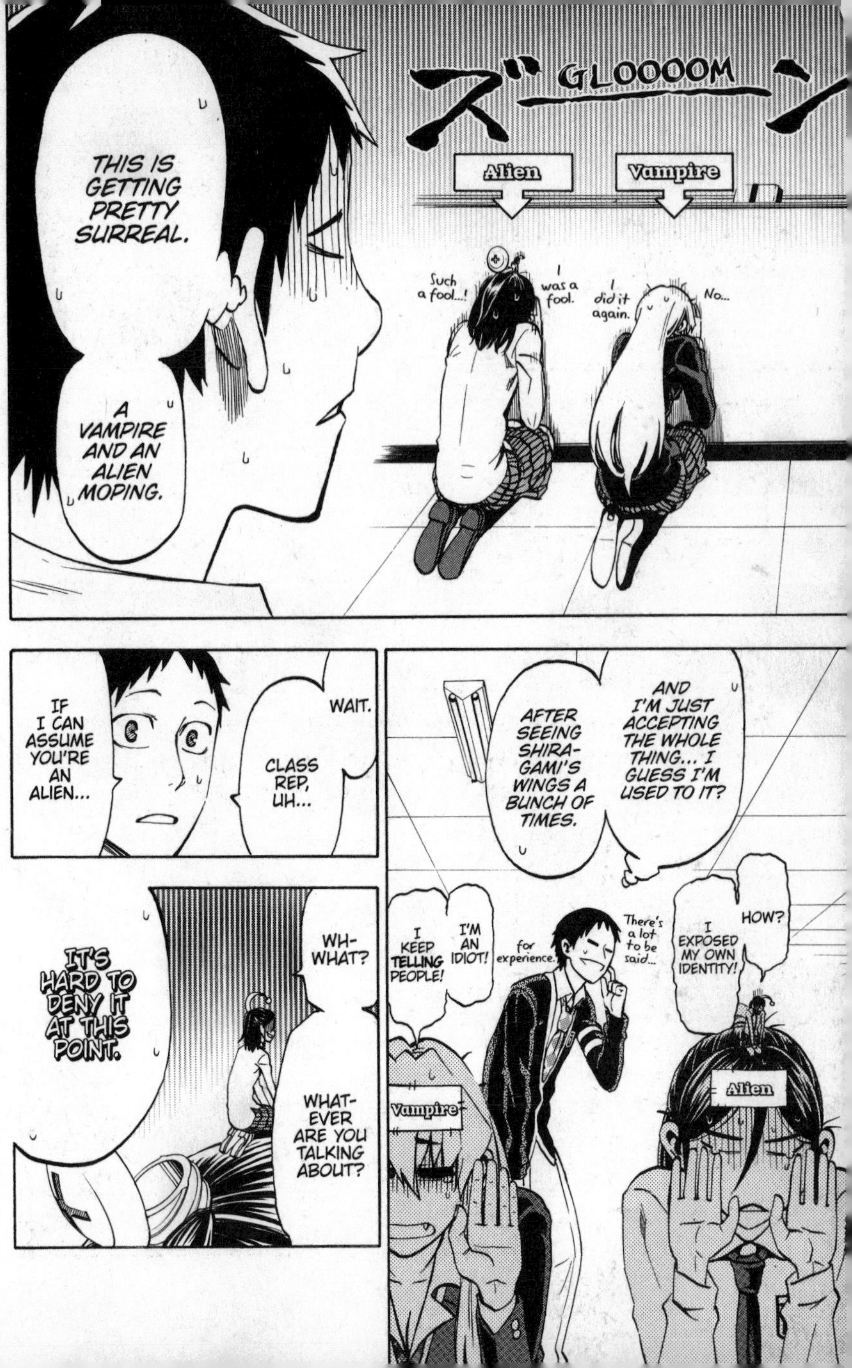
GLOOOOM
Alien
Vampire
No...
I did it again.
I was a fool.
Such a fool...!
THIS IS GETTING PRETTY SURREAL.
A VAMPIRE AND AN ALIEN MOPING.
AND I'M JUST ACCEPTING THE WHOLE THING... I GUESS I'M USED TO IT?
AFTER SEEING SHIRA-GAMI'S WINGS A BUNCH OF TIMES.
HOW?
I EXPOSED MY OWN IDENTITY!
There's a lot to be said...
for experience.
I'M AN IDIOT!
I KEEP TELLING PEOPLE!
Alien
Vampire
WAIT.
CLASS REP, UH...
IF I CAN ASSUME YOU'RE AN ALIEN...
WH-WHAT?
WHAT-EVER ARE YOU TALKING ABOUT?
IT'S HARD TO DENY IT AT THIS POINT.

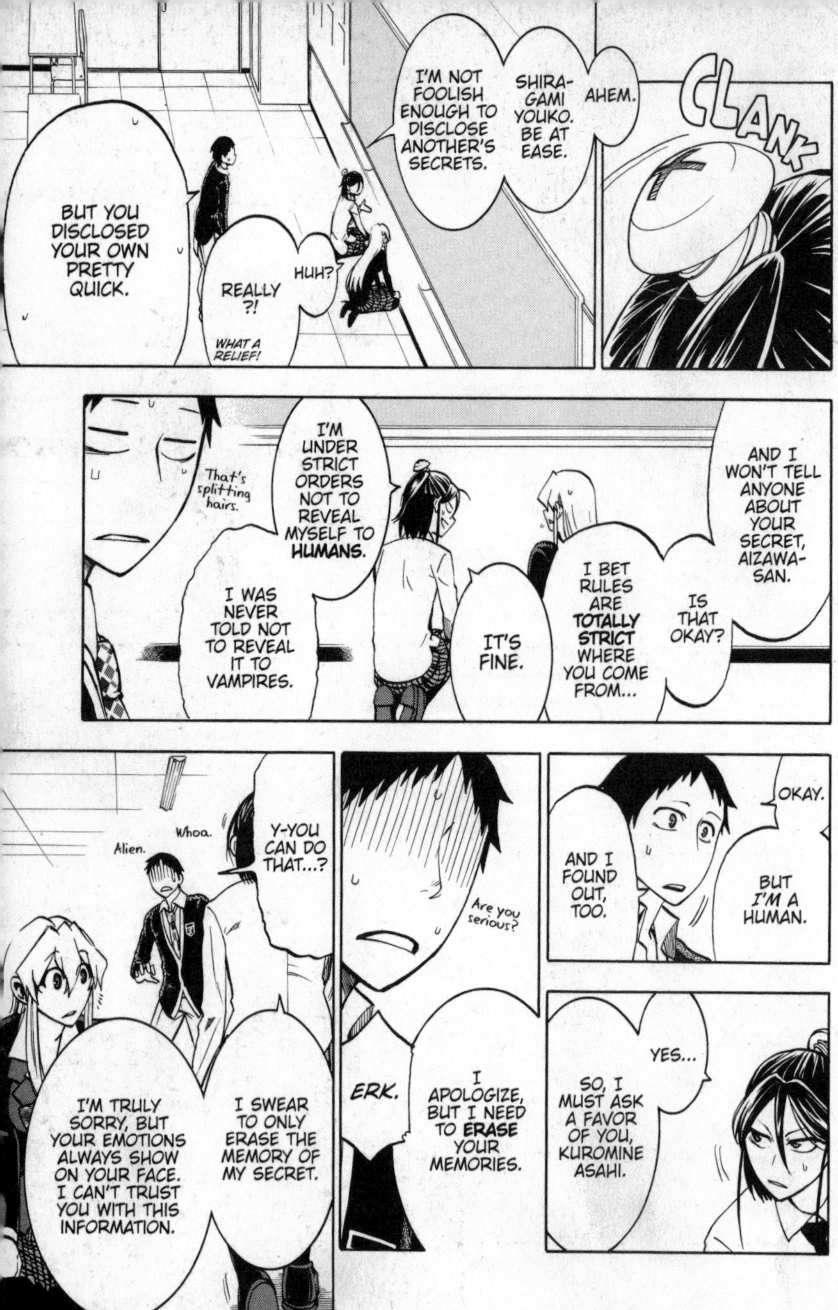
CLANK
AHEM.
SHIRAGAMI YOUKO. BE AT EASE.
I'M NOT FOOLISH ENOUGH TO DISCLOSE ANOTHER'S SECRETS.
HUH?
REALLY ?!
WHAT A RELIEF!
BUT YOU DISCLOSED YOUR OWN PRETTY QUICK.
AND I WON'T TELL ANYONE ABOUT YOUR SECRET, AIZAWA-SAN.
IS THAT OKAY?
I BET RULES ARE TOTALLY STRICT WHERE YOU COME FROM...
IT'S FINE.
I'M UNDER STRICT ORDERS NOT TO REVEAL MYSELF TO HUMANS.
I WAS NEVER TOLD NOT TO REVEAL IT TO VAMPIRES.
That's splitting hairs.
OKAY.
BUT I'M A HUMAN.
AND I FOUND OUT, TOO.
YES...
SO, I MUST ASK A FAVOR OF YOU, KUROMINE ASAHI.
Are you serious?
I APOLOGIZE, BUT I NEED TO ERASE YOUR MEMORIES.
ERK.
Y-YOU CAN DO THAT...?
Whoa.
Alien.
I SWEAR TO ONLY ERASE THE MEMORY OF MY SECRET.
I'M TRULY SORRY, BUT YOUR EMOTIONS ALWAYS SHOW ON YOUR FACE. I CAN'T TRUST YOU WITH THIS INFORMATION.

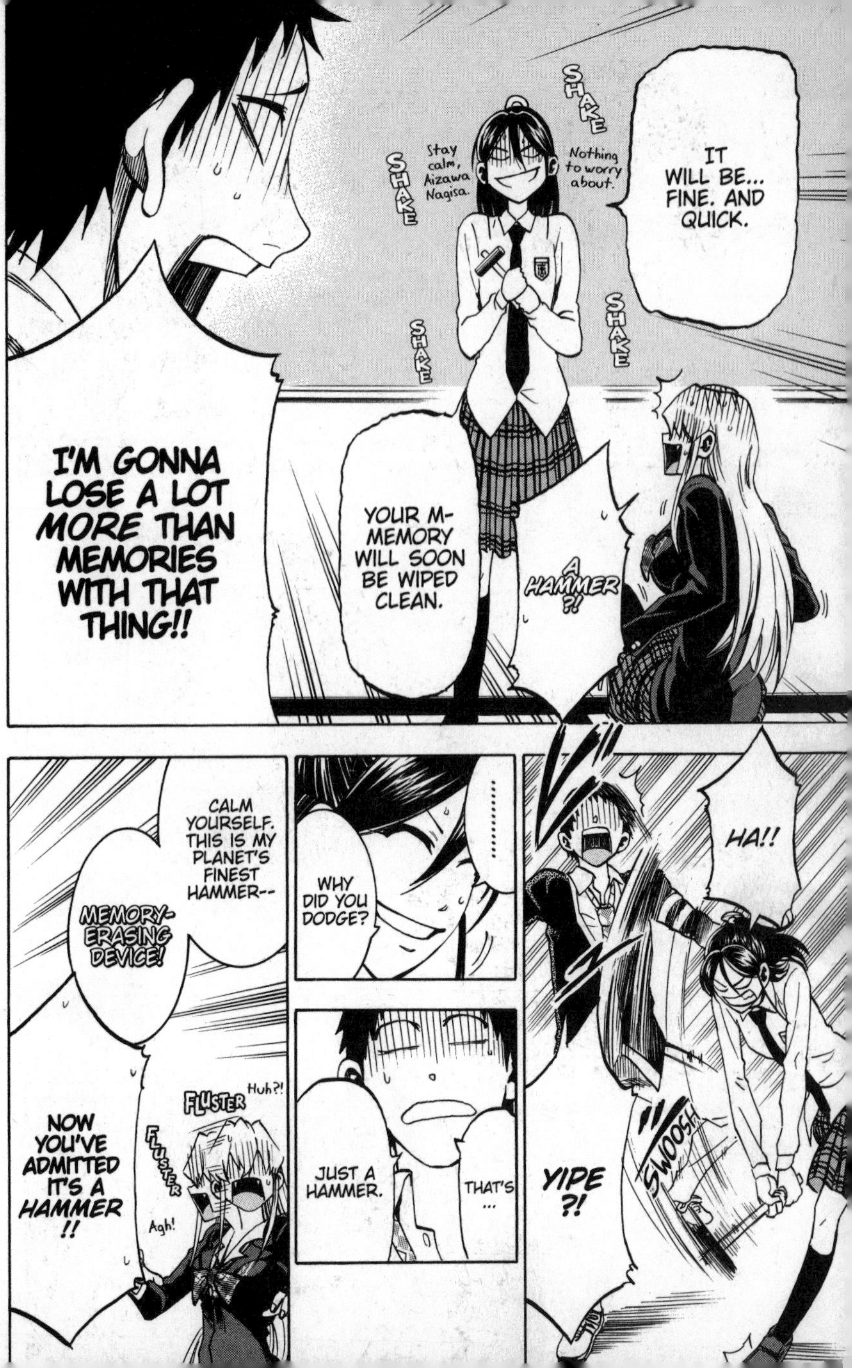
IT WILL BE... FINE. AND QUICK.
SHAKE
Nothing to worry about.
SHAKE
Stay calm, Aizawa Nagisa.
SHAKE
SHAKE
YOUR M-MEMORY WILL SOON BE WIPED CLEAN.
A HAMMER ?!
I'M GONNA LOSE A LOT MORE THAN MEMORIES WITH THAT THING!!
HA!!
SWOOSH!!
YIPE ?!
....
WHY DID YOU DODGE?
THAT'S ...
JUST A HAMMER.
CALM YOURSELF. THIS IS MY PLANET'S FINEST HAMMER--
MEMORY-ERASING DEVICE!
FLUSTER
Huh?!
FLUSTER
Agh!
NOW YOU'VE ADMITTED IT'S A HAMMER !!

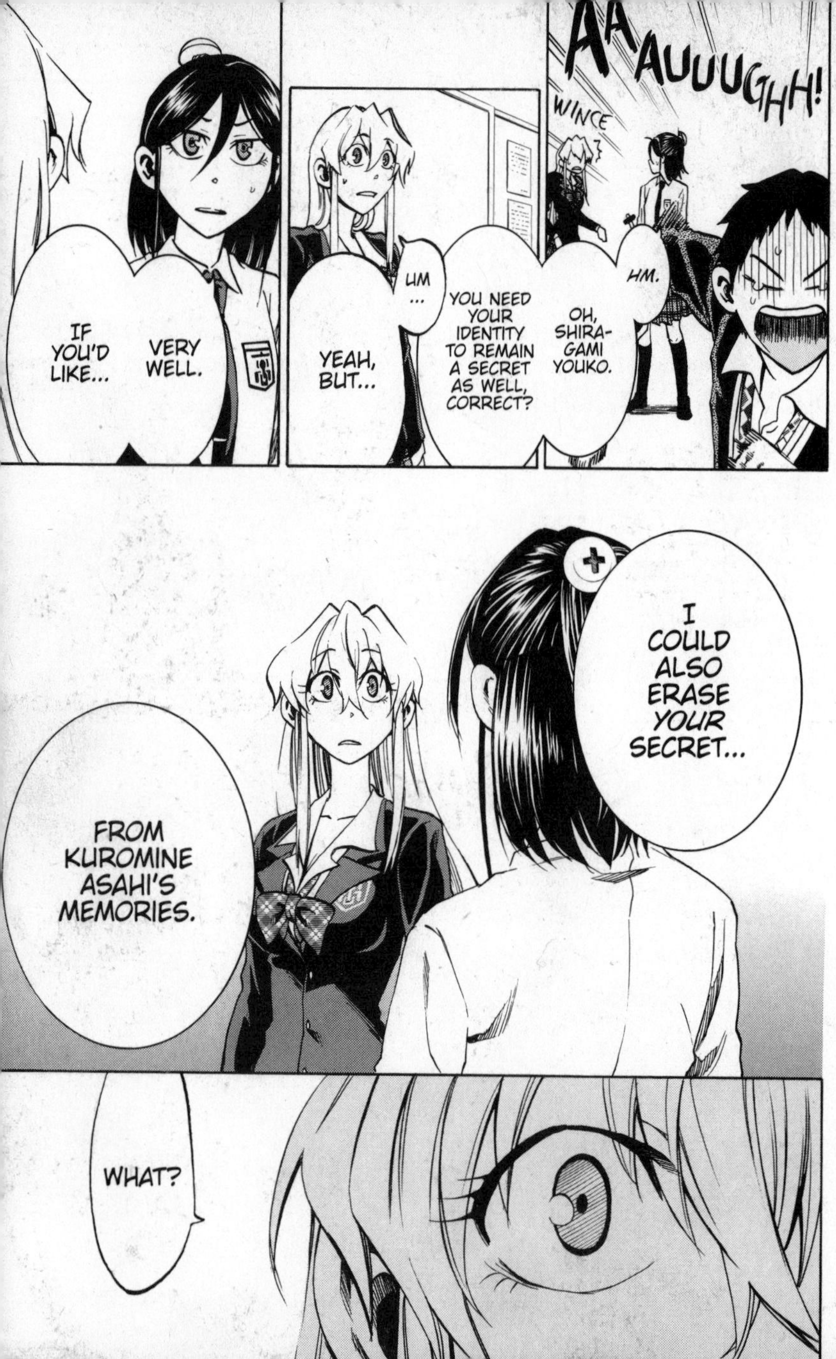
AAAUUUGHH!
WINCE
HM.
OH, SHIRAGAMI YOUKO.
YOU NEED YOUR IDENTITY TO REMAIN A SECRET AS WELL, CORRECT?
UM ...
YEAH, BUT...
VERY WELL.
IF YOU'D LIKE...
I COULD ALSO ERASE YOUR SECRET...
FROM KUROMINE ASAHI'S MEMORIES.
WHAT?

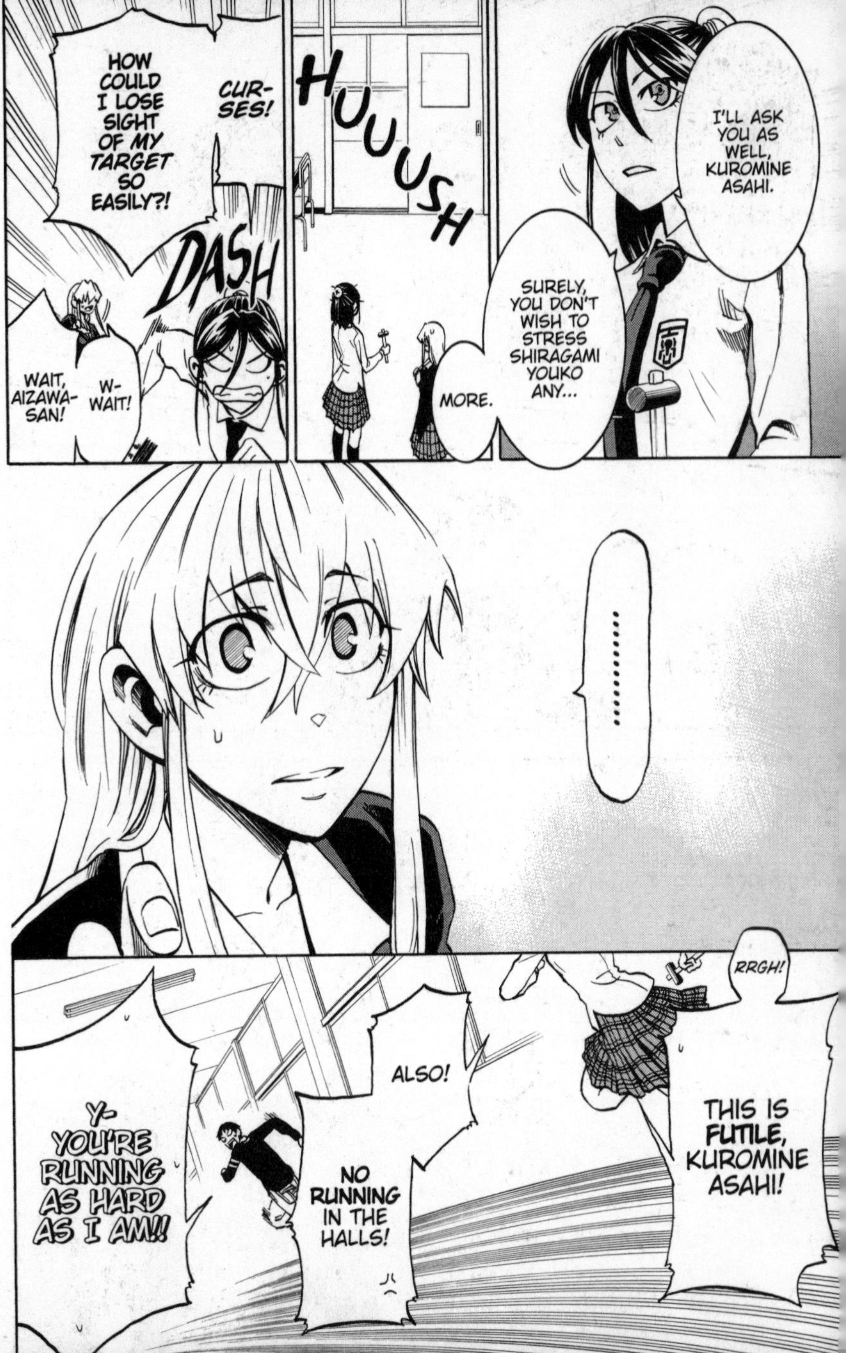
I'LL ASK YOU AS WELL, KUROMINE ASAHI.
SURELY, YOU DON'T WISH TO STRESS SHIRAGAMI YOUKO ANY...
MORE.
HUUUSH
CUR-SES!
HOW COULD I LOSE SIGHT OF MY TARGET SO EASILY?!
DASH
W-WAIT!
WAIT, AIZAWA-SAN!
......
RRGH!
THIS IS FUTILE, KUROMINE ASAHI!
ALSO!
NO RUNNING IN THE HALLS!
Y-YOU'RE RUNNING AS HARD AS I AM!!

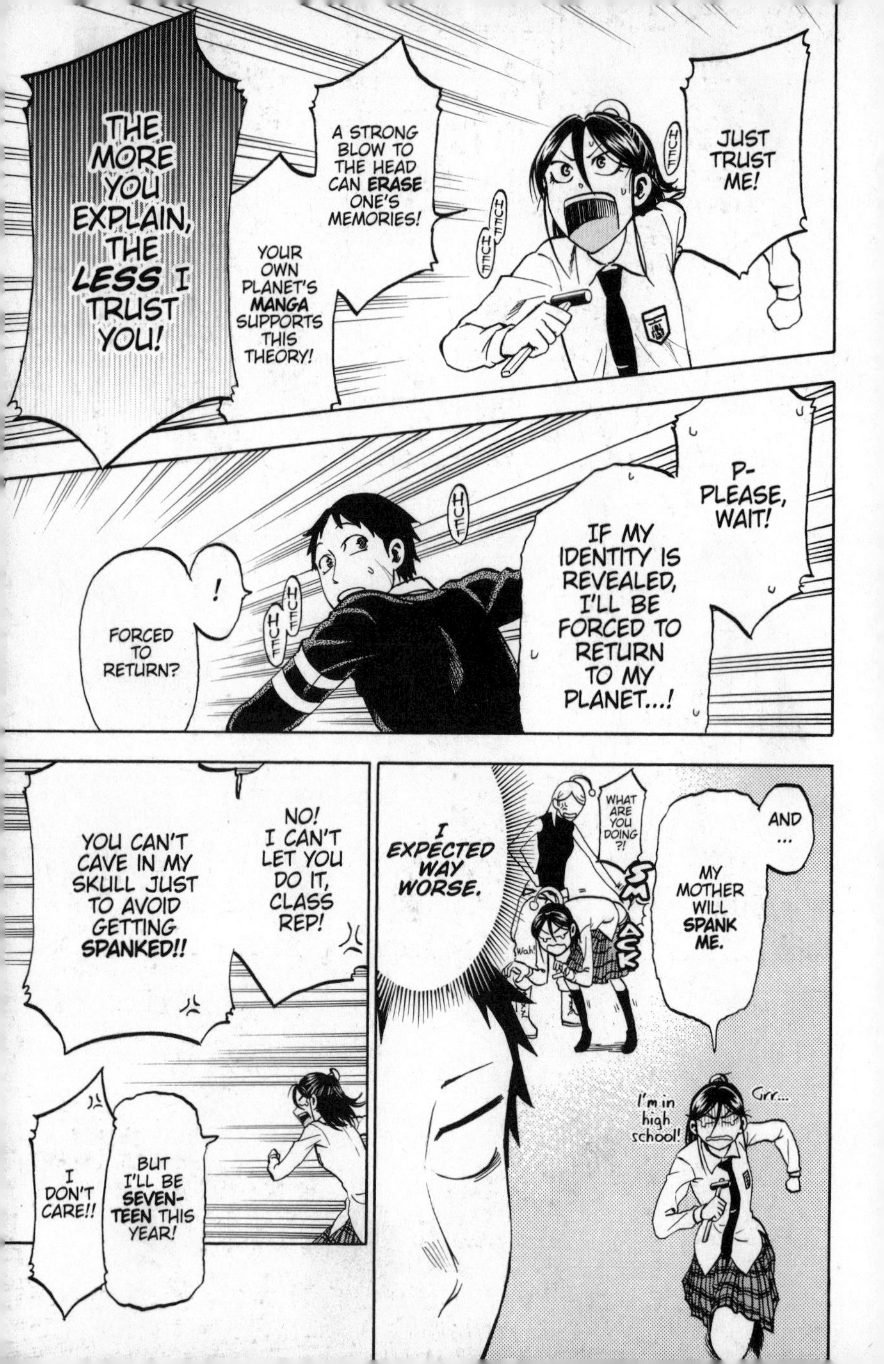
JUST TRUST ME!
HUFF
HUFF HUFF
A STRONG BLOW TO THE HEAD CAN ERASE ONE'S MEMORIES!
YOUR OWN PLANET'S MANGA SUPPORTS THIS THEORY!
THE MORE YOU EXPLAIN, THE LESS I TRUST YOU!
P-PLEASE, WAIT!
IF MY IDENTITY IS REVEALED, I'LL BE FORCED TO RETURN TO MY PLANET...!
HUFF
HUFF HUFF
!
FORCED TO RETURN?
AND ...
MY MOTHER WILL SPANK ME.
WHAT ARE YOU DOING?!
SMACK
Wah!
I EXPECTED WAY WORSE.
Grr...
I'm in high school!
NO! I CAN'T LET YOU DO IT, CLASS REP!
YOU CAN'T CAVE IN MY SKULL JUST TO AVOID GETTING SPANKED!!
BUT I'LL BE SEVENTEEN THIS YEAR!
I DON'T CARE!!

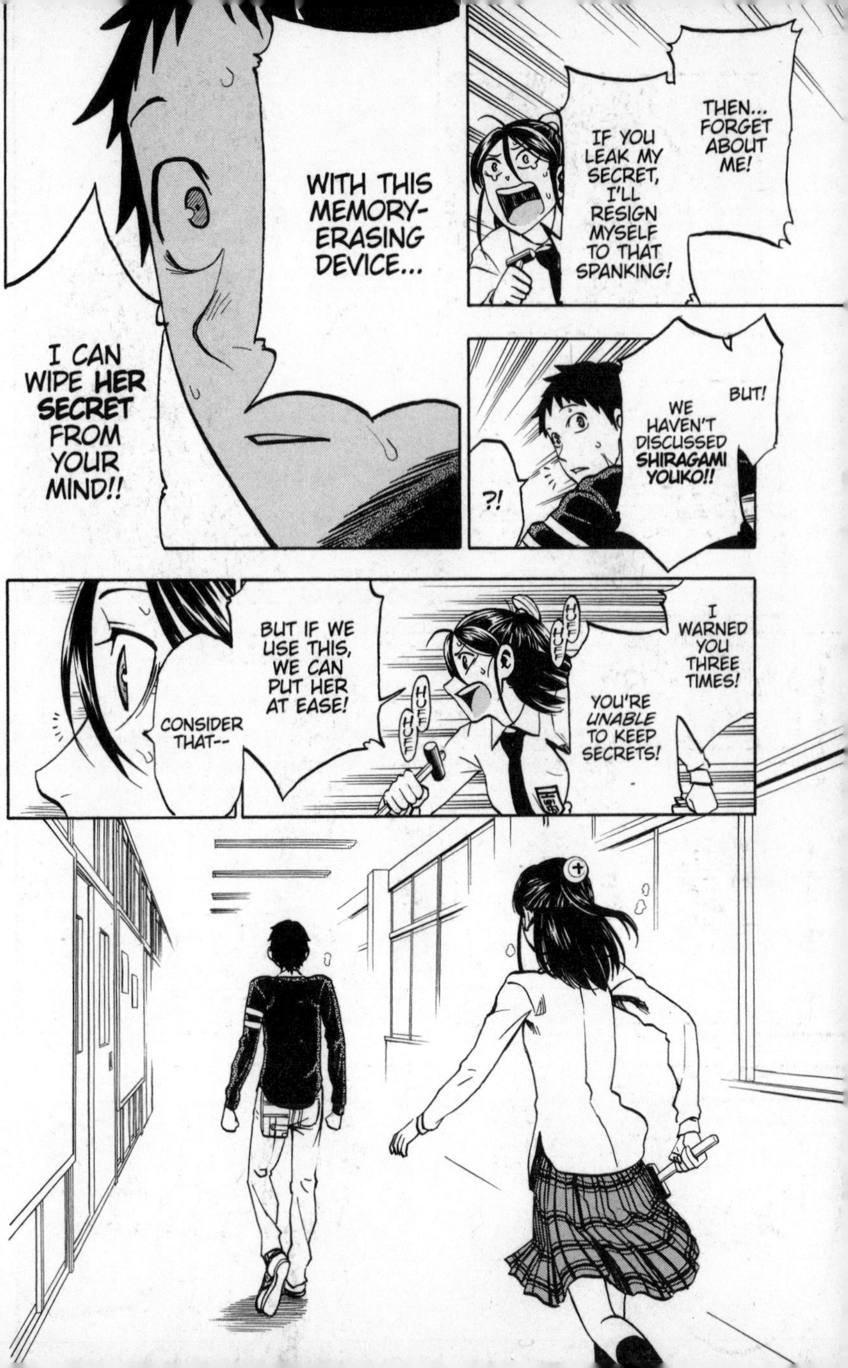
THEN... FORGET ABOUT ME!
IF YOU LEAK MY SECRET, I'LL RESIGN MYSELF TO THAT SPANKING!
WITH THIS MEMORY-ERASING DEVICE...
BUT!
WE HAVEN'T DISCUSSED SHIRAGAMI YOUKO!!
?!
I CAN WIPE HER SECRET FROM YOUR MIND!!
I WARNED YOU THREE TIMES!
YOU'RE UNABLE TO KEEP SECRETS!
HUFF HUFF
HUFF HUFF
BUT IF WE USE THIS, WE CAN PUT HER AT EASE!
CONSIDER THAT--

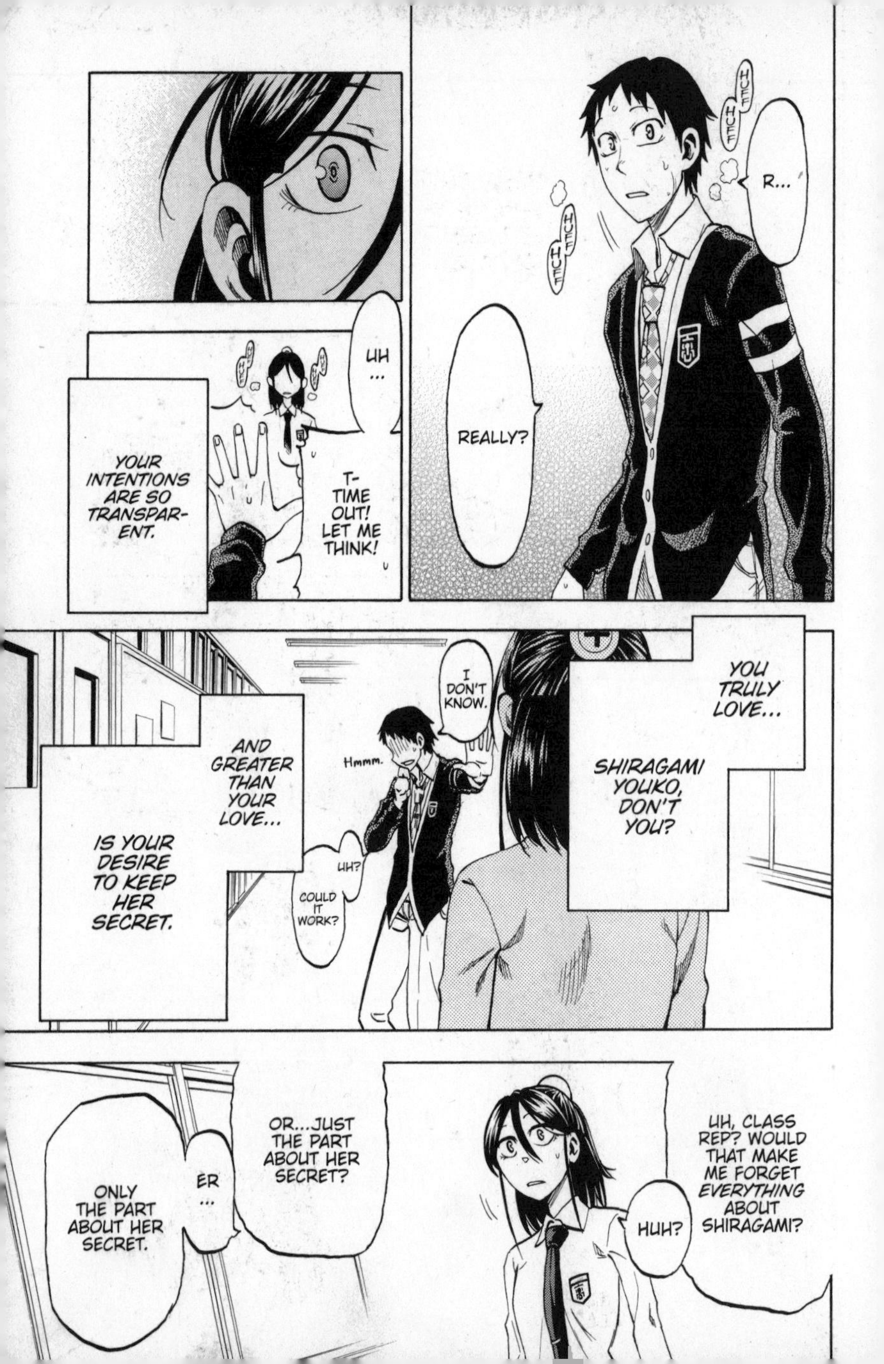
R...
HUFF HUFF
HUFF HUFF
REALLY?
UH ...
T-TIME OUT! LET ME THINK!
YOUR INTENTIONS ARE SO TRANSPAR-ENT.
HUFF
HUFF
YOU TRULY LOVE...
SHIRAGAMI YOUKO, DON'T YOU?
I DON'T KNOW.
Hmmm.
AND GREATER THAN YOUR LOVE...
IS YOUR DESIRE TO KEEP HER SECRET.
UH?
COULD IT WORK?
UH, CLASS REP? WOULD THAT MAKE ME FORGET EVERYTHING ABOUT SHIRAGAMI?
HUH?
OR...JUST THE PART ABOUT HER SECRET?
ER ...
ONLY THE PART ABOUT HER SECRET.

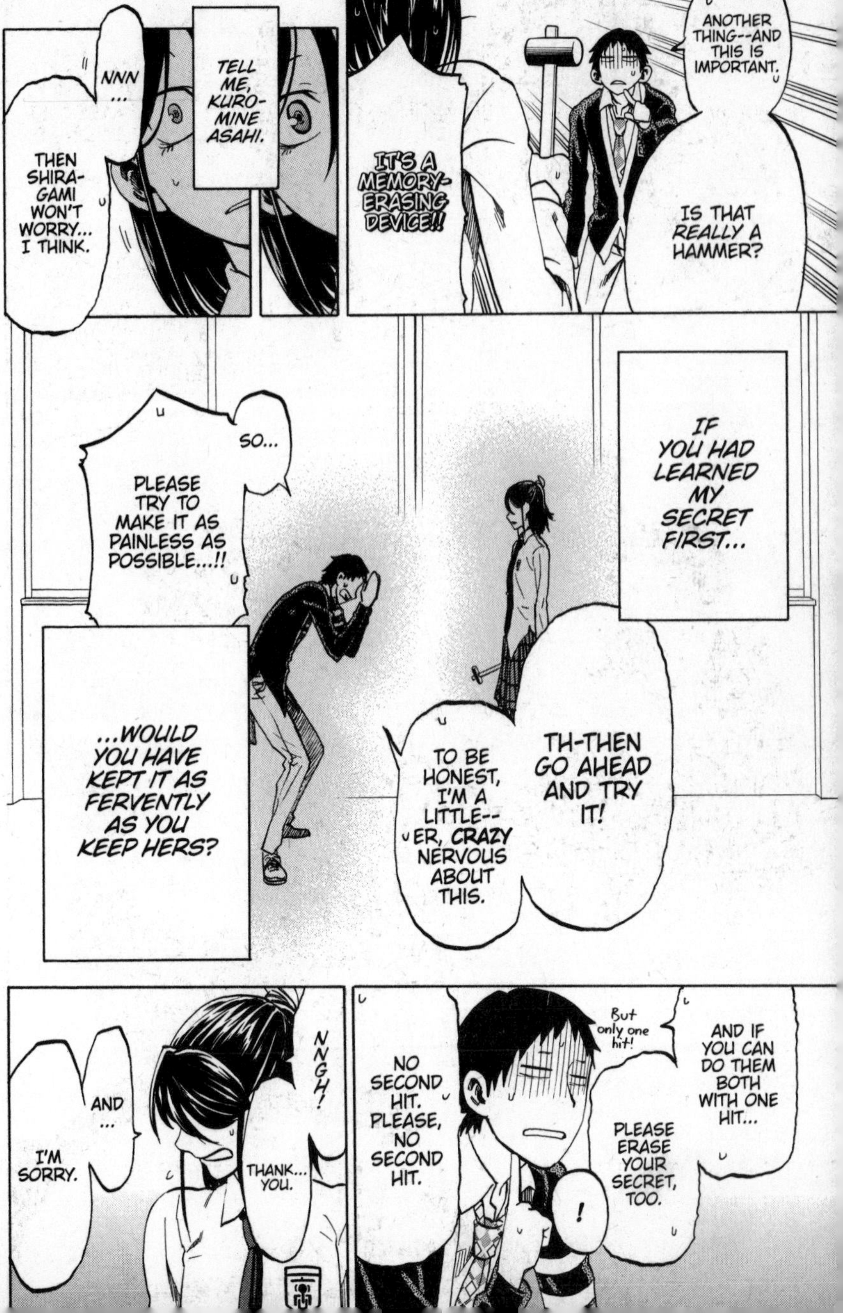
ANOTHER THING--AND THIS IS IMPORTANT.
IS THAT REALLY A HAMMER?
IT'S A MEMORY-ERASING DEVICE!!
TELL ME, KURO-MINE ASAHI.
NNN...
THEN SHIRA-GAMI WON'T WORRY... I THINK.
IF YOU HAD LEARNED MY SECRET FIRST...
...WOULD YOU HAVE KEPT IT AS FERVENTLY AS YOU KEEP HERS?
TH-THEN GO AHEAD AND TRY IT!
TO BE HONEST, I'M A LITTLE-- ER, CRAZY NERVOUS ABOUT THIS.
SO...
PLEASE TRY TO MAKE IT AS PAINLESS AS POSSIBLE...!!
AND IF YOU CAN DO THEM BOTH WITH ONE HIT...
But only one hit!
PLEASE ERASE YOUR SECRET, TOO.
!
NO SECOND HIT. PLEASE, NO SECOND HIT.
NNGH!
THANK... YOU.
AND...
I'M SORRY.

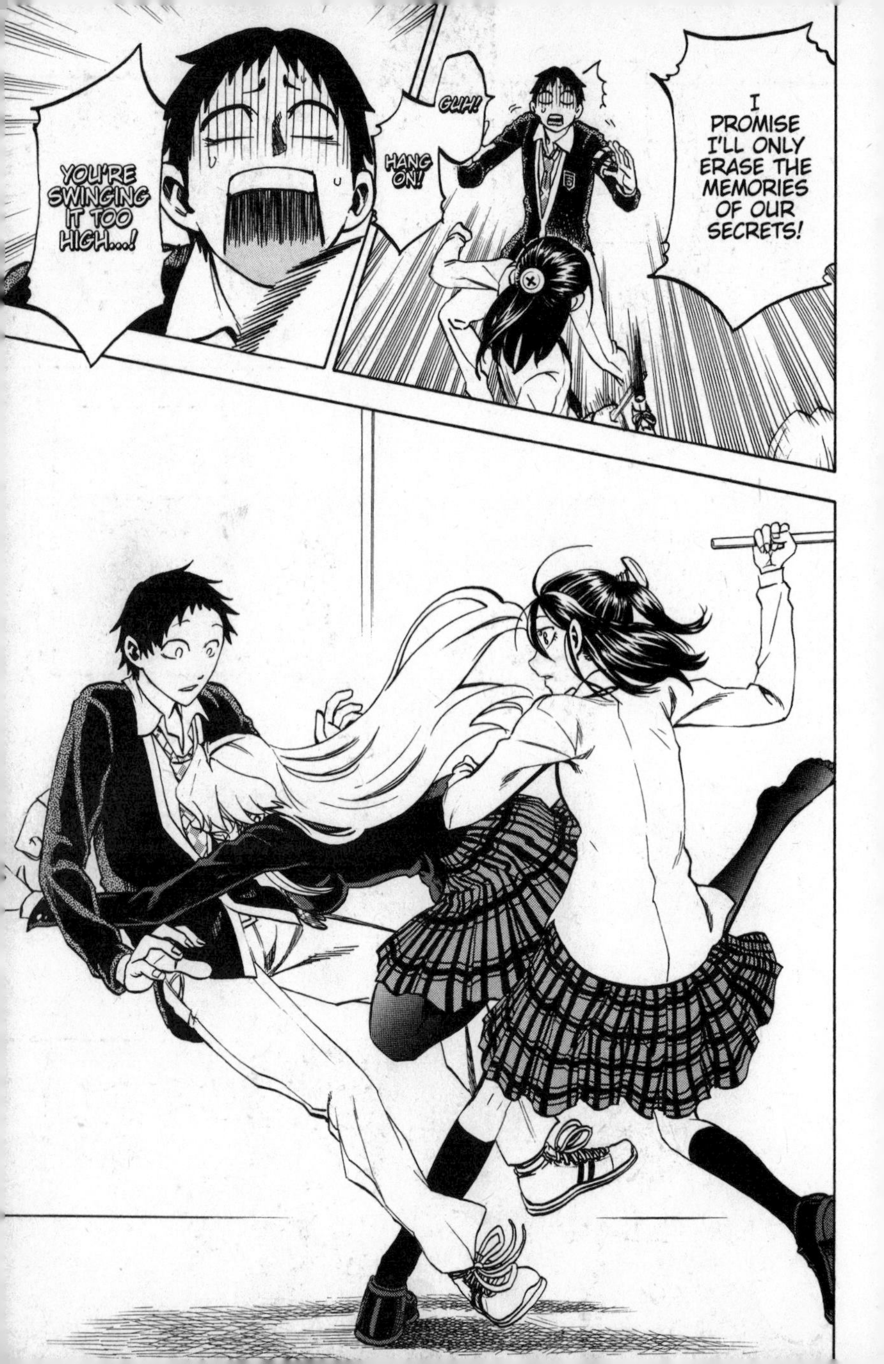
I PROMISE I'LL ONLY ERASE THE MEMORIES OF OUR SECRETS!
GUH!
HANG ON!
YOU'RE SWINGING IT TOO HIGH...!

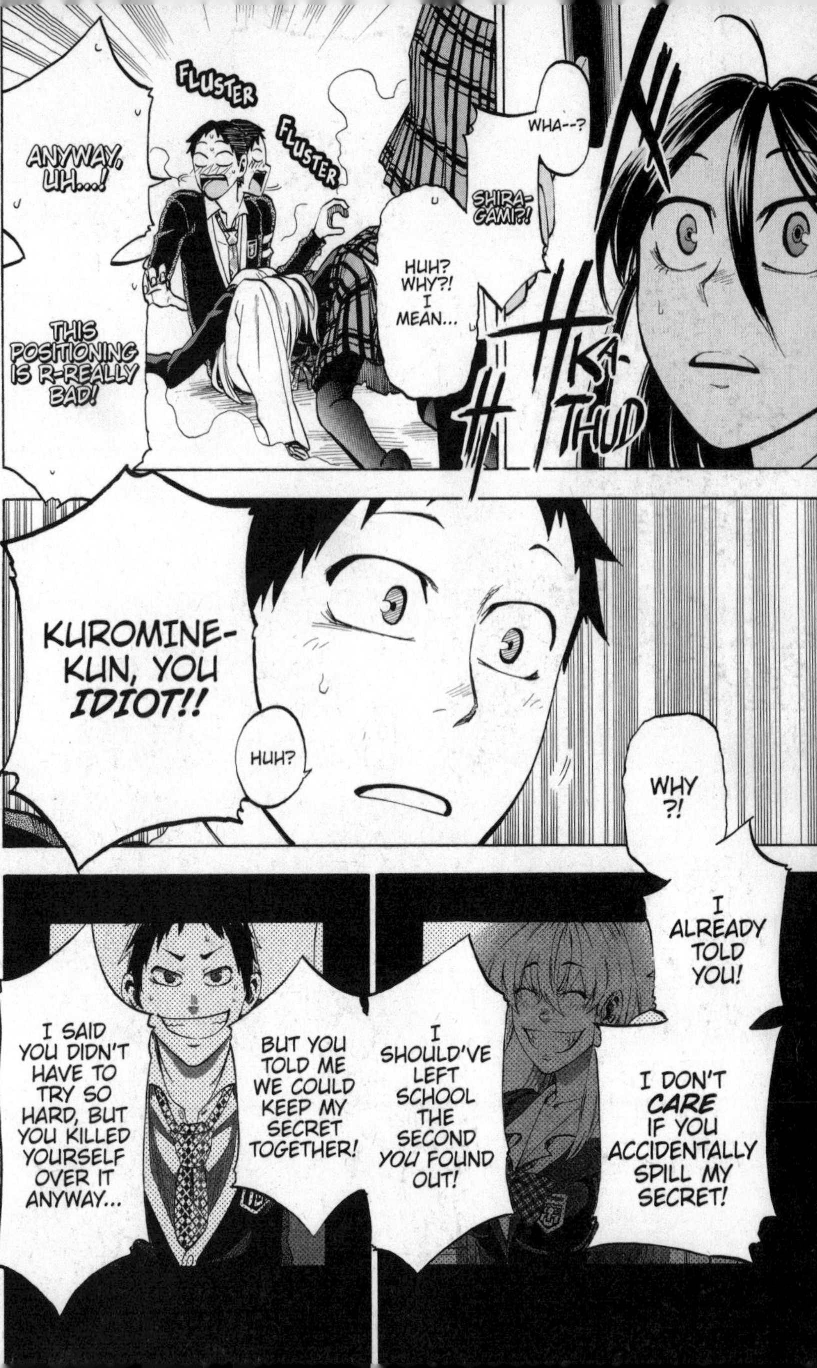
KA-THUD
WHA--?
SHIRA-GAMI?!
HUH? WHY?! I MEAN...
FLUSTER
FLUSTER
ANYWAY, UH...!
THIS POSITIONING IS R-REALLY BAD!
WHY ?!
HUH?
KUROMINE-KUN, YOU IDIOT!!
I ALREADY TOLD YOU!
I DON'T CARE IF YOU ACCIDENTALLY SPILL MY SECRET!
I SHOULD'VE LEFT SCHOOL THE SECOND YOU FOUND OUT!
BUT YOU TOLD ME WE COULD KEEP MY SECRET TOGETHER!
I SAID YOU DIDN'T HAVE TO TRY SO HARD, BUT YOU KILLED YOURSELF OVER IT ANYWAY...

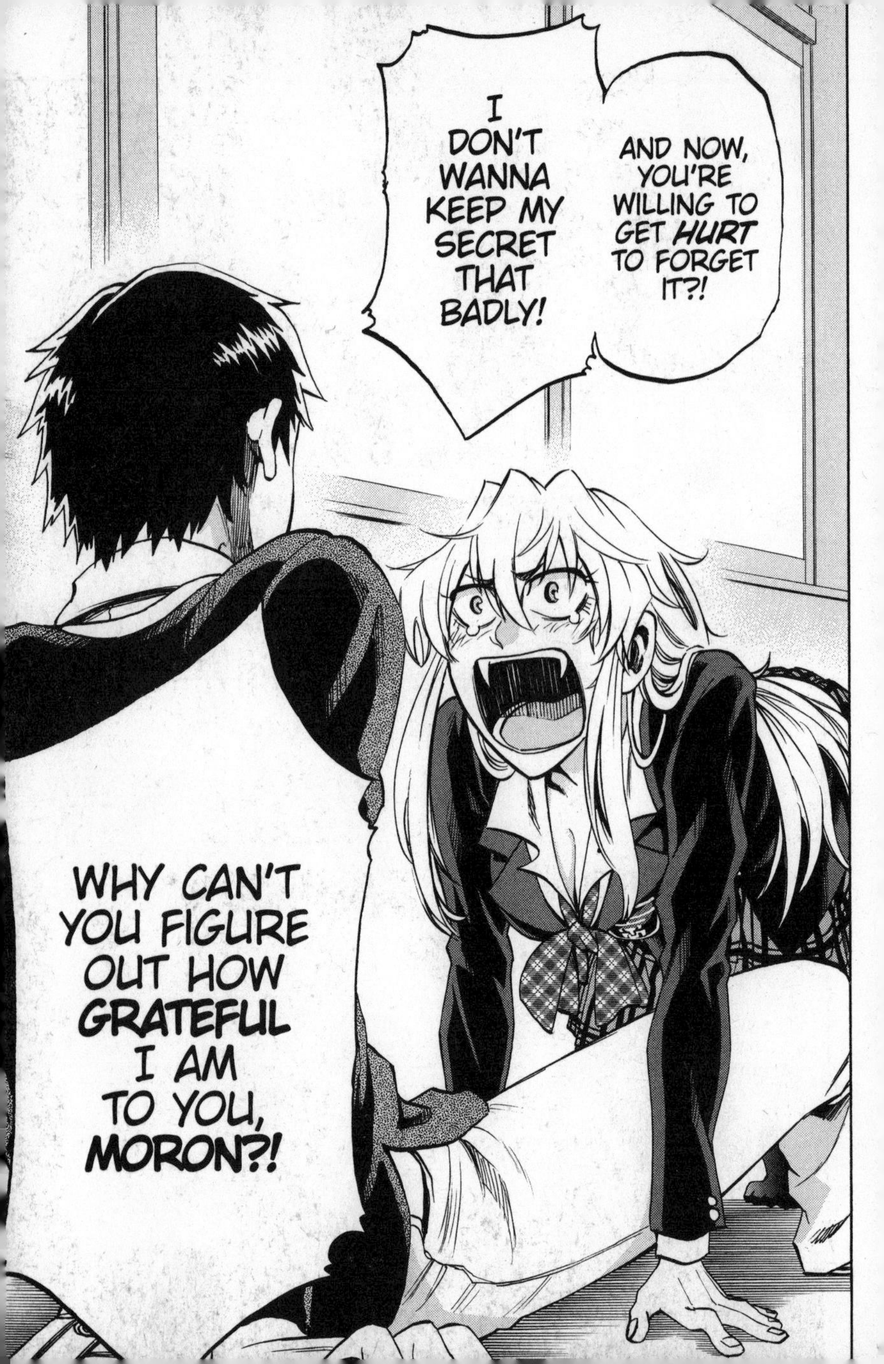
AND NOW, YOU'RE WILLING TO GET ***HURT*** TO FORGET IT?!
I DON'T WANNA KEEP MY SECRET THAT BADLY!
WHY CAN'T YOU FIGURE OUT HOW **GRATEFUL** I AM TO YOU, **MORON?!**

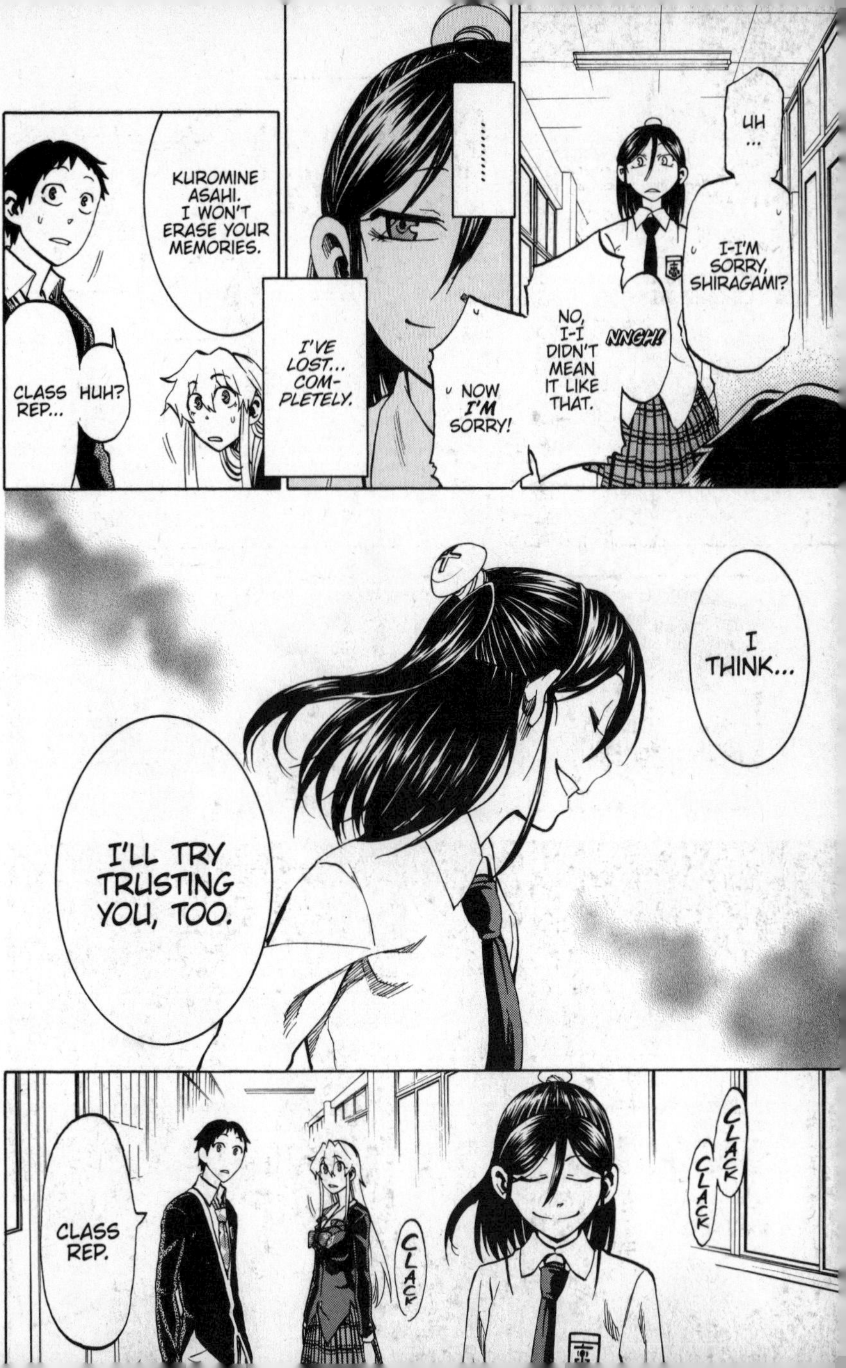
UH ...
I-I'M SORRY, SHIRAGAMI?
NNGH!
NO, I-I DIDN'T MEAN IT LIKE THAT.
NOW I'M SORRY!
......
I'VE LOST... COM-PLETELY.
KUROMINE ASAHI. I WON'T ERASE YOUR MEMORIES.
HUH?
CLASS REP...
I THINK...
I'LL TRY TRUSTING YOU, TOO.
CLACK
CLACK
CLACK
CLASS REP.

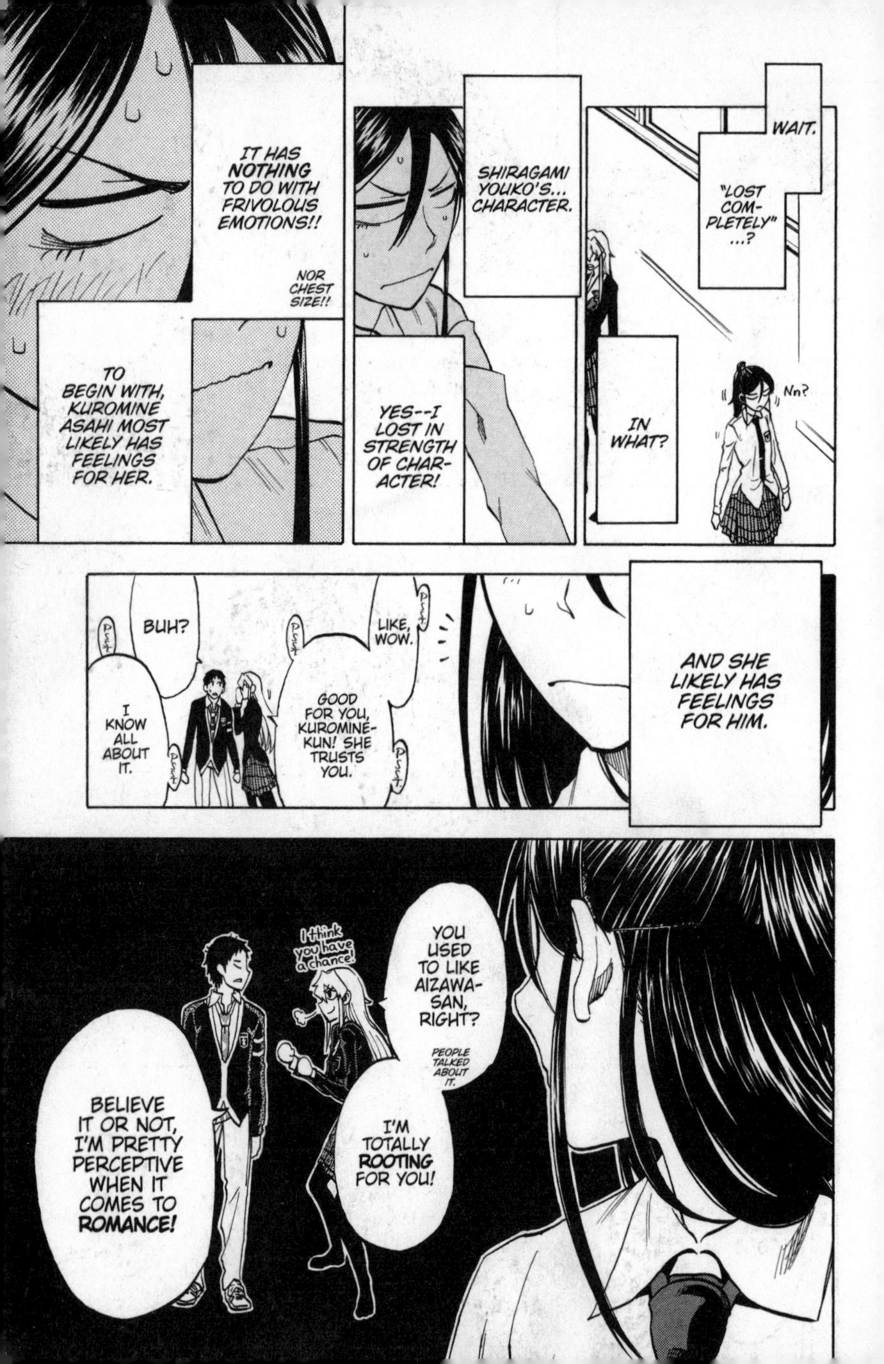
WAIT.
"LOST COMPLETELY" ...?
IN WHAT?
Nn?
SHIRAGAMI YOUKO'S... CHARACTER.
YES--I LOST IN STRENGTH OF CHARACTER!
IT HAS NOTHING TO DO WITH FRIVOLOUS EMOTIONS!!
NOR CHEST SIZE!!
TO BEGIN WITH, KUROMINE ASAHI MOST LIKELY HAS FEELINGS FOR HER.
AND SHE LIKELY HAS FEELINGS FOR HIM.
LIKE, WOW.
GOOD FOR YOU, KUROMINE-KUN! SHE TRUSTS YOU.
BUH?
I KNOW ALL ABOUT IT.
YOU USED TO LIKE AIZAWA-SAN, RIGHT?
I think you have a chance!
PEOPLE TALKED ABOUT IT.
I'M TOTALLY ROOTING FOR YOU!
BELIEVE IT OR NOT, I'M PRETTY PERCEPTIVE WHEN IT COMES TO ROMANCE!

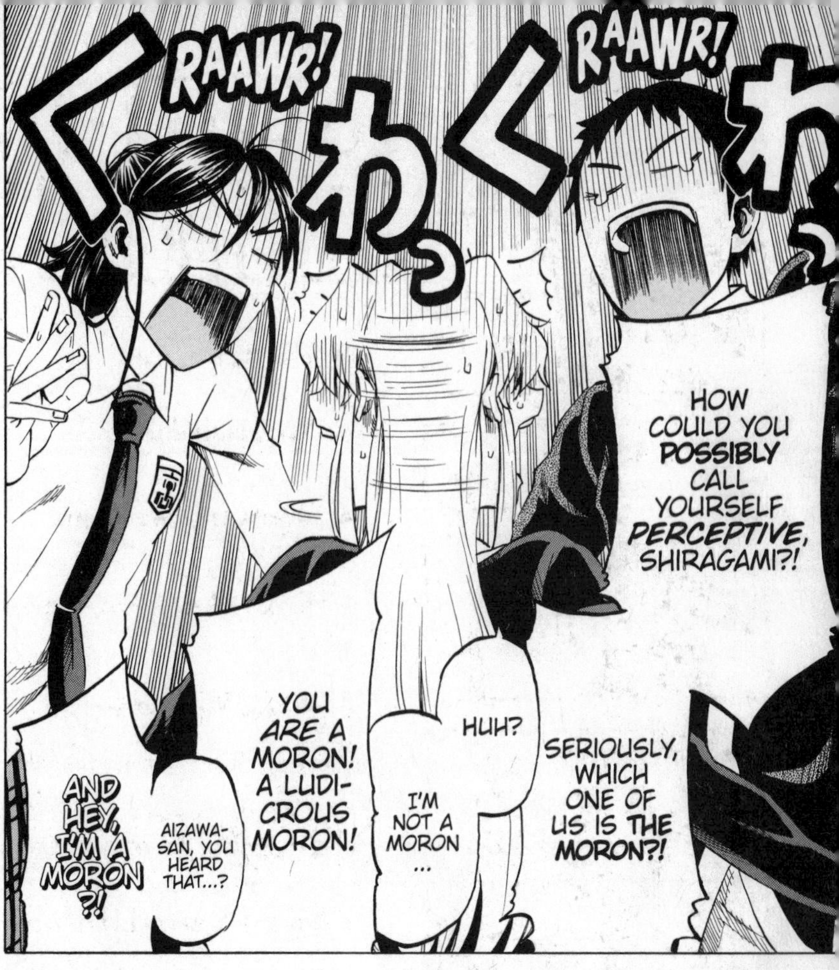
RAAWR!
RAAWR!
HOW COULD YOU POSSIBLY CALL YOURSELF PERCEPTIVE, SHIRAGAMI?!
SERIOUSLY, WHICH ONE OF US IS THE MORON?!
HUH?
I'M NOT A MORON ...
YOU ARE A MORON! A LUDI-CROUS MORON!
AIZAWA-SAN, YOU HEARD THAT...?
AND HEY, I'M A MORON ?!

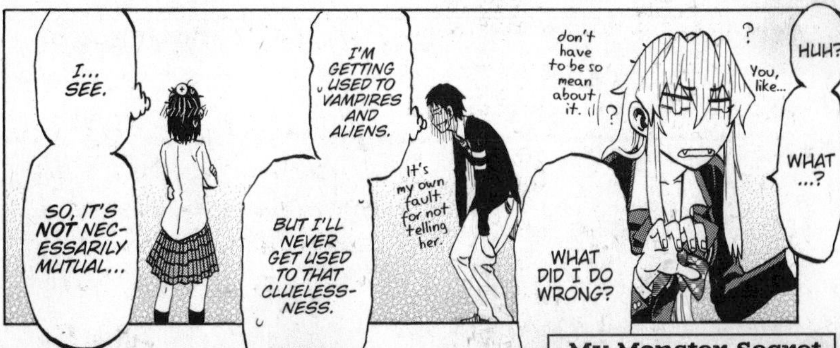
HUH?
You, like...
WHAT ...?
don't have to be so mean about it.
?
WHAT DID I DO WRONG?
I'M GETTING USED TO VAMPIRES AND ALIENS.
It's my own fault for not telling her.
BUT I'LL NEVER GET USED TO THAT CLUELESS-NESS.
HA HA HA...
I... SEE.
SO, IT'S NOT NEC-ESSARILY MUTUAL...

My Monster Secret
Volume 1 / End

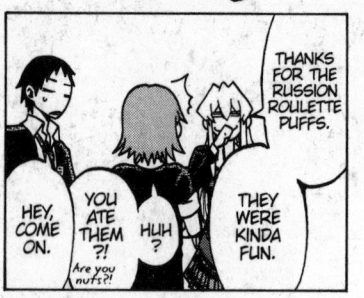

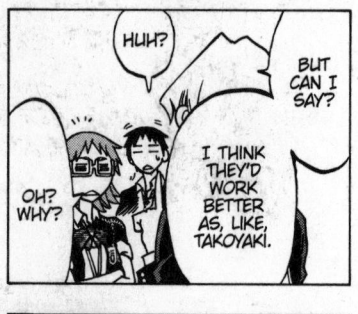

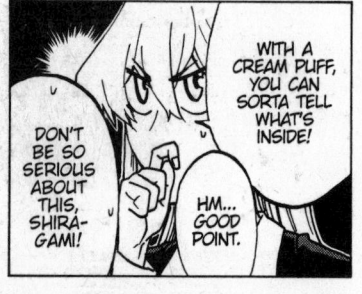

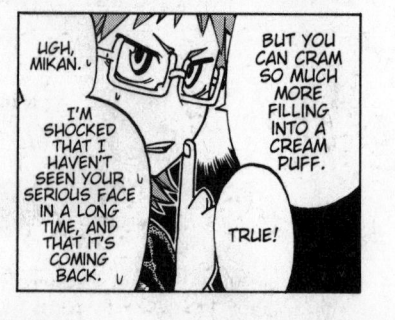

STAFF.

- Akutsu-san
- Shuumeigiku-san
- Seijun Suzuki-san
- Hiroki Minemura-san
- Junko Yamada-san

(in syllabary order)

SPECIAL THANKS.

- Youhei Yamashita-san

Editor: Mukawa-san

I give my thanks to those of you holding this book right now and everyone who let me and this work be a part of their lives.

増田英二.
Eiji Masuda

Bonus ①

THANKS FOR THE RUSSION ROULETTE PUFFS.
THEY WERE KINDA FUN.
HUH?
YOU ATE THEM ?!
Are you nuts?!
HEY, COME ON.
BUT CAN I SAY?
HUH?
I THINK THEY'D WORK BETTER AS, LIKE, TAKOYAKI.
OH? WHY?
WITH A CREAM PUFF, YOU CAN SORTA TELL WHAT'S INSIDE!
DON'T BE SO SERIOUS ABOUT THIS, SHIRA-GAMI!
HM... GOOD POINT.
BUT YOU CAN CRAM SO MUCH MORE FILLING INTO A CREAM PUFF.
UGH, MIKAN.
I'M SHOCKED THAT I HAVEN'T SEEN YOUR SERIOUS FACE IN A LONG TIME, AND THAT IT'S COMING BACK.
TRUE!

Bonus ②

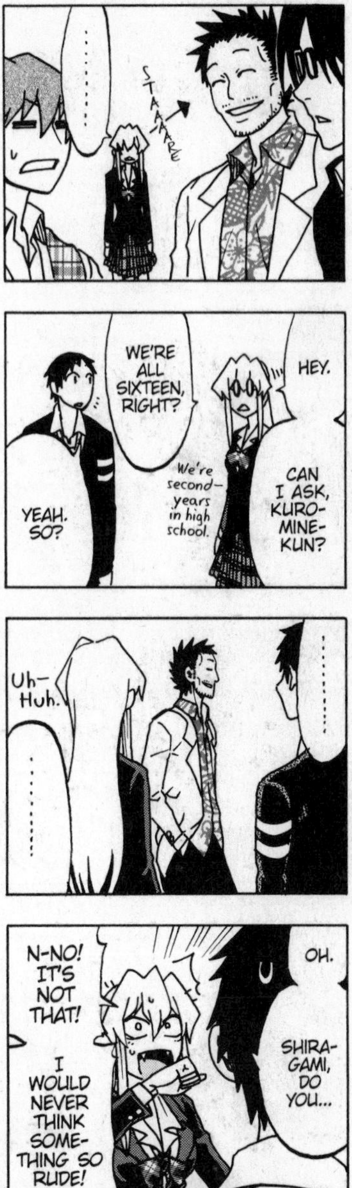
......
STAAAARE
HEY.
WE'RE ALL SIXTEEN, RIGHT?
CAN I ASK, KUROMINE-KUN?
We're second-years in high school.
YEAH. SO?
......
Uh-Huh.
......
OH.
N-NO! IT'S NOT THAT!
SHIRAGAMI, DO YOU...
I WOULD NEVER THINK SOMETHING SO RUDE!

Bonus ③

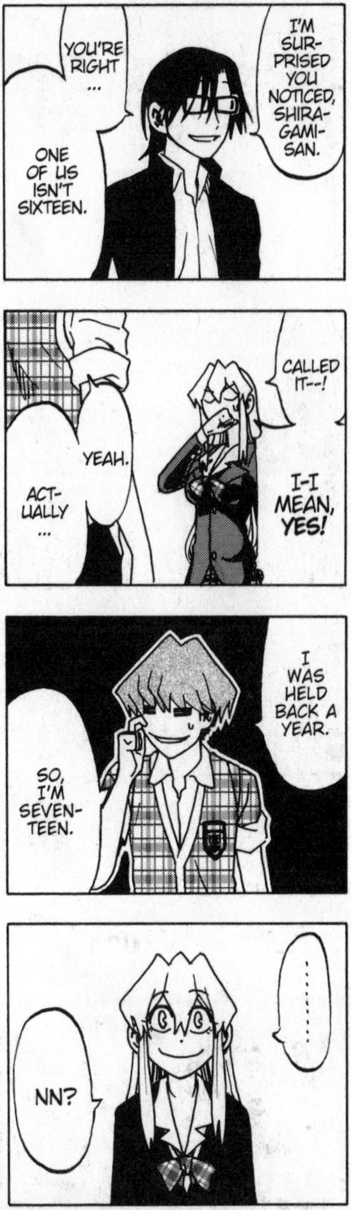
I'M SURPRISED YOU NOTICED, SHIRAGAMI-SAN.
YOU'RE RIGHT ...
ONE OF US ISN'T SIXTEEN.
CALLED IT--!
YEAH.
I-I MEAN, YES!
ACTUALLY ...
I WAS HELD BACK A YEAR.
SO, I'M SEVENTEEN.
......
NN?

Bonus ④

THIS IS A MEMORY-ERASING DEVICE.
BY NO MEANS IS IT A HAMMER.
HM.
GOOD.
GULP!
AGH!
I KNEW IT!
N-NO!
IT'S NOT WHAT YOU THINK!!
Gasp!

Bonus ⑤

THIS IS A MEMORY-ERASING DEVICE.
IT'S DEFINITELY NOT A HAMMER.
HM.
TAP TAP
SOME-THING ISN'T QUITE RIGHT IN MY SHOULDER SECTOR.
....
TAP
Oh...
TAP
That actually...
GULP!
AGH!
IF THAT DIDN'T ERASE YOUR MEMORY ...
N-NO!
I SIMPLY TURNED IF OFF FIRST!
Gasp!

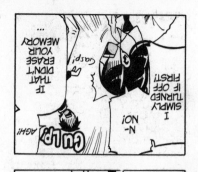

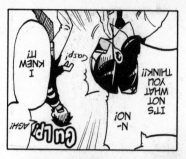

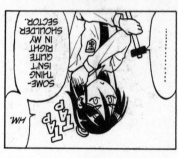

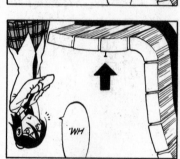

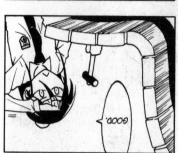

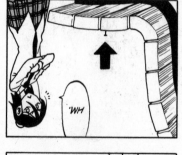

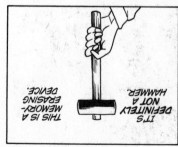

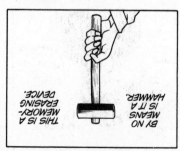

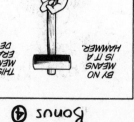